S0-BBC-399

AFRICAN HISTORICAL DICTIONARIES

Edited by Jon Woronoff

1. *Cameroon,* by Victor T. Le Vine and Roger P. Nye. 1974. *Out of print. See No. 48.*
2. *The Congo,* 2nd ed., by Virginia Thompson and Richard Adloff. 1984. *Out of print. See No. 69.*
3. *Swaziland,* by John J. Grotpeter. 1975.
4. *The Gambia,* 2nd ed., by Harry A. Gailey. 1987.
5. *Botswana,* by Richard P. Stevens. 1975. *Out of print. See No. 70.*
6. *Somalia,* by Margaret F. Castagno. 1975.
7. *Benin (Dahomey),* 2nd ed., by Samuel Decalo. 1987. *Out of print. See No. 61.*
8. *Burundi,* by Warren Weinstein. 1976. *Out of print. See No. 73.*
9. *Togo,* 3rd ed., by Samuel Decalo. 1996.
10. *Lesotho,* by Gordon Haliburton. 1977.
11. *Mali,* 3rd ed., by Pascal James Imperato. 1996.
12. *Sierra Leone,* by Cyril Patrick Foray. 1977.
13. *Chad,* 3rd ed., by Samuel Decalo. 1997.
14. *Upper Volta,* by Daniel Miles McFarland. 1978.
15. *Tanzania,* by Laura S. Kurtz. 1978.
16. *Guinea,* 3rd ed., by Thomas O'Toole with Ibrahima Bah-Lalya. 1995.
17. *Sudan,* by John Voll. 1978. *Out of print. See No. 53.*
18. *Rhodesia/Zimbabwe,* by R. Kent Rasmussen. 1979. *Out of print. See No. 46.*
19. *Zambia,* 2nd ed., by John J. Grotpeter, Brian V. Siegel, and James R. Pletcher. 1998.
20. *Niger,* 3rd ed., by Samuel Decalo. 1997.
21. *Equatorial Guinea,* 3rd ed., by Max Liniger-Goumaz. 2000.
22. *Guinea-Bissau,* 3rd ed., by Richard Lobban and Peter Mendy. 1997.
23. *Senegal,* by Lucie G. Colvin. 1981. *Out of print. See No. 65.*
24. *Morocco,* by William Spencer. 1980. *Out of print. See No. 71.*
25. *Malawi,* by Cynthia A. Crosby. 1980. *Out of print. See No. 54.*
26. *Angola,* by Phyllis Martin. 1980. *Out of print. See No. 52.*
27. *The Central African Republic,* by Pierre Kalck. 1980. *Out of print. See No. 51.*
28. *Algeria,* by Alf Andrew Heggoy. 1981. *Out of print. See No. 66.*
29. *Kenya,* by Bethwell A. Ogot. 1981. *Out of print. See No. 77.*
30. *Gabon,* by David E. Gardinier. 1981. *Out of print. See No. 58.*

31. *Mauritania,* by Alfred G. Gerteiny. 1981. *Out of print. See No. 68.*
32. *Ethiopia,* by Chris Prouty and Eugene Rosenfeld. 1981. *Out of print. See No. 56.*
33. *Libya,* 3rd ed., by Ronald Bruce St John. 1998.
34. *Mauritius,* by Lindsay Riviere. 1982. *Out of print. See No. 49.*
35. *Western Sahara,* by Tony Hodges. 1982. *Out of print. See No. 55.*
36. *Egypt,* by Joan Wucher King. 1984. *Out of print. See No. 67.*
37. *South Africa,* by Christopher Saunders. 1983. *Out of print. See No. 78.*
38. *Liberia,* by D. Elwood Dunn and Svend E. Holsoe. 1985.
39. *Ghana,* by Daniel Miles McFarland. 1985. *Out of print. See No. 78.*
40. *Nigeria,* 2nd ed., by Anthony Oyewole and John Lucas. 2000.
41. *Côte d'Ivoire (The Ivory Coast),* 2nd ed., by Robert J. Mundt. 1995.
42. *Cape Verde,* 2nd ed., by Richard Lobban and Marilyn Halter. 1988. *Out of print. See No. 62.*
43. *Zaire*, by F. Scott Bobb. 1988. *Out of print. See No. 76.*
44. *Botswana,* 2nd ed., by Fred Morton, Andrew Murray, and Jeff Ramsay. 1989. *Out of print. See No. 70.*
45. *Tunisia,* 2nd ed., by Kenneth J. Perkins. 1997.
46. *Zimbabwe,* 3rd ed., by Steven C. Rubert and R. Kent Rasmussen. 1998.
47. *Mozambique,* by Mario Azevedo. 1991.
48. *Cameroon,* 2nd ed., by Mark W. DeLancey and H. Mbella Mokeba. 1990.
49. *Mauritius,* 2nd ed., by Sydney Selvon. 1991.
50. *Madagascar,* by Maureen Covell. 1995.
51. *The Central African Republic,* 2nd ed., by Pierre Kalck; translated by Thomas O'Toole. 1992.
52. *Angola,* 2nd ed., by Susan H. Broadhead. 1992.
53. *Sudan,* 2nd ed., by Carolyn Fluehr-Lobban, Richard A. Lobban, Jr., and John Obert Voll. 1992.
54. *Malawi,* 2nd ed., by Cynthia A. Crosby. 1993.
55. *Western Sahara,* 2nd ed., by Anthony Pazzanita and Tony Hodges. 1994.
56. *Ethiopia and Eritrea,* 2nd ed., by Chris Prouty and Eugene Rosenfeld. 1994.
57. *Namibia,* by John J. Grotpeter. 1994.
58. *Gabon,* 2nd ed., by David E. Gardinier. 1994.
59. *Comoro Islands,* by Martin Ottenheimer and Harriet Ottenheimer. 1994.

60. *Rwanda,* by Learthen Dorsey. 1994.
61. *Benin,* 3rd ed., by Samuel Decalo. 1995.
62. *Republic of Cape Verde,* 3rd ed., by Richard Lobban and Marlene Lopes. 1995.
63. *Ghana,* 2nd ed., by David Owusu-Ansah and Daniel Miles McFarland. 1995.
64. *Uganda,* by M. Louise Pirouet. 1995.
65. *Senegal,* 2nd ed., by Andrew F. Clark and Lucie Colvin Phillips. 1994.
66. *Algeria,* 2nd ed., by Phillip Chiviges Naylor and Alf Andrew Heggoy. 1994.
67. *Egypt,* 2nd ed., by Arthur Goldschmidt, Jr. 1994.
68. *Mauritania,* 2nd ed., by Anthony G. Pazzanita. 1996.
69. *Congo,* 3rd ed., by Samuel Decalo, Virginia Thompson, and Richard Adloff. 1996.
70. *Botswana,* 3rd ed., by Jeff Ramsay, Barry Morton, and Fred Morton. 1996.
71. *Morocco,* 2nd ed., by Thomas K. Park. 1996.
72. *Tanzania,* 2nd ed., by Thomas P. Ofcansky and Rodger Yeager. 1997.
73. *Burundi,* 2nd ed., by Ellen K. Eggers. 1997.
74. *Burkina Faso,* 2nd ed., by Daniel Miles McFarland and Lawrence Rupley. 1998.
75. *Eritrea,* by Tom Killion. 1998.
76. *Democratic Republic of the Congo (Zaire)*, by F. Scott Bobb. 1999. (Revised edition of *Historical Dictionary of Zaire*, No. 43)
77. *Kenya*, 2nd ed., by Robert M. Maxon and Thomas P. Ofcansky. 2000.
78. *South Africa,* 2nd ed., by Christopher Saunders and Nicholas Southey. 2000.
79. *The Gambia,* 3rd ed., by Arnold Hughes and Harry A. Gailey. 2000.
80. *Swaziland*, 2nd ed., by Alan R. Booth. 2000.
81. *Republic of Cameroon,* 3rd ed., by Mark W. DeLancey and Mark Dike DeLancey. 2000.

Historical Dictionary of the Republic of Cameroon

Third Edition

Mark W. DeLancey
Mark Dike DeLancey

African Historical Dictionaries, No. 81

The Scarecrow Press, Inc.
Lanham, Maryland, and London
2000

SCARECROW PRESS, INC.

Published in the United States of America
by Scarecrow Press, Inc.
4720 Boston Way, Lanham, Maryland 20706
http://www.scarecrowpress.com

4 Pleydell Gardens, Folkestone
Kent CT20 2DN, England

British Library Cataloguing in Publication Information Available

Library of Congress Cataloging-in-Publication Data

DeLancey, Mark.
Historical dictionary of the Republic of Cameroon.—3rd ed. / Mark W. DeLancey & Mark Dike DeLancey.
p. cm.—(Historical dictionaries of Africa ; no. 81)
Rev. ed. of: Historical dictionary of the Republic of Cameroon. 2nd ed. / by Mark W. DeLancey and H. Mbella Mokeba. 1990.
Includes bibliographical references.
ISBN 0-8108-3775-7 (cloth : alk. paper)
1. Cameroon—Historical—Dictionaries. I. DeLancey, Mark D. II. Title. III. African historical dictionaries ; no. 81.
DT563.D45 2000
967.11'003—dc21 99-086621

∞™ The paper used in this publication meets the minimum requirements of American National Standard for Information Sciences—Permanence of Paper for Printed Library Materials, ANSI/NISO Z39.48-1992.
Manufactured in the United States of America.

Contents

Acknowledgments	ix
Editor's Foreword, *by Jon Woronoff*	xi
Acronyms and Abbreviations	xiii
Maps	xxiii
Chronology of Cameroon History	xxvii
Introduction	1
THE DICTIONARY	11
Bibliography	287
About the Authors	359

Acknowledgments

It is difficult to thank all of those who have assisted us over the many years, in so many ways, and at so many locations. Drs. Martin Njeuma and Victor Ngoh, now both at the University of Buea, have always been ready to assist and advise. Ms. Catherine (Kitty) Russell, now doing field research in Cameroon; Ms. Wendy Brown; and Mr. W. Wang provided invaluable word-processing help. Special gratitude is expressed for the assistance of Mr. Thomas Ngomba Ngali, of the University of Buea, who made strenuous efforts in updating materials. Numerous scholars in Cameroon, Europe, and America have given of their time and knowledge. Authors of earlier editions of the *Historical Dictionary of Cameroon*—Victor LeVine, Roger Nye, and H. Mbella Mokeba—deserve special thanks for the work they have done.

Editor's Foreword

Cameroon is one of the most intriguing countries in Africa. As the authors of this book demonstrate, it truly is an "Africa in Miniature." Geographically, it comprises very different regions; economically, it covers a broad mix of products and sectors; ethnically, it includes an amazing number of groups living within a fairly small area. It brings together major strands: Christian, animist, and Islamic religions; English- and French-speaking populations; and parts of the former French and British colonial empires, most of which were initially held by Germany.

Being "Africa in Miniature" is great for tourism. For virtually everything else, it only creates complications and problems. The political ones have been fairly evident, involving friction along the various dividing lines—ethnic, religious, and linguistic. Yet Cameroon has held together, and stability has become a hallmark under just two leaders (in fact, perhaps more stability than was good for it, to judge by a still unconvincing experiment in multipartyism). The economy also is undergoing a difficult transition from stultifying African socialism to freer private enterprise, and any educational and social progress has been slow and unsteady. Despite these obvious drawbacks, Cameroon has done better than most of its counterparts in Africa.

How this happened, and much more, is shown by this latest edition of the *Historical Dictionary of the Republic of Cameroon.* It reaches far back into early history, covers the colonial era extensively, and then continues on to the present period. It looks at the many groups that make up the Republic of Cameroon and focuses on individuals who have played a notable role. It also delves into political, economic, social, cultural, and other aspects. This is tied together neatly by the introduction and an up-to-date chronology as well as a bibliography that directs readers to other pertinent works.

This new edition was written by two men who know the country well. Mark W. DeLancey, professor of government and international studies at the University of South Carolina, has spent extended periods in Cameroon and has taught at the University of Yaoundé. He has published numerous books and articles on African politics and international relations, including

Cameroon, Dependence and Independence. He was also the lead author of the second edition. This time he is joined by Mark Dike DeLancey, a specialist in Cameroon art history and another frequent visitor to Cameroon. Mark Dike DeLancey is currently conducting research in Ngaoundéré on Islamic influences on palace architecture in northern Cameroon. Building on the first two editions, this thoroughly updated and extensively revised third edition provides a very solid and substantial guide to Cameroon.

Jon Woronoff
Series Editor

Acronyms and Abbreviations

AAC	All Anglophone Conference
ACAP	Agence Camerounaise de Presse
ACP	African, Caribbean, and Pacific countries
AEF	Afrique Equatoriale Française/French Equatorial Africa
AFC	African Football Federation
AFC	Allied Front for Change
ALCAM	Assemblée Législative du Cameroun
ALNK	Armée de Liberation Nationale du Kamerun/ National Army of Kamerun Liberation
ALUCAM	Société Aluminium du Cameroun
ANCAM	Assemblée Nationale du Cameroun
ARC-CNS	Alliance for the Reconstruction of Cameroon by a Sovereign National Conference
ARCAM	Assemblée Représentative du Cameroun
ATCAM	Assemblée Territoriale du Cameroun
BCD	Banque Camerounaise de Développement
BCEAC	Banque Centrale des Etats de l'Afrique Equatoriale et Centrale
BCUF	Bakweri Cooperative Union of Farmers
BDC	Bloc Démocratique Camerounais
BDEAC	Banque de Développement des Etats d'Afrique Centrale
BEAC	Banque des Etats de l'Afrique Centrale
BEPC	Brevet d'Etudes du Premier Cycle
BICIC	Banque Internationale pour le Commerce et l'Industrie du Cameroun
BMM	Brigades Mixtes Mobiles
CACEU	Central African Customs and Economic Union (*see* UDEAC)
CAM	Cameroon Anglophone Movement
CAMAIR	Cameroon Airlines
CAMRAIL	Cameroon Railway Company
CAMSUCO	Cameroon Sugar Company

CAPME	Centre National d'Assistance aux Petites et Moyennes Entreprises
CAPSU	Cameroon Public Service Union
CAPTA	Confederation of Anglophone Parents and Teachers Associations
CAR	Central African Republic
CBA	Cameroon Bar Association
CBC	Cameroon Baptist Convention
CBLT	Commission du Bassin du Lac Tchad
CCAST	Cameroon College of Arts, Science, and Technology
CCCE	Caisse Centrale de Cooperation Economique
CCFOM	Caisse Centrale de la France d'Outre-Mer
CCSC	Confédération Camerounaise des Syndicats Croyants
CDC	Cameroon Development Corporation
CDCWU	Cameroon Development Corporation Workers Union
CDF	Cameroon Democratic Front
CDP	Cameroon Democratic Party
CDU	Cameroon Democratic Union
CEAN	Centre d'Etudes d'Afrique Noire
CEE	Communauté Economique Européen (*see* EEC)
CEEAC	Communauté Economique des Etats de l'Afrique Centrale
CELLUCAM	Cellulose du Cameroun
CENADEC	Centre National de Développement des Entreprises Coopératives
CENAM	Centre National d'Administration et de Magistrature
CENER	Centre National des Etudes et des Recherches
CEPE	Certificat de Fin d'Etudes Primaire Elémentaire
CEPEC	Centre d'Education pour la Promotion Collective
CEPED	Centre Français sur la Population et le Développement
CEPER	Centre for the Publication of School Textbooks
CEPMAE	Centre de Production de Manuels et d'Auxiliaires de l'Enseignement
CFA	Colonies Françaises d'Afrique or Communauté Financière Africaine
CFAO	Compagnie Française de l'Afrique Occidentale
CFDT	Compagnie Française pour le Développement des Textiles
CFTC	Confédération Française des Travailleurs Chrétiens Camerounais

CGT	Confédération Génerale du Travail
CHOCOCAM	Chocolaterie–Confiserie Camerounaise
CICAM	Cotonnière Industrielle du Cameroun
CIMENCAM	Cimenteries du Cameroun
CIRAD	Centre de Coopération Internationale en Recherche Agronomique pour le Développement
CNCC	Conseil National des Chargeurs du Cameroun
CND	Centre National de Documentation
CNF	Cameroons National Federation
CNPS	Caisse Nationale de Prévoyance Sociale
CNR	Caisse Nationale de Reassurance
CNU	Cameroon National Union (*see* UNC)
COCAM	Contreplaques du Cameroun
COLICITE	Comité pour la Libération du Citoyen Titus Edzoa
COTCO	Cameroon Oil Transportation Company
CPDM	Cameroon People's Democratic Movement (*see* MDPC)
CPNC	Cameroons People's National Convention
CPO	Cameroon Patriotic Opposition
CRATRE	Cercle d'Réflexion et d'Action pour le Triomphe du Renouveau
CRTV	Cameroon Radio and Television
CTUC	Cameroon Trade Union Congress
CUC	Cameroon United Congress
CUN	Courant d'Union Nationale
CUSS	Centre Universitaire des Sciences de la Santé
CWU	Cameroon Welfare Union
CYL	Cameroons Youth League
DC	Démocrates Camerounais
DES	Diplôme d'Etudes Supérieure
DIRDOC	Direction Générale des Etudes et de la Documentation
ECSCA	Economic Community of the States of Central Africa
EDF	European Development Fund (*see* FED)
EEC	European Economic Community
EMIAC	Ecole Militaire Inter-Armes du Cameroun
ENAM	Ecole Nationale d'Administration et de Magistrature
ENFOM	Ecole Nationale de la France d'Outre-Mer
ENS	Ecole Normale Supérieure
ESOCAM	Evolution Sociale Camerounaise

ESSTI	School of Journalism and Information Sciences
EU	European Union
FAC	Fonds d'Aide et de Coopération
FAC	Front of Allies for Change
FEANF	Fédération des Etudiants d'Afrique Noire en France
FECAFOOT	Fédération Camerounaise de Football
FED	Fonds Européen de Développement (*see* EDF)
FEMEC	Femmes Ecrivains
FENASCO	Fédération National des Sports Scolaire et Universitaire
FIDES	Fonds d'Investissement pour le Développement Economique et Social
FNEC	Fédération Nationale des Etudiants Camerounais
FNU	Front National Unifié
FODIC	Fonds de Développement de l'Industrie Cinématographique
FOGAPE	Fonds de Garantie et d'Aide aux Petites Entreprises (Fonds d'Aide et de Garantie des Credits aux Petites et Moyennes Entreprises)
FONADER	Fonds National de Développement Rural/National Fund for Rural Development
FPUP	Front Populaire de l'Unité et la Paix
FSC	Fédération des Syndicats du Cameroun
FSLC	First School Leaving Certificate
GCE	General Certificate of Education
GETRAM	Société Générale des Travaux Metalliques
GPC	Groupe des Progressistes du Cameroun
HDRG	Human Rights Defence Group
HEVECAM	Hévéa-Cameroun
ICBC	International Centre of Bantu Civilizations
IFAN	Institut Français d'Afrique Noire
IFORD/CEPED	Institute for Demographic Studies/Centre Français sur la Population et Développement
IHEOM	Institut des Hautes Etudes d'Outre-Mer
IIAP	Institut International d'Administration Publique
IMF	International Monetary Fund
INDECAM	Coordination des Indépendants Camerounais
INTELCAM	International Telecommunications Company of Cameroon/Société des Télécommunications Internationale du Cameroun

IRA	Institut de Recherche Agronomique
IRCAM	Institut de Recherche Scientifique du Cameroun
IRIC	Institut des Relations Internationales du Cameroun
ISH	Institut des Sciences Humaines
IUCN	World Conservation Union
JDC	Jeunesse Démocratique Camerounaise
JEUCAFRA	Jeunesse Camerounaise Française
KNC	Kamerun National Congress
KNDP	Kamerun National Democratic Party
KPP	Kamerun People's Party
KUNC	Kamerun United National Congress
KUP	Kamerun United Party
LCBC	Lake Chad Basin Commission
MAETUR	Mission d'Aménagement et d'Equipment des Terrains Urbains et Ruraux
MAGZI	Mission d'Aménagement et de Gestion des Zones Industrielles
MANC	Mouvement d'Action Nationale du Cameroun
MDP	Movement for Democracy and Progress
MDPC	Mouvement Démocratique du Peuple Camerounais (*see* CPDM)
MDR	Movement for Defence of the Republic
MIDENAO	Northwest Development Authority
MIDEVIV	Mission de Développement des Cultures Vivrières, Maraichères, et Fruitières
MINAT	Ministry of Territorial Administration
MINFOC	Ministry of Culture
MINREST	Ministry of Scientific and Technical Research
MP	Mouvement Progressiste
NA	Native Authority
NBC	Native Baptist Church
NCDM	National Coordination for Democracy and a Multiparty System
NCNC	National Council of Nigeria and the Cameroons
NCOPA	National Coordination of Opposition Parties and Associations
NCPD	National Civic Centre for Participation in Development
NCSPD	National Civic Service for Participation in Development
NKDP	North Kamerun Democratic Party

NPMB	National Produce Marketing Board
NUCW	National Union of Cameroon Workers
NUDP	National Union for Democracy and Progress
OAC	Organisation Animiste Camerounaise
OAMCE	Organisation Africaine et Malgache pour la Coopération Economique
OAU	Organization of African Unity
OCALIP	Organisation Camerounaise pour la Liberté de la Presse
OCAM	Organisation Commune Africaine et Malgache Organisation Commune Africaine et Mauricienne
OCAMM	Organisation Commune Africaine, Malgache, et Mauritienne
OCB	Office Camerounais de Bananes
OFRDPC	Organisation des Femmes du Rassemblement Démocratique du Peuple Camerounais
OJRDPC	Organisation des Jeunes du Rassemblement Démocratique du Peuple Camerounais
OK	One Kamerun Party
ONAREST	Office National des Recherches Scientifique et Technique d'Outre-Mer
ONCPB	Office National de Commercialisation des Produits de Base
ONDF/ONADEF	Office National de Développement des Forêts
ONES	Office National des Equipements Sportifs
ONPC	Office National des Ports du Cameroun
ONPD	Office National de Participation au Développement
ORSTOM	Office de la Recherche Scientifique et Technique Outre-Mer
OSUSC	Office of Schools and University Sports Competition
OUA	Organisation de l'Unité Africaine (*see* OAU)
PAID	Pan-African Institute for Development
PDC	Parti des Démocrates Camerounais
PI	Paysans Indépendants
PMC	Permanent Mandates Commission
PME	Petites et Moyennes Entreprises
PSC	Parti Socialiste du Cameroun
PSP	Parti de la Solidarité du Peuple
PTC	Parti Travailliste Camerounais

PWD	Public Works Department
RACAM	Rassemblement Camerounais
RAPECA	Rassemblement du Peuple Camerounais
RDA	Rassemblement Démocratique Africain
RDPC	Rassemblement Démocratique du Peuple Camerounais
Regifercam	Régie Nationale des Chemins de Fer du Cameroun
RENAICAM	Renaissance Camerounais
RPC	Rassemblement du Peuple Camerounais
SACTA	Société Camerounaise des Tabacs
SAFACAM	Société Agricole, Forestière, et Africaine du Cameroun
SAP	Société Africaine de Prévoyance Structural Adjustment Program
SCAC	Southern Cameroons Advisory Council
SCARM	Southern Cameroons Restoration Movement
SCB	Société Camerounaise de Banque
SCM	Société Camerounaise des Minoteries
SCNC	Southern Cameroons National Council
SCOA	Société Commerciale de l'Ouest Africain
SCOLMA	Standing Conference on Library Materials on Africa
SCPC	Southern Cameroons Peoples Conference
SCT	Société Camerounaise de Tabacs
SDF	Social Democratic Front
SEBC	Société d'Exploitation des Bois du Cameroun
SEDOC	Service de Documentation
SEGAZCAM	Société d'Etude pour la Mise en Valeur du Gaz Naturel Camerounais
SEMRY	Société d'Expansion et de Modernisation de la Riziculture de Yagoua
SGMC	Société Grand Moulin du Cameroun
SIC	Société Immobilière du Cameroun
SIP	Société Indigène de Prévoyance
SNC	Sovereign National Conference
SNEC	Société Nationale des Eaux du Cameroun
SNH	Société Nationale d'Hydrocarbures
SNI	Société Nationale d'Investissement
SOCADRA	Société Camerounaise des Droits d'Auteurs
SOCAME	Société Camerounaise des Engrais
SOCAPALM	Société Camerounaise de Palmeraies
SOCATRAL	Société Camerounaise de Transformation de l'Aluminium
SOCOODER	Société Coopérative de Développement Rural

SOCOPED	Société Coopérative d'Epargne et de Développement
SODEBLE	Société de Développement pour la Culture et la Transformation du Blé
SODECAO	Société de Développement du Cacao
SODECOTON	Société de Développement du Coton
SODENKAM	Société du Développement du Nkam
SODEPA	Société de Développement et d'Exploitation de la Production Animale
SODEPALM	Société de Développement du Palmeraies
SODEPAR	Société de Développement et d'Exploitation des Productions Animales
SODERIM	Société de Développement de la Riziculture de la Plaine des Mbo
SOFIBEL	Société Forestière et Industrielle de Belabo
SONARA	Société Nationale de Raffinage
SONEL	Société Nationale d'Electricité du Cameroun
SOPECAM	Société de Presse et d'Editions du Cameroun
SOSUCAM	Société Sucrière du Cameroun
SOTUC	Société de Transports Urbains du Cameroun
SRCC	Société de Recouvrement des Créances du Cameroun
STPC	Société de Tanneries et Peausseries du Cameroun
SWELA	South West Elites Association
SYNDUSTRICAM	Syndicat d'Industriel du Cameroun
TAC	Teachers Association of Cameroon
UAM	Union Africaine et Malgache
UC	Union Camerounaise
UCCAO	Union Centrale des Coopératives de l'Ouest or Union des Coopératives de Cafe Arabica de l'Ouest
UDC	Union Démocratique Camerounaise (*see* CDU)
UDE	Union Douanière Equatoriale
UDEAC	Union Douanière Economique de l'Afrique Centrale (*see* CACEU)
UDFC	Union Démocratique des Femmes Camerounaises
UFC	Union of Forces for Change
UN	United Nations

UNC	Union Nationale Camerounaise (*see* CNU)
UNDP	United Nations Development Program
	Union Nationale pour la Démocratie et le Progrès (*see* NUDP)
UNEK	Union Nationale des Etudiants Kamerounais
UNESCO	United Nations Educational, Scientific, and Cultural Organization
Unicafra	Union Camerounaise Française
UNITAR	United Nations Institute for Training and Research
UNTC	Union Nationale des Travailleurs du Cameroun
UNVDA	Upper Noun Valley Development Authority
UPC	Union des Populations du Cameroun
USAC	Union des Syndicats Antonômes Camerounais
USC	Union Sociale Camerounais
USCC	Union des Syndicats Confédéres du Cameroun
WAPV	Westafrikanische Pflanzungsverein
WCNU	Women's Cameroon National Union
WCPDM	Women's Cameroon People's Democratic Movement
WCTUC	West Cameroon Trade Union Congress
YCNU	Youth's Cameroon National Union
YCPDM	Youth's Cameroon People's Democratic Movement
ZAPI	Zone d'Actions Prioritaires Intégrées
ZOPAC	Zone de Pacification

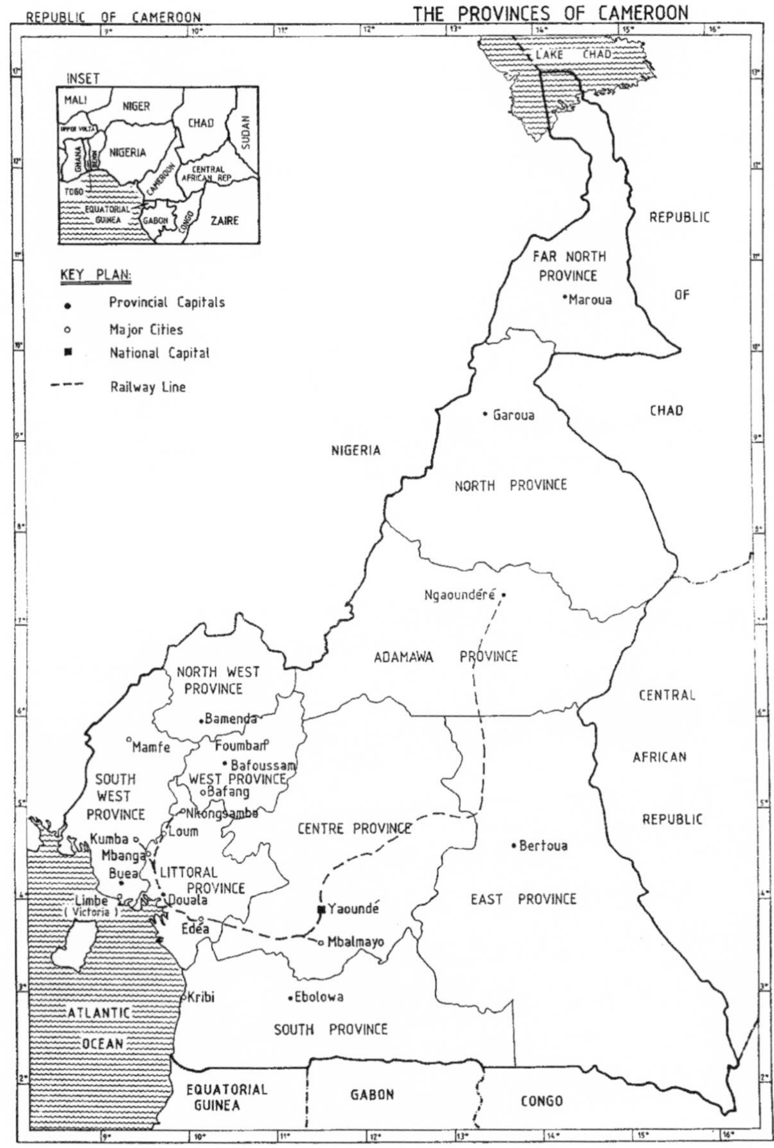
REPUBLIC OF CAMEROON
THE PROVINCES OF CAMEROON
INSET
MALI
NIGER
CHAD
SUDAN
NIGERIA
GHANA
TOGO
CAMEROON
CENTRAL AFRICAN REP.
EQUATORIAL GUINEA
GABON
CONGO
ZAIRE
KEY PLAN:
Provincial Capitals
Major Cities
National Capital
Railway Line
LAKE CHAD
REPUBLIC OF CHAD
FAR NORTH PROVINCE
Maroua
Garoua
NIGERIA
NORTH PROVINCE
Ngaoundéré
ADAMAWA PROVINCE
NORTH WEST PROVINCE
Bamenda
Mamfe
Foumban
Bafoussam
WEST PROVINCE
Bafang
SOUTH WEST PROVINCE
Nkongsamba
Loum
Kumba
Mbanga
Buea
LITTORAL PROVINCE
Limbe (Victoria)
Douala
Edéa
CENTRE PROVINCE
Yaoundé
Mbalmayo
CENTRAL AFRICAN REPUBLIC
Bertoua
EAST PROVINCE
Kribi
Ebolowa
SOUTH PROVINCE
ATLANTIC OCEAN
EQUATORIAL GUINEA
GABON
CONGO

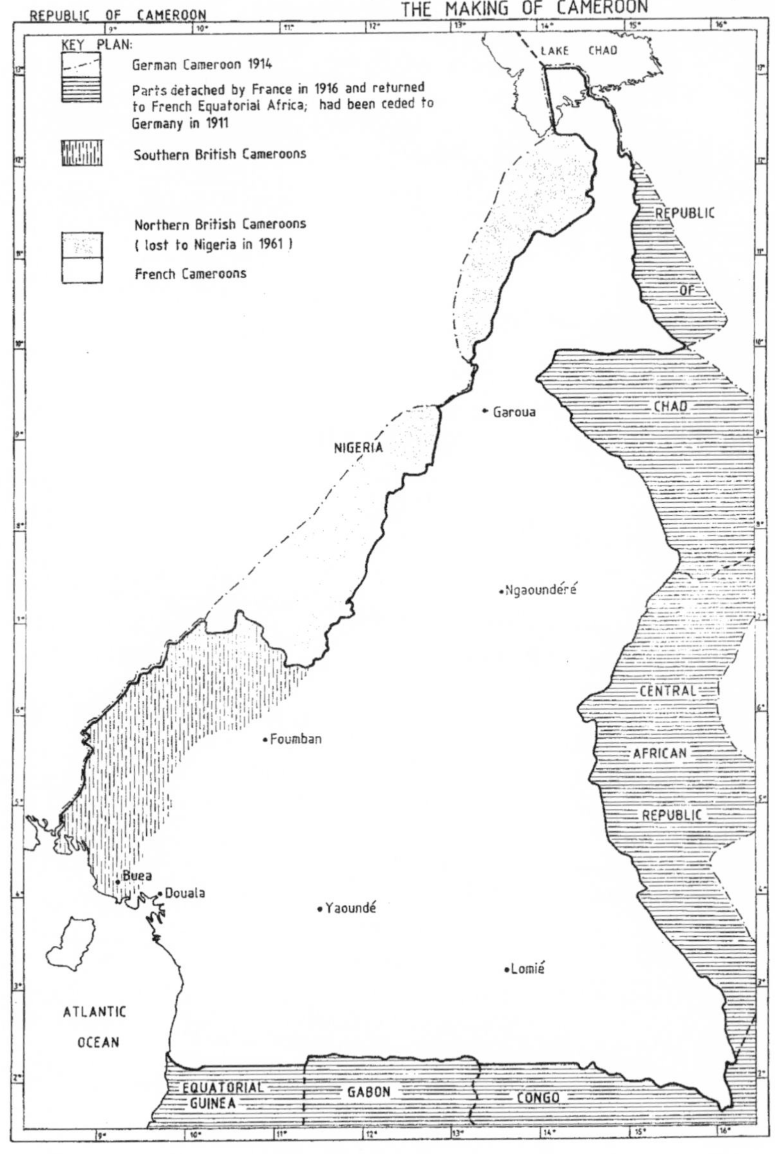
REPUBLIC OF CAMEROON
THE MAKING OF CAMEROON
KEY PLAN:
German Cameroon 1914
Parts detached by France in 1916 and returned to French Equatorial Africa; had been ceded to Germany in 1911
Southern British Cameroons
Northern British Cameroons (lost to Nigeria in 1961)
French Cameroons
LAKE CHAD
REPUBLIC OF CHAD
NIGERIA
Garoua
Ngaoundéré
CENTRAL AFRICAN REPUBLIC
Foumban
Buea
Douala
Yaoundé
Lomié
ATLANTIC OCEAN
EQUATORIAL GUINEA
GABON
CONGO

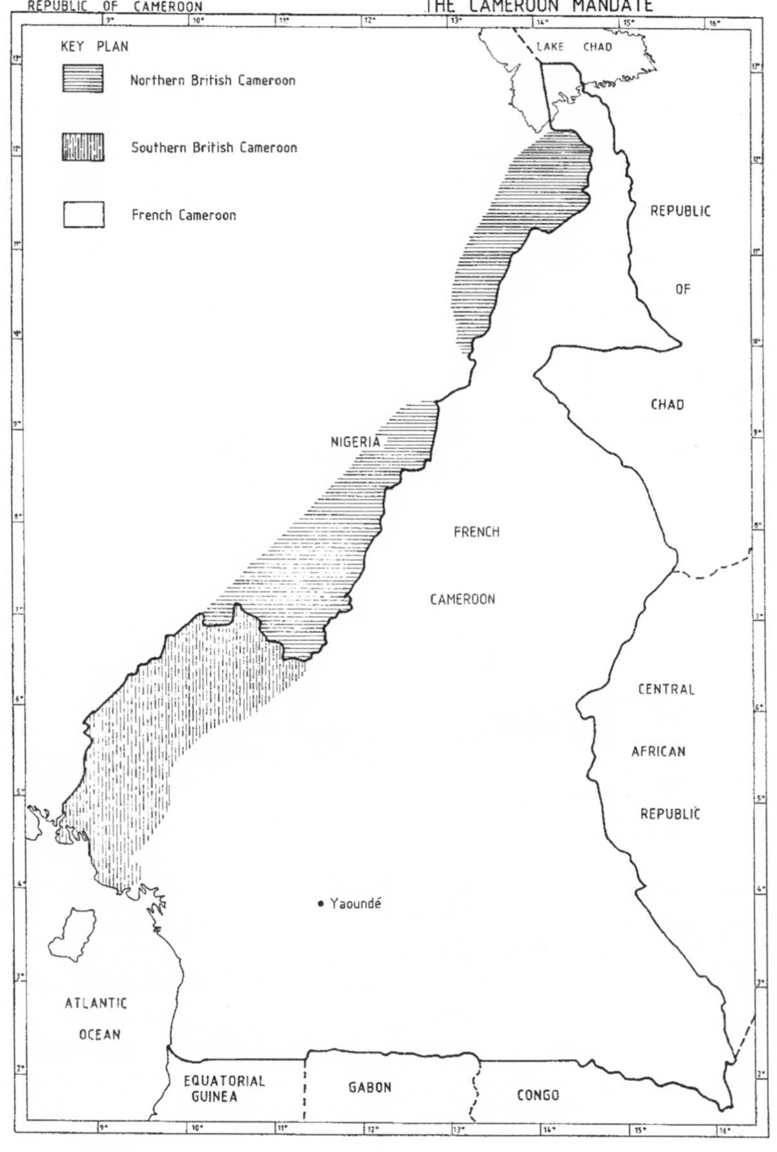
REPUBLIC OF CAMEROON
THE CAMEROON MANDATE
KEY PLAN
Northern British Cameroon
Southern British Cameroon
French Cameroon
LAKE CHAD
REPUBLIC OF CHAD
NIGERIA
FRENCH CAMEROON
CENTRAL AFRICAN REPUBLIC
Yaoundé
ATLANTIC OCEAN
EQUATORIAL GUINEA
GABON
CONGO

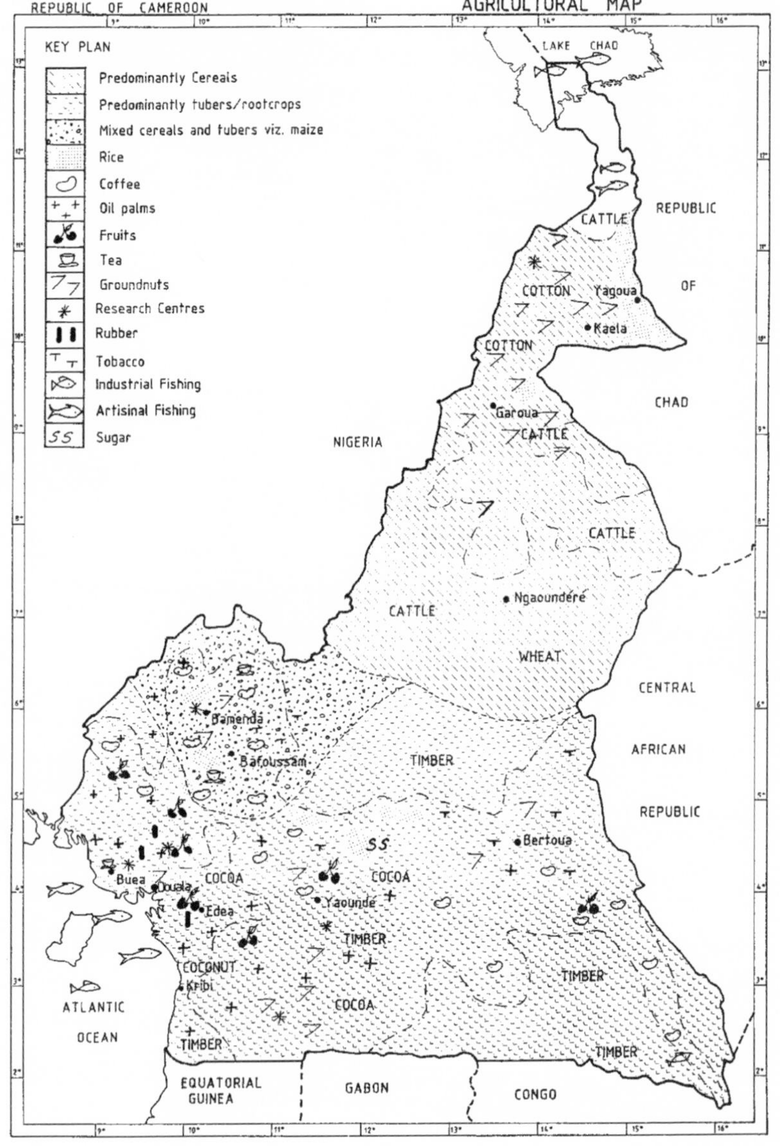
REPUBLIC OF CAMEROON
AGRICULTURAL MAP
KEY PLAN
Predominantly Cereals
Predominantly tubers/rootcrops
Mixed cereals and tubers viz. maize
Rice
Coffee
Oil palms
Fruits
Tea
Groundnuts
Research Centres
Rubber
Tobacco
Industrial Fishing
Artisinal Fishing
Sugar
LAKE CHAD
REPUBLIC OF CHAD
NIGERIA
CENTRAL AFRICAN REPUBLIC
ATLANTIC OCEAN
EQUATORIAL GUINEA
GABON
CONGO
CATTLE
COTTON
WHEAT
TIMBER
COCOA
COCONUT
Yagoua
Kaela
Garoua
Ngaoundéré
Bamenda
Bafoussam
Bertoua
Buea
Douala
Edea
Yaounde
Kribi

Chronology of Cameroon History

5th c. B.C. Hannon (Hanno) sees Mount Cameroon eruption.

9th–15th centuries A.D. The Sao civilization flourishes in the northern portions of contemporary Cameroon.

1472 Portuguese explorers under leadership of Fernando Gomes find the Wouri River, which they name Rio dos Cameroes, or "Shrimp River."

1600s Nshare founds Bamoun dynasty.

1806 Modibo Adama founds Adamawa.

1817 Uthman Dan Fodio, Moslem religious and military leader, dies.

1843 Joseph Merrick, a Baptist missionary from Jamaica, establishes missions at Bimbia and Douala.

1847 Death of Modibo Adama.

1852

29 April Anglo–Duala Treaty to end slave trade is signed.

1858 Alfred Saker founds Victoria (Limbe).

1884

12 July Eduard Woermann signs protectorate treaties with Duala chiefs on behalf of Germany.

14 July Gustav Nachtigal arrives to establish German protectorate.

1885

26 February Congress of Berlin defines rules for European colonization in Africa (15 November 1884–26 February 1885).

21 April Great Britain agrees to turn over control of Victoria to Germany.

1888 Theodor Christaller opens first German school in Douala.

1890 Njoya's reign as 16th Sultan of Bamoun begins.

1891 Bakweri-German clashes begin (1891–94).

1899 Bulu-German clashes begin (1899–1901).

1900 Rabah conquers Mandara (1895–1900).

22 April Rabah is killed in battle with French near Kousseri.

1902 Slavery is abolished by the German administration.

1908 Lotin Same is ordained in Baptist church.

1909

26 April Mount Cameroon erupts.

1911

4 November France grants large amounts of territory to Kamerun to form New Kamerun.

1914

1 August Kamerun becomes involved in World War I.

8 August Executions of Martin-Paul Samba and Rudolf Douala Manga Bell by the Germans for treason.

1916

20 February The last German stronghold, at Mora, falls, and the war in Kamerun is over.

1922

22 February Mount Cameroon erupts, causing damage to plantations.

20 July The French and British mandates over their respective territories in Cameroon come into effect.

1927

27 August The construction of the railroad, begun by the Germans, reaches Yaoundé.

1931 Sultan Njoya is exiled to Yaoundé.

1933

30 May Sultan Njoya dies in exile.

1938

February Jeucafra is formed to combat pro-German sentiments.

1939

1 February St. Joseph's College, Sasse, the first anglophone secondary school admits first class.

1940

27 March Cameroons Youth League is formed in Lagos.

26–27 August General Philippe Leclerc arrives in French Cameroun to rally the territory to the side of General de Gaulle and the Free French.

1943

1 September Chief Charles Atangana dies in Yaoundé.

1944

30 January Brazzaville Conference opens.

1946

25 October L'Assemblée Représentative du Cameroun (ARCAM) is established.

13 December Mandate period ends and French and British trusteeship periods begin.

1947

1 January Cameroon Development Corporation begins its existence.

1948

10 April Union des Populations du Cameroun (UPC) is founded.

1952 ATCAM, l'Assemblée territoriale du Cameroun, comes into existence.

1954 Southern Cameroons attains semiregional status within Nigeria.

November Ronald Pré becomes French high commissioner for Cameroun.

1955

March Kamerun National Democratic Party (KNDP) is founded.

13 July UPC goes underground, and effective civil war begins.

1956

23 June Loi Cadre is approved by French National Assembly.

1957

22 February Statut du Cameroun is ratified providing for Cameroun independence.

May–June London Constitutional Conference grants Southern Cameroons full regional status within Nigeria.

9 May L'Assemblée Législative du Cameroun (ALCAM) comes into existence.

10 May Andre-Marie Mbida becomes prime minister of the first Cameroun government.

1958

18 February Ahmadou Ahidjo becomes prime minister after Mbida government falls.

May Union Camerounaise political party is established in Garoua.

13 September Reuben Um Nyobe is killed by a gendarme.

1959 Southern Cameroon gains full regional status within Nigeria.

1 January French Cameroun gains full self-government, just short of independence.

March Mount Cameroon erupts.

10–11 August Mamfe Conference of Southern Cameroon political parties is held.

1960

1 January French Cameroun becomes the fully independent Cameroun Republic; the constitution of the République du Cameroun becomes law.

21 February Independence constitution for the Cameroun Republic is approved.

10 April Elections for the National Assembly of the Cameroun Republic are conducted.

May Cameroons Peoples' National Convention (CPNC) is founded.

5 May Ahmadou Ahidjo is elected the first president of the Cameroun Republic.

3 November Felix-Roland Moumie, hero of Cameroun nationalism and a leader of the UPC, is murdered by a French agent in Switzerland.

1961

11 February Plebiscites are held in British Cameroons.
Northern Cameroons votes to join the Federation of Nigeria; Southern Cameroons votes to join the Cameroun Republic.

17–21 July Foumban Conference defines the structure of the new country.

1 October The Cameroun Republic and British Southern Cameroons are reunified to form the Federal Republic of Cameroon; a new constitution is enacted.

1962 University of Yaoundé is opened.

1964

1 January Union Douanière Economique de l'Afrique Centrale (UDEAC) is established.

1965

10 March President Ahidjo is reelected.

1966

1 September Union Nationale Camerounaise/Cameroon National Union (CNU) is formally established.

1967

31 December Tombel Massacre of Bamiléké migrants occurs.

1969

10–15 March UNC/CNU holds First Party Congress at Garoua.

1970

7 June National Assembly elections are conducted.

1971

6 January Bishop Ndongmo, M. Ouandie, and others are convicted and sentenced to death in Ndongmo affair.

2 April Cameroon establishes diplomatic relations with the People's Republic of China.

1972

20 May Referendum in favor of the formation of the United Republic of Cameroon.

2 June The Constitution of the United Republic of Cameroon dismantles the federal system.

1973

9 March Green Revolution to develop agriculture is opened by President Ahidjo.

18 May National Assembly elections are conducted.

18 October Cameroon breaks relations with Israel.

1975 Transcameroon Railway is completed.

5 April President Ahidjo is reelected to office.

30 June Paul Biya appointed to post of prime minister.

14 December Tonnerre Yaoundé wins the African Cup Winners Cup in football (soccer).

1976

April First National General Population and Housing Census is conducted.

1977

December Petroleum production begins.

1978

28 May Legislative elections are conducted.

1979

21–22 October Northern Massacre occurs when police clash with Dolle villagers in the Northern Province.

9 December Canon Yaoundé wins African Cup Winners Cup in football (soccer).

16 December Union Douala wins the African Champion Club Cup in football (soccer).

1980

13 February CNU/UNC holds Third Party Congress at Bafoussam.

5 April President Ahidjo is reelected with 99.99 percent of votes cast in his favor.

14 December Canon Yaoundé wins the African Champion Club Cup in football (soccer).

1981

May 10,000 Cameroonians are repatriated from Gabon after anti-Cameroon riots in Libreville and Port Gentil.

15 May–19 August Border dispute and crisis with Nigeria occurs after five Nigerian soldiers are killed in disputed area.

16 May SONARA oil refinery at Victoria/Limbe is inaugurated.

November Song-Loulou Dam comes into operation.

4 November Fifth Five-Year Development Plan (1981–86) is submitted to National Assembly.

1982

4 November President Ahidjo resigns as president of Cameroon.

6 November Paul Biya becomes president of Cameroon.

1983

January–February Nigeria expels approximately 120,000 Cameroonians living within its borders.

29 May National Assembly elections are held.

17 August Ahidjo resigns as chairman of CNU.

22 August Destabilization plot against state and dismissal of Prime Minister Bouba are announced. Maj. Ibrahim Oumharou and Capt. Ahmadou Salatou are arrested shortly thereafter.

22 August President Biya divides Northern Province into North, Extreme North, and Adamawa Provinces. Center South is also divided to become Center and South Provinces.

27 August Ahidjo resigns as chairman of CNU.

14 September Second Extraordinary Congress of CNU selects Paul Biya as party leader.

19 October Treaty is signed in Libreville to establish the Economic Community of the States of Central Africa.

1984 The Constitution of the Republic of Cameroon is enacted.

14 January Presidential elections bring Paul Biya a victory of 99.98 percent of the vote.

3 February Name of country becomes Republic of Cameroon.

28 February Plotters of 22 August 1983 affair are convicted, as is Ahmadou Ahidjo. All are sentenced to death.

14 March President Biya pardons death sentences of plotters.
Cameroon wins African Nations Cup in football (soccer).

6–7 April Major attempt at coup d'état under leadership of Col. Ibrahim Saleh and Issa Adoum fails, with many killed.

1985 Petroleum production reaches record level, estimated at 9.2 million tons.

25–28 February President Biya makes official visit to United States.

1 March National Population Commission is established.

21–24 March Bamenda Congress of the UNC inaugurates the Cameroon People's Democratic Movement (CPDM).

August Pope John Paul II visits Cameroon.

23 December Regular television transmission begins.

1986 Petroleum income suffers major decline.

12 January Multicandidate elections held for lower-echelon CPDM offices.

30 June CELLUCAM project is declared a total loss.

July Tillier affair damages Franco-Cameroon relations.

25 July Sixth Five-Year Plan is submitted to the National Assembly.

21–22 August Lake Nyos disaster kills more than 1,700 people.

26 August Diplomatic relations are restored with Israel.

27 August Bernard N. Fonlon, politician and intellectual leader, dies.

29 November President Biya inaugurates Lagdo Dam on the Benue River.

1987 Government announces that the country is in an economic crisis.

24–31 March President Biya makes official visit to the People's Republic of China.

August Economic austerity measures are instituted.

1988

27 March Cameroon wins African National Cup in football (soccer).

April S. T. Muna withdraws from politics.

24 April Legislative elections with multiple candidates within the single-party structure and presidential elections are held.

Biya is reelected with strong support, but considerable turnover occurs within the Assembly.

June E. M. L. Endeley, anglophone politician and first prime minister of Southern Cameroons, dies.

1989

30 November Ahmadou Ahidjo dies.

1990 Indomitable Lions win World Cup opener, qualify for quarterfinals.

19 February Yondo Manengue Black is arrested for trying to form a new party.

26 May Bamenda riots at Social Democratic Front (SDF) rally, leaving six dead.

12 June Foncha resigns as vice president of CPDM to protest government actions of 26 May in Bamenda.

19 December President Biya approves multiparty system.

1991

1 January Celestin Monga is arrested for open letter to Biya in *Le Messager*.

12 February First two new parties approved by Government-Union des Populations du Cameroon (UPC) and Integral Democracy in Cameroon.

March SDF is legalized.

22 April Office of Prime Minister is approved; Sadou Hayatou is appointed on 26 April.

26 May Most of country is placed under military control.

24 June Official start of Ghost Town (Ville Mortes) campaign.

2 October Fru Ndi is shot at during Bamenda rally; government helicopters drop grenades on crowd.

30 October Tripartite Conference opens in Yaoundé.

1992

29–31 January Fighting in Kousseri between Kotoko and Chaos Arabs kills around 100.

1 March First multiparty National Assembly elections are held; Cameroon People's Democratic Movement (CPDM) loses majority.

13 April Establishment of the six-university system.

21–27 May SDF has first national convention.

4 July Cameroon Anglophone Movement (CAM) holds first national convention.

11 October First multiparty presidential elections are held; Biya wins.

27 October State of emergency is declared in North West Province; lasts until 28 December.

29 October Fru Ndi is placed under house arrest.

1993

23 March Grand Débat is announced.

4 April The first All Anglophone Conference (AAC I) is held in Buea, resulting in First AAC Buea Declaration.

17 May "Preliminary Draft Constitution," or Owona Constitution, is published.

1994

20 February Cameroon announces decision to go to the International Court of Justice on the Bakassi peninsula issue.

29 April–2 May AAC II Conference is held, resulting in Bamenda Proclamation.

25–26 December Kotoko and Chaos Arabs fighting kills 50.

1995

25–27 May SDF Maroua Congress.

December Cameroon joins the Commonwealth, becoming its 52nd member.

1996

18 January A new constitution of the Republic of Cameroon is promulgated.

25 May Paul Isidore Soppo Priso dies in France.

8–10 July Organization of African Unity (OAU) Summit is held in Yaoundé.

1997

17 May National Assembly elections are held; CPDM wins majority.

12 October Presidential elections are conducted; Paul Biya wins.

1999

10 April John Ngu Foncha dies.

Introduction

BACKGROUND

Cameroon is a central African state just slightly to the north of the equator. This triangular-shaped country of some 183,600 square miles is surrounded by Nigeria, Chad, the Central African Republic, Congo, Gabon, Equatorial Guinea, and a 160-mile coastline on the Atlantic Ocean.

There are four major geographic zones in the country: the southern coastal lowlands, the western highlands, the central and southern plateaus, and the Chad basin in the far north. Climate is affected by altitude, distance from the sea, and the season, but in general the country is characterized by rainy and dry seasons. Near the coast rainfall may be more than 170 inches per year and spread over six to seven months, but inland there may be only 32 inches of rain limited to two or three months. The average temperature at Douala, on the coast and close to sea level, is 79 °F, but at Bamenda, inland and at a higher altitude, it is 66 °F.

These multiple geographic zones and differences in climate lead to a variety of vegetation types and the possibility of a diverse range of food crops and pastoral activities. Rain forest and swamps lie in narrow belts along the coast, with the forest extending inland in the southeast. The forest gives way to savanna toward the northern interior.

The country is divided into 10 provinces (termed *regions* in the constitution of 1996) for administrative convenience: the Littoral, East, Center, South, West, Adamawa, North, and Extreme North Provinces are francophone (French speaking); the North West and South West are anglophone (English speaking). This difference in language results from Cameroon's colonial experience. Each of these provinces is subdivided into several divisions, or *départements*.

The population of 15 million persons lives mainly in rural areas. It is a young population, with 46 percent 14 years old or younger. The population is increasing at about 2.81 percent per year. Although urbanization is occurring rapidly, only 45 percent of the people live in towns and cities. The major cities are Douala and Yaoundé; smaller cities include Limbe, Kumba,

Bamenda, Garoua, Maroua, Ngaoundéré, Foumban, Edea, and Bafoussam. About 77 percent of the workforce is in agriculture and forestry; only 6.8 percent is in industry and 16.9 percent in services.

The Cameroon people exist in numerous ethnic groups, most of which number fewer than 100,000 persons. Among the more well known of these are the Duala, Bamiléké, Bamoum, Fulani, Fang, and Bakweri. These ethnic groups include many of the major cultural types of the continent, leading tourism officials to describe the country as "Africa in Miniature." Many Cameroonians are Christians—Catholic and Protestant—but there is also a large Muslim minority. This minority, perhaps 20 percent of the population, is located mainly in the north. For most of the period since independence, the Muslim minority has held a disproportionate amount of political power.

HISTORY

Precolonial Period

Archaeologists, students of oral history, and scientists are helping to uncover the early history. But at this time in these efforts, much is still to be learned. Remains from the Neolithic period have been found in many parts of the country, suggesting that human beings have been here for many thousands of years, perhaps 50,000 years or more. The current population of Cameroon is ethnically diverse. Among the many groups are the pygmies, situated in the southeast corner of the country. Although now few in number, the pygmies and their lifestyle represent the most ancient of Cameroon populations.

Only recently have we begun to have information substantial enough to develop some conception of Cameroon's past. Some 500 years after the birth of Christ, an important civilization was developing in the interior of today's Cameroon. Around the shores of Lake Chad, the Sao civilization was becoming a large entity ruled by a king. Most of our knowledge of this civilization comes from the work of archaeologists. Over the years the Sao came into contact with the kingdom of Kanem, which eventually conquered Sao. By the 14th century Sao was reduced to a small entity replaced eventually by the Kotoko state.

At about this same time, Portuguese explorers were sailing along the western coasts of Africa, beginning the contacts that would lead to the slave trade and the eventual conquest and colonization of Africa—and Cameroon. At various times, Portuguese, Dutch, and British traders dominated the commerce along the Cameroon coasts, though in the end it was the Germans who colonized and established the entity now called Cameroon. In the latter part of the trading era, Christian missionaries, many of whom were of African descent, began their work establishing churches, schools, and communities, first along the coast and later inland. The Baptist Mission from London and the American Presbyterian Mission were the first of many groups to enter the country.

Significant events were occurring inland during this time period, too. The history of the Fulani, or Foulbé, people begins far from the boundaries of Cameroon, but by the 1800s these people were becoming an important factor in northern Cameroon. Many Fulani had settled into the northern grasslands by this time. Under the powerful leadership of Uthman Dan Fodio, a revolutionary Islamic influence was rapidly spreading among the Fulani. In 1896 Uthman began a holy war, or *jihad*. He appointed Modibo Adama to carry the war into Cameroon. Adama was highly successful in conquering the various Fulani and other societies and establishing a large empire, Adamawa. Maroua, Garoua, and Ngaoundéré became major centers in this entity, which was ruled from Yola in present-day Nigeria.

By this time a large number of states, kingdoms, and societies had been established over the area of Cameroon. Many of these entities, their customs, and the descendents of their rulers continue to be significant in Cameroon today. There is not space to discuss all of these, life within them, or the relations between them. Trade was widespread, diplomatic relations were well developed, and conquests and wars took place. Most well known of these are the various Bamiléké chiefdoms in today's West Province and the various Tikar societies of the Northwest and West. Bamoum, founded by Nshare, is one of the most famous of these societies.

One other important group, the Bantu, should be mentioned. The study of the Bantu peoples and their migrations over much of the African continent is a major topic in African history. Much research suggests that the origin of the Bantu is somewhere along the Cameroon–Nigeria border. Thus, many of the Bantu groups now found in Cameroon have been in their present locations for a long time. However, other groups moved into new locations in the recent past. The Fang and Beti were still spreading and settling in southeastern Cameroon at about the same time that American missionaries were establishing at Batanga.

Colonial Period

Regardless of the changing nationality of the predominant European traders along the coast, the Germans in 1884 managed to take the area for their empire. They did so only days before the British made a similar attempt. The Germans moved inland over the years, extending their control and their claims to land far beyond the Cameroon on today's map. Initially, their major dealings were with African traders, mainly Duala, along the coast. But German traders did not enjoy dealing with these "middlemen," for direct trade with the interior promised greater profits. So, colonial power was used to break the Duala monopoly.

A second major economic activity of the German era was plantation agriculture. Large estates were established, especially in the southwest of Kamerun (the German spelling), to provide a variety of tropical produce (e.g., cocoa, bananas, tea, rubber) to Germany. The traders, the plantation owners, and government officials competed for scarce labor, and force was necessary for the Germans to break the Africans away from their homes and farms. The labor system established was harsh and cruel, and many laborers died while serving German interests.

The events of World War I brought a swift end to German rule. British, French, and Belgian troops—mainly drawn from their African colonies—were used to successfully drive the Germans into exile on the Spanish island of Fernando Po. Thus began a period of British rule in small western and northern portions and French rule in a larger portion of the territory. These territories, "mandates" under the League of Nations and "trusts" under the United Nations, were usually referred to as French Cameroun and British Cameroons. The latter was in two parts—Southern and Northern Cameroons. A large piece of Kamerun, the New Kamerun, was given to the French to add to their colonies in French Equatorial Africa. This territory was never again considered to be part of Cameroon.

British rule in their territories is generally described as a period of neglect. The areas were attached to their colony, Nigeria, and, in the eyes of many Cameroonians, the British mandate/trust became the colony of a colony. This neglect, coupled with the influx of numerous Nigerian migrants into Southern Cameroons, caused great resentment. The major economic activity in Southern Cameroons was agriculture. Most of the German plantations were located here, and after a brief period of control by colonial officials, these returned to German control—which lasted until World War II. After the war, these were united into one entity, the Cameroon Development Corporation (CDC), which became a parastatal. Today, although portions have been privatized (sold or turned over to private enterprise), the CDC is the second largest employer in the country. Government is the largest. The railroad, like the CDC recently privatized, is the third largest employer.

Some development occurred in peasant agriculture, too, especially in the latter years of British rule. Cocoa became important in the 1930s; coffee and bananas, both for export, saw rapid growth after World War II as a result of Cameroonian initiatives—often with British opposition or reluctance. Little change of any type was fostered in Northern Cameroons.

Much greater agricultural development took place in French Cameroun. Limited industrial and infrastructural growth also occurred, again largely after World War II. The French took much greater interest in their mandate/trust than did the British. Much more capital was invested, and many French people (the *colons*) came to work in Cameroun. This greater French involvement meant that at independence French Cameroun had a much higher gross national product (GNP) per capita, higher education levels, better health care, and—although still rudimentary—a better infrastructure than British Cameroons. Note, however, that French interest concentrated in the region bounded by Douala, Yaoundé, Foumban, and Kribi. Outside this "Fertile Crescent" were large areas at least as underdeveloped as Southern and Northern Cameroons.

Although one may point to various differences in the colonial experiences of the French and British mandates/trusts, some powerful similarities are also evident. Most important, these rulers—and the Germans before them—continued the process of drawing the Cameroon people into the international capitalist economic system. By the time of independence, Cameroon had become an attachment to the economic system of Western Europe. More directly, the majority of Cameroon had become an appendix to the French economy. A dependent status had evolved whereby the trusts produced raw materials for use by European industries, but they produced little for Cameroon needs. The trusts were dependent on Europe/France for finished goods and for a market for the raw materials the inhabitants produced. This fragile, dependent economy continues to plague the people of Cameroon and their government to this day.

Although opposition to colonial rule was expressed from its onset, it was only after World War II that internal developments in Cameroon and Europe and changes in the world attitude toward colonialism were powerful enough to bring about independence. In British Cameroons the major question for the public was whether to remain with Nigeria or to rejoin Cameroun. In a United Nations–supervised plebiscite, Southern Cameroons decided to reunify with French Cameroun to become the Federal Republic of Cameroon. Northern Cameroons voted to join the Federation of Nigeria.

In French Cameroun the major question was the type and intensity of the relationship with France after independence. The first true nationalist party, the Union des Populations du Cameroun (UPC), and its leaders, Felix Moumie and Um Nyobe, demanded a thorough break with France and the construction of a socialist economy. French officials opposed and suppressed the UPC, leading to a bitter civil war. The French encouraged alternative political parties and leaders as they gradually granted increasing power to elected assemblies. Eventually, independence was granted, with Ahmadou Ahidjo to become first president. Ahidjo and his ruling party, the Union Camerounaise, pledged to build a capitalist economy and, in a series of secret agreements, to maintain very close political, economic, and cultural ties to France. On 1 January 1960, the independent Republic of Cameroon came into existence. On 1 October 1961, it joined with Southern Cameroons to become the Federal Republic of Cameroon.

Independent Cameroon

From independence until 1982, Cameroon was ruled by President Ahidjo. In this period he centralized power in the capital, Yaoundé, and in one person, himself. He used the economic power of the state to reward followers and used the police and the security apparatus to punish his enemies. Cameroon was an authoritarian, single-party state in which civil rights held little sway. The civil war with the UPC was ended slowly and brutally, but the state of emergency declared during the war continued for years beyond the conclusion of the struggle. Ahidjo declared nation building to be a major goal, for—as in much of Africa—there was fear that the country's multiethnic population might owe greater loyalty to ethnic groups than to the nation. He used the fear of ethnic conflict to justify authoritarian government. In his effort to centralize power, he ended the federation in 1972, replacing it with a highly centralized government; eliminated all political parties except his own, the Cameroon National Union (CNU); and on several occasions altered the constitution to concentrate power in the presidency.

The government's economic policy of planned liberalism aimed to encourage private investment, local and foreign, but government was to play a strong, significant role in guiding development into sectors of the economy and into geographic areas deemed as priorities. To this end, the government became a partner in numerous economic enterprises, the parastatals.

Initially, Cameroon relied on the export of cash crops—cocoa, coffee, bananas, rubber, timber, palm products, cotton—to provide the foreign capital needed for development expenditures. Much emphasis was placed on the expansion of the production of these crops, often while ignoring food crops. In addition to export crops, some emphasis was placed in import substitution crops such as sugar, wheat, and rice, which had become popular in Cameroon but were not grown in sufficient quantity locally to provide for the country's needs. With the announcement of the Green Revolution at the Buea Agropastoral Show in 1973, it was acknowledged that attention must be given to indigenous food crops, too. Not only was the country to be self-sufficient in food, but it was also to become the food source for many of its neighbors. Although today Cameroon agriculture continues to be plagued by low productivity and outdated technology, it has been successful in fostering growth and development in food and export crops. Some major failures have taken place in attempts to develop import substitution crops.

The discovery of exploitable petroleum reserves in the 1970s was initially a great boost to the Cameroon economy. Once into production, petroleum soon became the country's most valuable export. Petroleum revenues were used to give higher prices to farmers, thus encouraging increased agricultural output. Petroleum money was used to pay the costs for the imports of materials and technical skill needed for many development projects. And petroleum earnings were used to build financial reserves for difficult times that might arise in the future. Sadly, petroleum income was also used to pay the costs of many large, badly planned projects. Much of the income was poorly used. It is difficult to accurately state the size of the petroleum income, for until recently this figure has been known only to the president's office. The earnings were not included in the annual budget and were spent at the discretion of the president.

Attempts to foster industrial development have met with less success. For many years the emphasis was on large-scale projects such as the Cellucam paper pulp facility. Numerous problems in respect of planning, technology transfer, and market research have plagued these projects, and large amounts of capital have been lost. In addition to other problems, these parastatals were often used as political resources. Management positions were given to reward political friends, regardless of any business skill they might lack. Many unnecessary employees were taken on for political purposes, as patronage. Corrupt practices enriched many in management but bankrupted the businesses. More success has been found in assisting the growth of small and medium-sized enterprises producing goods for local use. But to a large extent the country still depends on the purchase abroad of industrial goods. Large-scale and significant exceptions to this have taken place with respect to refined petroleum products, cement, fabric and finished clothing, beverages, and aluminum. Some success has also been met in the development of agrobusiness, processing agricultural products for domestic use or export.

Although a first-time visitor to Cameroon may view the transportation system as inadequate, the government has made significant progress since independence in extending the road, rail, and air services. Telephone facilities have multiplied rapidly. National radio broadcasting covers the entire country, and television is available in most areas. With the construction of large-scale hydroelectric projects in the coastal region and in the north, the country has multiplied several times its electricity-generating capabilities. The most important success in infrastructure building has been in education. Relative to many African countries, Cameroon had a high proportion of children in school at the time of independence, but shortages of appropriately trained men and women was then—and is now—a major restraint on growth and development. Tremendous growth in facilities and number of staff and students has taken place in the last three decades.

In 1982, Cameroon underwent a dramatic and obvious political change, but equally important though less obvious economic changes were under way, too. On 4 November, President Ahidjo resigned his government office and turned the presidency over to his legal successor, Paul Biya, but Ahidjo retained his leadership position in the Cameroon National Union, the country's sole political party. In recent African history, such a peaceful change of government was rare. Sadly, the tranquil nature of the transfer did not last long. Ahidjo's retention of control of the CNU along with other evidence suggest that he had no real intention of giving up his domination of the Cameroon political system. Rather, he wished to move in to the background, keeping overall control but turning over lesser duties to President Biya. In effect, Biya was to be Ahidjo's puppet. However, Biya turned out to have a mind and a will of his own, and conflict between the two men became obvious. The showdown took place when Ahidjo tried to assert party domination over the government, claiming that the party would select the president of the country. However, Biya had used his time in office to build a coalition that was sufficient to overwhelm Ahidjo, and Ahidjo resigned from the party. A minor coup attempt, and then on 6 April 1984 a bloody uprising by the Republican Guard, probably in favor of if not directed by Ahidjo or his supporters, followed, but Biya prevailed.

Early in his presidency, Biya seemed to desire the development of a freer, more democratic society in Cameroon. Within the confines of a one-party system, Biya allowed competitive elections for party offices and for the National Assembly. He experimented with more freedom of speech and press. However, the conflict with Ahidjo and the severity of the 1984 coup attempt brought back some of the restrictions of the Ahidjo era. Events since that time make clear that whatever democratic intentions Biya may have had, these intentions have been overwhelmed by his desire to stay in power.

Biya's reactions to two overlapping political issues have shown his autocratic nature. Cameroon, like much of the world, has come under intense pressure to develop a more democratic society. At the same time, discontent among the anglophone members of Cameroon society has become intense. The two pressures unite in the demand for greater anglophone control over matters affecting their part of the country. A more democratic society is seen as a means of bringing greater autonomy to the anglophones—or even independence for their portion of Cameroon. In general, democracy is seen as a preferable way to exist. From 1989 until the turn of the century, these two pressures on the Biya government have led to periods of political instability, at times almost chaos, and the threat of civil war.

These pressures have also led to some important changes in the political system of the country. As of December 1990, Cameroon is a mulitiparty state. Since then, numerous parties have emerged, most based on ethnic or regional concerns. Two parties, the Social Democratic Front (SDF), led by Fru Ndi, and the National Union for Democracy and Progress (UNDP), led by Maigari Bello Bouba, have become significant challengers of Biya's ruling party, the Cameroon People's Democratic Movement (CPDM). Since 1992, multiparty elections have been held for the National Assembly and for the presidency. Biya and the CPDM have managed to maintain power, much to the frustration of opponents who believe (correctly so) that the elections are rigged and that they do not face a fair fight in their struggle for power. Less progress has been made in resolving the anglophone problem.

Anglophone leaders in general give strong support to the idea of returning the country to a federal situation, but a federation in which the states would have considerably more self-governance than in the original Federal Republic of Cameroon. Some anglophones have given up on the idea of Cameroon and have begun to demand independence as the Republic of Ambazonia. There is little if any support for the idea of rejoining Nigeria. Biya rammed through a new constitution in 1996 to answer anglophone demands, but it failed to quell their anger. Instead of a federation it established a weak sort of decentralization that left the central government and the president clearly in control of all matters.

The economy has presented major problems for the Biya government, a factor that has exacerbated the political demands. In some respects, Ahidjo resigned at the right moment, for a severe economic crisis was just to emerge. In the eyes of many Cameroonians, the blame for that crisis is placed on President Biya. Corruption, bad planning, and the use of government money to enrich government personalities and serve patronage purposes are important causes of the crisis. But the economic crisis is partly the result of international economic conditions and the weak, brittle, and dependent economy that Biya inherited on coming to office. The infamous African drought of the 1980s caused export crop production to decrease at a time when prices for coffee, cocoa, and other agricultural exports were in decline.

More significant was the drop in prices and demand in world petroleum markets. Cameroon's income, dependent on exports, dropped rapidly. For a short period, this loss of revenue was covered by drawing on reserves built up in the first years of petroleum exports. These funds were quickly exhausted, and by 1987 the government admitted that the country faced an economic crisis. Cameroon had become a debtor nation. Budget cuts were necessary, and the ripple effects of this have been felt throughout the economy. Under pressure from the International Monetary Fund (IMF), the World Bank, and aid-giving countries, Cameroon has been forced to accept structural adjustment programs. In return for financial assistance, the government must undertake stringent economic and important political reforms.

While the economic demands may in the long run benefit the country, the short-term effect is hardship for the majority of the population. Cutbacks in spending on education and health care, reduction of salaries and number of employees, and closure and privatization of many of the parastatals have been accompanied by a reduction in the quality of life for all but the wealthiest and most politically connected of Cameroonians. The meaning of this crisis is clear: Although Cameroon has made economic progress since independence, it has not been able to change the dependent nature of its economy.

As Cameroon enters the 21st century, its prospects for political stability, justice, and prosperity are dimmer than they have been for most of the country's independent existence. Compared to many African countries, Cameroon remains a relatively successful state. But compared to itself two decades ago, most Cameroonians have a sense of failure and foresee a gloomy future for the country.

The Dictionary

– A –

ABBIA. *Abbia: Cameroon Cultural Review* is a journal uniquely expressing Cameroonian culture and **bilingualism**.* Founded by the father of Cameroon bilingualism, **Bernard Fonlon**, this cultural review has successively brought about greater collaboration among Cameroonian elites as vanguards of the bilingual ideal. However, since 1963, *Abbia* has experienced a rough life cycle. Its future became even more bleak with Fonlon's death in August 1986. The name *Abbia* is taken from a game of chance common among certain peoples in the south of Cameroon, particularly the **Beti** who come from the **Yaoundé** area. The game pieces, Abbia stones, are the carved pits of the fruits of the Mimusops Congolensis tree. An Abbia stone as well as a few lines of the **Bamoum** script, ***shu mom***, invented by **Sultan Njoya,** are used to decorate the cover of the journal.

ABJOUDI, HAMADJODA. *See* HAMADJODA ABJOUDI.

ACCORD DE COOPERATION ECONOMIQUE MONETAIRE ET FINANCIERE. This bilateral agreement between **France** and the new **République du Cameroun** was signed in November 1960. This monetary agreement was one in a series of conditions under which Cameroun's independence was granted by France. By the accord, Cameroun entered the **franc zone** under a monetary structure of a fixed exchange rate of 50 Cameroon francs to one French franc. All gold and foreign exchange reserves of the franc zone were to be held in Paris as a joint pool. The establishment of the **Bank of Central African States (BEAC)**, functioning in close cooperation with the French Treasury, led to further agreements on monetary cooperation in November 1972, the Convention

---

*Users of this volume should note that cross-references in each dictionary entry are printed in boldface type.

of the Operations Accounts of December 1973, and the Amendment to the Reserve Exchange Guarantee in 1975. There has been a lively debate in scholarly circles on the merits and demerits of such a dependent monetary situation and an internationally recognized and easily transferable currency. *See also* CFA FRANC.

ACHU, SIMON ACHIDI (1934–). Although his true home is Santa, Achu was born on 5 November 1934, at **Bamenda**, Mezam Division, in the **North West Province**. He attended primary school in Bamenda before entering Cameroon Protestant College (CPC) in Bali. On completion, he served as an accounts clerk with a commercial house before joining the Widekum Council. He then moved to the **Cameroon Development Corporation (CDC)** but later did a one year course in economics in the Faculty of Economic Sciences at the University of London. On his return, he was appointed assistant manager in training in one of the CDC's large plantations.

While in Cameroon, Achu gained a scholarship to continue his studies in economics, in the Federal **University of Yaoundé**. He later suspended his studies in **Yaoundé** and proceeded to the University of Besançon in France, where in 1963 he graduated with diplomas in the **French** language and literature. On his return home in October 1963, Achu continued with his study in law and economics at the Federal University of Yaoundé. After his university studies in Yaoundé, he gained admission into the magistracy section of the National School of Administration and Magistracy (ENAM). Between October 1965 and October 1966, he was a magistrate.

On completion at ENAM, Achu worked at the Presidency as a translator and interpreter from 1966 to February 1968. While in the Presidency, he also performed the functions of state inspector until 30 April 1971. Between May and October 1971, he worked as secretary-general in the Ministry of the Public Service and later became minister delegate at the General State Inspection. In July 1973, Achu was appointed minister of justice and keeper of the seals, a post he held until 1977. He then retired to become a businessman. On 9 April 1991, in an apparent attempt to calm **anglophone** agitation and cries of marginalization, Achu was called back to government and appointed prime minister. He served in this post until 19 September 1996, when he was dropped in favor of another anglophone, **Peter Mafany Musonge**.

ACT OF BERLIN. The text of the Congress of Berlin of 1884–85 sanctioned the partition of Africa by European powers. Intense rivalry and suspicion characterized the activities of European powers in their quest for territories in Africa. The Act of Berlin established consensus among contending European powers who struggled to get treaties with local populations on the coast. The principal rivals for the Cameroon territory were the English and the Germans, but the territory became a German **protectorate** after the visit of **Gustav Nachtigal** to the coastal area.

ADAMA, MODIBO (1786–1847). A learned Muslim scholar and holy warrior, he established the **Adamawa** Kingdom of north Cameroon. Son of another learned man, Hassana, Adama studied in Bornou and gained a high reputation for his mystic fervor. In 1806, he received the blessing from **Uthman dan Fodio** to launch the holy war and become the military, political, and religious leader of the believers. Adama established his headquarters in Yola in today's Nigeria and named the kingdom Adamawa after him. It was from this kingdom that the **Fulani,** concentration in today's northern Cameroon, expanded. Under Adama, the various animist groupings such as the Bata, Fali, and Moundang were subjected to constant wars and Islamic pressure.

ADAMAWA. The Adamawa plateau is about 1,100 meters high. One of five geographic zones of the country, the plateau flanks the middle of Cameroon and forms the water reservoir of the country. The Adamawa Division was previously an administrative region in North Cameroun inhabited mainly by the **Kirdi** peoples and the Muslim **Fulani**. The name *Adamawa* is derived from the chief figure in the spread of Fulani hegemony, **Modibo Adama**. The division existed until August 1983 when the **Adamawa Province** replaced the division as part of the administrative reform undertaken by President **Paul Biya** to preserve the peace and unity of the country. Adamawa Province was created out of the split-up of the former **Northern Province** of Cameroon.

ADAMAWA PROVINCE. This province covers a surface area of 69,339 square kilometers and consists of five divisions, 11 subdivisions, and one district. Its relief corresponds to the **Adamawa** plateau of humid tropical climate and savannah vegetation. The estimated population in 1976, the latest available estimate, was 552,500, most of whom are engaged in agriculture and animal breeding. Adamawa consists of the Djerem, Faro and Deo, Mbere, Mayo Danyo, and Vina Divisions. The province is administratively headed by a **governor** appointed by the president. The headquarters of the province is **Ngaoundéré** in the Vina Division. Other important towns include Tibati (Djerem Division) and Meiganga (Mbere Division). The province was created by presidential decree of 23 August 1983.

ADMINISTERING AUTHORITIES. European countries were empowered to exercise control of respective territories under the auspices of the **League of Nations** and the United Nations. The former German **protectorate** of **Kamerun** was turned over to administering authorities at the end of **World War I**. Under the League of Nations **mandate system,** the territory was unequally partitioned between France (four-fifths of the territory) and Great Britain (one-fifth of the territory) as administering authorities. Both powers continued in this status under the **trusteeship system** of the United Nations. Although administering authorities accepted a special responsibility of leading their territories toward self-government and independence, the Cameroon territories experienced a system of control similar to other French and British colonies in Africa. This distortion of the legal status of the Cameroon territories became a driving theme among early nationalists. Administering authorities ceased to exist with the attainment of independence.

ADOUM, ISSA (?–1984). A former director of **National Fund for Rural Development (FONADER)** (the farmer's bank) and presumed civilian leader of the failed **coup attempt of 6 April 1984**, Issa Adoum was born in Mokolo. He trained as a customs inspector in the National School of Administration and Magistry (ENAM) and underwent specialized studies in France. He served successively as secretary-general of the **National Water Corporation of Cameroon (SNEC)**, as deputy director general of **Crédit Foncier**, and as managing director of FONADER. It was in this last post, on the eve of the coup, that he is alleged to have stealthily withdrawn funds that were used to entice rebel forces against the security of the state. He is also alleged to have hurriedly written and edited the proclamation of the coup message that was read by Captain Abale over the local channel of Radio Cameroon on Friday, 6 April 1984. Although Issa Adoum was reportedly addressed as "Mr. President" by rebel forces, he attempted to escape as loyal forces gained military control. He was arrested on the run in Bangangté (**Western Province**) on 7 April. After secret trials by a military tribunal, Issa Adoum was executed on 2 May 1984.

ADVISORY COUNCIL (GOUVERNEMENTSRAT). This council was established as part of the **protectorate** government in German

Kamerun. The Advisory Council was created in July 1885 on the initiative of German traders who largely comprised its membership. This council functioned in a purely advisory manner; its decisions had no binding effect on the governor. Given the major role played by trading firms in securing Kamerun as a German protectorate, the traders' opinion was vital in the early stages of administration and consolidation. Later in the period, the Advisory Council failed to function, and its necessity was the subject of debate in the Kolonialrat in 1903. The Kolonialrat approved the continuous functioning of the advisory councils under conditions that indigenes be exempted, members be named by the governor, and preference be given to colonial settlers living near centers of administration.

AFANA, OSENDE (1930–1966). This radical Cameroon nationalist and economist was born in Ngoksa in the **East Province**. He was remarkable in his student epoch in Cameroon as a classic instigator and troublemaker against the French colonial regime. He left for further studies in Paris and became a leading organizer of the French section of the **Union des Populations du Cameroun (UPC)** exile movement. He also served as editor in chief of the journal *L'Etudiant d'Afrique Noire*. In 1957, his scholarship was withdrawn for participating in a UN debate in favor of immediate independence for Cameroun. He moved to Cairo and Conakry to join the exile UPC movement. During this period, he worked on his thesis and concentrated on the political rebellion against the **Ahmadou Ahidjo** regime. He was elected UPC secretary-general and was widely considered an intellectual at the service of the masses. He joined and led underground insurgency operations of the **National Army of Kamerun Liberation (ANLK)** from the borders between Cameroon and **Congo** Brazzaville, where he was killed on 15 March 1966, by government troops. His thesis, *L'Economie de l'Ouest-Africain*, was published in 1966 and 1977. The book contains a strong attack against bourgeois imperialist theories.

AFO A KOM. This news review of Cameroon art and culture was first published in May 1982 by the Cameroon Society for Authorship Rights (SOCADRA) under the auspices of the Ministry of Information and Culture. It aims at sensitizing the public, both at home and abroad, on the diverse aspects of the country's cultural personality through its expressions and daily manifestations. The review usually contains an editorial and news about Cameroon **music** and its stars, its literature and its authors, its **theaters** and dance groups, and its arts and artists.

The journal is named in honor of a sculpture, the Afo A Kom, that was stolen from the court of Kom in 1966. The name literally means "a thing of Kom." The sculpture is one of a set of three beaded, wooden statues. After extensive diplomatic negotiations, the Afo A Kom was returned to Kom in 1973.

AFRICA IN MINIATURE. This popular touristic phrase is often used to describe Cameroon, designating the country as a microcosm of nearly all Africa. The catch phrase signifies that all aspects of the African continent are found in a single triangle. The government's tourist industry makes reference to the vegetational, climatic, ethnological, and language variegation of the country to attract foreign visitors.

AFRICAN SOCIALISM. The first development ideology of independent Cameroon was elaborated in Ebolowa in 1962 as part of the statement on general policy at the fourth Congress of the **Union Camerounaise**. Underlying this philosophy was the denial of the existence of social classes in Africa. This policy of progress for the less privileged groups was aimed at promoting the interests of farmers, workers, **women,** and the unemployed. **Ahmadou Ahidjo** distinguished classical socialism that emphasized nationalization from African socialism based on village communities, collective labor, and human resources investment. African socialism was abandoned as a philosophy in 1965. One could assume it was one step, in a series of moves, to offset the socialist orientation of the **Union des Populations du Cameroun (UPC)**. Following poor dividends African socialism was replaced by a policy of **planned liberalism**.

AGRICULTURAL POLICY. Agriculture is the centerpiece of Cameroon's economic growth and development. Some 70 percent of the country's population is engaged in agriculture. Consequently, the first five-year development plan was styled the "farmers' plan." The strategy toward agricultural development has included the establishment of a new type of relations between the administration and farmers, the setup of structures to develop agricultural zones, and the improvement of living conditions and productivity in rural areas. Over the years, however, there has been greater promotion of export-oriented crops. This led to rural poverty and a lag in food production. The term "**Green Revolution**" is often used to denote government agricultural policy.

Agriculture growth slumped during the late 1970s with the exportation of **petroleum**. This was the case despite government efforts not to neglect agriculture or to depend on its depletable oil resource. Higher prices are now paid to farmers, and **food self-sufficiency** has been maintained. Cameroon remains heavily dependent on the export of agricultural products such as **coffee**, **cocoa**, **timber,** and **bananas** to earn the foreign exchange needed to purchase imports and finance development projects. The government also promotes the export of food crops to neighboring countries. *See also* COOPERATIVES; PALM OIL; RUBBER; SELF-RELIANT DEVELOPMENT; TEA; WHEAT.

AGROINDUSTRY STRATEGY. The development of agriculturally related industries is conceived as a decisive means for speeding up the country's growth and **self-reliant development**. State support for agroindustrial ventures began in 1968 with the creation of the Palm Grove Company (SOCAPALM). Many other agroindustrial ventures have been established. They are designed to set up industries for the processing of principal agricultural products in a bid to change the country's status from a raw material exporter. Agroindustrial ventures therefore seek to transform Cameroon's traditional agriculture through industrialization, to enhance rural development, to escape from the strong dependency on export crops, and to ameliorate the quality of Cameroon export and major domestic crops. Despite the backing of foreign consultants, constructors, and financers, agroindustry has failed to meet government's expectations and has not yet had a substantial impact on Cameroon's agriculture or economy in general. The government's decision to outlaw the export of raw timber in 1999 is an example of this strategy. The expectation is that finished lumber and wood products will be exported. New industrial jobs will appear as timber-processing factories are enlarged and established. *See also* AGRICULTURAL POLICY.

AGROPASTORAL SHOW. This national event showcases Cameroon's agricultural productivity. The most outstanding farms and livestock are rewarded to encourage competition and excellence. Agricultural shows existed at divisional and local state levels up to 1972. With the establishment of the unitary state, the first National Agricultural Show was held in **Buea** in March 1973. On this occasion, **Ahmadou Ahidjo** launched the **Green Revolution** aimed at maintaining **food self-sufficiency** in a bid to become the storehouse of central Africa.

Since Buea in 1973, agropastoral shows have been held in several cities. Agropastoral shows are jointly organized by the Ministeries of Agriculture and Livestock, Fisheries and Animal Industries. These shows, in much the same fashion as the party congresses, have provided a rationale for the government to provide extensive modern amenities to the towns wherein the shows have been located. *See also* AGRICULTURAL POLICY.

AHIDJO, AHMADOU (1924–1989). The first president of Cameroon resigned on 4 November 1982, to later become persona non grata in the country following a severe rupture with his designated constitutional successor, Pres. **Paul Biya**. Ahidjo was born in August 1924 in **Garoua** to an essentially single-parent home. It was Ahidjo's mother who catered for his livelihood. After primary education, Ahidjo attended the Ecole Primaire Supérieure in **Yaoundé** and in 1941 was trained and served as a post office radio operator in the Posts and Telegraph Service in **Douala.** He later became the leader of the Jeunes Musulmans movement

Ahidjo then engaged in a serious political career that began with his election as delegate to the first Assemblée Représentative du Cameroun (ARCAM) in 1947. In 1952, when ARCAM was restyled the **Assemblée Territoriale du Cameroun (ATCAM)**, Ahidjo was reelected. He also served as a member of the Assembly of the French Union from 1953 and became its vice president in 1956. In May 1957, he was appointed vice premier in **André-Marie Mbida's** government in **French Cameroun**. Mbida's blunders and shortcomings brought Ahidjo his lifetime opportunity. He founded the **Union Camerounaise** and, in February 1958, he replaced Mbida as French Cameroun's second prime minister.

With Ahidjo at the helm of the state, the **République du Cameroon**, which became independent in January 1960, reunited with the British **Southern Cameroons** in 1961. Before and after independence, Ahidjo faced severe challenges. These included the growing guerilla resistance to his rule by the **Union des Populations du Cameroun (UPC)**; the loss of British **Northern Cameroons** to **Nigeria** during the reunification **plebiscite**; a tarnished international image due to his poor human rights record; and an underdeveloped economy and an acute **nation-building** problem, which was aggravated by the **anglophone**-versus-**francophone** cleavages. By crushing the UPC rebellion with the help of French troops, Ahidjo improved the political stability of the country, which was crucial for Cameroon to obtain the necessary foreign assistance for its development. Even though he adopted an anti-UPC stand partly because the party called for **reunification**, he later adopted the idea and included it as one of the top priorities of his government in 1958. After talks with Southern Cameroons' politicians between 1959 and 1961, a UN-sponsored plebiscite took place on 11 February 1961, leading to the reunification of French Cameroon and British Southern Cameroons. Ahidjo became the first president of the **Federal Republic of Cameroon**.

Ahidjo had longer-range objectives in terms of the country's unification process and his eventual consolidation of power. Following his reelection in March 1965, he carried his one-party Union Camerounaise in **East Cameroon** toward a new party structure for the entire country. This meant the dissolution of the three major parties of **West Cameroon**: **Kamerun National Democratic Party (KNDP)**, **Cameroons Peoples' National Convention (CPNC)**, **Cameroon United Congress (CUC)**. Through pressure and persuasion, this became reality on 1 September 1966, with President Ahidjo as chairman of the one-party structure, the **Cameroon National Union (CNU)**.

Ahidjo was reelected in 1970, and after having silenced the guerrilla movement with the execution of **Ernest Ouandie** on 15 January 1971, he channeled his energies toward changing the political structure of Cameroon from a federal to a unitary state. In May 1972, therefore, the Federal Republic of Cameroon became the **United Republic of Cameroon**, with Ahidjo as the father of the nation.

To do this, Ahidjo acknowledged and displayed a fundamental attachment to the doctrine of the ends justifying the means. For many critics, Cameroon has since earned the reputation of a "not free state." Restriction of civil liberties, including freedom of speech and movement as well as detention without trial, were common features of the Ahidjo regime. Ahidjo argued that repression took place because certain individuals sacrificed the collective interest in the quest for personal political designs. Ahidjo used these various tactics to make Cameroon one of Africa's most "stable" countries. It was this disputable element of stability that assisted Cameroon's very promising economic prospects. Agricultural production increased, and petroleum exploitation helped to sustain the country's economy to one of the highest levels of performance on the African continent.

Consequently, by the time Ahidjo left office, Cameroon was a country with high marks on several fronts in a troubled continent. His departure produced a surprise of significant proportions. No one took his word for truth when he declared on multiple occasions after 1975 that "I will not remain in power for eternity." Although the entire nation was caught off guard on his resignation announcement, the population and his successor reserved for the former president superlative eulogies befitting his 24 years in politics following his resignation. What followed Ahidjo's resignation was a melodramatic demonstration of power and political succession of an unusual kind. Ahidjo's greatest undoing was that he never left power completely. Ahidjo continued to retain the influential position of chairman of the CNU with President Biya as head of state and government. Such a situation inevitably created a struggle for position and influence between Ahidjo and Biya. Two conspiracy theories have been elaborated to explain the goings-on: the first assuming that Ahidjo strongly wanted to return to power or that he expected Biya to be a mere caretaker president of limited tenure; the second holding that the Biya entourage created an uncompromising situation for the former president.

Ahidjo, who had taken refuge in **France**, resigned from his party post on 27 August 1983 and predicted a gloomy future for his country and the people he had ruled for over two decades. In August 1983 he was implicated in a plot to overthrow Biya and on 27 February 1984, was tried in absentia and sentenced to death. President Biya later commuted the sentence to life imprisonment and suspended the pursuit of the case a month later. Ahidjo was later accused of being behind the **coup attempt of 6 April 1984** in Cameroon.

Ahidjo took up residence in Dakar, Senegal, but made regular visits to France. He also attended the gathering of Former Heads of State and Governments, which discusses contemporary world issues. Before his death in Dakar on 30 November 1989, several abortive attempts were made to reconcile him and his predecessor. Despite his disappearance, Ahidjo's legacy will continue to characterize Cameroon politics for a long time. *See also* AHIDJO–BIYA RUPTURE.

AHIDJO–BIYA RUPTURE. Political disagreement and suspicion followed the transition of power between former president **Ahmadou Ahidjo** and his designated constitutional successor, **Paul Biya**. Although the initial process of transition was peaceful and orderly, the clash of the two personalities became inevitable. Ahidjo resigned as head of state in favor of President Biya but retained the chairmanship of the **Cameroon National Union (CNU)**. For the first time in its history, Cameroon was faced with political dualism. Whereas Ahidjo believed the party defined the guidelines of the nation's policy and the government merely implemented this policy, President Biya argued that the constitution granted the president the prerogative to define the policy of the country. This conflict also magnified itself in trivial aspects like protocol treatment, picture on party uniforms, and decision-making formalities.

The Ahidjo–Biya rupture could also be understood in terms of the dynamics of Cameroon's cultural politics. It was believed that Ahidjo retained many of his close collaborators in key government positions, which made it difficult for President Biya to function effectively without turning to Ahidjo collaborators in high places. Moreover, it was argued that President Biya resented the endless consultation with Ahidjo before taking decisions. Consequently, political associates close to President Biya questioned the sincerity of Ahidjo in resigning from office. Ahidjo's actions left room for suspicion. In January 1983 he visited only six of the then seven provinces of the country to urge for more respect and support for President Biya. He failed to go to the North, his province of origin. In June 1983 he held a secret conclave with Muslim and Northern ministers to advocate their collective resignation from the Biya government. From his exile home in **France**, he allegedly sent a loyal aide to Cameroon with instructions for a **destabilization plot** against President Biya. He also issued statements and declarations from France injurious to the new head of state. Under pressure from President Biya, Ahidjo was forced to resign from the party chairmanship on 27 August 1983. Attempts by Pres. François Mitterrand of France and other African leaders as well as the president of Cameroon's **National Assembly** to reconcile the two men were unsuccessful.

In January 1984 President Biya distanced himself further from the Ahidjo heritage by seeking an independent mandate of his own in anticipated presidential elections. The peak of the Ahidjo–Biya rupture was the public trial of February 1984 in which the former head of state (in absentia) and other close collaborators were sentenced to death. President Biya later commuted the sentences and suspended the further pursuit of the case. Another serious phase in the rupture was the **coup attempt of 6 April 1984** in which the Republican Guard loyal to the former president attempted to overthrow President Biya. After the incident, Biya fully consolidated his position and power in the country's politics. In 1985, he distanced himself further from the Ahidjo regime by changing the name of the one-party structure to the **Cameroon Peoples Democratic Movement (CPDM)**. *See also* COLLECTIVE RESIGNATION PLOT; DESTABILIZATION PLOT OF 22 AUGUST 1983.

AIDS-HIV. Although Cameroon is not among the most severely affected of African countries, AIDS-HIV is a substantial problem for the country. Because of the low quality of medical care and inadequate health records, it is difficult to give an accurate assessment. Gotlieb Monekosso, minister of health, stated on 14 April 1999, that 6.5 percent of the population was HIV-positive but that in specific sectors the rate was much higher. In the military, a 15 percent rate was noted. Other high-level groups included transportation workers, prostitutes, and youth. Among infants (0–4 years), 13,000 cases had been diagnosed. Visits to medical centers indicate that these numbers are much lower than reality. Many cases go undiagnosed or are attributed to other causes. In rural areas there is little attempt to diagnose cause of death. Several problems accompany the AIDS epidemic. Many children are orphaned as the parents die of AIDS. There is inadequate funding for the treatment of AIDS patients. There is tremendous shame associated with having AIDS, and patients are often shunned by family and former friends. In addition, there has been considerable difficulty in convincing people that AIDS exists and how it is caused.

AISSATSU, YAOU (1951–). Aissatsu was the first minister of **women**'s affairs and president of the women's wing of the national party, the **Cameroon People's Democratic Movement (CPDM)**. Born on 28 November 1951 in Cheboa near **Garoua** in the **North Province**, she completed primary school in Cheboa and began secondary education in Garoua, which she completed in Lycée Technique in **Douala**. She enrolled in the University of Rouen in France and graduated in 1975 with a *licence* in economics. After a short experience in the **National Investment Company (SNI),** she moved to the United States, from where she obtained a master's degree in finance in 1979. She returned to the SNI, serving as deputy director of finance until her appointment as minister of women's affairs in February 1985. After the party congress in **Bamenda**, she replaced **Delphine Tsanga** as president of the women's wing of the party in March 1985. In May 1988, when the Ministry of Women's and Social Affairs was created, Aissatsu remained at the head. She is currently the minister of women's affairs, following the split of the Ministry of Women's and Social Affairs in 1997.

AKWA. This is one of many lineage groupings among the coastal **Duala** peoples. The Akwa became prominent in the precolonial and colonial periods through their learning of European languages, the art of governing, and significant trading skills. The Akwa clan provided leadership among coastal peoples through its king. This leadership role facilitated communication and authority in the dealings between the Duala and European governments. The **Anglo–Duala treaty (29 April 1852)** and the **protectorate** treaty with Germany (German–Douala treaty) were signed by King Akwa.

The Akwa town on the east side of the **Wouri River** was projected for inland relocation by the Germans in 1909. This hated German policy of expropriation was the source of considerable protest and debate against German rule. Protests and petitions against German land policy were a spur to the rise of nationalism in Cameroon. *See also* MANGA BELL, DOUALA RUDOLF.

AKWA, BETOTE (1892–1965). An early **Duala** politician in the independence period, Betote Akwa was born 15 August 1892, in **Douala**. He became King of the **Akwa** clan and was instrumental in organizing the cultural–political organization, **Ngondo**. He served in the **East Cameroon** Legislature from 1959 to 1960 and as a minister of state without portfolio in Prime Minister **Ahmadou Ahidjo**'s cabinet. He retired from politics to resume business activities following his electoral defeat in 1960.

AKWA, DIKA MPONDA. This traditional **Duala** chief was one of the main signatories of the German **protectorate** treaty of 12 July 1884, but he died shortly thereafter.

ALIMA, GIBERING BOL. *See* BOL ALIMA, GIBERING.

ALL ANGLOPHONE CONFERENCES. The first All Anglophone Conference (AACI) was held in **Buea** on 2–3 April 1993. It was convened in response to Pres. **Paul Biya**'s announcement in November 1992 to organize a national debate (**Grand Débat**) on constitutional reform in Cameroon. AACI was the first attempt since the introduction of multiparty politics in Cameroon in 1993 that **anglophones** had come together to discuss their fate. In fact, AACI was the culmination of efforts by anglophones, either as individuals or as groups, to seek for the redress of injustices committed against them by the **Yaoundé** government. As part of these efforts pressure groups were formed such as the **Cameroon Anglophone Movement (CAM)** and the South West Elite Association (SWELA).

In 1991, the government convened the **Tripartite Conference,** and anglophones were, inadvertently, brought together under the canopy of the Constitutional Committee. The latter, which was set up to draft a new constitution reflecting the multiparty situation in Cameroon, contained four anglophone jurists: Benjamin Itoe, Carlson Anyangwe, Sam Ekontang Elad, and Simon Munzu. Being the only anglophones on the committee and representing the political and constitutional aspirations of their kith and kin, the four anglophones presented a draft constitutional proposal on a new federal structure that came to be styled the **EMIA** (an acronym for Elad, Munzu, Itoe, and Anyangwe) **constitution**. Itoe was later dropped in a subsequent cabinet shakeup, allegedly because he participated in producing such a document, even though he never signed the final draft. The announcement of an imminent national debate by President Biya shortly after the **elections for the president in 1992** galvanized anglophone Cameroons into convening a much larger meeting. Thus, the AACI was convened in Buea in April 1993. Among its aims were:

1. to adopt a common anglophone stand on proposed constitutional reforms;
2. to air anglophone grievances (political, economic, social) with the hope that their grievances would be solved within the framework of the new constitution; and
3. to put an end to Anglophone marginalization.

Proposals were put forward in the **Buea Declaration** at the end of the conference.

In 1994, the AACII met in **Bamenda**. At the end of its deliberations, the conference issued the **Bamenda Proclamation**, stating that if the government failed to address the problems of the anglophones, they would eventually proclaim, unilaterally, the independence and sovereignty of the anglophone territory. Meanwhile, on 19 August 1994, an AACII resolution created the Southern Cameroons Advisory Council (SCAC). The aim of the SCAC, the resolution stated, was to serve as the principal adviser to the governing body of the AAC. It was made up of 33 members, including traditional rulers, elder statesmen, senior citizens, leading politicians, and religious authorities.

ALLIANCE FOR THE RECONSTRUCTION OF CAMEROON THROUGH THE SOVEREIGN NATIONAL CONFERENCE (ARC-SNC). This was an alliance of opposition parties that hoped to change the sociopolitical–economic situation in Cameroon through the convening of a sovereign national conference, as a first step toward solving the country's political–economic crisis. The ARC-SNC included a group of a dozen opposition parties, otherwise known as the hard-core opposition parties, with the **Social Democratic Front (SDF)** at the head. They constituted themselves into the Union for Change group, which envisaged change through a three-point agenda: the resignation of the **Biya** government, the formation of a transitional government that would convene a sovereign national conference, and the establishment of genuinely democratic institutions. **John Fru Ndi** was elected chairman of the ARC-SNC. Other prominent opposition politicians in the alliance included **Maigari Bello Bouba** of the **National Union for Democracy and Progress (NUDP)** and **Adamu Ndam Njoya** of the **Cameroon Democratic Union (CDU)**.

In anticipation of the October 1992 presidential elections, the alliance chose Fru Ndi as a single candidate for the opposition. This did not help the alliance because various political parties in the alliance presented their own candidates. Consequently, the alliance's attempt to present a single presidential candidate failed.

This was the beginning of cracks in the alliance. The cracks became more visible when the government refused to give in to any of the alliance's demands. The result was that prominent parties within the alliance, notably Bouba Bello's NUDP, began identifying itself with the party in power, eventually entering into a coalition with that party after the 1997 presidential elections. The failure of opposition parties to adopt a common strategy in dealing with the government's intransigence made the alliance redundant.

ALLIED FRONT FOR CHANGE. *See* FRONT OF ALLIES FOR CHANGE (FAC).

ALUCAM. *See* ALUMINUM.

ALUMINUM. Aluminum is a significant export of the Cameroon economy. Although Cameroon has extensive deposits of bauxite in the north and east of the country, aluminum is now produced from bauxite imported from Guinea. This dependent trend began since the aluminum industries were established in **Edea** in 1957. The origin of this industry in Cameroon is based on the relative low-cost electricity produced by **hydroelectric** projects on the **Sanaga River**. It is the government's intention to extend the **Transcameroun** railroad to enable exploitation of local bauxite deposits in the future.

The ALUCAM Company that produces Cameroon's aluminum exists as a subsidiary of the French Pechiney–Ugine industrial group. Cameroon is one of Africa's principal producers of aluminum. ALUCAM capacity is presently 86,000 tons per year, but with the planned expansion of electricity supply, this may increase to 135,000 tons per year. Another company, Kaiser Aluminum, has considered opening operations in Cameroon.

AMADOU, ALI (1943–). Amadou Ali was born in 1943 in Kolofata in present-day **Extreme North Province**. Amadou Ali did his primary school studies in Kolofata, Mora, before proceeding to Lycée de **Garoua** for secondary education. He began official service as an administrative assistant in 1961 and rose to the rank of subdivisional officer of Kaele. He proceeded to the National School of Administration and Magistry (ENAM) in **Yaoundé** and to the International Institute of Public Administration in Paris. He earned diplomas from both institutions in 1970 and 1971, respectively.

From 1971 to 1972, he served as first assistant divisional officer in **Ngaoundéré**. He was later transferred to Yaoundé where from 1972 to 1982 he was secretary-general in the Ministry of Public Service. He worked for a short period as delegate-general for tourism, and between 1983 and 1985, was delegate-general for the National **Gendarmerie**. During a major cabinet shakeup in August 1985, Amadou Ali retained his duties as delegate-general for the National Gendarmerie when the latter post was retitled secretary of state for defense. In 1996 Ali was appointed secretary-general at the Presidency, a post he held until 7 December 1997, when he was appointed minister delegate at the Presidency in charge of defense.

AMBAS BAY. Early Portuguese navigators referred to the inhabitants of the islands in the Bay of Victoria as the Ambos. This is the most plausible historical derivation of the contemporary title, Ambas Bay. It was after initial settlement in Ambas Bay that the land area today known as Victoria, presently **Limbe,** was cleared and founded by **Alfred Saker**. It was the site of one of the early trading networks established on the Cameroon coast by the British. In the 1990s, the term **Ambazonia** came into use as a name for a proposed independent country, within the boundaries of the old **Southern Cameroons**.

AMBAZONIA. This term is used to denote the former **Southern Cameroons** as an independent country, the Republic of Ambazonia, as envisioned by the more radical of **anglophone** separatists. The term is derived from **Ambas Bay**, the name given to the bay on which **Limbe** is located. *See also* ZERO OPTION.

AMERICAN PRESBYTERIAN MISSION. The American Presbyterian Mission, one of the earliest Christian groups in Cameroon, continues its presence in the 1990s. Work began in 1875 at Batanga near the coast. By 1889, agreements were reached with the new German administration, and in 1890, the mission began to expand inland, with a major station at Lolodorf. The mission's work centered among the **Bulu** and **Bassa**. Many believe that the mission's education role was a factor explaining the rise of nationalist fervor and the rise of the **Union des Populations du Cameroun (UPC)** in this area.

AMINOU, OUMAROU (1943–1998). The former delegate-general of tourism and minister delegate of foreign affairs, Oumarou Aminou was born in Tignére (**Adamawa**) on 20 February 1943. After early education in Tignère (1952–58) and secondary studies in **Garoua** and **Maroua** (1958–62), Aminou proceeded to the famous Institute of International Public Administration in Paris, where he specialized in diplomacy. On his return home, he was admitted to the National School of Administration and Magistry (ENAM) in **Yaoundé** and graduated with a diploma in January 1964. He was attached to the Ministry of Territorial Administration, serving in varying capacities in Yaoundé and Batouri. From 1970 to 1972, he was chief of administrative and judicial affairs and later secretary-general in the Federal Inspectorate of Administration in Garoua. For 10 years he was **commissioner** and later delegate-general of tourism. In January 1982 he was appointed as vice minister of foreign affairs. Under the presidency of **Paul Biya,** the post was retitled minister delegate to the minister of foreign affairs, and he served here until July 1984. Aminou was also prominent in party circles, serving as a central committee member and organizing secretary of the **Cameroon National Union (CNU)** from 1975 to 1984 and later as administrative secretary until March 1985. From 1972 to 1987, he served as head of the Islamic Association of Cameroon. These crucial roles placed him at the center stage in the controversy and discord of the **Ahidjo–Biya rupture**. However, Aminou emerged from this difficult period to be appointed ambassador to Saudi Arabia. He was subsequently dropped as ambassador in favor of **Mohamadou Labarang**. His final appointment was as **governor** of the **West Province** (until January 1992). He died on 2 August 1998.

ANDZE TSOUNGUI, GILBERT (1930–). Born in 1930 in Nkolondom, near **Yaoundé**, Andze Tsoungui was a civil administrator and the first minister of Cameroon's armed forces not of northern origin. He served in this post during the **coup attempt of 6 April 1984**. Tsoungui studied law by correspondence from the University of Dakar, Senegal. In 1955 he did law practice and administrative ethics. He later served as senior divisional officer for Mungo Division before being appointed as **federal inspector of administration** in the Littoral and in the Western Region until 1972.

Under the **Ahmadou Ahidjo** government, Tsoungui served in various capacities: as minister delegate at the State Inspectorate, minister of agriculture in 1975, minister of justice in 1980, and under the **Paul Biya** government as minister of armed forces from August 1983 until November 1985. During the foiled military **coup attempt of 6 April 1984**, Tsoungui set up a secret command post to organize the recapture of strategic locations by loyal forces. The army mutiny reinforced Tsoungui's position, and he emerged as a powerful figure calling for vigilance and firmness and contradicting President Biya with the assertion that all rebel forces hailed from the North. In November 1985, he was replaced when the ministry was attached to the Presidency and the post retitled minister delegate at the Presidency, in charge of defense. In April 1989, he was appointed delegate-general for national security, a post he held until he was appointed deputy prime minister in charge of territorial administration on 27 November 1992. On 7 December 1997, Andze Tsoungui was dropped from government.

ANGLO–DUALA TREATY (29 APRIL 1852). The export of Cameroon slaves to foreign countries was abolished by this treaty. The treaty was to be enforced by the king and chiefs of Cameroon who were mainly the **Duala** coastal leaders. The British were to expel any Europeans who settled and made a living out of the slave trade in the territory. The Anglo–Duala treaty also granted the most favored nation (MFN) status in open commercial trade to Britain. Signatories were the British resident agent, trade, missionary and military officials for Britian and King **Akwa** and his subordinate chiefs for the Duala. *See also* SLAVE TRADE.

ANGLOPHONE. This term denotes Cameroonians whose secondary medium of expression is the English language, and it refers to the portions of the country previously under British rule. Historically, the grouping corresponds to the population subjected to the British **mandate** and **trusteeship systems**. Today, anglophones mostly occupy the **North West** and **South West Provinces** of Cameroon and constitute about one-fifth of the country's population.

ANGLOPHONE POLITICAL PRESSURE GROUPS. The introduction of multiparty democracy in December 1990 reawakened the **anglophone problem**. The political liberalization that came in the wake of the introduction of multiparty politics in the early 1990s provided an opportunity for the **anglophones** to create pressure groups that would address their plight. Consequently, there was a proliferation of pressure groups with contrasting views on how to tackle the anglophone problem. While some felt that anglophone grievances could be redressed through a return to the federal system of government as it was between 1961 and 1972, others held the view that the secession of anglophone Cameroon from the rest of the country—the so-called **zero option**—was the only solution. *See also* ALL ANGLOPHONE CONFERENCE; CAMEROON ANGLOPHONE MOVEMENT.

ANGLOPHONE PROBLEM. The anglophone problem has to do with the cultural identity of English-speaking (**anglophone**) Cameroonians, who form a minority in the **Republic of Cameroon**. This group of Cameroonians argues that as citizens of the Republic of Cameroon, they reserve the right to be treated equally with their French-speaking counterparts (**francophones**). Unfortunately, many anglophones believe that this has not been the case since **reunification**. Many anglophone Cameroonians see themselves being marginalized in all aspects of national life. The anglophone problem is said to have been brought about by three factors: the Anglo–French partition of German Cameroon after **World War I,** which split the territory into British and French spheres; the conditions under which anglophone Cameroon achieved independence in 1961, which included the fact that they achieved independence from a position of weakness vis-à-vis **French Cameroun**; and the price the territory had to pay as one of the two states of the **Federal Republic of Cameroon** from 1961 to 1972.

Anglophone grievances with the francophone-dominated leadership have been centered on the centralization and monopolization of power by government and the accusation that anglophones had been reduced to a second-class status, in violation of the 1961 agreement that established a federal union of equal federal status. Anglophone exclusion from effective power sharing and consequently policy making in the country, the economic exploitation of the anglophone territory, and the fear of the eventual suppression of their cultural identity (language and educational system) by the francophones are aspects of the problem.

In an attempt to redress these grievances, anglophone Cameroonians have formed both political and social groupings to fight for their cause. In reaction, the government has tried to satisfy anglophone grievances by appointing anglophone **prime ministers**, gaining admission of the country into the **Commonwealth**, creating the English-speaking university in **Buea**, establishing a separate examination board for anglophone examinations, and drawing up a new constitution that makes provision for minority problems. *See also* ALL ANGLOPHONE CONFERENCES; ANGLOPHONE POLITICAL PRESSURE GROUPS.

ANGLOPHONE STANDING COMMITTEE. *See* SOUTHERN CAMEROONS NATIONAL COUNCIL.

ANLU. This traditional **women**'s society among the Bikom women, similar to women's associations among other **Grassfield** groups, was mobilized and developed as a tool of modern politics during the days of multiparty government in **West Cameroon**. It played a significant role in supporting the **Kamerun National Democratic Party (KNDP)** but was also active in supporting the interests of women at the local level. *See also* TAKEMBUNG.

ANTI-BAMILEKE INCIDENTS. The **Bamiléké** settlement and prowess in commerce and trade have led to significant incidents with host ethnic groups. In 1956, Bamiléké market stalls were scattered and pillaged in Sangemelima. In 1960, at least 19 Bamiléké lost their lives, and a Bamiléké residential area was severely burned down, leaving about 5,000 homeless in an anti-Bamiléké rage in **Douala**. On 31 December 1967, 236 Bamiléké were slaughtered by the Bakossi in the **Tombel Massacre**. On the national level, there is a widely held belief that government discriminates against the Bamiléké, or "Bami."

ARMED FORCES. The Cameroon Armed Forces is made up of the ground forces, the marines, the air force, and paramilitary forces. As of 1996, it consisted of some 23,000 persons (substantially larger than the 7,500 persons in 1986). The Ministry of Defense also holds a respectable position in terms of budgetary allocation. As such, the armed forces is well equipped, largely with French materials since independence and increasingly with Israeli defensive and offensive weapons. The **People's Republic of China** and the **United States** also play significant roles in the Cameroon armed forces.

Since 1960, Cameroon politics has been reflected in the armed forces. With **Ahmadou Ahidjo** in power until 1982, the posts of minister and secretary-general of the ministry had been held by Ahidjo loyalists from the North. Following the strains in relationship with the former leader, **Paul Biya** introduced southern loyalists as bosses of the ministry. The president also set up an Armed Forces General Staff to enable the military to carry out their task of national defense and the protection of the legality of the republic in a more coherent and efficient manner. Moreover, to reduce the influence and power of the minister of armed forces, the post was renamed minister delegate at the Presidency in charge of defense. This gives the president a direct hold over the most sensitive cabinet post.

ARTISANAL INDUSTRIES. These consist of the major activities dealing with arts and crafts work. They are a significant form of traditional genius and creativity serving commercial, ritual, and aesthetic purposes. Centers of artisanal industry exist in nearly all parts of the country. They serve the needs of a growing tourist industry as well as for domestic trade. The government shows considerable interest in these industries as demonstrated in the activities of the Ministry of Information and Culture. Various craft cooperatives have been developed in recent years to serve local and export markets, and these have brought about a significant revitalization of skilled artisans in rural areas. Wood sculptures, cast bronze, leather work, textiles, baskets, and jewelry are among the many items produced.

ASSALE, CHARLES (1911–). Former **prime minister** of the **République du Cameroun**, Assale was born on 4 November 1911, at Mefo, Ebolowa. He trained as a nurse at Ayos before serving in that capacity for 10 years. A leading nationalist, he began politics through the trade union movement. In 1946, he played a key role in organizing the French Cameroon branch of the French Confédération Générale de Travail (CGT) and a year later became a representative of the French Economic Council. In 1948, Assale helped the **Union des Populations du Cameroun (UPC)** and was instrumental in preparing the declaration "Appel au Camerounais" in 1948. In 1957, however, he left the UPC. In 1949, he founded the Union Tribale Ntem-Kribi and participated in the creation of the Courant d'Union Nationale. At various times after 1948, he was elected to the **Assemblée Territoriale du Cameroun**, the **Assemblée Législative du Cameroun,** and the **National Assembly** in 1960. He also joined the **Mouvement d'Action Nationale Camerounaise (MANC)**.

After serving as finance minister in French Cameroun from February 1958, he was appointed prime minister of the **République du Cameroun** in 1960. He served in this capacity until 1961 when, following **reunification** and the creation of a federal government, he became prime minister of the state of **East Cameroon**, 1961–65. Assale was adviser and member of the Central Committee when the **Cameroon National Union (CNU)** party was formed in 1966. He remained in this post until the **Bamenda Congress** of March 1985. His last post was as mayor of Ebolowa in 1987.

ASSEMBLEE LEGISLATIVE DU CAMEROUN (ALCAM). This was the name of **French Cameroun's** legislature during the period of self-government between 9 May 1959 and 10 April 1960. Important day-to-day government decisions, except for defense and foreign relations, were deliberated by ALCAM. Although ALCAM provided self-rule governments under **André-Marie Mbida** between May 1957 and February 1958 and **Ahmadou Ahidjo** until February 1960 and left Cameroon out of the **French Union**, Cameroun was still represented in the French National Assembly. On 22 November 1958, ALCAM voted in favor of the new French statute for the transition period into independence. The new status provided full internal autonomy for the territory, and Cameroun was no longer represented in the French parliament in Paris.

On 30 October 1959, ALCAM provided the groundwork for the future Cameroun polity with the election of a 21-member consultative committee to draft the constitution of the new **République du Cameroun,** the **constitution of 1960**. ALCAM gave way to the **Assemblée Nationale du Cameroun (ANCAM)** following the general elections of 10 April 1960.

ASSEMBLEE NATIONALE DU CAMEROUN (ANCAM)/NATIONAL ASSEMBLY OF CAMEROUN. ANCAM was the legislative body of the **République du Cameroun** from April 1960 until October 1961. ANCAM was the historic successor of **Assemblée Législative du Cameroun (ALCAM)**. It came into existence following the general election of 10 April 1960, with the **Union Camerounaise** as the dominant party. ANCAM was a unicameral legislature and had legislative powers over persons and property rights, political, administrative, judicial, and security matters as well as on socioeconomic and financial policies.

ASSEMBLEE TERRITORIALE DU CAMEROUN (ATCAM). ATCAM was the legal successor of Assemblée Représentative du Cameroun (ARCAM) in 1952. ATCAM possessed more than just advisory functions in that it provided an indigenous legislative structure in the governing process of the territory. The number of members was increased from 34 to 50, but this still included about one-third European members who constituted the "first electoral college." Following the passage of the **Loi Cadre** in 1956, lesser restrictions were imposed on its recommendations and decisions. ATCAM decisions, however, did not automatically become law. They were subject to approval by the Conseil d'Etat in Paris.

The territorial assembly played the role of a melting pot for future Camerounian politicians. Except for the **Union des Populations du Cameroun (UPC)**, which was virtually excluded from gaining political representation even though it participated in elections, other leaders such as **Louis Paul Aujoulat**, **Ahmadou Ahidjo**, **Rene-Guy Charles Okala,** and **Paul Soppo Priso** began their active national political careers in ATCAM. Following the abolition of the dual college electoral system in the Loi Cadre, universal suffrage became the basis for election. Before the dissolution of ATCAM in November 1956, voter registration had reached a peak of nearly two million Camerounians. Cameroun gained a new status that allowed for a greater measure of autonomy and led to the replacement of ATCAM by the **Assemblée Législative du Cameroun (ALCAM)** on 9 May 1957. ALCAM provided the opportunity for preindependence self-rule headed by **André-Marie Mbida** as first prime minister of the coalition government.

ASSIMILATION POLICY. This major determinant of French colonial theory prevailed throughout the 19th century. Its philosophical origins are to be found in the Enlightenment, with its belief in the power of reason and the concept of the universal equality of all men. This led to the *mission civilisatrice et providentielle* (the civilizing and providential mission) that aimed at making colonial peoples assimilate French habits and beliefs and stressed oneness between France and its empire. The educated elites were the main propagators of assimilation. Although the policy of assimilation was enshrined in Article 109 of the 1848 French constitution, a troubling divergence between policy and practice was easily detectable. By the early decades of French rule, this policy, which was applied in Cameroon despite the territory's unique character, was under severe assault. It was replaced by the **association policy**.

ASSOCIATION POLICY. French association policy was aimed at cooperation and solidarity between the ruler and ruled during the colonial period. It replaced the policy of **assimilation** that prevailed throughout the 19th century. Association was to give higher regard for indigenous institutions and the values of inhabitants that had been degraded under assimilation. Throughout the 20th century, the French preached the doctrine of association as a means of enabling Africans to develop within the context of their own milieu. Rather than using educated elites, the French created traditional chiefs to uphold local populations and create stability. This participation of local leaders appeared to make French rule more secure, practical, and economical. The French also used association as a belated means to work toward economic development in their colonies. These assumed goals of association did not, however, eliminate the traces of assimilation that continued to persist through French paternalism, education, and cultural control. The association policy, like that of assimilation before it, was rooted in the Enlightenment ideas. The common distinctions made between the policies of association and assimilation were not very significant. *See also* MISE EN VALEUR.

ASSOCIATION POLICY OF THE EUROPEAN ECONOMIC COMMUNITY (EEC). The association policy is an integral part of the Treaty of Rome, which established the **European Economic Community (EEC)** in 1957. At that time African territories were still under the yoke of colonialism, and no adequate thought was given to the eventual independence of the colonies. Through the association policy, the French insisted on provisions in the EEC Treaty (Articles 131–136) that would provide for a wider economic sphere, high level of freedom, and effective financial assistance for its African territories. Consequently, the six members of the EEC and 14 associated African States and Madagascar (AASM) signed the **Yaoundé Agreements** in 1964 and 1969. This association policy, which allowed African states to benefit from certain advantages with member states of the EEC, was regarded by critics as a subtle progression from the isolated imperialism of France to a "joint imperialism" of the EEC over its former colonies. Since 1975, Cameroon has been a signatory of the several **Lome Agreements** between the EEC and the African, Caribbean, and Pacific countries (ACP), which continue under the EEC's successor, the European Union.

ATANGANA, CHARLES (1885–1943). Atangana was paramount chief of the **Beti**, the major ethnic group of the **Yaoundé** area. Atangana, rather than being a romantic reactionary, was more a sophisticated collaborator with succeeding European administrations in Cameroon. This does not make him less of a nationalist. Born in Mvoly and introduced to the German explorer, Major Hans Dominik, Atangana gained proficiency in German and served in multiple functions as a schoolteacher, an infirmary assistant, and an interpreter under the Germans.

During punitive expeditions into the interior of the country, Atangana is credited with intervening to save the lives of some local chiefs. He received first-class treatment during his stay in **Germany** beginning in 1911 and was later crowned as paramount **chief**. Atangana's loyalty with the Germans survived the turmoil of World War I when he flew with his defeated masters to the Spanish island of Fernando Po.

When the French allowed Atangana's return from exile, he was put to test in directing forced-labor workers in Dschang. His never-failing loyalty allowed him to regain primacy among the French. In his unswerving attachment to colonial authorities and wide-ranging support among his people, Atangana amassed substantial wealth and became a powerful figure in his own right.

After years of eclipse, in which dead leaders were simply forgotten, Atangana's legacy has recently been revived in the scholarship of Cameroon nationalism.

ATLANTIKA MOUNTAINS. One of the mountain ranges of the mountainous chain of the **West**. The Atlantika served as a significant dividing line between the two parts of British **Northern Cameroons** territories at the **Benue River**.

AUJOULAT, LOUIS PAUL (1910–?). One of the principal figures of preindependence politics, this French medical doctor was born 28 August 1910, in Saida, Algeria. Although the early part of his life involved the medical practice and lay ministry activities, he is largely remembered in Cameroon history as a politician. After his arrival in Cameroon in 1936, he won continuous elections into the Cameroon Assembly and the National Assembly in Paris from 1946 to 1956. He was cofounder of the Catholic Mission Society Ad Lucem and formed a political party, the **Bloc Démocratique Camerounais (BDC)**, in 1951. As secretary of state for overseas France in the Mendès–France government, Aujoulat was instrumental in passing the Overseas Labor Code in 1952. Before Aujoulat's retirement in 1957, he had schooled future Cameroon leaders such as **André-Marie Mbida** and **Ahmadou Ahidjo** toward a reformist and evolutionary stance in politics. It was this legacy that made Aujoulat's BDC a fervent opponent to the more radical **Union des Populations du Cameroun (UPC)** during the era of decolonization.

AWANA, CHARLES ONANA. *See* ONANA AWANA, CHARLES

AWUNTI, JOSEPH CHONGWAS (1932–1987). Awunti, a former minister delegate at the Presidency in charge of relations with Parliament and the **Economic and Social Council**, died in office in October 1987. Born on 20 December 1932, in Kedjom Ketinguh of the Tubah district in Mezam Division, the late minister schooled in Ndop and later in the Cameroon Protestant College, Bali (1948–53). On completion he trained in forestry, attending the Dean School and Oxford University and graduating with a master's degree in 1964. He served in the West Cameroon Forestry Department prior to his appointment to the federal government as pioneer research officer. With the advent of the unitary republic in 1972, he joined the government as vice minister of agriculture (1972–79); and then was vice minister of territorial administration (1979–84); minister delegate at the Presidency in charge of state inspection and administrative reforms (1984–85); and minister delegate at the Presidency in charge of relations with Parliament and the **Economic and Social Council** until his death. Awunti was also a member of the Central Committee of the **Cameroon People's Democratic Movement (CPDM)** for which he served as secretary for administrative and financial inspection.

AYANG, LUC (1947–). A former interim **prime minister** and current president of the **Economic and Social Council**, Luc Ayang was born in 1947 in Doukoula, Mayo Danai Division, in the **Extreme North Province**. After primary and secondary education in Doukoula and **Ngaoundéré**, he enrolled in the **University of Yaoundé** in 1968 reading law. Following graduation in 1972, he served at the Presidency of the Republic as chief of service for regulations and control. In 1976, he was appointed assistant senior divisional officer for the Adamawa Division; in 1978, he joined the cabinet as minister of livestock and fisheries. In August 1983, he was named acting prime minister to replace **Maigari Bello Bouba** who had fallen out of favor as a result of the **Ahidjo–Biya rupture**. With the constitutional amendment abolishing the post of **prime minister** in January 1984, Ayang was nominated to the powerful position of president of the **Economic and Social Council**, a post he still held in January 2000. In May 1984, he joined the Central Committee and Bureau of the **Cameroon National Union (CNU)**.

AYMERICH, JOSEPH GEORGES (1858–1937). General Aymerich led the French forces during the **Kamerun** Campaign of **World War I,**

1914–16. He and his forces stormed German Kamerun from the southeastern border with French **Congo**. He also led the administrative control of the areas captured by the French. He left Cameroon following its partition in October 1916.

– B –

BACCALAUREAT. This certificate is awarded at the end of the second cycle of general or technical secondary **education** in **francophone** areas. Students sit for the *baccalauréat* three years after the **Brevet d'Etudes du Premier Cycle (BEPC)**. The examination has written and oral parts. Success in both parts of the examination leads to the award of the certificate and an automatic entry into the university. Admission into other professional institutions of higher learning requires an additional competitive examination, the ***concours,*** after the *baccalauréat*. For educational and employment purposes, the baccalauréat is the direct equivalent of the Advanced Level **General Certificate of Education (GCE)** in **anglophone** Cameroon. In 1984, the government created the Baccalauréat Board to organize and manage the examination.

BAFIA. An ethnic group, predominantly of the Middle Cameroon **Bantu** stock, found around the center–east of the country. Other important subgroupings of the Middle Bantu include the Ponek, Omand, Banend, Njabeta, and Yambessa. The Bafia were presumably pushed from the northern areas by the **Fulani** and Sudanese pressure. The Bafias today settle around the Mbam and **Sanaga River** zones and are mostly fishermen and farmers in their daily occupation. The usually strong dualism of sexes common in most Cameroon groupings is not popular here. Their monistic tendency lies in the fact that men and **women** share the same names and compete equally for livelihood and existence.

BAFOUSSAM. This city in the Mifi Division is the capital of the **West Province**. Its 1976 census population was 62,239, making it the sixth largest city of the country. Populated mainly by **Bamiléké** people, this city was a scene of much activity during the **Union des Populations du Cameroun (UPC)** rebellion. Bafoussam has been the site of several significant meetings, such as the 1965 congress of the **Union Camerounaise** and the 1980 congress of the **Cameroon National Union (CNU)**. Today the city is a major center of commerce and an important road transport hub.

BAFUT. The Bafut, a **Tikar** ethnic group of the **North West Province**, are spread across the upward areas of the Mezam Division and are organized in subchiefdoms of Babanki, Babanki-Tungo, Bafreng, Bambui, Bamendankwe, and Bambili. They come under the suzerainty of a paramount chief—the **fon**. The Fon of Bafut has spiritual, legislative, and executive roles in the society. Although the system is deeply rooted in tradition and values, the current fon is a graduate of the **University of Yaoundé** and reigns as a secular monarch preserving the values and integrity of his people.

BAKARY, ISSA. *See* ISSA BAKARY.

BAKASSI DISPUTE. The **Nigeria**–Cameroon border has never been completely demarcated. This provides opportunities for conflict. The Bakassi Peninsula in the Gulf of Guinea is apparently rich in petroleum and has become the setting for sporadic clashes between the military and police forces of the two countries for many years. These clashes became more severe in the 1990s, resulting in several deaths. The case has been taken to the International Court of Justice. In 1999, **Equatorial Guinea** joined the case, arguing that it was an interested party as resolution of the case would define portions of its maritime borders with Cameroon and Nigeria. *See also* BORDER CONFLICTS.

BAKOKO. *See* BASSA-BAKOKO.

BAKOSSI. The Bakossi are on the northwestern **Bantu** borderline sharing boundaries with the Mbo and **Bamiléké** of the **Littoral** and **Western Provinces**. The Bakossi are **anglophone** and inhabit mostly the greater parts of Meme Division in the **Mungo River** valley, especially the Tombel, Bangem, and Nguti subdivisions. Consequently, interactions with the neighboring **francophones** have not been particularly harmonious, as exemplified in the **Tombel massacre** of 1967. In general, the Bakossi people, including the Bassosi subgroup, number about 100,000 and are surrounded by two significant physical structures: the Kupe and Manengouba Mountains.

BAKWERI. This group of noncentralized peoples lives in villages on the slopes of **Mount Cameroon** and coastal environs. The Bakwerians are a cluster consisting of the Kpe, Moboko, Isuwu, and Wovea grouping, but no elaborate, overarching system of political authority exists. Their settlement is largely the result of **Bantu** migration from the mid-18th century. Early European settlement in the Bakweri region was a source of both indignation and pride among the people. The major towns—**Buea** (first German capital in **Kamerun**), Victoria (now **Limbe**, a seaport and plantation center), and **Tiko** (trade and seaport center)—have grown into administrative, commercial, and social agglomerations for anglophone Cameroon. The Bakweri suffered substantial losses of land due to the development of plantations in the German era.

BAKWERI COOPERATIVE UNION OF FARMERS (BCUF). A large and progressive indigenous **cooperative** exporter of **bananas** in former West Cameroon, BCUF was formed in 1954 under the leadership of **Emmanuel M. L. Endeley**. After the rise of national banana organizations in the 1970s, the BCUF largely ceased to exist.

BAKWERI LAND CLAIM COMMITTEE. Much of the land now occupied by the **Cameroon Development Corporation (CDC)** was originally owned by the **Bakweri** people. It was taken from them by force and without adequate compensation during the era of German rule. During the period of **trusteeship** this committee was established under the leadership of **Emmanuel M. L. Endeley** as part of a campaign to rectify the problem. The committee petitioned the Trusteeship Council without success, but the existence of the committee must be seen as part of the political mobilization of the peoples of **Southern Cameroons** and as an early contributor to the growth of the independence movement.

BALANCED DEVELOPMENT. This development philosophy aimed at spreading progress throughout Cameroon by redressing existing inequalities. The idea involved regional, sectoral, and personnel aspects. The regional aspect consisted of a judiciously balanced allocation of programs across the geographic areas of the country. The sectoral aspect concerned the redistribution of the country's economic potential across the agricultural, industrial, extractive, and tertiary sectors of the economy. In terms of personnel, balanced development aimed at equalizing opportunities for post allocation among various regional and ethnic interests. Such a policy of development required enormous state intervention, falsified the economic rational in location of industries, and sometimes led to administrative mediocrity. The government defended the balanced development option as an aspect of planning and as such, a necessity for a young developing country.

The origins of the imbalances that exist in the country are a part of the colonial legacy. In the colonial period, economic activity as well as missionary and Western education developments were concentrated near the coast and especially in the **"Fertile Crescent"** bound by **Douala**, **Edea,** and **Yaoundé**. However, implementation of balanced development in the **Ahidjo** era led to dissatisfaction in southern parts of the country, as Ahidjo placed heavy emphasis on projects in the northern areas. By the 1990s, little was heard of this philosophy in government circles.

BALI. A major ethnic group of the Bamenda **Grassfield** area, the Bali have a hierarchical political structure headed by a king or **fon**. The Bali are part of the **Tikar** and were the major ally of the Germans during the period of German conquest of the **Bamenda** region. The memory of Bali's cooperation with the Germans lingers on in Cameroon, and many Bali believe they are discriminated against because of this history.

BAMBILI. This roadside village in the Bamenda **Grassfield** became the heartland of **anglophone** education in Cameroon. The creation of the Cameroon College of Arts, Science and Technology (CCAST) was the first step in Bambili's renown. Established under federal control, CCAST Bambili prepared students in a two-year course leading to the advanced-level GCE. Bambili's prominence widened with the opening of the National College of Agriculture, which prepared supervisors and technical experts, as well as a branch of the Ecole Normale Supérieure, an advanced teacher-training institution of **francophone** orientation. With the opening of nearby **Bamenda University of Science and Technology**, a private institution, the educational significance of the region has been enhanced.

BAMENDA. Bamenda is the common name given to the **Grassfield** highlands of northwestern Cameroon and the name of the main city that is in that area. The name was also used by the British for one of the four major administrative districts into which they divided the **Cameroons Province**. After 1949, Bamenda became a separate province in the British territory. According to the 1976 census, the city of Bamenda had 48,111 inhabitants and ranked as the seventh largest city in the country. Today the city serves as the capital of the **North West Province**, and, as one of the major cities in the country, has been the venue of important events. In 1984, it hosted the **agropastoral show** and the following year was the venue for the last congress of the **Cameroon National Union**

(CNU), during which the new party, the **Cameroon People's Democratic Movement (CPDM)**, was formed.

Bamenda has also played a prominent role in the prodemocracy movement in Cameroon. It was here that the **Social Democratic Front (SDF)** was launched in 1990. Bamenda has remained a political hotbed since then. It is the seat of the SDF. After the proclamation of the October 1992 presidential election, violent protests and demonstrations erupted in Bamenda and other parts of the North West Province, leading to the declaration of a state of emergency, which was only lifted after Christmas 1992.

BAMENDA "ALL-PARTY" CONFERENCE. This conference was convened for political leaders of **Southern Cameroons** between 26 and 28 June 1961, in a bid to create consensus prior to the important consultation and negotiation with politicians of the **Ahmadou Ahidjo** government. The Southern politicians set forward proposals calling for a loose federation of legislative powers. Despite this common ground, disunity continued to characterize relations within the Southern Cameroons camp.

BAMENDA CONGRESS. This was the fourth ordinary congress of the **Cameroon National Union (CNU)** held in **Bamenda**, the capital of the **North West Province**, 21–25 March 1985. In terms of political significance, the Bamenda Congress (christened the Congress of the **New Deal**) outweighs all others held previously. The Bamenda Congress was the first held in the country under the leadership of Pres. **Paul Biya**. It came on the heels of a political rupture between former party chief **Ahmadou Ahidjo** and Biya. Moreover, the Bamenda Congress led to the birth of a new party, the **Cameroon Peoples Democratic Movement**, from the ruins of the CNU. In terms of orientation, the Bamenda Congress heralded the promise of a more open and pluralistic political structure in the country. Moreover, the Bamenda Congress was the first congress of the one-party regime held in the **anglophone** part of the country. It opened a flurry of new hopes and aspirations. The Bamenda Congress witnessed the consolidation of President Biya's power and the enunciation of his doctrine of **communal liberalism**.

BAMENDA IMPROVEMENT ASSOCIATION. One of the early nationalist movements in **British Cameroons**, the association was formed by Cameroon elites resident in Lagos, Nigeria, by the mid-1940s. It was a protonationalist organization calling for **Southern Cameroon's** autonomy and demanding **reunification**. The Bamenda Improvement Association was a founding member of the coalition that later established the **National Council of Nigeria and the Cameroons** in 1944.

BAMENDA PROCLAMATION. This proclamation was the result of the Second **All Anglophone Conference**, held in **Bamenda** in 1994. The essence of its message was the determination of the **anglophones** to declare independence from the **Republic of Cameroon** if the government failed to address the problems defined in the first All Anglophone Conference and the **Buea Declaration**. *See also* ZERO OPTION.

BAMENDA UNIVERSITY OF SCIENCE AND TECHNOLOGY (BUST). This private institution was formed by opposition leaders in the 1990s who were angered by the **Cameroon People's Democratic Movement (CPDM)**–dominated government's failure to open a state university in the **North West Province**. That government did open the **anglophone** University of **Buea** in the **South West Province**. In many people's minds, this was a deliberate move to punish the North West, the center of opposition to CPDM. **John Fru Ndi** and **John Ngu Foncha**, who chaired the board of the university, were among its many supporters.

BAMILEKE. This generic term is commonly used to refer to several ethnic groups in the **West Province**. Each Bamiléké group is headed by a **chief** who has strong powers, particularly with respect to land distribution. This is reflected architecturally in the massive size of the chief's compound with respect to all others. There is a dense population in most of the area occupied by Bamiléké, and this fact in conjunction with other factors has caused many Bamiléké to migrate to the urban areas of the country. The Bamiléké have a reputation of being excellent farmers and businessmen and -**women**. While they have become a significant factor in the national economy, their success has also generated some jealousy and resentment, especially among the original inhabitants of areas to which Bamiléké migration has occurred. The Bamiléké were also one of the major ethnicities involved in the **Union des Populations du Cameroun (UPC)**. *See also* ANTI-BAMILEKE INCIDENTS; TOMBEL MASSACRE.

BAMOUM (BAMUM). This major ethnic group is found in the **West Province** around the historic town of **Foumban**. The Bamoum dynasty was founded about 400 years ago by Nchare Yen, son of a **Tikar fon**. The Bamoum are believed to be descendants of Prince Rifun and were the most southerly group to have accepted **Islam** toward the end of the

jihad period. They have been involved in several wars with neighboring groupings and even experienced a civil war against dynastic rule. The monarchy has remained the source of Bamoum pride in addition to its highly developed oral tradition and fascinating culture. In 1896, the sultan developed a new alphabet and art of writing known as ***shu mom***. The Bamoum crafts and architecture are well known and have been the subject of numerous studies. They have also provided an important contribution to Cameroon's tourism. *See also* NJOYA (SULTAN); NJOYA, SEIDOU NJIMOLUH.

BANANA. The intensive production of bananas began under the German administration. Today, plantations account largely for export production and small farmers' produce for the local market. The most significant areas of banana production are in the **Littoral** and **South West Provinces**.

The Office Camerounais de Bananes (OCB) was given national control of banana issues, but it was closed in 1987 as part of the austerity measures to fight the economic crisis. Private companies such as Del Monte, Dole, and Compagne Fruitière have taken over most of the government-owned banana plantations. In 1977–78, 83,000 tons of bananas were exported, but by the late 1990s this number had risen to about 200,000 tons per year. Total production of bananas was estimated by the Food and Agriculture Organization to be about 986,000 tons in 1998.

BANDJOUN. Bandjoun is one of the larger of the **Bamiléké** chiefdoms in the **West Province** and the name of one of the subdivisions of the Mifi Division of that province. In the 1976 census, the Bandjoun Subdivision had a population of 49,300 persons. The palace at Bandjoun is a major tourist attraction.

BANDOLO, HENRI (1943–1997). Henri Bandolo was the chief editorialist of the national daily, ***Cameroon Tribune***, deputy director of the Cameroon Publishing Company (SOPECAM), and a supplementary member of the national party's central committee. He was born on 15 September 1943, in **Douala**.

Bandolo trained in France from 1966 to 1968 after entering the journalistic profession as a local radio announcer in 1964. By 1974, he had risen to the rank of chief of service for news in Radio Cameroon and was considered the most popular journalist in the country. In 1975, he returned to France for studies at the Sorbonne for two years and headed the

French-language programs on return. His popularity was eclipsed in 1979 when he moved to the remote Eastern Province to serve as provincial delegate. He returned to prominence in 1980 as deputy director of *Cameroon Tribune,* a post in which he has easily turned his credentials from the most popular to the most powerful journalist.

His critical and sometimes partisan editorials, his interviews of former president **Ahmadou Ahidjo**, his friendship with then prime minister **Maigari Bello Bouba,** and his sentiments and attachment for Pres. **Paul Biya** placed him at center stage during the political crisis from 1982 to 1984. He was named to the Central Committee at the **Bamenda Congress** of the party in 1985 and became minister of information and culture in April 1988. On leaving government, he was appointed chairman of the board of Cameroon Radio and Television (CRT) until his death.

BANK OF CENTRAL AFRICAN STATES/BANQUE D'ETATS DE L'AFRIQUE CENTRALE (BEAC). This bank replaced the Central Bank of the States of Equatorial Africa and Cameroon, which had replaced the Institut d'Emission de l'Afrique Equatoriale Française established in 1955 to issue currency for French colonies in **French Equatorial Africa (AEF)** and the mandate territory of Cameroon. The BEAC, established on 23 November 1972, is controlled by a Council of Administration, a governor, national monetary committees, and a College of Censors, which regularly supervises the activities and the books of the bank. The council is the governing body. Cameroon and **France** each have four seats on the council; the rest of the members share four seats. The current membership includes all of the former French colonies in the AEF (**Central African Republic**, **Chad**, **Congo**, **Gabon**), Cameroon, and **Equatorial Guinea**, a former Spanish colony. The **Development Bank of Central African States** is associated with the BEAC, and both are affiliated with the **Union Douanière Economique du Cameroun (UDEAC)**. The headquarters is in **Yaoundé**. *See also* ACCORD DE COOPÉRATION ECONOMIQUE, MONÉTAIRE ET FINANCIÈRE; MONETARY UNION OF EQUATORIAL AFRICA AND CAMEROON.

BANK CRISIS. One of the major aspects of Cameroon's **economic crisis** was the almost total collapse of the country's banking system in 1989. Numerous banks were underfunded, several had made large loans that could not be recovered, there was a tendency to overstaff, and management was frequently inadequate. Paribas Cameroon, Cameroon Bank, and the development bank (Banque Camerounaise de Développement) were liquidated. A large scandal was created when rumors spread that the **Société Camerounaise de Banque (SCB)** had been undermined by bad loans to the spouse of President **Biya**. The government was a major investor in the four collapsed banks. In addition to internal problems, the banks were hit heavily by the overall economic crisis facing the country. A Société Financière de Recouvrement (SFR, sometimes titled Société de Recouvrement des Créances du Cameroun) was established to assist in the liquidation of the banks. As people lost confidence in the formal banking system, many withdrew their funds and turned to the informal system, the ***tontines*** or *njangis*.

BANQUE DE DEVELOPPEMENT DES ETATS DE L'AFRIQUE CENTRAL. *See* DEVELOPMENT BANK OF CENTRAL AFRICAN STATES.

BANQUE D'ETATS DE L'AFRIQUE CENTRALE (BEAC). *See* BANK OF CENTRAL AFRICAN STATES.

BANTU. The Bantu are one of the major cultural groupings of Africa. Its unity is derived from genetic and cultural ties, though the term is often used to suggest the existence of a Bantu "race." Recent research reveals that the cradle of Bantu settlement was the Nigeria–Cameroon coastal borders from where the Bantu migrated and diffused into southern, western, and eastern parts of Africa. Eventually this great movement of culture and people returned to Cameroon as Bantu groups migrated into southeastern portions of the country. Most of the ethnic groupings in Cameroon southern regions are of Bantu stock.

BAPTIST MISSION. The Baptists were the first Christian mission in Cameroon. They began work in Cameroon as the Baptist Missionary Society of London in 1846. The idea to evangelize in Africa grew out of its early experience in Jamaica. Various teams of English and Jamaican preachers, **Alfred Saker** (English), Jackson Fuller, and **Joseph Merrick** (Jamaican) arrived in Fernando Po from where they paid visits to Bimbia and **Douala**.

The Baptist Missionary Society of London remained the most active Christian mission on the Cameroon coasts. It established churches, ordained pastors, and evangelized widely in Cameroon until the advent of the German **protectorate** in 1884 and the **Basel Mission** in 1886. Later, in 1890, a Committee of Assistance to the Baptist Churches of Cameroon was founded in Berlin. Following the 1914–18 war, the German Baptists left the territory, leading to the establishment of the Paris Evangelical Missions in the French-speaking Cameroun and the American Baptists in the English part. *See also* NATIVE BAPTIST CHURCH.

BASEL (BASLER) MISSION SOCIETY. This German–Swiss mission began operation in Cameroon in 1886 on request of the German government following the acquisition of **Kamerun** as a **protectorate** in 1884. They replaced the English **Baptist Mission,** which had arrived in 1846. Although designed as an arm of the German administration in Kamerun, the Basel Mission defended the interests of the indigenous peoples against the usually harsh and unjust policies of the colonial administration.

The mission had expanded greatly by 1914 when, with **World War I**, it lost its vast holdings. It resumed activities in the country in 1924 under the British administration. It reestablished a wider network of churches, schools, bookshops, handicraft stores, teacher training, and leprosy centers in the British **trust/mandate**.

These institutions were gradually turned over to the **Presbyterian Church** in Cameroon in 1957 and 1966 without seriously affecting the strong Swiss–German connection. In the French part of Cameroun, the Basel Mission activities were mostly restricted to the coastal **Duala**, **Bassa,** and **Bulu** areas. They promoted much of the relative educational advancement of the population and are reputed, along with the **American Presbyterians**, to have developed radicalism and individualism, particularly among the Bassa.

BASSA–BAKOKO. This ethnic grouping of **Bantu** stock was located around the coastal regions for centuries before being displaced by the **Duala**. The Bassa–Bakoko consequently suffered exploitation from the Duala middlemen role during the period of contact with the Europeans. Their early occupation as subsistence farmers and fishermen was less widely carried out under the colonial periods.

The Bassa–Bakoko emerged as fierce anticolonialists. They fought successive battles against German inland penetration but had to succumb to defeat and a rigorous regime of forced labor on the Douala–Yaoundé "Mittel Kamerun" railway. Although they suffered economic stagnation, they were very advanced in the field of education through the activities of Protestant missionary activities. It is believed that the **American Presbyterian Mission** was instrumental in sharpening the Bassa political and intellectual consciousness. In the period of the preindependence nationalist struggle, the Bassa–Bakoko region was the seat of radical nationalism represented by the **Union des Populations du Cameroun (UPC),** and it also hosted the early messianic movement led by **Thong Likeng**. Industrial activities that developed around the main city of **Edea** were a radical inspiration in the ensuing years of labor unrest. The entire Sanaga–Maritime Division was the setting of virtual civil war between Bassa–Bakoko elements of the UPC spiritually led by **Reuben Um Nyobe** and **Theodore Mayi-Matip** and Cameroon soldiers guided by French troops. By the mid-1960s, the UPC rebellion around Bassa country had been crushed, but the belief of many Bassa–Bakoko in a "Nka Kunde" (liberation toward independence) lives on.

BASSONG, ISABELLE (1937–). Bassong served as secretary of state for public health from 1984 to 1988. Born in Ebolowa in the **South Province** of Cameroon on 9 February 1937, she did her secondary education in New Bell, **Douala**, and later in France. Her university studies took her successively to the University of Paris (Sorbonne), Indiana University, and the University of Denver in the United States. She holds a *licence* in modern letters and a *diplome d'études supérieure* (DES) in English. Prior to her nomination to the Ministry of Public Health, she was a translator at the **National Assembly**. She is a member of the Central Committee of the **Cameroon People's Democratic Movement (CPDM)** and serves as assistant secretary for press, information, and propaganda. Bassong is currently Cameroon's ambassador to Belgium.

BAYANG (BANYANG, BANYANGI). This is the major ethnic group in Manyu Division. They occupy the central portion around the upper **Cross River** that flows into **Nigeria**. Bayangs have language and cultural affinity to groupings beyond the Nigerian border. Although they are made up of 14 clans, no knowledge of common descent exists, making language and cultural values the principal features of Bayang identity. The village is the ultimate level of authority for their diffuse political system. The Bayang were heavily influenced by colonialism. After early years of conflict, they succumbed to the Germans in 1909. The Germans named the area Ossindinge Division, which was changed to **Mamfe** under the British and became the Manyu Division in 1972. Mamfe town itself has been largely deserted since the colonial era, with males moving to cities or taking up plantation employment. Many Bayang live in major cities of the country and maintain quarters bearing their name. They are reported to have a higher proportion of educated elites than other groups from the **South West Province**. Leading figures include **Emmanuel Egbe-Tabi**, W. N. O. Effiom, M. T. Kima, and S. E. Ncha. The name "Bayang" is often known as "Banyang."

BEBEY, FRANCIS (1929–). A Cameroonian artist of many talents, he was born in **Douala** and educated in Paris (at the Sorbonne) and the United States. On the invitation of Kwame Nkrumah—to all Africans of nonindependent territories—he moved to Ghana in 1957 to serve as a broadcaster. He left Ghana and returned to France in the early 1960s to begin a superb career as an artist.

Bebey served for UNESCO as a consultant while undertaking his performances as author, sculptor, and musician. His most famous book, *Agatha Moudio's Son*, was also produced as a popular song. His songs, often of a very innovative nature, are directed to the listener's mind and intellect but also contain humor and seriousness. His other specialty is the use of traditional instruments to blend the sound of his music. Nevertheless, his guitar and the microphone are the most significant tools while on stage. The ease with which the author creates scenes and imagery from his poems and twists his voice and guitar to depict reality gives his **music** a distinctive touch and finesse. *See also* MAKOSSA.

BEBEY-EYIDI, MARCEL (1914–1966). This physician and opposition politician was born on 21 November 1914, in **Douala**. He was educated in **Yaoundé** and Jos before proceeding to Paris for medical studies. He served in the Free French Force during **World War II** and later as a medical practitioner and adviser to **Louis Paul Aujoulat** between 1951 and 1955. He opened a private clinic in Douala in 1956 but became more popular as a leading figure of the political opposition than as a medical officer. Bebey-Eyidi published *l'Opinion au Cameroun* as an opposition journal and petitioned in the United Nations against French rule. He won elections into the **Assemblée Nationale du Cameroun (ANCAM)** in 1960 but was tried, convicted, and jailed with three other prominent politicians in 1962 for conspiracy and sedition. Bebey-Eyidi opposed **Ahmadou Ahidjo's** proposal to form a ***parti unifié*** as dictatorial. His small **Parti Travailliste Camerounais** was disbanded following his imprisonment. Released in 1965, Bebey-Eyidi died in Douala in 1966.

BEECROFT, JOHN (1790–1854). This British agent of African descent settled along the coastal areas of **Nigeria** and Cameroon and served as governor of the British on Fernando Po, an island off the coast of

Cameroon. He was important in the development of British trade with Cameroon in the precolonial period. In 1856, he established a **Court of Equity** in **Douala** to resolve conflict between the **Duala** traders and British merchants.

BELL, DOUALA RUDOLF MANGA. *See* MANGA BELL, DOUALA RUDOLF.

BELLO BOUBA, MAIGARI (1947–). Bello Bouba became **prime minister** of Cameroon after the resignation of Pres. **Ahmadou Ahidjo** and the accession of former prime minister **Paul Biya** to the presidency in November 1982. An Ahidjo loyalist, Bello Bouba was dismissed in August 1983 in the tense atmosphere of the **Ahidjo–Biya rupture**.

Born in 1947 in Bascheou in the Benue Division of the **North Province**, he attended primary and secondary school in **Garoua**. In 1966, he entered the National School of Administration and Magistracy (ENAM) in **Yaoundé** and, on graduation in 1970, he enrolled in the Institute of International Public Administration in Paris. He began his work career as an attaché at the General Secretariat at the Presidency then under Secretary-General Paul Biya. He was later moved to the Ministry of Armed Forces as secretary-general before returning to the residency in 1974. He earned successive promotions to the rank of vice minister and minister in his post as assistant secretary-general at the Presidency. In this capacity he earned the reputation of a key Ahidjo confidant, serving as special envoy in several diplomatic initiatives. In January 1982, he was appointed minister of economy and planning, a post that he occupied until he became prime minister in November 1982.

As prime minister, Bello Bouba was a politician with a difference with his youth, devotion, and **bilingualism** making him a popular figure. His undoing, however, was his solidarity with the North and his unflinching dedication to former president Ahidjo at an unfortunate juncture in Cameroon's political history. It was even rumored in many circles that there was a plan to nominate him as president when President Biya completed Ahidjo's mandate in 1985. This could be done through the **Cameroon National Union (CNU)** party, which was then under the chairmanship of former president Ahidjo. President Biya, it was alleged, was only a transitional figure and Bello Bouba the rising star. As prime minister, Bello Bouba sided openly with the former head of state, allowing regional solidarity to override concern for statehood and national unity. He participated actively in the dramatic move by ministers from the North to resign en masse from the Biya government in June 1983, the **collective resignation plot**, but finally signed an individual letter of resignation. His contention was the failure of President Biya to inform him of a cabinet reshuffle that was announced shortly after their meeting. Although Bello Bouba retained his post, he believed there was lack of trust between the president and he as the prime minister. He was finally dismissed as prime minister on 22 August 1983. A non-Muslim from the North, **Ayang Luc**, was named as interim prime minister. Because of his participation in the secret meeting of northern ministers, Bello Bouba was charged in the plot against the security of the state, although on 14 March 1984 President Biya stopped all proceedings related to the trial.

Shortly after this, Bello went on self-exile to **Nigeria,** where he remained until the liberalization of the political climate in 1990. In August 1991, he returned to Cameroon and together with **Samuel Eboua** formed the **National Union for Democracy and Progress** (Union Nationale pour la Démocratie et le Progrès, UNDP). Since then, Bello has remained a controversial politician. Despite the decision by the Coordination of Opposition Parties, to which Bello Bouba belonged, to boycott the 1992 legislative elections, Bello's party participated in those elections and won 68 seats. He moved into Parliament and in October 1992 ran as a candidate for the presidential elections. Bello remained as a UNDP parliamentarian until December 1997 when he joined President Biya's 22d government as **minister of state** in charge of industrial and commercial development. As minister of state, as opposed to just a minister, Bello Bouba had become very senior in the government.

BENUE RIVER. The Benue River is a major tributary of the Niger River. The Benue originates in the heart of **Adamawa,** north of **Ngaoundéré.** The Benue is navigable up to **Garoua** during the rainy season. Until the construction of the railroad to Ngaoundéré, this port served to evacuate **cotton** and other exports of northern Cameroon and **French Equatorial Africa.** Today, the port is not in use. Cameroon is a member of the **Niger Basin Authority.**

BERLIN CONFERENCE. *See* CONGRESS OF BERLIN.

BERTOUA. Bertoua has been the capital of the **Eastern Province** of Cameroon since 1972. Bertoua was a relatively backward city that has progressively developed over the years with the hosting of national events such as the **agropastoral show** and the schools and university games competition. It has a population of over 20,000, employed mostly in administrative services and in an expanding groundnut-oil mill.

BETI. This **Fang–Pahouin** subgroup is located essentially in the Mfoundi, Lekie, Mfou, Nyong and So, and Ocean divisions of the **Center Province**. There is no consensus among researchers on the origin or ethnographic composition of the Beti. Despite the confusion, the Beti have a well-developed oral literature and traditional art as well as song and games. In terms of the visual arts, they are best known for their carved game pieces called **Abbia** Stones. The renowned writer **Mongo-Beti** belongs to this group.

BIKUTSI. Originating in the traditional balafon **music** of the **Beti**, located around **Yaoundé**, bikutsi pop began to be recorded in the 1940s by Anne-Marie Nzie. Other early pioneers were Messi Me Nkonda Martin and Los Camaroes in the 1960s and 1970s and Les Vétérans in the 1980s. Pres. **Paul Biya**, a Beti himself, later lent his support to the bikutsi group Les Têtes Brulées who gained international acclaim.

BILINGUALISM. Article 3 of Part 1 of the **constitution of 1996** stipulates that **French** and **English** are the official languages of Cameroon. Cameroon's bilingual status is rooted in the joint supervision of the territory by France and Great Britain from 1916 until 1960. Bilingualism helps Cameroon to solve a huge problem of **nation building** caused by its over 300 linguistic groupings. However, the reality of bilingualism is alarming. Only a small portion of the country's population speaks both French and English; a majority probably speaks neither. Despite increasing attempts at integration, the **anglophone** and **francophone** sectors are distinct and jealously preserve their colonial attributes. Attempts are made to promote bilingualism, even though progress has been made very slowly. The number of bilingual schools is increasing. The **University of Yaoundé** has been decentralized, and other universities have been created, some of which offer courses in both French and English. The anglophone University of **Buea** is an example. Linguistic centers for the teaching of French and English have gone into operation in some provinces. As if to demonstrate and promote the bilingual nature of the country, Cameroon recently joined **La Francophonie**, an association grouping French-speaking countries, and the **Commonwealth** of Nations. These efforts notwithstanding, bilingualism as a goal is still distant. *See also* FRANGLAIS; PIDGIN ENGLISH.

BINDZI, BENOIT (1924–1997). A former foreign minister, Bindzi was born in 1924 and attended schools in Mbalmayo, **Yaoundé,** and Akono. He received professional training in the French Foreign Ministry and later at the French Embassy in Bonn, West Germany. He headed Cameroon's delegation to the United Nations from 1961 to 1964 and in 1966. He was elected vice president of the 18th session of the UN General Assembly in 1963. He was appointed minister of information in 1964 and served there until July 1966 when he became minister of foreign affairs (1966–67).

BIYA, PAUL (1933–). President Paul Biya was born of humble parents on 13 February 1933, in Mvomeka'a around Sangmelima in the **South Province**. Although he hails from the Yezum clan of the **Bulu** ethnic group, historical findings have traced the ties of his family to other regions of the country. After a successful primary education, he entered the seminary in Edea and Akono, and it was widely expected that be would end up in the priesthood. He finally enrolled in **Lycée Leclerc** in **Yaoundé** from where he obtained his ***baccalauréat*** in 1956. His university education was done in France at the Lycée Louis-le-Grand in Paris, the law faculty of the University of Sorbonne, the Institute of Political Studies, and the prestigious Institut des Hautes Etudes d'Outre-Mer (IHEOM). From these institutions, he obtained a degree (L.L.B.) and a postgraduate diploma in public law in 1960 and 1963, respectively, as well as two diplomas from the Institute of Political Studies and IHEOM in 1961 and 1962. Like several powerful figures in Cameroon, Biya is a member of the **Rosicrucian Order**.

On his return to Cameroon, Biya served in multiple administrative and governmental posts. In October 1962 he was chargé de mission at the Presidency of the Republic until January 1964, when he was appointed director of cabinet to the then minister of education, youth, and culture, **William-Aurelian Eteky Mboumoua**. He returned to the Presidency in December 1967 as director of the civil cabinet of Pres. **Ahmadou Ahidjo** and became secretary-general at the Presidency in addition to his director functions in January 1968. His post of secretary-general was elevated to ministerial status in 1968 and was further adorned with the higher designation of **minister of state** in June 1970. He remained in his post during the constitutional transition from a federal to a unitary structure in 1972. Following a constitutional amendment in June 1975 reinstating the post of **prime minister**, Biya was appointed the first prime minister of the United Republic of Cameroon. In 1980, the prime minister was declared constitutional successor to the president of the Republic in case of death, resignation, or permanent inability of the incumbent to perform his duties.

When President Ahidjo surprisingly resigned from office on 4 November 1982, Biya became his constitutional successor two days later in an initially peaceful transition of power. Thereafter, a difficult period of struggle for power and influence between the head of state, President Biya, and Ahidjo, who retained his post as **Cameroon National Union (CNU)** party chief, ensued. Ahidjo finally gave up his party leadership on 27 August 1983. President Biya was elected by an extraordinary congress of the party to succeed Ahidjo in September 1983. Having assumed full powers to determine the destinies of the country and unwilling to continue the tenure of his predecessor, Biya called presidential elections on 14 January 1984. He later distanced himself from Ahidjo by forming his own national party, the **Cameroon People's Democratic Union (CPDM)** out of the remnants of the CNU party in March 1985. In a bid to allow the presidential mandate to run concurrently with that of the legislature, elections were again held on 24 April 1988, in which Biya was unanimously reelected.

Since assuming the supreme office of the country, Biya has set for himself an agenda of a new society based on **rigor and moralization.** His economic philosophy is based on the idea of **communal liberalism,** which foresees a profound transformation of the present political principles and institutions in a bid to build a new political society. He also called for rigor and moralization. However, debate continues to grow on the extent of change that has taken place in post-Ahidjo Cameroon. Given the very high expectations of the Cameroonian masses and intellectuals, change has been very minimal. In addition, the Biya regime suffers against a background of an unfortunately bloody but unsuccessful coup attempt, a crushing **economic crisis,** and a image of indecision and contradiction.

Biya's greatest strength, however, has been his ability to weather the storms and defy critiques that have predicted ill and written him off as "unprepared for office." In the 1990s, Biya proved to be adept at delaying and manipulating domestic and international pressures for greater democracy and transparency in government. Although agreeing to allow a multiparty system to develop, he has managed to stay in office and in power. *See also* COUP ATTEMPT OF 6 APRIL 1984.

BIYIDI ALEXANDRE. *See* MONGO-BETI.

BLACK, YONDO MANDENGUE. Black, a lawyer and former president of the Cameroon Bar Association, is viewed by many as one of the early heroes in the democracy movement. Late in 1989, he and several others formed a political organization, the National Coordination for Democracy and a Multiparty System (NCDM). In February 1990, Black and other members of NCDM were arrested under a variety of charges, in essence for forming a political party in a one-party state. The trial of the "Douala Ten," as the arrested persons became titled, brought bad publicity to Cameroon at home and abroad. The trial that followed, before a military court, was a mockery of justice, but it had the positive result of further stimulating demands for an end to the one-party system and alerting international humans rights organizations to the deplorable conditions in Cameroon.

BLOC DEMOCRATIQUE CAMEROUNAISE (BDC). Founded in 1951 under the leadership of **Dr. Louis Paul Aujoulat**, the Bloc Démocratique Camerounais was a political party with a difference. Unlike most other parties formed between 1949 and 1954, there was no specific ethnic group as the base of its creation. Social reform and progress toward political evolution within the French union were major demands advocated by its leader. The BDC, however, had a weak local base concentrating mostly in the **Yaoundé** area and among the elites. Dr. Aujoulat was the party's greatest asset. When he succumbed to electoral defeat in January 1956, the party's fortunes faded from the political scene.

BOL ALIMA, GIBERING (1942–1999). The first minister of higher education and scientific research, a reputed agronomist, ambassador to **Great Britain**, Bol Alima was born on 20 February 1942, in Mbanga. He was a Muslim from Bafia in the Mbam Division. After primary education in Bafia, he proceeded to **Lycée Leclerc** from 1955 to 1962 and later to the Faculty of Science of the **University of Yaoundé** from 1962 to 1966. Thereafter he gained a year of professional experience in Abong-Mbang before embarking on a long trail of specialized education in France, Ivory Coast, and Great Britain. He earned his Ph.D. in crop physiology at the University of London in 1978.

Dr. Alima later occupied important academic, ministerial, and party functions. He was director of the National School of Agronomy from 1975 to 1979 and the first director-general of the University Centre of Dschang from August 1978 to April 1983. His ministerial functions have included minister of planning and industry from April 1983 to February

1985 and minister of the newly created Ministry of Higher Education and Scientific Research from February 1984 to August 1985. From 1975 to 1983, he served as adviser to the **Economic and Social Council** and has occupied many local party posts since 1971. Between 1980 and 1985, Dr. Alima was a member of the **Cameroon National Union (CNU)** Central Committee and played the role of rapporteur of the historic 14 September 1983 extraordinary congress of the party.

An accomplished scholar, Dr. Alima was named Cameroon's ambassador to **Great Britain** in January 1987, where he remained until November 1994, when he was replaced by Samuel Libok-Mbei. He died on 30 July 1999.

BORDER CONFLICTS. Recurrent disputes in the delineation of national frontiers between Cameroon and its neighbors led to occasional discord with **Nigeria**, **Congo,** and **Gabon**. The root of border conflict in contemporary Africa is a legacy of colonial rule. The old borders of Africa were created exclusively by European powers based on decisions of the **Congress of Berlin (1884–85)** and were largely arbitrary. With independence, African countries did not change their old boundaries. International law made the existing boundaries sacrosanct, but the actual boundaries were not clearly delineated. The 1970s were marked by persistent conflict between Cameroon and the countries to the south, Gabon and Congo, while the persistent quarrel with Nigeria reached a peak in May 1981 when five Nigerian soldiers were shot down on the coastal fringes of the two countries. War appeared imminent, but Cameroon apologized to the Nigerian government and paid compensation for the victims. Nigeria continues to accuse Cameroon **gendarmes** of making incursions into Nigerian territory and mistreating Nigerian citizens living in the border areas, especially on the coastal fringes. Cameroon denies these charges, although occasionally, as in 1988, admitting to incursions. Delineation has been slow, thereby increasing the potential for further conflict. In December 1993, hostilities broke out again along the Cameroon–Nigeria border, when Nigerian troops attacked and occupied parts of the Bakassi Peninsula. *See also* BAKASSI DISPUTE.

BOTANICAL GARDENS. Established in Victoria (now **Limbe**) by the Germans during the tenure of Governor Soden (1885–91), its principal aim was to assist planters in the economic exploitation of **Kamerun**. This was carried out through experimentation with various tropical crops, trees, and plants to test their adaptability and commercial potential. Other substations of the Victoria Botanical Garden were opened in major administrative and military headquarters. Specialists in the Victoria center worked closely with the central Botanical Bureau in Berlin for research and investigation. Favorable research results turned the Victoria Botanical Gardens into a profit-making arm of the **protectorate**.

The defeat and the departure of the Germans after **World War I** led to the slow but gradual decline of the Botanical Gardens both as a research station and as a resort for natural beauty under the British and the later Cameroon administrations. The headquarters building of the gardens became a hospital for whites during the British era and an expensive tourist hotel after independence. In 1988, the British government began to provide financial assistance for the restoration of the gardens. By the 1990s, the gardens had returned to their original glory and had become an important tourist stop.

BOUBA, MAIGARI BELLO. *See* BELLO BOUBA, MAIGARI.

BRAZZAVILLE CONFERENCE. This important political conference of **French Equatorial Africa** in January 1944 defined the postwar evolution of various African territories. It was organized by supporters of the Free French under Charles de Gaulle and presided over by the governor of Chad, Félix Eboue. The conference recommended the continuation of French **assimilation policies** and rejected the idea of autonomy for these territories. The most significant recommendation was the abolition of the ***indigénat*** and elimination of the cosmetic distinctions between *citoyens* and *sujets*.

BREVET D'ETUDES DU PREMIER CYCLE (BEPC). This is one of the major examinations for secondary schools in **francophone** Cameroon. Students take the BEPC four school years after the **Certificat de Fin d'Etudes Primaires Elémentaires (CEPE)**. The BEPC sanctions the end of the first cycle of secondary **education**. Success in the written part of the examination allows for admission into the oral exam. Generally, the national performance rate in the Brevet d'Etudes du Premier Cycle is not very remarkable. In terms of comparative equivalent for public service employment, the BEPC is ranked the same as the Ordinary Level **General Certificate of Education** in **anglophone** Cameroon.

BRIQUETERIE. Briqueterie is a district of **Yaoundé.** A large proportion of the Muslim population of the city resides here, but it is also known as a rather dangerous neighborhood in terms of thievery and violence.

BRITISH CAMEROONS. The British Cameroons existed as a **mandate** from 1916 to 1945 and as a **trust** territory from 1946 to 1961. Despite this special status, **Great Britain** ruled its Cameroon territory as an ordinary British colony. For administrative purposes, British Cameroons was not only tied to the adjoining colony of **Nigeria** but separated between a **Northern** and **Southern Cameroons** without any connecting ties between them. The British justified their action based on the sparse population of the territory and the need to restore historic connections between ethnic groups in Nigeria and Cameroon. Thanks to this connection, many Nigerians migrated to work in Cameroon, and many Cameroonians studied in Nigerian schools and colleges. The British imposed their policy of **indirect rule,** determining all aspects of political development in the territory. By 1959, various parts of British Cameroons were allowed to operate as self-governing entities under a premier. In the 1961 **plebiscite**, Northern Cameroons voted to join with Nigeria, while Southern Cameroons voted for reunification with the **République du Cameroun**.

BUEA. The provincial capital of the **South West Province** and capital of the former **West Cameroon**, Buea was also capital of German **Kamerun**. The town is essentially a **Bakweri** stronghold. The main elders of the group and the recognized elites were mainly born in this town. Its altitude and climate largely accounted for its administrative significance throughout the country's history. Structures left behind by German administrators were utilized by the British, as well as by the postcolonial authorities of the former West Cameroon. Apart from its political importance, Buea remains of little commercial interest. However, with a population estimated at 24,584 inhabitants in 1976, it is among Cameroon's 17 towns with over 20,000 people. The centralization of political structures in 1972 led to the decline of its administrative role. The creation of the University of Buea has boosted social and economic activities in the town. This notwithstanding, the town remains in dire need of a host of other attractions that higher education itself does not provide. Local initiative and government action need to be channeled toward the rebirth of a historic town in decline.

Once every year, the town hosts the Guinness **Mount Cameroon** Race. The race has become a popular international sporting event. Contestants run from Buea to the top of the mountain, from 1,030 meters to 4,080 meters in altitude, and back to town, with the best of times under four hours.

BUEA DECLARATION. The **All Anglophone Conference** held in **Buea**, 2–3 April 1993, produced the Buea Declaration. This document expresses the view, widely held among **anglophones** at the time, that the union of **French Cameroun** and **Southern Cameroons** had failed, with the **francophone** domination and exploitation of the anglophone areas a major issue. The document argues that in fact the unitary state imposed in the **constitution of 1972** was illegal and that the federal form of government must be restored. Other demands were made concerning education issues, including the opening of an anglophone university and the reestablishment of various anglophone institutions.

BULU. A part of the wider sociocultural **Beti** group, the Bulu are located in the deep south of Cameroon and trace kin and language affinity to the **Fang** and **Ewondo** people in the region. Their main activity is agriculture around the predominantly rich cocoa-producing towns of Ebolowa, Sangmelima, and Djoum. With only about 150,000 people, they constitute a minority even among the Beti. Historically, the Bulu served as middlemen in the European **slave trade** and were defeated in their attempt at armed rebellion against German penetration in the coastal south.

The Bulu have a record of uneasy relationship with the neighboring **Bassa–Bakoko** group and rose against **Bamiléké** success in trade and petty commerce around the southern regions of the country in 1956. Despite their small numbers and weak sense of community, they have gained leadership through the personalities of **Charles Assale** (former **East Cameroon prime minister**) and Pres. **Paul Biya**.

– C –

CAMEROON ANGLOPHONE MOVEMENT (CAM). The CAM was among the pressure groups that held that a return to the federal system of government was the solution to the **anglophone problem**. This group, founded in 1991, regards itself as the symbol of the **anglophone** struggle. It was the brainchild of the **All Anglophone Conference** (AAC). In 1992, CAM declared 20 May as Cameroon's National Day, Slavery Day. According to the CAM, it was on this day that anglophones moved from independence to slavery. It called on anglophones to observe 20 May as a mourning day. In October 1993, both CAM and the AAC sent a delegation to the Nicosia **Commonwealth** Summit in an attempt to have that organization put pressure on the Cameroon government to accelerate constitutional and democratic reforms. Other profederalist pressure groups include the Teachers Associations of Cameroon (TAC) and the Confederation of Anglophone Parents–Teachers Association of Cameroon (CAPTAC), both of which are concerned with the improvement of the educational system of anglophone Cameroon. The creation of the GCE Board in 1993 was partly due to the activities of the TAC and CAPTAC. *See also* ZERO OPTION.

CAMEROON CULTURAL REVIEW. *See* ABBIA.

CAMEROON DEMOCRATIC UNION (CDU)/UNION DEMOCRATIQUE CAMEROUNAISE (UDC). This small party originated with the return to a multiparty system. It is led by Adamou Ndam Njoya and finds its major support in **Foumban**, **West Province**. The party philosophy is in many ways similar to that of the **Social Democratic Front (SDF),** and an alliance between the two parties would benefit both. However, there is a substantial difference of view on the issues of a new constitution and the question of federalism versus decentralization. In the early 1990s, the parties often worked together, even sharing rallies. Both boycotted the **elections for the National Assembly (1992)**. The CDU leader did run in the **elections for president (1992)**, receiving 3.2 percent of the vote. In the elections of 1997 for the **National Assembly**, the CDU won five seats, all in Foumban. The CDU boycotted the **elections for president (1997)**. Most of the party's support comes from the **Bamoum** people, although the current sultan, Ibrahim Mbombo Njoya, supported the **Cameroon People's Democratic Movement (CPDM).**

CAMEROON DEVELOPMENT CORPORATION (CDC). The CDC is the biggest agroindustrial company in the Central African region and the largest statutory organization in Cameroon. It was created in December 1946 by an ordinance of the Nigerian colonial authorities to manage and develop the large expanses of former German plantations. In reality, therefore, the CDC is the direct legacy of a long-dating colonial venture. It remained the most significant economic and social feature of the former **West Cameroon**, although its activities were initially concentrated in the Fako and Meme Division area. Activities have now expanded into the **North West**, with a tea estate at Ndu; the **West**, with a tea estate at Djuttitsa; and the **Littoral Province**, with a rubber estate at Kompina.

This expansion was achieved after multiple setbacks and difficulties at the early stages. The CDC faced a rather hostile **Bakweri Land Claim**

Committee that requested the return of expropriated land to its indigenous owners. It also had to struggle with uncertain budgetary subsidies from Great Britain, **Nigeria,** and the **Commonwealth** in the early period to survive. Moreover, following independence and **reunification**, its lifeblood was only secured with heavy loans from the **European Economic Community**'s development fund, the **World Bank**, the International Development Association, and the Commonwealth Development Corporation. In another attempt to rescue the CDC from its problems, the government of Cameroon took control of its operations in 1962.

The CDC is the second largest employer in the country, after the government, with about 13,000 workers. Its main activity is in the domain of agriculture by which it accounts for much of Cameroon's total production of crops such as **bananas**, **rubber**, **palm products**, **tea**, and pepper. This notwithstanding, the corporation also provides services such as hospitals and health care, schools and technical training, roads, as well as sponsoring sports teams and conducting engineering and maritime activities.

The corporation's products find their way into the national and international markets. Apart from exporting the bulk of its products to other countries, the CDC supplies local industries with raw materials such as palm oil and palm kernels for chemical complexes and rubber for the footwear industry. It also supplies the local population with palm oil for consumption. Its tea products are widely used in Cameroon and neighboring countries.

Fako Division continues to be the mainstay of the CDC, with its headquarters established in Bota on the outskirts of **Limbe**. Even though **Tiko** lost significance with the takeover of the hospital facilities by the government and privatization of the company's football (soccer) club, the town has regained its status as the headquarters of the company's health facilities. It hosts a modern hospital.

In contrast to the early period when the company was run by British and Nigerian staff, the CDC at present has been indigenized. It is currently run by a board of directors, headed by a chairman who is appointed by the government. **Fon Victor Mukete** became the first indigenous chairman of the company. Other Cameroonians have succeeded him as chairman: Justice S. M. L. Endeley, Gov. John E. Ngole, Gov. Sigfried Etame Massoma, and Honorable **Nerius N. Mbile**, who is the current chairman. In the same manner, the post of general manager, in charge of the day-to-day business of the company, has been held by a number of indigenes since 1973—for example, John Niba Ngu, who ruled from April 1973 until his appointment in May 1988 as minister of agriculture, and **Peter Mafany Musonge** from August 1988 to September 1996, when he was appointed **prime minister**. It should be noted that Musonge combined the posts of prime minister and general manager, until Henry Njalla Quan, current general manager, was appointed on 10 March 1998, to head of the company. Since its creation, the CDC has had seven chairmen, 10 general managers, six deputy general managers, and 104 board members. In November 1997, the company celebrated its 50th anniversary. In an effort to increase efficiency, various sectors of the company are presently being privatized.

CAMEROON MOUNTAIN. *See* MOUNT CAMEROON.

CAMEROON NATIONAL ANTHEM. As stated in Part 1, Paragraph 6, of the **constitution of 1996**, the national anthem of the country is "O Cameroon, Cradle of Our Fathers." The national anthem is a symbol of the country's sovereignty. Although critics believe it bears a melodic resemblance to the French hymn "La Marseillaise," the Cameroonian national anthem was actually composed in 1928 at the Foulassi Teacher Training College near Sangmelima in the **South Province**. The words of the song were selected by Jam Afane and the lyrics composed by Minkyo Bamba. The song was heard in public for the first time during the visit of the French governor to the Protestant Mission Teacher Training College in 1928. The song was gradually propagated as teachers left this institution to begin their careers elsewhere. It later became representative and symbolic of the nationalist aspiration of the people. In 1960, it was proclaimed the national anthem of the Republic by Cameroon's first Constituent Assembly. The English version (not a translation) is widely attributed to **Bernard Fonlon**. The words of the first verse were changed in 1972 by a special commission and later made official by the head of state. The tune has always remained true to the original.

Cameroon National Anthem (French)
O Cameroun berceau de nos ancêtres,
va debout et jaloux de ta liberté,
comme un soleil ton drapeau fier doit être,
un symbole ardent de foi et d'unité,
Chorus:
Chère Patrie, Terre chérie,
Tu es notre seul et vrai bonheur,
Notre joie, notre vie,

En toi l'amour et le grand honneur.
Que tous tes enfants du Nord et Sud,
De l'Est à l'Ouest soit tout amour,
Te servir que ce soit le seul but,
Pour remplir leur devoir toujours.
Cameroon National Anthem (English)
O Cameroon, Thou Cradle of our Fathers
Holy Shrine where in our midst they now repose,
Their tears and blood and sweat thy soil did water,
On thy hills and valleys once their tillage rose.
Dear Fatherland, thy worth no tongue can tell!
How can we ever pay thy due?
Thy welfare we will win in toil and love and peace,
Will be to thy name ever true!
Chorus:
Land of Promise, land of Glory!
Thou, of life and joy, our only store!
Thine be honor, thine devotion
And deep endearment, for evermore.
From Shari, from where the Mungo meanders
From along the banks of lowly Boumba Stream,
Muster thy sons in union close around thee,
Mighty as the Buea Mountain be their team;
Instill in them the love of gentle ways,
Regret for errors of the past;
Foster, for Mother Africa, a loyalty
That true shall remain to the last.

CAMEROON NATIONAL UNION (CNU)/UNION NATIONALE CAMEROUNAISE (UNC). The CNU was the first one-party structure in independent Cameroon. It was formed on 1 September 1966 to forge greater national unity and consolidate **Ahmadou Ahidjo**'s political hold on the country. The main parties of the two federal states—the **Union Camerounaise (UC)** in **East Cameroon**, headed by Ahidjo, as well as the **Kamerun National Democratic Party (KNDP)**, the **Cameroon United Congress (CUC),** and the **Cameroons Peoples' National Convention (CPNC)** in **West Cameroon**—met in **Yaoundé** on 11 June 1966, to reach an agreement in favor of a unified movement. Consequently, the main party in East Cameroon and the three major parties of West Cameroon agreed to declare their dissolution by 31 August.

On 1 September, the CNU party came into being as a party for all Cameroonians, supposedly able to bridge barriers between the rich and poor and to integrate ethnic groups and religions for the attainment of common objectives. These objectives included:

- the consolidation of the union of all Cameroonians;
- the contribution of civic and political education; and
- the promotion of the economic and social interests of Cameroonian people.

The CNU had two ancillary organs, the youth wing (YCNU) and the **women**'s wing (WCNU). Its four central organs at the national level were the National Congress, the National Council, the Central Committee, and the Political Bureau. The motto of the party was Union–Truth–Democracy. However, throughout its 19 years' existence, the CNU hardly succeeded in its objectives. It was not a true reflection of the unity of peoples. It was a major propaganda institution of government, and democracy was only defined in the narrow interest of the party leadership. Indeed, membership in the high organs of the party was identical to membership in the national government, the **National Assembly**, and the **Economic and Social Council.**

The National Congresses, held every five years in different towns of the country, marked the most lively periods in the party's existence. These brought the party a little closer to the people as suspense arose over the choice of presidential candidate in the upcoming election. Until his resignation as head of state in 1982, Ahidjo was the sole candidate of the party. While virtually unchallenged, President Ahidjo always delayed the acceptance of the candidacy to the very last minute of the congress.

Following his resignation in November 1982, Ahidjo retained the post of chairman of the CNU, plunging the party and the country into political debate. He argued as ex-president of the country that the party, of which he was still chairman, determined and guided government policy under Pres. **Paul Biya**. President Biya, for his part, emphasized government's autonomy. The animosity and suspicion surrounding this issue led to Ahidjo's announcement from France of his resignation as party boss on 27 August 1983. President Biya was hurriedly mandated to replace him in an Extraordinary Party Congress in **Yaoundé** on 14 September 1983. Biya served in this post until the March 1985 **Bamenda Congress** that led to the formation of the **Cameroon People's Democratic Movement (CPDM)**.

CAMEROON OIL TRANSPORTATION COMPANY. *See* PIPELINE.

CAMEROON OUTLOOK. This controversial anglophone newspaper has been published since 1969. Unlike the early ***Cameroon Times***, the

Cameroon Outlook was not tied to any political establishment and remained fearless in its public attacks on **corruption**, tribalism, discrimination, and inefficiency. It became a ready target for governmental censorship and frequently appeared with blank spaces on its pages. Its most popular column was known as "Ako-Aya," believed to represent the view of the editor and publisher of *Cameroon Outlook*, Tataw Obenson. "Ako-Aya" mirrored gossip from political, social, and cultural settings and was particularly appealing to the person on the street. The newspaper survived the death in 1978 of its publisher but has declined in popular appeal and now appears irregularly. At its peak periods, *Cameroon Outlook* had a circulation of nearly 10,000 copies. *See also* CAMEROON TIMES; CAMEROON TRIBUNE, L'EFFORT CAMEROUNAISE; LE MESSAGER.

CAMEROON PEOPLES DEMOCRATIC MOVEMENT (CPDM)/ MOUVEMENT DEMOCRATIQUE DU PEUPLE CAMEROUNAIS (MDPC). As of 1999, the dominant party of the **Republic of Cameroon**, the CPDM is a successor of the **Cameroon National Union (CNU)**. The CPDM was formed at the end of the fourth ordinary congress of the CNU in **Bamenda**, 24 March 1985.

The CPDM represents President **Biya**'s desire to create his party in his image following the continuous identification of the CNU with the former **Ahidjo** regime. It is representative of the **New Deal** era that became the symbol of Biya's rule. The party attempts to distinguish itself from the past through its new emblem made of a flame protected by two black hands on a blue field encircled by the initials of the party. Its motto is Unity–Progress–Democracy. The party strives in its objectives to mobilize the population of the country to:

- consolidate national unity, integration, and independence;
- promote a democratic system of government as well as rapid economic growth; and
- contribute to the civic political education of nationals and promote their economic and social interest.

However, the CPDM has equally been characterized by striking resemblances to the CNU party. Like its predecessor, the CPDM has annex organizations like the Youth and Women's wings of the party. Its structures are a standard carbon copy of the past from the lowest organ (the cell) to its highest organ (the national congress). Like the CNU of yesterday, the CPDM remains highly elitist.

In the 1990s, the CPDM's monopoly of political power was challenged with some success, by increasing demands for democracy and transparency in government. New parties have formed, in particular the **Social Democratic Front** (SDF) led by **John Fru Ndi** and the **Union for Democracy and Progress** led by **Maigari Bello Bouba**. While the CPDM's presidential candidate, Paul Biya, was successful in retaining the office of the national president, the party lost its domination of the National Assembly and was forced to form a coalition.

While the CPDM now does face competition, it retains tremendous advantages in terms of the very large infrastructure it obtained during the years of one-party rule (offices, vehicles, telephones, etc.) and as a result of President Biya's control of relatively huge patronage resources (jobs, contracts, location of development projects, etc.).

CAMEROON TIMES. This **anglophone** newspaper was launched in Victoria (now **Limbe**) as a weekly on 9 December 1960. The *Kamerun Times* was established with the financial assistance of the **Douala**-based business magnate, **Paul Soppo Priso**. It became known as *Cameroon Times* in 1961 and supported the **Kamerun National Democratic Party (KNDP)** political platform in the early independence era. The newspaper ceased publication in April 1968 but resumed operations twice or thrice weekly in 1969. The *Cameroon Times* was now associated with a more centrist viewpoint, especially with the rise of other rival **anglophone** newspapers. It folded for a while in the 1970s but in the 1980s recruited younger editors who stirred controversy with the new **Paul Biya** regime in an open, critical letter to the president. The editors were detained but later released. The *Cameroon Times* now appears either weekly or sporadically. *See also CAMEROON OUTLOOK; CAMEROON TRIBUNE; L'EFFORT CAMEROUNAIS; LE MESSAGER.*

CAMEROON TRADE UNION CONGRESS (CTUC). The CTUC was established as the official forum for Cameroon workers in 1985, replacing the **National Union of Cameroon Workers**. It was made up of the national congress, the national council, and the executive bureau. Members of the union were drawn from national and section syndicates as well as professional groups in the country. In the first congress of the CTUC in December 1985, the executive bureau was formed, and a journalist, **Dominique Foude Sima**, was elected its first president. In June 1992, the CTUC was dissolved and replaced by the **Confederation of Cameroon Trade Unions** (**CCTU**).

CAMEROON TRIBUNE. The government's national daily newspaper came into existence in 1974 to replace the previous daily, *La Presse du Cameroun*. Published in **Yaoundé,** the *Cameroon Tribune* belongs to the national editing and publishing company, SOPECAM. Because it is an official government newspaper, editors are not allowed to give their viewpoints; they are charged to mirror the viewpoint of the government and party. This makes the newspaper unexciting to readers. However, compared to other newspapers of the country, the *Cameroon Tribune* is a better written and more educative newspaper particularly designed for the nation's elite. Most of the *Cameroon Tribune* staff writers are trained in the Yaoundé Advanced School of Mass Communications. The editors are regularly furnished with reports from the Cameroon News Agency (CAMNEWS), correspondents in the provinces, and wireless world news services from abroad. However, the most popular parts of the *Cameroon Tribune* are the sports and culture pages as well as public announcements and frequent publication of entire texts of presidential decrees and appointments. In 1988, the new director of SOPECAM, **Paul Tessa**, and the editor in chief, **Henri Bandolo,** were appointed to high government posts. Since its inception, the *Cameroon Tribune* has been a daily newspaper only in the French language. The English edition of the newspaper progressed from a weekly into a biweekly publication in August 1986. *See also CAMEROON OUTLOOK; CAMEROON TIMES; L'EFFORT CAMEROUNAIS; LE MESSAGER.*

CAMEROON VERSUS THE UNITED KINGDOM. *See* NORTHERN CAMEROONS CASE.

CAMEROON UNITED CONGRESS (CUC). This splinter group from the **Kamerun National Democratic Party** (KNDP) emerged as a parliamentary faction and developed into a small but influential party in 1965. Its main leader and founder was the then federal minister, **Solomon Tandeng Muna**. The CUC was designed to sensitize Cameroonians to the need for greater political unity and harmony east and west of the **Mungo River**. The birth of the party was the result of a constitutional controversy in the KNDP on the appointment of the **West Cameroon** premier. Muna asserted the prerogative of the federal president (**Ahmadou Ahidjo**) over the party president (**John Ngu Foncha**). This led to the definitive rupture between Muna and Foncha. Along with another federal minister, **Emmanuel Egbe-Tabi**, Muna made the CUC the opposition party in the West Cameroon House of Assembly in 1965.

In opposition, the CUC championed the call for the immediate formation of a national party, a timely appeal as the single unified party, the **Cameroon National Union (CNU)**, was founded in September 1966.

CAMEROON WELFARE UNION (CWU). Formed in late 1939 as an early political group in **Southern Cameroons**, its leaders were mainly Western-educated Southern Cameroonians, which made the CWU an essentially elite gathering. Its main purpose was the quest for an identity for the region and recognition for its leaders. It therefore advocated direct representation of Southern Cameroons in the Nigerian central legislature in Lagos. The British turned down the request denying claims of any autonomy for the territory. **Chief Manga Williams** played a leading role in the early stages of the movement. In the later periods, more sophisticated politicians such as **Emmanuel Endeley**, **John Ngu Foncha**, and **P. M. Kale** provided leadership for the union. The CWU was essentially short-lived as a political grouping, but much of its designs were carried forward in the scheme of the **Cameroons Youth League**.

CAMEROONIAN PATRIOTIC OPPOSITION. A brief-lived coalition of 11 (and at times 13) opposition parties formed under the leadership of **Ndam Amadou Njoya** of the **Cameroon Democratic Union (UDC)**.

CAMEROONS NATIONAL FEDERATION (CNF). This political grouping in **Southern Cameroons** brought together various interests in local government issues in a May 1949 conference in **Kumba**. Its leader was **Emmanuel M. L. Endeley** and it included other personalities such as **Solomon Tandeng Muna**, **Sampson A. George,** and **Nerius Mbile**. The aim was to discuss issues on tribal development initiatives through improvement unions, agrarian grievances of the land committees, and employment issues of the **CDC Workers Union**. These questions were to serve as the basis of a petition to the 1949 United Nations Visiting Mission to the territory. The CNF expressed local neglect of the region by the British and the frustration of the population to the UN trust authority. The group also embraced collaboration with **French Cameroun** groupings resident in the territory and advocated evolutionary **reunification**. Its memoranda on reunification envisaged the abolition of the intra–Southern Cameroons and interfrontier boundary regulations, the teaching of compulsory **English** and **French** with equal emphasis in all schools of Kamerun, and the nondiscriminatory treatment of French Camerounians in all aspects of life in **British Cameroons**. A federal or unitary political state was to emerge from these concrete arrangements.

The CNF thus became a leading laboratory to experiment with the reunification idea. It resulted in major divergences among the leadership and conflicting options like the separationists (led by Endeley), the secessionists (under **P. M. Kale**'s guidance), the reunificationists (championed by Dibongue) and the ultra-anti-imperialists (spearheaded by **Ntumazah Ndeh**). Although the CNF continued collaboration with the **Union des Populations du Cameroun (UPC)**, both saw reunification not as an ideal in itself but as a means to an end. *See also* TRUSTEESHIP SYSTEM.

CAMEROONS PEOPLES' NATIONAL CONVENTION (CPNC). The CPNC was formed in May 1960 as a result of the fusion between the **Kamerun National Congress** (led by **Emmanuel Endeley**) and the Kamerun Peoples Party (under **Nerius Mbile**, **P. M. Kale,** and Peter Motomby-Woleta). If the **Kamerun National Democratic Party (KNDP)** is largely identified as a **Grassfield** party, the elite leadership of the CPNC brands it as a forest-dominated party. In reality, the CPNC was formed to put an end to the resounding electoral victories of the KNDP that permitted the latter's political hegemony over other parties in **Southern Cameroon**.

CAMEROONS PROVINCE. This was the official administrative title of **Southern Cameroons** between 1916 and 1949. The Cameroons Province was first administered as a province of the Southern Provinces of **Nigeria** and later became part of Eastern Nigeria. The entire province consisted of the Victoria (**Limbe**), **Kumba**, Ossidinge (**Mamfe**), and **Bamenda** Divisions. In April 1949, Bamenda became a province in its own right. The Cameroons Province was ruled by a **resident** responsible to the lieutenant governor and the governor general in Nigeria. **Buea** was the capital of Cameroons Province.

CAMEROONS YOUTH LEAGUE (CYL). Founded in Lagos in 1939, the Cameroons Youth League is among the earliest expressions of **Southern Cameroon** nationalism. It was formed in reaction to, and as a model of, the Nigerian Youth Movement and brought together leading figures who later commanded the destinies of **West Cameroon** such as **P. M. Kale** as its president, **Emmanuel M. C. Endeley** as secretary, and **John Ngu Foncha**. In this respect, the CYL resembled the **Jeunesse Démo-**

cratique Camerounaise (Jeucafra) of **French Cameroun**. Most CYL leaders were students in Nigeria, who, on return home, founded local branches of the organization as did Foncha in Bamenda by 1943.

The CYL was a social and political movement. As a social movement, it sought to develop fraternal ties among Cameroonians in Nigeria and foster their welfare, employment, and social consciousness. As a political movement, it awakened Cameroonians' sense of awareness and stimulated political participation. The CYL was the catalyst for Cameroonian participation and identity in the **National Council of Nigeria and the Cameroons (NCNC)**. The league's leader, P. M. Kale, played an active role in the NCNC. Given the early period of its formation, the CYL, like Jeucafra, did not foresee **reunification**, which later became a leading theme for major political parties. Unlike Jeucafra, which was a creation of the French and entertained francophile fantasies, the CYL was an indigenous creation of Southern Cameroonians.

CAMEROUN. The French appellation and spelling for Cameroon. About four-fifths of the German **Kamerun protectorate** was administered by the French under the **mandate** and **trusteeship** agreements between 1916 and 1960. Consequently, this appellation and spelling is still often utilized specifically to identify the French epoch in Cameroon history. In addition, since independence and **reunification**, most references to the country use the French spelling partly as a recognition of a greater **francophone** presence.

CAMEROUN ACTUALITES. The national cinematographic agency, created in 1962, was charged with the production of all varieties of films, their sales and distribution, as well as their use and projection in movie theaters and the national television. All commercial, industrial, and artisanal operations dealing with the cinematographic industry work closely with Cameroon Actualités. Given the relative underdevelopment of the indigenous cinematographic industry, Cameroun Actualités prevails in the mind of the average citizen who visits movie and theater halls in the country. Short segments of presidential and governmental activities are usually displayed on screen by Cameroun Actualités to serve as prelude to the programmed Western films. *See also* FILM INDUSTRY.

CAMEROUN ORIENTAL. *See* EAST CAMEROON.

CAMSUCO. *See* SUGAR.

CASSAVA (MANIHOT ESCULENTA, POPULARLY KNOWN AS MANIOC). It originated from Central America as a root crop grown in the fertile lowland tropics. The soils of the rain forest regions are particularly suited for root-crop production. Cassava in Cameroon grows well in the **Littoral**, **East**, **Center**, **South,** and **South West** provinces. Consequently, the people of these areas depend heavily on cassava for livelihood. It can be boiled in water and eaten with sauce or pounded to make *fufu,* soaked to prepare water *fufu*, or grated to make popular foodstuffs such as miondo and bobolo. Cassava can also be turned to starch, which is used for laundry in many Cameroonian homes.

CATHOLIC CHURCH. The Catholic Church was established in Cameroon by several missionary groups and missionaries from many countries. In the German period the Pallotine Mission, mainly Germans and Swiss, began operations in 1880 under the leadership of Mgr. Heinrich Vieter. Sacred Heart missionaries joined the Pallotines in 1912 to begin work in Kumbo in today's **North West Province**. World War I interrupted the work of the Pallotines, who took refuge on Fernando Po in 1916 when the Germans were defeated in Cameroon. By 1922, the Church in France had appointed Mgr. François-Xavier Vogt to take charge of Catholic activities in **French Cameroun**. The Holy Ghost Fathers (Pères du St. Esprit) replaced the Pallotines, and Holy Ghost nuns arrived in 1924. Also from France came members of the Sacred Heart order in 1922 to replace German members of the order driven out in World War I. From Great Britain came the Mill Hill Fathers, led by Rev. William Campling to work in the British mandate of **Southern Cameroons**. Franciscan and Patricoft sisters, Benedictine fathers, the Oblates of Mary Immaculate, and the Daughters of the Holy Spirit were other groups involved in the Cameroon mission.

The first Cameroonian to join the church was Andres Ludwig Kuo a Mbangue, baptized 6 January 1889. **Charles Atangana** was another early convert. Mgr. Paul Etoga was the first Cameroonian bishop, consecrated 30 November 1955. Among other well-known figures in the church are Mgr. **Jean Zoa**, first Cameroonian archbishop of **Yaoundé**; Mgr. **Paul Verdsekov**, archbishop of **Bamenda**; and Mgr. **Christian Tumi**, who has held posts at **Garoua** and **Maroua** and is now cardinal. As with other Christian organizations in Cameroon, the Catholic Church has played important roles in education, health care, and economic development. **St. Joseph's College** in Sasse, Collège Libermann in **Douala**, and the Collège Sacre-Coeur in Makak near Yaoundé are among the most famous schools. In 1995, it was estimated that about 20 percent of Cameroon's population, about 2.8 million people, followed the Catholic faith.

CDC WORKERS UNION. This major trade union was formed in the **British Cameroons** in 1947 to cater for the needs of workers employed by the **Cameroon Development Corporation (CDC)** in the plantations and in its related health, administrative, education, and engineering services. The first secretary-general was **Emmanuel M. L. Endeley** who later rose to become premier of the territory.

CELLUCAM. *See* CELLULOSE DU CAMEROUN.

CELLULOSE DU CAMEROUN (CELLUCAM). The Cameroon pulp and paper industry is located in **Edea** in the **Littoral Province** and designed to cut down and replant the forest for the production of paper. CELLUCAM began its operation in November 1980 with a capital of 202 billion CFA francs, the first factory for the production of pulp and paper in francophone Africa. By June 1982, CELLUCAM had produced only 49,487 tons of paper, almost half its anticipated capacity. By the end of 1982, the company had lost over 23 billion CFA francs and was heavily in debt. This poor performance was due partly to the weak sales of its product and two accidental explosions suffered at its main chemical bleaching plant. An Austrian firm, Voest Alpina, built and ran the firm, while Cameroon held 57 percent of the shares. Difficulties in repairing the damaged plant, falling production and export, and expected bankruptcy led the government to finally terminate the project in 1986. In November 1991, the remnants of CELLUCAM were sold to an Indonesian firm, Gudang Garam, which intends to resuscitate the project.

CELLUCAM was the result of the government's drive to implement an interventionist industrial strategy in its fourth five-year development plan. Its demise and closure are largely seen as a microcosm of the many problems inherent in developing economies: heavy dependence on foreign input, careless feasibility studies, failing managerial and expert skills, and low quality of finished products.

CENTER PROVINCE. The Center Province covers a surface area of 74,050 square kilometers and occupies the south central part of the country. The province consists of eight divisions, 39 subdivisions, and five districts. Much of the province is located on a low plateau at an elevation of 200 to 600 meters. The vegetation represents two distinct zones: the secondary forest in the South and the savannah zone in the North. Unlike other regions of the country, the province has an equatorial type climate of two dry seasons and two rainy seasons. Over 1,690,000 inhabitants live in the province. Agriculture is the principal occupation of the population, especially in the growing of key exports such as **cocoa** and **coffee**. Industrial, educational, commercial, transport, and hotel activities have been greatly expanded, especially in **Yaoundé,** which is the capital of the province and the country. Other important towns include Mbalmayo (Nyong and Soo Division), Akonolinga (Nyong and Mfoumou Division), Eseka (Nyong and Kelle Division), Mfou (Mefou Division), Bafia (Mbam Division), Monatele (Lekie Division), and Nanga Eboko (Upper Sanaga). The Center Province was established on 23 August 1983. Previously, it was part of the **Center South Province**.

CENTER SOUTH PROVINCE. This was Cameroon's second largest province between May 1972 and August 1983. The province gained added significance as host to the capital city, **Yaoundé**, and a multiplicity of institutions that have been established in and around the city. The province had a sparse population density with a total population of 1,393,608 in 1976. There were 11 administrative divisions headed by various ***préfets*** under the supervision of a **governor**. In August 1983, Pres. **Paul Biya** divided the province into the **Center** and **South Provinces** in the wake of the **destabilization plot**.

CENTRAL AFRICAN CLEARING HOUSE. It was founded in 1979 as an affiliate of the **Bank of Central African States** and the Central Bank of Zaire. It encourages monetary cooperation among the members and assists in financial transactions between them. The headquarters is in **Yaoundé**.

CENTRAL AFRICAN CUSTOMS AND ECONOMIC UNION (CACEU). *See* UNION DOUANIERE ET ECONOMIQUE DE L'AFRIQUE CENTRALE (UDEAC).

CENTRAL AFRICAN MONETARY UNION/UNION MONETAIRE DE L'AFRIQUE CENTRALE/ZONE MONETAIRE CENTRAFRICAINE. It was founded on 22 November 1972 to coordinate and harmonize the monetary policies of the member states—Cameroon, **Central African Republic**, **Chad**, **Congo**, **Equatorial Guinea**, and **Gabon**. **France** is a participant. The headquarters is in **Yaoundé**. The common currency, the **CFA franc**, is issued by the **Bank of Central African States**. *See also* CENTRAL AFRICAN CLEARING HOUSE; CENTRAL AFRICAN CUSTOMS AND ECONOMIC UNION.

CENTRAL AFRICAN REPUBLIC. This country to the east of Cameroon has a population of about 3.4 million people. Cameroon is an important trading partner, facilitated by common membership in **Union Douanière Economique de l'Afrique Centrale (UDEAC)** and the **franc zone**. Civil unrest has prevailed in the country since 1996, causing some disruptions in trade and sending refugees to Cameroon.

CENTRAL BANK OF THE STATES OF EQUATORIAL AFRICA AND CAMEROON. *See* BANK OF CENTRAL AFRICAN STATES.

CENTRE NATIONAL DES ETUDES ET DES RECHERCHES (CENER). *See* FOCHIVE, JEAN.

CERTIFICAT DE FIN D'ETUDES PRIMAIRES ELEMENTAIRES (CEPE). This certificate is awarded at the end of the primary or elementary school **education** in **francophone** Cameroon. Depending on the aptitude of the child, primary education lasts from six to eight years. Success in the CEPE allows for an automatic entry into an institution of general or technical education. It is the equivalent of the **First School Leaving Certificate (FSLC)** in **anglophone** Cameroon.

CFA FRANC. The CFA franc is the currency used in most French-speaking countries of Africa. CFA stands for the *Communauté Financière Africaine*. In 1948, financial arrangements between France and its colonies tied the CFA to the French franc, fixing the parity at one French franc to 50 CFA francs. At independence in 1960, the currency became the official legal tender in the **République du Cameroun**. The currency was introduced in the **anglophone** part of the country on 2 April 1962. Prior to the introduction of the CFA franc, the Nigerian pound was legal tender in the former **British Cameroons**. Consequently, the CFA franc became the first tangible economic reality of Cameroon's **reunification**. Since then, the merits and demerits of the CFA franc in the unstable international monetary system have been vastly discussed. The falling economic fortunes of most Third World countries from the late 1980s, however, put the stability of the CFA franc into question, and on 12 January 1994, the CFA was devalued and fixed at 1 French franc to 100 CFA francs. *See also* ACCORD DE COOPÉRATION ECONOMIQUE, MONETAIRE, ET FINANCIERE; BANK OF CENTRAL AFRICAN STATES.

CHAD, REPUBLIC OF. To the east of Cameroon is the landlocked country of Chad, with a population of 7.2 million. A large proportion of Chad's imports and exports must pass through Cameroon, a source of some income for Cameroon. Petroleum deposits will soon be exploited near Lake Chad. The petroleum will be exported via a **pipeline** to **Kribi** in eastern Cameroon; construction was under way in the late 1990s. Much of Chad's history as an independent country has been plagued with civil war. Refugees have fled to Cameroon, and in recent years a very high instance of banditry in the northern parts of Cameroon has been blamed on Chadians. Chad is a member of **Union Douanière Economique de l'Afrique Centrale (UDEAC)** and the **franc zone**.

CHAD BASIN COMMISSION. *See* LAKE CHAD BASIN COMMISSION.

CHARI RIVER. *See* LOGONE AND CHARI RIVERS.

CHIEF (TRADITIONAL, PARAMOUNT, APPOINTED). This term is used to designate the ultimate source of authority in most ethnic groupings throughout the country. Chiefs exist for both centralized and "stateless" societies; they existed in the precolonial and colonial eras and play a role in independent Cameroon. Colonialism was the intermediary agent that distinguished among the various forms of chieftaincy. Only very few ethnic groupings survived the destruction of precolonial structures. These were essentially centralized societies for which genealogy could be retraced and political systems reinstated. Under these conditions, rulers retained their spiritual and noble attributes to serve as traditional rulers.

In collectively linked societies in which several subunits exist over which a singular source of authority operates, this ruler is designed as "paramount chief." Paramount chiefs could exist among stateless societies (e.g., the **Bakweri** with the Mboko, Isuwu, Wovea subgroupings) as well as in centralized societies (e.g., the **Bafut** with control over the Bafreng, Nkwen, and Bambili subethnicities). While such chiefs are selected on the basis of traditional law and custom, they must receive government approval before taking office.

Appointed chiefs prevail in societies in which traditional political structures were not visible to colonial authorities or were destroyed by colonialism and where European powers or latter-day independence authorities merely selected leaders based on certain preferences. The most remarkable reflection of this amalgam of chieftaincy types was the **West Cameroon House of Chiefs**. In the 1990s, many chiefs faced a serious dilemma. The **Cameroon People's Democratic Movement (CPDM)**–dominated government demanded their allegiance and support, but many of their constituents supported other parties. This was particularly acute in the **North West Province**, where support for the **Social Democratic Front (SDF)** was very strong, and in the northern provinces, where the **Lamido** faced a similar circumstance with respect to the **National Union for Democracy and Progress (UNDP)**. *See also* FON; INDIRECT RULE; NATIVE AUTHORITIES.

CHINA. *See* PEOPLE'S REPUBLIC OF CHINA.

CHRISTALLER, THEODOR (1840–1896). This German administrator came to **Kamerun** in 1887 and is credited with having opened the first German school in **Douala** in 1888. He later managed to spread German institutions in other towns of the **protectorate** and established a school curriculum for Kamerun. Christaller also compiled the first German–Duala dictionary and encouraged learning in the **Duala** and German languages.

CHRISTIANITY. The Christian belief was spread on the Cameroon coasts by missionaries in the early 19th century. In 1844, **Joseph Merrick**, the Jamaican Baptist missionary, laid the groundwork that was later concretized by the English Baptist missionary, **Alfred Saker**.

Various colonial powers later encouraged the establishment of particular missions in the territory. The **Basel Mission** and the Catholic Pallotin Fathers were established in 1886 and 1889, respectively, under the German administration. Under the **mandate** and **trusteeship systems**, the French missionary societies of the Holy Fathers and the Sacred Heart were established in the area. An equally significant development was the operation of the **American Presbyterian Mission** in the **Bassa** country in 1875. Schism in the ranks of the French Protestant missions gave birth to the purely **African Native Baptist Church** led by **Lotin Same** in 1922. The messianic movement of **Thong Likeng** also drew its inspiration from Christian teaching.

A major activity of Christian missions in Cameroon is in the domain of education. Various primary and secondary institutions in the country are owned and supervised by religious missions. There is now a Catholic university in **Yaoundé.** Although these religious institutions levy higher fees, they are reputed to provide quality education to students at all levels. Some missions have also established hospitals and other health care facilities.

Among the various Christian churches and missions in Cameroon are the **Catholic Church**, the Cameroon Baptist Convention, the Presbyterian Church of Cameroon, the Evangelical Church, the Lutheran Evangelical, the Apostolic Church, the True Church of God, the Greek Orthodox, the Seventh Day Adventist, the Coptic Church, and the African Protestant Church. Although these are all Christian institutions, there is no common bond of unity between them.

Christianity became strongly identified with politics between 1970 and 1971 during the arrest and trial of Bishop Albert Ndongmo (see NDONGMO AFFAIR) for complicity to overthrow the government. Since 1990, various church leaders have been active proponents of democracy in Cameroon.

The Baha'i and Islamic faiths are also practiced in Cameroon. *See* ISLAM.

CIMENTERIES DU CAMEROUN (CIMENCAM). CIMENCAM, a cement manufacturer, is one of the few industrial complexes able to show satisfactory economic performances. The company was established in 1970–71 with a 51,211-ton production. In the 1985–86 budget year, production had risen to 807,328 tons, compared to 753,455 tons in 1984–85. The CIMENCAM company plays an important role in the rapid urbanization and the amelioration of housing conditions for a growing number of Cameroonians. The major industrial units of CIMENCAM are found in Figuil (North Cameroon) and in the **Douala**–Bonaberi region. However, the company is unable to fill the demand for its product, so imported cement plays an important role. **Smuggling** cement from **Nigeria** is also a problem.

CIRCONSCRIPTION. *See* DIRECT RULE.

CIRE PERDU CASTING. A method of brass casting widely used in Cameroon, this three-step process involves first making a model in wax of the object to be cast. The wax model is then covered with clay and baked, causing the wax model to melt. This baked clay mold is then filled with molten brass, which after cooling forms the desired object.

COCOA. Cameroon cocoa was regarded of superior quality by the Germans, who previously imported large amounts of the crop from Central and South America. Efforts were intensified in the German era to bring about large-scale production. The French administration took particular interest in cocoa and carried out important measures to ensure its growth.

Today, Cameroon cocoa is widely grown in the moist land around the coast, in the **South**, **Center**, **Littoral**, **North West**, **South West,** and **West** Provinces in essentially family enterprises. Unlike other crops, cocoa is mainly considered an African crop despite the presence of Greek, Lebanese, and Syrian traders in the local market.

Much of Cameroon cocoa is destined for export and prior to petroleum its production represented over 30 percent of Cameroon's export volume. There has been substantial domestic manufacture of chocolate products since independence by the CHOCOCAM company, whose products are widely distributed in the country. According to the Food and Agriculture Organization, Cameroon produced 130,000 tons of cocoa in 1998, 126,000 in 1997, and 125,726 in 1996.

COCOYAM (COLOCASIA OR TARO). This root crop with large green leaves is grown especially in the coastal regions of the country. After harvest, cocoyam is cooked before being used for human consumption or feeding livestock. Otherwise, boiled cocoyam may be pounded and made into ***fufu*** or grated raw and cooked into other edible varieties such as *ekpan* or *kwacoco*. The leaves are used for cooking. Schoolchildren and those in rural areas use cocoyam leaves as shelter from a surprise downpour of rain.

COFFEE. Coffee is grown extensively in Cameroon. The major areas include the **South**, **Center**, **Littoral**, **South West**, **North West,** and **Western** Provinces of the country. The extensive production of this crop for export makes many indigenous families depend on the world market for their livelihood. There are also large expanses of plantations growing coffee in which European settlers played a major development role. In 1957, these settlers produced about 25 percent of Cameroon's coffee.

Two varieties of coffee are grown in the country: Robusta, mostly cultivated in the coastal areas, and Arabica, which is widely grown in the western highlands of Cameroon. Much of Cameroon's production is the Robusta variety. According to the Food and Agriculture Organization, Cameroon coffee production in 1998 was 102,000 tons, up from 52,648 in 1996.

COLLECTIVE RESIGNATION PLOT. This plot was one of the high points of the **Ahidjo–Biya rupture**. Following Pres. **Paul Biya**'s surprise cabinet reshuffle of 18 June 1983, former president **Ahmadou Ahidjo** called a secret conclave of ministers from the **North Province** at his official residence on the same day to request their collective resignation. Ahidjo considered the reshuffle "a declaration of war" against the North because many of his close associates were dropped from government and President Biya did not consult him on his plans. Non-Northern ministers, including the Muslim from Foumban, Mbombo Njoya, and non-Muslims from the North attended the meeting but did not yield to Ahidjo's call for resignation. Prime Minister **Maigari Bello Bouba** signed a separate resignation letter to the head of state during the secret meeting.

The military aspect of the resignation plot was directed by Armed Forces Minister Maikano Abdoulaye later in the night of 18 June 1983. He informed top-level military officials from the North of the impending political situation. Although the former head of state desired to create an explosive situation of ungovernability, various other personalities, including **Sultan Njoya** of **Foumban**, Governor **Usman Mey** of the North Province, and a former cabinet regular, **Sadou Daoudou**, managed to quell the fury and the vengeance of the former head of state and avert a difficult political outcome. The collective resignation plot was an important component of the public trial of February–March 1984.

COMMISSIONERS AND HIGH COMMISSIONERS OF FRANCE IN CAMEROON (1916–1959). Commissioners and high commissioners were the leading political and administrative authorities during the **mandate** and **trusteeship** periods of the French in **Cameroun**. Consequently, they played a prominent role in determining the course of, and the forces that affected, Cameroun's evolution to independence. The following officials served in Cameroun between 1916 and 1959 (the dates indicate the year of their arrival in Cameroun):

Aymerich, Joseph Georges, 1916
Fourneau, Lucien-Louis, 1916
Carde, Jules, 1919
Marchand, Theodore-Paul, 1923
Bonnecarrere, August François, 1932
Repiquet, Jules, 1934
Boissson, Pierre, 1936
Brunot, Richard, 1938
Leclerc, Philippe, 1940
Cournarie, Pierre, 1940

Carras, Hubert, 1943
DeLavignette, Robert, 1946
Hofherr, René, 1947
Soucadaux, André, 1949
Pre, Roland, 1954
Messmer, Pierre, 1956
Ramadier, Jean, 1958
Torre, Xavier, 1958

COMMONWEALTH. This is a loose, rather informal grouping of many of the countries that were once colonies of Great Britain, as well as **Great Britain** itself. The closest thing to a constitution for this organization is the Declaration of Commonwealth Principles adopted in 1971 at a meeting in Singapore. The most important structure is the Commonwealth Heads of Government Meeting (CHOGMs), conducted every two years in a Commonwealth country. Economic questions and the winding down of the British empire are the major topics of these meetings. Thus, the CHOGMs have become a major source of discussion between the nonindustrialized or southern countries and the industrialized or northern countries. In the past, South African apartheid and Commonwealth reactions to it, including sanctions, were a major topic. Rhodesia (Zimbabwe) and its Unilateral Declaration of Independence (UDI), the South West Africa/Namibia problem, and economic relations between the rich and the poor states have been other topics of discussion.

A second significant structure is the Commonwealth Secretariat. In addition to planning and organizing the CHOGMs, the secretariat is responsible for many of the activities of the organization, including the Human Resource Development Group (HRDG), the Commonwealth Fund for Technical Cooperation (CFTC), and the science division. There are also divisions for legal affairs, law, and economic cooperation. The HRDG maintains programs in education, fellowships and training, management development, health, **women** and development, and youth. The CFTC has a Technical Assistance Group, a General Technical Assistance Division, and an Industrial Development Unit.

In addition, there are more than 40 Commonwealth-related organizations dealing with agriculture and forestry, **education**, communications, health, information and the media, law, science and technology, and other subjects. Regular meetings at the ministerial level are also held, annually in some cases (finance ministers), less often in others (education ministers every three years).

In December 1995, Cameroon became the 52d member of the Commonwealth at the Auckland, New Zealand, CHOGM. Prior to this, Cameroon had not joined the Commonwealth or several of the similar French organizations in deference to domestic political considerations. The situation changed in the late 1980s. English-speaking Cameroonians began exerting pressure on the **Biya** government for Cameroon's admission into the Commonwealth, given its British colonial heritage. But Cameroon's membership of the Commonwealth was contingent on its **human rights** record, democratization, and good governance. In principle, Cameroon's membership was tied to its respect for and adherence to the Harare Declaration of 1991, whose fundamental goals are to promote the political values of the Commonwealth, democracy and democratic processes, the rule of law and the independence of the judiciary, just and honest government, fundamental human rights—including equal rights and opportunities for all citizens regardless of race, color, creed, or political belief—and the environment. Admission had been denied for several years on the basis of Cameroon's failure to meet these standards. Some **anglophone** organizations supported this denial as a means of pressuring the government to reform.

COMMONWEALTH OF INDEPENDENT STATES. Although postindependence Cameroon faced problems from radical nationalists of communist inspiration, the Soviet Union granted early recognition to the first Cameroon government of 1960 under **Ahmadou Ahidjo**. Trade was the essential link between the two countries, with the Soviet Union emerging as the fifth largest foreign trading partner of Cameroon in the late 1960s. Cultural exchanges developed through scholarships and sports assistance. While Cameroon used the early support of the Soviet Union to weaken the diplomatic strength of the **Union des Populations du Cameroun (UPC)** and carry out its task of **nation building**, it never used Moscow to juggle between superpowers, as was common with the foreign policies of some other African states. Despite its professed policy of nonalignment, the country remained tied to the West in terms of financial, cultural, and political relationships. Cameroon has continued to maintain cordial relations with the Commonwealth of Independent States.

COMMUNAL LIBERALISM. The political philosophy of Pres. **Paul Biya** is based on the dual dimensions of community and freedom that are rooted in the culture and vision of the country. The society of communal liberalism is based on openness toward a more interdependent humankind, a new political society at the service of people, and a policy of social justice designed to bring about equality and greater humanness. In the process, the Biya vision seeks to lead Cameroonians from their ethnic cultures into a national culture characterized by tolerance, freedom, and sharing. President Biya outlined this vision in his book *Communal-Liberalism* (Editions Faure, ABC and Macmillan, 1987).

COMMUNAUTE/COMMUNITY. The French Community was a short-lived attempt to maintain an integrated structure between **France** and its former colonies. In 1958, the colonies were allowed to vote to decide whether they wished to remain directly linked to France. In Africa, all colonies except Guinea voted to remain with France. They then became part of the Community, as described in the constitution of the Fifth Republic. By 1960, almost all of the territories had decided to leave the Community and become independent states. Indirect means of retaining some of the links were established in the African and Malagasy Union formed in 1961. The Community might be viewed as a federation of France and the former colonies, but in fact control of the most significant aspects of government remained with France. There were Community organs, but these had only a consultative role. *See also* FRANCO-AFRICAN SUMMIT; FRANCOPHONE SUMMIT; LA FRANCOPHONIE.

COMMUNAUTE ECONOMIQUE DES ETATS DE L'AFRIQUE CENTRALE (CEEAC)/ECONOMIC COMMUNITY OF THE CENTRAL AFRICAN STATES (ECCAS). The Economic Commission for Africa and the Lagos Plan called for the construction of regional organizations to include all of the states of Africa. CEEAC is a result of this call. CEEAC's goals are to establish a customs union leading to eventual economic integration. Yet while CEEAC was founded in 1983, it has failed to accomplish much.

The CEEAC possesses economic potential, for it has a large population, contains several petroleum producing countries, and has other resources. However, it also includes several countries with critical political problems and several very poor countries. Members are Cameroon, **Central African Republic (CAR)**, **Chad**, **Congo**, Democratic Republic of the Congo, **Equatorial Guinea**, Rwanda, and Sao Tomé and Principe. Its membership thus includes states that are also members of other, smaller regional groupings. CEEAC structures include a Conference of Heads of State and Government, a Council of Ministers, a general secretariat, technical committees, and a consultative commission. There is also a Court of Justice. The headquarters is in Bangui, CAR. *See also* UNION DOUANIERE ECONOMIQUE DE L'AFRIQUE CENTRALE (UDEAC).

COMMUNAUTE FINANCIERE AFRICAINE. *See* CFA FRANC.

COMPTE HORS BUDGET. This term (meaning "account outside of the budget") refers to the practice initiated by Pres. **Ahmadou Ahidjo** and continued by Pres. **Paul Biya** of not including the revenues received from Cameroon's **petroleum** production in the national accounts. Petroleum revenue was then spent at the discretion of the president in addition to funds spent within the announced budget. In 1995, petroleum revenue was included for the first time in the national budget.

CONCOURS (COMPETITIVE ENTRANCE EXAMINATION). This French term is used widely in Cameroon to designate special competitive entrance examinations for recruitment into particular positions in the public service or admission into various professional institutions of higher learning. Usually, the number of candidates required is set before the exam is taken, independent of the number of applicants. This makes the performance level highly competitive. Announcements for the *concours* are made publicly in the national media and results are announced in the same fashion. Supervision of public service *concours* are organized by the Ministry of Public Service, while academic *concours* are set by the various institutions. Despite the high level of competitiveness required, the public has expressed doubts about the level of fairness involved in the final selections in various *concours*. *See also* BACCALAREAT.

CONDOMINIUM, THE (1914–1916). This was the period of joint Franco–British administration of the **Kamerun** territory following the capture of **Douala** from the Germans by the West African Expeditionary force during **World War I**. In reality, the Franco–British device was never a joint administrative arrangement in the true sense of the term. For several reasons, the British carried the burden of the administration. In terms of personnel and resources, the British were better endowed in the development of major services. In terms of proximity and knowledge, the British had a better knowledge of the area, given their closer contact to the local population in the preannexation era and their more powerful presence in neighboring **Nigeria**. In addition, the British had in Gen. **Charles Dobell** a military strategist and administrator of the first order. Consequently, the proposed Condominium was only short-lived, and it was followed by the partition of the territory. The irony of the partition exercise was that the British, who prevailed during the Condominium, ended up with a tiny portion of the Kamerun territory as compared to the French.

CONFEDERATION OF ANGLOPHONE PARENTS-TEACHERS ASSOCIATIONS OF CAMEROON (CAPTAC). *See* CAMEROON ANGLOPHONE MOVEMENT.

CONFEDERATION OF CAMEROON TRADE UNIONS (CCTU). The CCTU replaced the **Cameroon Trade Union Congress** (CTUC) in June 1992. The CCTU, which is the umbrella for different trade unions, is not much different from the defunct CTUC. Its president, Etame Ndedi Samuel, is a member of the Central Committee of the **Cameroon People's Democratic Movement (CPDM)**.

CONFERENCE OF HEADS OF STATE OF EQUATORIAL AFRICA/ CONFERENCE DES CHEFS D'ETAT DE L'AFRIQUE EQUATORIALE (CCAE). The title occasionally appears as the Conference of Equatorial Africa and Cameroon Heads of State. The conference brought together the heads of state of the independent countries that emerged from the colonial **French Equatorial Africa** and the **trust territory** of Cameroon. From this conference arose the Union Douanière Equatoriale (UDE) and several related organizations. Cameroon membership in the conference may have been temporary, as later reports (1969) do not include this country. *See also* UNION DOUANIERE ECONOMIQUE DE L'AFRIQUE CENTRALE (UDEAC).

CONGO, REPUBLIC OF. Cameroon's southern neighbor has a population of two million. The country is a member of the **franc zone,** and in the late 1990s internal conflict has destabilized the country and caused serious economic decline. The railroad was rendered inoperable for some time; the landlocked countries of **Chad** and **Central African Republic** have been forced to conduct more of their trade through Cameroon as a result. Cameroon is a major trading partner of Congo.

CONGRESS OF BERLIN (1884–1885). This infamous international conference was held in Berlin between 15 November 1884, and 26 February 1885 to establish a process to parcel out the territories in Africa for various European powers. The process, generally regarded as the "Partition of Africa," led to the creation of small territorial entities for European colonial designs on the African continent.

Fourteen countries attended the conference, including **France**, **Great Britain**, the **United States**, **Germany**, Belgium, and Spain; observers from Russia also participated. They were summoned to this gathering by the German empire under Bismarck to settle accounts and reach common agreement to prevent further colonial rivalry among them. The colossal injustice of the Congress of Berlin was the absence of any representatives from the African continent. Of relevance to Cameroon history, the congress not only regulated navigation on the Congo and Niger Rivers but also solidified German annexation of **Kamerun**, which had been the subject of controversy, especially from the French and British, since 12 July 1884.

CONSTITUTION OF THE FEDERAL REPUBLIC OF CAMEROON (1961). This constitution was the result of the **Foumban Conference** between **Southern Cameroons** representatives and the government of the **République du Cameroun**. The constitution came into effect on 1 October 1961, with the birth of the **Federal Republic of Cameroon**. The federal system consisted of two states, **East** and **West Cameroon**, each with its own government headed by a prime minister and a legislature. In addition, the West Cameroon system retained the institution of a **West Cameroon House of Chiefs** in a quasi-bicameral legislature.

The federal structure consisted of a government headed by the president and assisted by the vice president as well as a cabinet and federal legislature of 50 seats. The **francophone** president had an **anglophone** vice president, while the seats at the federal assembly were distributed on a 4:1 ratio between East Cameroon and West Cameroon. The federal government had broad-ranging powers and could intervene in the domains of each federated state.

There were two amendments to the federal constitution. The 1969 amendment prolonged the life of the federal assembly and changed procedures for selecting the prime ministers of the federated states; the 1970 amendment made the position of vice president of the Republic incompatible with any other governmental office. Previously, the vice president of the Federal Republic was concurrently the prime minister of West Cameroon. This constitution ceased to exist in 1972, with the inauguration of a unitary system of government. *See also* CONSTITUTION OF THE UNITED REPUBLIC OF CAMEROON (1972); CONSTITUTION OF

THE REPUBLIC OF CAMEROON (1984); CONSTITUTION OF THE REPUBLIQUE DU CAMEROUN (1960); CONSTITUTION OF THE REPUBLIC OF CAMEROON (1996); CONSTITUTIONS.

CONSTITUTION OF THE REPUBLIC OF CAMEROON (1984). The issue underlying the constitution of 1984 was the quest for popular legitimacy by Pres. **Paul Biya**. In addition to his constitutional mandate, Biya gained an electoral mandate in early presidential elections of 14 January 1984, with 99 percent of the electorate. He used this opportunity to revise the constitution.

The new constitution varied in several ways from the 1972 constitution. The major changes were Articles 1, 5, and 7. In Article 1, the new official name of the republic was simply reduced to the Republic of Cameroon. It continued to retain its unitary structure. In Article 5, the post of prime minister was abolished. Article 7 stipulated that any member of government could be granted expressed delegation of powers in the case of the temporary absence of the head of state. The speaker of the National Assembly would exercise presidential powers until a new president was duly elected. The interim president could not modify the constitution, change the composition of government, or call for a referendum. In addition, he could not become a candidate for the office of the president of the Republic. *See also* CONSTITUTION OF THE FEDERAL REPUBLIC OF CAMEROON (1961); CONSTITUTION OF THE UNITED REPUBLIC OF CAMEROON (1972); CONSTITUTION OF THE REPUBLIQUE DU CAMEROUN (1960); CONSTITUTION OF THE REPUBLIC OF CAMEROON (1996); CONSTITUTIONS.

CONSTITUTION OF THE REPUBLIC OF CAMEROON (1996). According to law Number 96/06 of 18 January 1996, a new constitution was adopted for Cameroon. The issue underlying the constitution of January 1996 was the need for a constitution that reflected the attempts at democratization and decentralization in Cameroon since 1990. Thus, the 1996 constitution could be linked to Pres. **Paul Biya**'s quest for popular legitimacy. The new constitution differs in several aspects from the 1984 constitution. Article 6 puts the term of office for the president at seven years, with the right to be reelected once. Article 6 also stipulates that the president of the Senate or his vice president would exercise presidential power until a new president was duly elected, after the expiration of the term of office of the previous president. Article 14 creates a two-chamber legislature for Cameroon comprising a National Assembly and a Senate.

A further innovation in the new constitution is the replacement of provinces by **regions** (Article 61). *See also* CONSTITUTION OF THE REPUBLIQUE DU CAMEROUN (1960); CONSTITUTION OF THE FEDERAL REPUBLIC OF CAMEROON (1961); CONSTITUTION OF THE UNITED REPUBLIC OF CAMEROON (1972); CONSTITUTION OF THE REPUBLIC OF CAMEROON (1984); CONSTITUTIONAL COUNCIL; CONSTITUTIONS.

CONSTITUTION OF THE REPUBLIQUE DU CAMEROUN (1960). This was a hurried draft written by a 1959 consultative committee to meet the 1 January 1960 independence deadline for **French Cameroun**. The constitution created a unitary structure with a unicameral parliament elected by direct universal suffrage. The president of the Republic had identical powers to those of the president of the Fifth Republic in France, who served as a model for newly independent francophone countries in Africa. The constitution was in effect for only 21 months. *See also* CONSTITUTION OF THE FEDERAL REPUBLIC OF CAMEROON (1961); CONSTITUTION OF THE UNITED REPUBLIC OF CAMEROON (1972); CONSTITUTION OF THE REPUBLIC OF CAMEROON (1984); CONSTITUTION OF THE REPUBLIC OF CAMEROON (1996); CONSTITUTIONS.

CONSTITUTION OF THE UNITED REPUBLIC OF CAMEROON (1972). The 1972 constitution was promulgated by decree 72–270 of 2 June 1972. This followed a massive approval by the Cameroonian electorate on 20 May 1972 to a presidential intention to dismantle the federal structure. The federalism of 1961 was now replaced by the unitarism of 1972. The new **United Republic of Cameroon** prescribed a monolithic political structure headed by the president of the Republic, who was head of state and head of government. He could prevail over a monocameral **National Assembly** of 120 members, an integrated judiciary, and the centralized governmental institutions. The 1972 constitution was illustrative of presidential power at its superlative. In this tight political setup, the speaker of the National Assembly was the constitutional successor to the head of state.

Two major amendments were introduced to the constitution of the United Republic. On 9 May 1975 the post of **prime minister** was created and on 29 June 1979 the prime minister was declared constitutional successor to the head of state in case of death, resignation, or permanent impairment from attending to his duties.

The 1972 constitution was Cameroon's most enduring constitutional arrangement since independence. It experienced its decisive moment with the orderly and constitutional transfer of power between former president **Ahmadou Ahidjo** and former prime minister **Paul Biya** in November 1982. Thereafter, contradictory interpretation of party versus executive function characterized relations between the two leaders. This led to a lasting rupture and feud that paved the way for a new constitution in 1984. *See also* CONSTITUTION OF THE FEDERAL REPUBLIC OF CAMEROON (1961); CONSTITUTION OF THE REPUBLIC OF CAMEROON (1984); CONSTITUTION OF THE REPUBLIQUE DU CAMEROUN (1960); CONSTITUTION OF THE REPUBLIC OF CAMEROON (1996); CONSTITUTIONS.

CONSTITUTIONAL COUNCIL. Part VII of the **constitution of 1996** establishes the Constitutional Council, which has jurisdiction in matters pertaining to the constitution. It rules on the constitutionality of laws, treaties, and international agreements. The council "ensures the regularity of presidential elections, parliamentary elections and referendum operations." It announces the results of such elections. It has 11 members appointed by the president for nine-year terms.

CONSTITUTIONS. Cameroon has had five constitutions since independence in 1960. The constitutions define existential and operational aspects of the Cameroon political system. The Cameroon constitution consists of a preamble outlining the guiding national, external, and developmental beliefs of the state, as well as a set of proclamations reiterating principles of religious, social, and political significance. The preamble has remained intact since 1960, while various other articles of the constitutions have changed over time. *See also* CONSTITUTION OF THE REPUBLIQUE DU CAMEROUN (1960); CONSTITUTION OF THE FEDERAL REPUBLIC OF CAMEROON (1961); CONSTITUTION OF THE UNITED REPUBLIC OF CAMEROON (1972); CONSTITUTION OF THE REPUBLIC OF CAMEROON (1984); CONSTITUTION OF THE REPUBLIC OF CAMEROON (1996).

COOPERATIVES. Cooperatives have been important institutions for agricultural development. They are found across the country as small- and large-scale organizations for farmers, planters, and agricultural brokers designed to increase their strength and solidarity vis-à-vis the general public. The major cooperatives in Cameroon concentrate on export crops such as **cocoa**, **coffee**, or **bananas**. One important cooperative, the Union

Centrale des Coopératives Agricoles de l'Ouest (UCCAO), was established in 1958 by the **Bamiléké** and developed into a federation. Its membership has increased to over 100,000 farmers. The service of Cooperatives and Mutualities in the Ministry of Agriculture handles cooperative activities in the country, while various foreign agencies and international institutions provide education and training of cooperative cadres. In 1969, the Centre National de Développement des Enterprises Coopératives (CENADEC) was created to increase the range of activities undertaken by cooperatives, including the commercialization of their products. Given the importance of the rural population, the government set up the Sociétés Coopératives de Développement Rural (SOCOODER) to improve on rural cooperative activities.

Cameroon counts on the cooperative movement for the full realization of its agricultural potential and policy. However, despite the widespread influence of the cooperative movement, they are more developed in the **West** and **North West Provinces** than in other parts of the country. Cooperatives suffer from government interference, operating more as tools of the government than as independent, member-run institutions.

CORN. *See* MAIZE.

CORRUPTION. Corruption is a major problem in Cameroon, affecting people in all walks of life. Police and **gendarmes** constantly harass people for small bribes. One scholar estimates that some 2.5 billion CFA francs was removed from motorists in this manner in 1994. Corruption reaches to the highest levels, in the granting of government contracts, in the affairs of government-owned banks, and in the very significant **smuggling** operations in which government officials are thought to play a major role. In surveys of international business persons, Cameroon often ranks as one of the most corrupt countries in which to do business. Government attempts to overcome this problem have met with little success.

CORVEE. *See* FORCED LABOR.

COTONNIERE INDUSTRIELLE DU CAMEROUN (CICAM). The Cameroon Textile Industry was founded in 1964 by the government and operated through international cooperation. **Germany**'s Deutsche-Entwicklungs-Gesellschaft and French private groupings represented by Copartex own 35 percent of the shares each; the Cameroon government represented by **Société Nationale d'Investissement (SNI)** owns

26.15 percent of shares; while **Chad** owns 3.85 percent. There are two production units of the **cotton** industry in **Douala** and **Garoua** producing colorful prints. The industry consumes cotton fiber produced by the SODECOTON company. CICAM employs about 1,800 people, with the majority in the Garoua unit, the biggest textile unit of French-speaking black Africa. Over 85 percent of CICAM's production is absorbed by the **Union Douanière Economique de l'Afrique Centrale (UDEAC)** market and the rest is exported to Europe. Two subsidiary units have been created to cater to growing demands. These include the SYNTECAM (1972) and the SOLICAM (1979). CICAM faces increased challenges from a Lebanese commercial firm CONFITEX, which was established in Cameroon in 1985, and from cheaper Nigerian goods, often **smuggled** into Cameroon.

COTTON. Production of this crop is concentrated in the less humid northern regions of the country. Like other export crops, the cultivation of cotton was the result of colonial interest. Actual production was delayed because of the difficulty of the colonial powers to penetrate the interior. When this was done, **Garoua** in northern Cameroon became the center of cotton production. Under the French administration, cotton was only marginally encouraged in Cameroon. **Chad** was charged with cotton production for much of Equatorial Africa. Cotton production improved since 1950 with the direct participation of the Compagnie Française pour le Développement des Fibres Textiles (CFDT) and the postindependence parapublic, the Cotton Development Company, SODECOTON, set up with headquarters in Garoua. Most production is now used by Cameroon textile companies, such as **Cotonnière Industrielle du Cameroun (CICAM)**. Production varies greatly from year to year due to climate and other factors. Cameroon produced 192,000 tons in 1998, 140,000 in 1997, and 218,336 tons in 1996.

COUNCILS OF NOTABLES. Between the two world wars, the French attempted to establish structures of local government based on what they considered to be local elites. Councils of Notables were established as part of this effort and as part of an attempt to divert nationalist and independence aspirations.

COUP ATTEMPT OF 6 APRIL 1984. Rebel Republican Guards attempted a takeover of the government on this day. For once, since the difficult early years of independence, uncertainty reigned over the political stability and future of Cameroon. This development did not occur in a single day; it was the accumulation of months of suspicion and animosity that had characterized Cameroon politics since the constitutional change of 5 November 1982. Underlying this climate of tension was the personality conflict between **Ahmadou Ahidjo** and **Paul Biya**. It was settled by gunfire. Republican guards who were more loyal to former president Ahidjo rebelled against President Biya, who had the full support of the army. Although able to seize control of strategic locations in the capital, the rebellious Republican Guards and units of the gendarmerie were overcome by the numerically superior and better-coordinated armed forces in a battle that ensued late into Saturday, 7 April. Government estimates of 70 dead in the skirmishes have been contradicted by accounts that rank this coup attempt as one of the bloodiest foiled coup d'états in Africa. *See also* AHIDJO–BIYA RUPTURE.

COUPEURS DE ROUTE. In the late 1980s and into the 1990s, bandits frequently attacked vehicles on the roads of the **Extreme North**, **North,** and **Adamawa Provinces**. Referred to as *coupeurs de route* (highway robbers), they were thought to be from **Chad** and **Nigeria** as well as Cameroon. Their actions were highly disruptive of transport, tourism, and commerce and caused the government to organize convoys with armed guards in the region.

COURANT D'UNION NATIONALE (CUN). This political movement was formed on 6 June 1956 to unite all political parties in **French Cameroun** toward a common "minimum program." Led by **Paul Soppo Priso,** the movement was opposed to the **Loi Cadre**, advocated the **reunification** of the Cameroons, and favored a general amnesty for the banned **Union des Populations du Cameroun (UPC)** movement. The CUN attracted a wide membership but quickly disappeared in November 1956. Despite its short existence, the party was instrumental in bringing diverse national groupings together in the quest for common objectives.

COURT OF EQUITY. This mechanism was devised to settle disputes between white traders and **Duala** chiefs in the mid-1800s on the Cameroon coast. The court had the power to levy taxes or penalties on guilty partners and maintain the steady exchange of goods between Europeans and Africans. British leadership in the Court of Equity initially survived the German **protectorate** treaty of 1884 until it was forcibly abolished in December 1884. The Court of Equity was another proof of English hegemony on the Cameroon coast prior to German annexation. The German administration replaced the Court of Equity with a dual court system for different races to handle trade disputes.

COURT OF IMPEACHMENT. According to the **constitution of 1996**, this body has jurisdiction to try the president for high treason and the **prime minister** and other senior officials for conspiracy against the security of the state.

COURTS. *See* JUDICIARY.

COUSCOUS. *See* FUFU.

CREDIT FONCIER. This specialized institution is designed to facilitate the financing of housing projects in the country. Created by the Cameroon government in 1977, the Crédit Foncier aims at providing Cameroonians with decent housing through repairs, construction, or acquisition of buildings from private citizens by housing corporations. Crédit Foncier also helps to finance the purchase of land necessary for housing development. *See also* NATIONAL FUND FOR RURAL DEVELOPMENT.

CREDIT UNIONS. These primary institutions developed especially among farmers, peasants, and professional groups such as police and teachers for the generation of savings and surplus funds. The first credit unions in Cameroon were established in 1963 in the Bamenda area of the **North West Province** by Roman Catholic clergymen from Canada and the United States. In 1968, the West Cameroon Credit Union League was formed and received assistance from national and foreign associations. Initially, these credit unions thrived on the already existing traditional saving institutions known varyingly as the *njangi, esusu,* or ***tontine*** across the country. Such increased funds allow ordinary farmers to gain access to important material needs and property and foster social projects, including education of children. The success of local *njangis, tontine,* and credit union activity has improved the fortunes of the **cooperative** movement and Cameroon's rural development. For many years, American **Peace Corps** volunteers played a significant role in credit union growth and development.

CROSS RIVER REGION. This region of southeastern Nigeria and southwestern Cameroon has closely related cultures. These cultures are located in the basin of the Cross River in eastern Nigeria. The Cameroonian area includes such cultures as the Ejagham, Bangwa, **Bayang**, Ekwe, Keaka, Anyang, and Widekum. Perhaps the most obvious cultural tie is provided by the "Leopard cult" known as **Ngbe** among the Ejagham. It is also known as "Ekpe" and by various permutations of these two terms in other localities. Also common to, and peculiar to, many cultures in the Cross River region is the use of skin-covered masks.

CULTURAL RENEWAL. This represents part of the triple revolution embarked on by Cameroon in 1972, alongside political and economic revolutions. The aim is to make Cameroon's culture its symbolic identity as an aspect of life capable of differentiating between human beings from elsewhere. The cultural variety of the country led to the delay of endeavors toward a national cultural renewal. Culture was conceived not only as the legacies of the traditional thought but also as all external givens of Cameroon's historical experience. In 1976, as the first step toward this cultural renewal, a prestigious artistic prize christened after the head of state was awarded to a sculptural piece by Gideon Mpando. The **University of Yaoundé** was awarded a prize for scientific discovery in 1979.

A major step toward cultural renewal was the establishment of a National Ensemble consisting of a national orchestra, a ballet school, and a dance group. Begun in 1978, the National Ensemble is a creation of the Council of Cultural Affairs, presided over by the head of state, which seeks to enhance the cultural identity of Cameroon by a melange of the various dance, music, and choreographic patterns for public pride, delight, and appreciation. In 1982, the week preceding 20 May was instituted as the National Cultural Week of Cameroon. *See also* CULTURE.

CULTURE. Cameroon considers the culture of a people as its identity card in the forum of nations. Over 200 distinct ethnic groups with their particular cultural patterns exist in the country. Despite this diversity, the government continues to emphasize culture as anything rooted in life and values of the people that gives meaning to their existence. Consequently, the government considers every ethnic culture indispensable in the understanding and appreciation of the country's cultural heritage. It utilizes other cultural universals, such as **music** and **sports**, to fight parochial tendencies and tribalism.

The government proclaimed a cultural renovation era in 1974 and a National Council of Cultural Affairs presided over by the head of state. By 1979, the Ministry of Information and Culture had created a National

Ensemble consisting of a national orchestra, a national ballet, and a theater group. Since 1982, the week preceding the national day, 20 May, is observed as National Culture Week. Many intellectuals and artists within and outside the country are encouraged to become part of this process of cultural renewal to create a common set of social values, norms, and customs from a diverse cultural background. Pres. **Paul Biya** defined the country's cultural policy in terms of an "ideology of cultural spiritualism" whereby the moral, academic, civic, political, and aesthetic aspects of culture are emphasized. *See also* CULTURAL RENEWAL; FILM INDUSTRY; THEATER.

– D –

DAN FODIO, UTHMAN. *See* UTHMAN DAN FODIO.

DAOUDA, YOUSSOUFA (1942–). A former minister and director-general of Cameroon Airlines, Daouda was born on 29 September 1942, in **Garoua**, capital of the **North Province**. From 1972 he served successively as minister of husbandry, fisheries, and animal industries; minister of industrial and commercial development (1973); minister of the economy and planning (1975–82); minister of public service (1982); and minister of state planning and territorial development (1983).

Youssoufa Daouda was the only Northern minister to have survived the **Ahidjo–Biya rupture** of 1983 and the **coup attempt of 6 April 1984**. He was finally dropped from government in 1985. In 1986, he was appointed managing director of the National Railway Corporation and in 1987 to his post at Cameroon Airlines.

DAOUDOU, SADOU (1926–). Daoudou was Cameroon's minister of the armed forces from 1961 until July 1980. He was born in 1926 in **Ngaoundéré** and studied at local schools in **Garoua** before proceeding to the Collège de Bongo in neighboring **Chad**. He later served in administrative positions as an administrative assistant in **Maroua** and as deputy subdivisional chief of Kaele from 1948 to May 1957.

He moved to **Yaoundé** in 1958, where he served as chef du cabinet to the prime minister and won a seat to the **National Assembly** as a representative of the **Adamawa** Division in 1960. In May 1960, Daoudou earned his first cabinet rank appointment as secretary of state for information, but it was in his capacity as minister of the armed forces from June 1961 that he made his mark in Cameroon politics.

His major significance lies in his political longevity in a most sensitive office for 19 years, an exceptional feat. Thereafter, Daoudou did not disappear from the political scene. He was named civil service minister from 1980 until January 1982 and later moved to the Presidency of the Republic as assistant secretary-general. In the November 1982 government—formed after the resignation of Pres. **Ahmadou Ahidjo**—Daoudou climbed to the powerful post of secretary-general at the Presidency under Pres. **Paul Biya**. He stayed in this office until he was dropped from government on 18 June 1983, at the onset of the **Ahidjo–Biya rupture**. During his political career, Daoudou received the title of minister of state and was generally ranked at the top of official protocol listings of cabinet ministers. In addition to his ministerial duties, he also served in the executive committee and political bureaus of the **Cameroon National Union (CNU).**

DEBT. For most of its history as an independent country, Cameroon had no national problem with debt. However, with the advent of the economic crisis in the mid-1980s, Cameroon rapidly became a major debtor country—on a per capita basis one of the world's worst. In 1996, the official national debt was estimated at $10 billion. **World Bank**, Paris Club, and various countries have reduced and rescheduled that debt, but repayment remains a major problem.

DeLAVIGNETTE, ROBERT (1897–1976). A French colonial administrator and publicist, DeLavignette served as high **commissioner** in Cameroun between 1945 and 1947 after successful service in Niger and Upper Volta. During his rule in **Cameroun,** he played a significant role in warding off attempts by French *colons* (settlers) to institutionalize a system similar to apartheid in the territory and opposed the initial formation of **Rassemblement Camerounais (RACAM)** as too ambitious. Unlike other colonial administrators, DeLavignette argued that colonies were not arenas for exploitation but regions to which the French were to be called upon to fulfill long-term obligations. He was appointed director of the Colonial School in Paris and was instrumental in making the curriculum of the institution more relevant to practical realities of the colonial world. DeLavignette also made a name as a significant author and publisher. His work *Paysans Noirs* (1931) won the award for the best novel with a colonial theme, while his *Service Africain* (1946) was translated into *Freedom and Authority in West Africa* (1968) and serves as the only French classic on colonial administration, comparable to Lord Lugard's *Dual Mandate in Tropical Africa*.

DEMOCRACY. Cameroon considers itself a democracy, one that is truly adapted to the needs of the country and is inspired by the will of the people. For the Cameroonian leadership, there is no universal standard of democracy. Under Pres. **Ahmadou Ahidjo**, the political system was commonly defined as a "ruling democracy" void of paralyzing rifts of popular opinion and conflicts of interest. Pres. **Paul Biya** initially conceived of a strong democracy based on a national charter of freedom and operating on a temporary platform of a one-party system. Such a truly democratized party structure could allow for free and competitive election of officials and serve as a prelude to multipartyism. As a follow-up to this idea and with pressure from forces within Cameroon, President Biya reinstituted multiparty politics in Cameroon in December 1990. In March 1992, the first legislative elections were held to elect a multiparty parliament. The result was that for the first time since the collapse of multiparty democracy in Cameroon in 1966, Cameroon's **National Assembly** became a multiparty assembly with four parties; the **Cameroon People's Democratic Movement (CPDM)**, the **Union Nationale pour la Démocratie et le Progrès (UNDP)**, the **Union des Populations du Cameroun (UPC),** and the **Mouvement pour la Défence de la République (MDR)**.

DESTABILIZATION PLOT OF 22 AUGUST 1983. In a nationwide broadcast, Pres. **Paul Biya** revealed that the security police had arrested several persons plotting to "attack the security of the Republic." Although the people were unidentified, it was generally known that the plotters, Ibrahim Oumharou and Ahmadou Salatou, were key aides of former president **Ahmadou Ahidjo**. It was alleged that President Biya would have been assassinated in the course of his official outing to preside over a sports festival. The head of state revealed that the persons had "confessed completely" to the plot and would receive "appropriate sanctions for their criminal activities."

The destabilization plot came at the height of the rupture between President Biya and his predecessor, less than a year after the transition of power. Consequently, President Biya used this opportunity to take important steps to preserve the peace and integrity of the Republic. He reshuffled the cabinet, creating a more united government team geared toward the objectives defined by the head of state. He split the **Center South** and **North Provinces** into two and three new provinces, respectively. An **armed forces** General Staff was set up to carry out the task of national defense and the protection of the legality of the Republic in a more coherent and efficient manner. Personalities implicated in the destabilization plot (including the former head of state in absentia) faced a public trial in **Yaoundé** in February 1984. *See also* AHIDJO–BIYA RUPTURE.

DEVELOPMENT BANK OF CENTRAL AFRICAN STATES/ BANQUE DE DEVELOPPEMENT DES ETATS DE L'AFRIQUE CENTRALE (BDEAC). The BDEAC was founded on 3 December 1975, with the same membership as the affiliated **Bank of Central African States.** The BDEAC's purpose is to promote cooperation between member states, to conduct research, and to mobilize the funds necessary for development projects in and among the member states. The ultimate goal is the integration of the member states. The headquarters is in Brazzaville, **Congo.** The bank is associated with the **Union Douanière Economique de l'Afrique Centrale.**

DEVELOPPEMENT AUTOCENTRE. *See* SELF-RELIANT DEVELOPMENT.

DIBANGO, MANU (1933–). Cameroon's most renowned musician was born 12 December 1933 in **Douala**. After early education, Emmanuel Dibango N'Djoké, or Manu Dibango, gradually took up music, an outgrowth of his choral experience as a youth. He left for France to begin a musical career but returned to Africa, where he spent time in Kinshasa to relate to the popular sounds of the then Congolese rhythms. He played his first songs in the company of leading Zairean artists.

Dibango returned to France and began an ambitious project at assimilating African rhythm to the popular beat in the West. He called this musical sophistication "soul **makossa**." The song earned Dibango a gold record because it sold more than one million copies in 1972. However, Dibango's greatest popularity was felt abroad more than at home. Inspired by the success of the *Soul Makossa* album, Dibango moved to the United States and began to work with leading jazz musicians as well as continuing his experiments with makossa. He became known as the "Makossa Man."

He has traveled to the Caribbean and fused makossa with reggae, as well as to Japan and Asia for greater exposure and exchange. He has won multiple international awards and was the first African to play in the famous French music hall, the Olympia. In the mid-1970s, he was employed by the Ivory Coast government to set up and train a national orchestra. Over the years, his songs have become popular in Cameroon, and he returned home in 1979 to establish his "Club Manu" but later returned to France, where he lives permanently. His favorite musical instrument is the saxophone, his hair is nearly always shaved to the skin, and his unmistakable concert attire is the grandiose embroidered West African gown.

DIBONGUE, R. JABEA K. (1896–1963). Robert Jabea Kum Dibongue was an active nationalist politician in **British Cameroons**. Born to the historically prestigious **Akwa** clan in **Douala**, **French Cameroun**, in October 1896, Dibongue received a classic German education in the country and rose to a high level in the German administrative hierarchy. As one of the most enlightened young elites during the period of German administration in Cameroon, he won the coveted Governor Puttkamer Prize in 1911. After his education, Dibongue entered the German administration, where he served as clerk to the Douala district **commissioner** until 1916. Before the ouster of the Germans from Cameroon in 1916, Dibongue had become one of the highest-ranking Africans in the German colonial government. In 1918, he migrated to the British Cameroons and served in the Nigerian Civil Service, rising to the rank of chief clerk in Enugu, Eastern Nigeria, by 1946. In 1947, he returned to Douala but later moved to **Buea** to join the **Cameroons National Federation**.

As a French Camerounian, he took a lead in advocating **reunification** between the two **trust territories**. He formed the French Cameroon Welfare Union to advance the interests of the **Duala**, **Bassa**, and **Bamiléké** living in the British Cameroons. Dibongue became the link to the exile **Union des Populations du Cameroun (UPC)** movement, which settled in **Kumba** for a short period after 1955, but he later fell out of favor with the UPC. By 1960, he was an advocate of British Cameroon's integration with the Nigerian Federation. He was at one time member of the Southern Cameroons Marketing Board and the Southern Cameroons Development Agency. When British Southern Cameroons voted to reunify with the Republic of Cameroon in 1961, Dibongue lost political clout in the new political setup of the country.

DIRECT RULE. In this system of colonial organization administrative units generally cut across traditional political or ethnic boundaries. The policy is generally ascribed to French colonial rule in Africa. In **French Cameroun**, the basic unit of administration was the *circonscription*. A *chef de région* commanded a particular *circonscription*.

The *circonscription* was further divided into cantons, which included traditional chiefdoms. Under the system of direct rule, the French colonial officials were in charge of order and security, the economy, social development, and the coordination of European activities in the field of health, education, and agriculture. Traditional leaders performed only ceremonial tasks and were often retained on stipends by the French. In 1931, **Sultan Njoya** of **Bamoum** was deposed and exiled to **Yaoundé**. In Northern Cameroon, the French allowed **indirect rule** to prevail as traditional rulers retained much power. The policy of direct rule recognized and absorbed trained African personnel, the *citoyens* or *évolués,* to serve in administrative positions over the *sujets*. Such a system of administrative control created a gulf between the educated, French-assimilated elite, and the common man.

DIRECTION GENERALE D'ETUDES ET DE LA DOCUMENTATION (DIRDOC). *See* FOCHIVE, JEAN.

DOBELL, CHARLES M. (1869–1954). Dobell was a British military strategist and administrator who launched the **World War I** seaborne expedition against the German **protectorate** in **Kamerun**. Through his commanding skills, the strategically important city of **Douala** fell to his troops on 26 September 1914. The capture of this port town was considered important given its powerful radio facilities, which the Germans used to monitor Allied shipping in the south Atlantic. Following the collapse of German resistance in 1916, a period of supposed joint administration between French and British officials took place. It was during this period that General Dobell displayed his administrative qualities by outmaneuvering the French in organizational tactics and initiatives. *See also* CONDOMINIUM.

DOO KINGUE, MICHEL (1934–). Doo Kingue has served as United Nations undersecretary-general and executive director of the United Nations Institute for Training and Research (UNITAR) since 1983. Born in **Douala** on 10 January 1934, he was one of the first Cameroonians sent to study in France after World War II. From 1947, he attended secondary school and the University of Paris, graduating as a chemical engineer in 1958. He later obtained a doctorate in physical chemistry in 1961. Thereafter, Doo Kingue taught in Paris and also gained recognition for his musical prowess. He was one of the early Cameroon musicians to blend the local **makossa** with traits of jazz music.

On his return to Cameroun in August 1961, he served as permanent secretary in the Ministry of Education under **William-Aurelian Eteky Mboumoua**. In November 1963, he returned to Paris to become special adviser on African affairs to the director-general of UNESCO and later served as director of relations with International Organizations and Programs. From May 1971, he headed the newly created Bureau for Africa at the Directorate of the United Nations Development Program (UNDP). He later became the first UNDP regional director for Africa with the rank of UN assistant secretary-general. In this capacity, he played a crucial role in setting development objectives of the continent and in seeking funds to implement various programs. He was appointed United Nations undersecretary-general and executive director of UNITAR on 4 December 1982. UNITAR is a world training center for diplomats and other specialists in international cooperation. In the execution of his duties, Doo Kingue has traveled widely, published extensively, and contributed to a clearer perception of issues relating to international development, social peace, and economic security.

DOUALA. This is the economic capital of Cameroon and headquarters of the **Littoral Province**. The history of this city dates back to the 18th century and coincides with the **Bantu** presence. It was a significant station for the **slave trade** across the Atlantic, and the towns in this area thrived in its early period due to this particular practice. By the 19th century, English influence prevailed over the Dutch on the Douala coast. Throughout this period, the Douala coast was significantly synonymous with the territory that later came to be known as Cameroon. It was from Douala that the Germans first established and penetrated into the interior through the use of bellicose strategies.

Except for the period during World War II, Douala was never the capital of Cameroon, but its coastal location and port facilities permitted easy access to the interior and the outside world. Foreign firms were established in large numbers and attracted labor from the country's interior, making Douala a cosmopolitan area in the colonial era. It had a substantial number of French *colons* (settlers), until the end of the French administration.

The infrastructure established under the colonial epoch was further developed at independence, confirming the city's vitality as the economic, communications, business, and social capital of the country. This has led to many social problems resulting from the massive influx of people from other areas in search of employment opportunities. New quarters are regularly established as the city continues to expand beyond its preindependence dimensions. The industrial zone in Bassa, the populous New Bell area of commerce and **Bamiléké** bustle, the clan strongholds in Diedo, Akwa, and Bonaberi, as well as the commanding impact of consulates, multinational corporations, and governmental services in Bonapriso, give the city a sophisticated outlook.

In 1983, Douala's population was estimated at 800,000, but in 1994, the population was estimated to be 1.2 million.

DOUMBA, JOSEPH-CHARLES (1936–). Former minister in charge of missions at the Presidency of the Republic, Charles Doumba was born on 2 February 1936, in Yabassi, in the **Littoral Province**. Doumba, however, has his home in Mbethen near Bertoua in the **Eastern Province**. After primary and secondary education, he enrolled in the **University of Yaoundé**, studying law and English. He holds a *licence* in law and a diploma for general literary studies in English. During this period, Doumba also studied in the National School of Administration and Magistracy (ENAM) and received specialized training in the School of Administration in Paris.

On his return home, he served as secretary-general to the vice prime minister of **East Cameroon** simultaneously with his posts as substitute general of the Federal Court of Justice and later as secretary-general of the **National Assembly** in 1973. He has since become a key member of government, serving as minister of information and culture (1974–75); minister of justice (1975–79), and then as minister in charge of missions at the Presidency. In this post, he is reputed to have served as the speech writer for the head of state. He also held important party posts as member of the Central Committee (1980–83) and director of the School for Party Cadres (1973–83). Doumba's key role in governmental and party circles suffered from the **Ahidjo–Biya rupture** leading to his dismissal from the party and government on 29 January and 12 April 1983, respectively. Doumba apparently resisted **Ahmadou Ahidjo**'s attempt to impose the primacy of the party over the government. His dismissal was proof of the enormous power Ahidjo wielded in the political system of the country even after his voluntary resignation as head of state.

In February 1984, following the eclipse of former president Ahidjo, Pres. **Paul Biya** appointed Doumba to government as minister in charge of missions at the Presidency of the Republic. Months later, he was appointed member of the Central Committee and the Political Bureau of the Party, where he served as organizing secretary. In May

1987, Doumba was appointed president of the Board of Administration of the Cocoa Development Corporation (SODECAO). In 1992, he took over from Ebenezer Njoh Mouellé as secretary-general of the **Cameroon People's Democratic Movement**. Prior to this, he served as president of two sport federations. Doumba has remained an accomplished writer with three major publications. He also heads the state publishing company, SOPECAM.

DUALA. This ethnic group of **Bantu** stock is located on the Cameroon coast. They were apparently the first to come in contact with Europeans in the precolonial period, and they eventually played a successful middleman role in the **slave trade** from the interior across the Atlantic. For this reason, early European traders regarded them as vigorous, enterprising, prosperous, and excellent collaborators.

The Duala king Manga Bell signed the annexation treaty with the Germans at a time when the Dualas were considered the all-powerful representative of Cameroon peoples. The Dualas later fell out with the Germans, who infringed on indigenous rights and violated the terms of the treaty. For the Dualas, the end of the slave trade and their short-term middleman role in legitimate trade was replaced by the sale of land. Initially, land was sold to Europeans who settled in the area and later to **Bamiléké** from the Cameroon interior attracted to **Douala** by economic opportunities.

Since independence, the Duala have gradually lost economic and political power in their area. Nonetheless, they continue to remain a cultural force. Thanks to closer collaboration with Europeans, missionaries translated the Bible and used Duala as the Christian lingua franca of the coastal people, including the **anglophone** coastal population. Moreover, in a country of great cultural diversity, the Duala dance and music style, the **makossa**, has been virtually adopted nationally and receives international acclaim. Leading Duala politicians and elites include **Paul Soppo Priso**, **Betote Akwa**, **William-Aurelian Eteky Mboumoua,** and **Felix Sengat-Kuo.**

– E –

EAST CAMEROON. This is the official name of the former **French Cameroun** and the **République du Cameroun** when it became a state in the **Federal Republic of Cameroon**. East Cameroon was the larger of the two federated states of the Federal Republic of Cameroon. It became a political entity in October 1961. The referendum in 1972 in favor of the **United Republic of Cameroon** led to the end of East Cameroon's legal existence. East Cameroon was headed by a government under a **prime minister** and a unicameral legislature. Various East Cameroon prime ministers included **Charles Assale**, Vincent de Paul Ahanda, and **Simon Pierre Tchoungui**.

EAST PROVINCE. It covers a surface area of 109,000 square kilometers, about one-quarter of the entire national territory. Located in the southeastern part of the country, the province consists of four divisions, 16 subdivisions, and three districts. It is made up of three broad vegetation zones: the forest, the savannah, and the transitional zones. The southern part of the province has a Guinean-type climate, and the northern part has a Sudanian-type climate of four seasons. There are 538,000 inhabitants in the province. This population is essentially rural and engaged predominantly in agriculture, forest exploitation, and animal breeding. Industrial, commercial, and touristic potentials are still to be developed. **Bertoua** (Lom and Djerem Division) is the provincial headquarters. Other important towns include Batouri (Kadey Division), Abong-Mbong (Upper Nyong Division), and Yokadouma (Boumba and Ngoko Division). It has existed as a province since 1972.

EASTERN NIGERIA. Prior to and for a few years after its independence in 1980, **Nigeria** was a federation with three regions: the Northern, Western, and Eastern Regions. Enugu was the capital of the Eastern Region. **Southern Cameroons** was attached to the Eastern Region, **Northern Cameroons** to the Northern Region. Nigeria was a colony of **Great Britain**, and the British found it convenient—and cheaper—to treat the **mandate/trust territories** of **British Cameroons** as parts of that colony rather than as separate entities. Considerable movement of goods and people took place between Eastern Nigeria and Southern Cameroons, and Cameroonians were represented in the elected bodies that governed Eastern Nigeria.

EBERMAIER, KARL. Ebermaier was the sixth and last German governor of **Kamerun** (1912–16). His tenure began with the worsening relations between the **Duala** and the Germans and culminated with the fall of the Kamerun territory to Allied Forces at the outset of **World War I**. It was during Ebermaier's period in office that two local chiefs, **Douala**

Rudolf Manga Bell and **Martin Samba,** were executed by the Germans. The hostility of the local population and the defeat from the Allied troops led Ebermaier and remaining German troops to flee to the Spanish colony at Rio Muni.

EBOUA, SAMUEL (1928–). Born in Njombe in the **Littoral Province**, Eboua studied in **Nkongsamba** and **Douala** before going to France for the advanced cycle of his secondary education. He did all of his university education in Paris, earning a *licence* and a *diplôme d'études supérieures* in geography from the Sorbonne and a diploma in political science from the University of Paris. He also did advanced training at the Fondation Nationale des Sciences Politique.

On return home, he was principal of the highly prestigious **Lycée Leclerc** in **Yaoundé** and later director of secondary education in the Ministry of National Education. He was also managing director of the Cameroon Airlines Company before he was called up for duties at the Presidency in 1969. He served successively as chargé de mission (1969–71), assistant secretary-general with rank of vice minister (1971–75), and secretary-general with rank of minister of state (1975–82). He was a powerful figure in the seven years in this post, virtually leading to the eclipse of the prime minister. When **Paul Biya** became president in 1982, he was moved to the Ministry of Agriculture until June 1983. In 1985, he was reappointed to his earlier post as chairman of Cameroon Airlines Company (CAMAIR).

When multiparty politics was relaunched in Cameroon, Eboua made a comeback by helping to found the **National Union for Democracy and Progress (UNDP)**. However, when Eboua was voted out of office as chairman of the UNDP in favor of **Maigari Bello Bouba**, he left the latter party and in March 1992 founded the Movement for Democracy and Progress (MDP). He contested the October 1992 presidential elections but later threw his weight behind **John Fru Ndi**. Eboua equally contended the 1997 presidential elections but lost. At various times he has chaired the Allied Front for Change also known as the **Front of Allies for Change (FAC)**, an organization attempting to unite the numerous parties and organizations that oppose the **Cameroon People's Democratic Movement (CPDM)**. Eboua also served as Chairman of the Board of REGIFERCAM, the national railroad.

ECOLE NATIONALE D'ADMINISTRATION ET DE MAGISTRATURE. *See* NATIONAL CENTRE FOR ADMINISTRATION AND MAGISTRACY.

ECONOMIC AND SOCIAL COUNCIL. The **constitution of 1996** (Part 9) continues the existence of the Economic and Social Council, without discussion of its structure or role. It is the consultative assembly of the republic on crucial economic and social issues. Its main functions are to improve collaboration between the political and socioeconomic institutions and to determine government's economic and social policy. The president of the Republic or speaker of the National Assembly forwards projects of study to the council. The council provides its opinion and options, which are made known to Parliament and the government. There are 85 members in the Economic and Social Council representing the salaried sector (14), commercial industrial activities (12), cooperatives (11), banking (4), agriculture (14), and other members chosen for their economic, social, and cultural competence (30). The council has a five-year life cycle and is presided over by an elected chairman in collaboration with four committees on the general economy, production and exchange, general affairs, and social and cultural affairs. Felix Sabal Lecco served as chairman of the council from 1972 to 1982, while **Luc Ayang** was appointed on 4 February 1984.

ECONOMIC COMMUNITY OF CENTRAL AFRICAN STATES (ECCAS). *See* COMMUNAUTE ECONOMIQUE DES ETATS DE L'AFRIQUE CENTRALE (CEEAC).

ECONOMIC CRISIS. The period from the mid-1980s to the turn of the century has been characterized by structural difficulties, falling revenues, trade imbalances, and rising costs in the production and supply of goods and services. The government finally admitted to a severe crisis early in 1987. In the words of Pres. **Paul Biya**, "all our export commodities fell at the same time." For this reason, the government portrays the cause of the crisis as largely considered to be external: the falling value of exports and especially the precipitate decline of the price of **petroleum** on the world market. Opponents of government tend to believe the cause of the crisis is political, especially the absence of shrewd economic management under the new leadership. To tackle the problem, Cameroon turned to its major foreign allies including **France**, **Germany**, and the **United States** for assistance. The industrialized countries made their assistance contingent on Cameroon's adherence to an **International Monetary Fund (IMF)** austerity program. Given the severe political consequences of an IMF deal, the government initially stepped in with economic reforms of its own.

For the first time since independence, the 1987–88 budget of the country was reduced, by 18 percent. High-powered delegations of the **Cameroon People's Democratic Movement (CPDM)** were sent to the provinces to explain the draconian steps announced by the head of state. These included forcing retirement of many civil servants; curtailing electricity, telephone, and housing facilities granted to top-level civil servants; selling many administrative vehicles; changing the official working schedule in a bid to bring about higher productivity; forcing the dissolution or **privatization** of unproductive parapublic enterprises; and closing certain costly economic missions in various Cameroon embassies abroad. Although the international community considered the Cameroon approach to be bold and assertive, the policy was not far-reaching enough in bringing corrupt officials to trial. Moreover, with the scarcity of revenue in society, the rate of armed robbery and theft from banks and government services increased.

These setbacks led Cameroon to sign an aid package of $150 million with the IMF in October 1988. The agreement led to a flow of another **structural adjustment program (SAP)** loan from the **World Bank** as well as expected assistance from the African Development Bank, the United Kingdom, Germany, and France. The government used this assistance to reduce its current balance of payment deficit and honor its foreign **debts**. Apart from its external commitment, the government has also initiated internal squeezes and freezes on the national economy by equating salaries of workers in public service with those in parapublic institutions and by eliminating any salary increase in the near future. In addition, government froze all new employment for the next few years.

EDEA. Edea is headquarters of the Sanaga Maritime Division in the **Littoral Province** and an important industrial center. Mostly **Bassa** and Bakoko lived there until the town was transformed by the **hydroelectric** dam and the **aluminum** complex in the 1950s into a lively urban city. Today, Edea provides the country with much of its supply of electricity. Edea is also the seat of the Alucam company established by the French to process imported bauxite from Guinea to produce various aluminum products. Politically, Edea remained an important stronghold of the **Union des Populations du Cameroun (UPC)** movement from 1948 to 1955. It remained under a virtual state of emergency until the mid-1970s.

EDUCATION. Cameroon's educational foundation is a complex mix of its colonial heritage and attempts to create an authentic national blend out of this legacy. Until 1999 the education system provided a two-year nursery school and a primary school of six years in the **francophone** area and seven years in the **anglophone** region. A five-year secondary school existed in anglophone Cameroon; secondary school lasted for six years in francophone parts of the country. A two-year preuniversity program exists at the high school, *or lycée,* in various parts of the country. The number of years spent in primary and secondary school was equalized in 1999.

The Ministry of National Education coordinates the different systems and grants graduating certificates. The ministry provides the grounds for **harmonization** and equivalence. Various examinations and certificates such as the **Certificat de Fin d'Etudes Primaires Eléméntaires (CEPE)** or the **First School Leaving Certificate (FSLC)** at the primary level, the **Brevet d'Etudes du Premier Cycle (BEPC),** or the **General Certificate of Education (GCE)** ordinary level at secondary schools, and the ***baccalauréat*** or the GCE advanced level at the *lycée* are all administered by the ministry.

Attempts in 1983 to restructure the GCE to resemble the French format were greeted by stiff protest by anglophone students at all levels. Government later allowed both systems to exist in their original forms. However, pupils and students in either system are gradually trained in French and English in the early stages of their education with the aim of creating a truly bilingual country.

Various religious bodies and private individuals also own schools and colleges to assist government in its task. Mission- and privately owned institutions levy high fees for pupils and students. Apart from classical learning, vocational, technical, and commercial institutions exist. Moreover, all educational institutions are mandated to provide agricultural training to introduce students to the practical realities of outdoor life. There is an extensive tertiary level of institutions including state and private universities, technical and professional institutions, and specialized programs. Although many Cameroonians go abroad for university education, the majority remain for study in Cameroon. Cameroon's literacy rate, the proportion of those over 15 years of age who can read and write, is about 63 percent. For males it is 75 percent, but only 52 percent for females. In 1995, about two million children were in primary and 560,000 in secondary schools. *See also* UNIVERSITY OF YAOUNDE.

EDZOA, TITUS. A specialist surgeon and a close confidant and personal friend to Pres. **Paul Biya**, Professor Edzoa was a very influential figure in Biya's government. In his 15 years of service under the Biya regime,

Professor Edzoa served as a high-ranking official. He first served as Biya's private physician before being appointed special adviser to the president. He was then moved to the post of secretary-general at the Presidency of the Republic and, in September 1996, was appointed minister of health. Like Biya, Edzoa is reputed to be a member of the **Rosicrucian Order**. On 20 April 1997, however, Professor Edzoa took a fateful decision to announce his resignation from government and his intention to run for the **elections for the president of 1997**. As an indication of his determination to challenge Biya's candidacy, he joined the Parti Ouvrier du Peuple Camerounais (POPC).

Edzoa's decision to run as a presidential candidate was, apparently, an embarrassment to the government, especially as it came from a close confidant of the president. The result was immediate arrest and detention, on 3 July 1997, of Professor Edzoa and his close associate, Michel Thierry Atangana, at the military headquarters on charges of embezzlement. In protest of the arrest, some **Béti** elites grouped themselves into the Comité pour la Libération du Citoyen Titus Eddzoa (COLICITE), under the leadership of the renowned writer **Mongo-Béti**. The aims of COLICITE were to ensure that Professor Edzoa ran for the presidential elections, that he be given a fair trial, and that he be released. COLICITE achieved none of these goals.

Professor Edzoa's application to run for the presidential elections was rejected on two accounts: first, that the file was incomplete; and second, that according to the law, he could not run for elections because he was under judicial investigation. These points notwithstanding, on 4 August 1997, the COLICITE sent a petition to the Ministry of Territorial Administration, denouncing the poor conditions under which Professor Edzoa was detained. The government did not budge. On the contrary, in October 1997, after what was widely considered a masquerade of justice, Professor Edzoa and Thierry Atangana were sentenced by a **Yaoundé** court of First Instance to 15 years' imprisonment, confiscation of their property, and payment of 350 million CFA francs, as damages. Even though this verdict was appealed, a subsequent verdict by a Yaoundé Court of Appeal upheld the 15-year prison sentence but canceled the confiscation of property and the payment of 350 million CFA francs.

L'EFFORT CAMEROUNAIS. This Catholic weekly newspaper founded in **Yaoundé** by the Paulist fathers in 1955 was reputed to be the most dynamic and provocative nongovernmental newspaper. It features commentaries and articles following a relatively liberal line. Issues of

L'Effort Camerounais are often confiscated or suppressed because they critically mirror the ills of society. The newspaper faced increased financial difficulty and was forced by government to discontinue its once popular column "Billet du Juré" in the early 1970s. In 1988, the editor in chief of the newspaper was assassinated by unknown gunmen. By the 1990s, ***Le Messager*** had become the most popular and famous of antigovernment newspapers. *See also CAMEROON OUTLOOK; CAMEROON TRIBUNE.*

EGBE-TABI, EMMANUEL (1929–). This long-serving former minister of state for posts and telecommunications was born on 24 May 1929, in Bachua-Akagbe near **Mamfe** in the **South West Province**. After primary education in Bali, he returned to Mamfe, where he taught in Tali until 1948, when he obtained the British Chamber of Commerce Certificate through correspondence. He later earned a Cambridge certificate in 1949. He served as treasury clerk in Mamfe in 1950 and later acquired a scholarship to study economics at Fourah Bay College in Freetown, Sierra Leone. Thereafter, he left Sierra Leone to study in the University of Durham in England, graduating with a degree in 1956.

On return home, Egbe-Tabi worked with the **Cameroon Development Corporation (CDC)** as assistant personnel manager before he earned a scholarship from the corporation to study law in London. On return to Cameroon in 1961, he was appointed legal adviser to the CDC and the speaker of the West Cameroon House of Assembly and the **West Cameroon House of Chiefs**. He became a deputy federal minister of justice following **reunification** and was appointed minister of posts and telecommunications on 12 June 1970. In 1975, he was raised to the rank of **minister of state** in the department and remained the sole **anglophone** minister of state under the **Ahmadou Ahidjo** presidency. He served as the minister of posts and telecommunications until January 1982.

Egbe-Tabi's status as a political heavyweight was also manifested in party circles. He was a member of the **Kamerun National Democratic Party (KNDP)** in the early years of independence before joining **Solomon Tandeng Muna** to form the **Cameroon United Congress** in 1964. When the **Cameroon National Union (CNU)** was formed in 1966, Egbe-Tabi held a steady seat in the Central Committee and served as party secretary for youth and propaganda affairs. Despite his failing health, he remained politically significant until the **Bamenda Congress** when he was replaced in high party functions by Tabong Kima. Thereafter, he was named roving ambassador.

EKANGAKI, NZO (1934–). Ekangaki was born on 22 March 1934, in Nguti in the **South West Province**. After primary school in Nguti and Besongabang, he entered Cameroon Protestant College, Bali (1949–53), and on completion enrolled at the Hope Waddle Training Institute in Calabar, Nigeria. In 1954, he was admitted to the University College of Ibadan, Nigeria, and later earned a bachelor of arts degree from Oxford University. He was very active in student bodies travelling across Europe for conferences. He won a scholarship from West Germany in 1960 where he studied diplomacy at the University of Bonn. On return home in 1961, he was elected to the Legislative Assembly on a **Kamerun National Democratic Party (KNDP)** ticket. A year later he became deputy minister of foreign affairs and in 1964 was made a full minister and elected to the **National Assembly**. Until his appointment as **Organization of African Unity (OAU)** secretary-general in 1972, Ekangaki remained a key member of the government serving as minister of health and population (1964–65) and minister of labor and social welfare (1965–72). Prior to the formation of the **Cameroon National Union (CNU)**, he had switched from the KNDP to form the **Cameroon United Congress** with **Solomon Tandeng Muna** and **Emmanuel Egbe-Tabi** in 1965. He became a member of the Political Bureau of the CNU, occupying important party duties on press, information, and propaganda.

His appointment as secretary-general of the OAU was aimed at transforming the office from one of policy making to an administrative coordinating role in continental politics. Determined to work as an international official responsible only to the OAU, Ekangaki ran into conflict with the African heads of state over the Lonrho affair. He selected Lonrho, a multinational organization with strong links to racist regimes in southern Africa and some other black African governments, as OAU consultant on matters of refining, storing, and distributing petroleum during the economic crisis. His decision was heavily criticized by the OAU summit, forcing his resignation as secretary-general in 1974. Another Cameroonian, **William-Aurelian Eteky Mboumoua**, succeeded him. Former president **Ahmadou Ahidjo**, who had kept a distance from Ekangaki because of his independent stance in his top continental job and the "disgrace" his resignation brought to Cameroon, marginalized him to an obscure post as technical adviser in the Ministry of Territorial Administration (1974–85). Three years into **Paul Biya**'s rule, Ekangaki received a comparatively prestigious job as adviser for administrative affairs at the Presidency of the Republic in 1985, where he remained until retirement in 1989.

EKHAH NGHAKY, NZO. *See* EKANGAKI, NZO.

EKO, CATHERINE (1938–). A professional nurse and former secretary of state for national education, Eko was born on 22 June 1938, in **Douala**. She did primary school at the Presbyterian Girls' School (1945–53) in Victoria (now **Limbe**) and secondary education in Uyo, **Nigeria** (1954–58). Her specialized education began in the School of Nursing of the University College Hospital, Ibadan, Nigeria (1959–62), followed by courses for a midwife and a midwife teacher's diploma in 1962–63 and 1977–78, respectively.

Eko held the post of dean of studies at the National School of Nursing from 1981 until her appointment in August 1985 as secretary of state in the Ministry of National Education. In 1992, she became deputy director of the Palais de Congrès.

EKPE. *See* NGBE.

ELANGWE, NAMATA HENRY (1932–). A former government minister, Elangwe was born on 28 September 1932, in Kake near **Kumba** in the **South West Province**. He attended primary education in Kake and Kumba before entering **St. Joseph's College**, Sasse, in **Buea** in 1947. Thereafter, he attended the Yaba School of Pharmacy in Nigeria, from which he qualified as a pharmacist in 1955. He worked briefly for the **Cameroon Development Corporation (CDC)** before settling as an independent pharmacist. Elangwe's first political role was as secretary of the **Kamerun People's Party** (1956–58) before joining the **Cameroons Peoples' National Convention (CPNC)** in 1960 as secretary-general. He became a member of the West Cameroon House of Assembly in 1961 and was secretary of state for finance in the **West Cameroon** government in 1968. In May 1970, he was deputy prime minister of West Cameroon and still held his finance portfolio. When the **United Republic of Cameroon** was formed in 1972, Elangwe was appointed minister of mines and energy in July and remained in this post until November 1979, when he was removed from government. He remained prominent in party circles as deputy treasurer and deputy political secretary of the **Cameroon National Union (CNU)** at various times between 1966 and 1985. He was reelected to the Central Committee of the **Cameroon People's Democratic Movement** at the end of the **Bamenda Congress** in March 1985. Elangwe is presently traditional ruler of the Bakundu of Kake.

ELECTIONS FOR PRESIDENT (1992). After several postponements, the first multicandidate presidential elections since independence were held on 11 October 1992. After some delay, the results were officially announced on 23 October. **Paul Biya** (**Cameroon People's Democratic Movement, CPDM**) won with 39.9 percent of the votes. **John Fru Ndi** (**Social Democratic Front, SDF**) was second with 35.9 percent. Other candidates were **Maigari Bello Bouba** (**National Union for Democracy and Progress, UNDP**), 19.2 percent; **Adamou Ndam Njoya** (**Union for a Democratic Cameroon, UDC**), 3.6 percent; Jean-Jacques Ekindi (Progressive Movement), 0.95 percent; and Ema Otou, 0.4 percent. About 72 percent of eligible voters participated.

The elections were viewed as rigged by members of the opposition and by foreign observers. Rioting broke out in several locations after the results were announced, and the government placed Fru Ndi under house arrest after he announced that he believed the vote had been miscounted and that he was the actual winner with 38 percent of the vote.

ELECTIONS FOR PRESIDENT (1997). The 12 October 1997 presidential elections were boycotted by the major opposition parties (**Social Democratic Front**, **SDF**; **National Union for Democracy and Progress, UNDP**; and the **Cameroon Democratic Union, CDU**) to protest government's refusal to establish an independent electoral commission. Amnesty International reported an increase in politically motivated arrests prior to the election; both domestic and international observers cautioned that the electoral process was not legitimate. Six candidates came forward, but other than Pres. **Paul Biya**, only Samuel Eboua was a well-known figure. Biya received 92.51 percent of the vote. Other candidates were Henri Hogbe Nlend, Albert Dzongang, Joachim Tabi Owono, Antoine de Pandoure Ndemanou, and Gustave Essaka.

ELECTIONS FOR THE NATIONAL ASSEMBLY (1992). Cameroon's first multiparty elections since the formation of the **Cameroon National Union (CNU)** took place on 1 March 1992. Some of the main opposition parties boycotted the elections claiming that they had been called without adequate time for opposition parties to prepare and that the electoral law favored the **Cameroon People's Democratic Movement (CPDM)**, the government party. Even with the boycott in place, the CPDM failed to gain a majority, winning only 88 of 180 seats. The **National Union for Democracy and Progress (UNDP)** won 68 seats; the **Union des Populations du Cameroun (UPC),** six; and a small group, the **Movement for**

the Defense of the Republic (MDR), six. The MDR joined in coalition with the CPDM to form a government.

ELECTIONS FOR THE NATIONAL ASSEMBLY (1997). The second multiparty elections for the **National Assembly** took place on 17 May 1997. About 1,800 candidates competed for 180 seats. Opposition parties and foreign observers, such as a **Commonwealth** team, declared the elections seriously flawed. However, the **Cameroon People's Democratic Movement (CPDM)** took 109 seats; the **Social Democratic Front (SDF)**, 43; the **National Union for Democracy and Progress (UNDP),** 13; and minor parties took the remainder. Results for seven seats were nullified due to irregularities and were rerun in August. Final results were announced on 18 August, with the CPDM now winning 116 seats.

EMIA–EMA CONSTITUTION. This was the name given by the **anglophone** public to the constitutional proposals tabled by anglophone members in the constitutional drafting committee, set up at the **Tripartite Conference** in **Yaoundé** between October and November 1991. EMIA, the acronym for Elad, Munzu, Itoe, and Anyangwe, all prominent anglophone jurists, was later reduced to EMA when Itoe refused to sign the final document that recommended a federal structure as a solution to Cameroon's political crisis.

The fundamental objective of the architects of the EMIA–EMA constitution was to replace the **constitution of 1961**, which, according to them, did not clearly define the scope of competence between the federal and state governments and did not adequately take care of minority (anglophone) problems. Thus, the EMIA–EMA group hoped to awaken the consciousness of anglophones to the benefits that could be achieved if a genuine federal structure was adopted for Cameroon.

The EMIA–EMA group, therefore, strove to create a balanced constitution that, on the one hand, gave adequate protection of the anglophone against **francophone** domination and, on the other hand, took care of the division between South Westerners and North Westerners in anglophone Cameroon. In this light, while the constitution created a federal state within anglophone Cameroon, so as to put to rest the South West–North West dichotomy, it provided for a House of Assembly for anglophone Cameroon with a presidency that rotated between the South Westerners and North Westerners. The same principle was recommended for the office of the national president, which had to rotate between the anglophones and francophones. As far as the term of office of the president was concerned, the constitution recommended a five-year term, renewable once. The constitution received the support, at least overtly, of the majority of anglophones and some francophones mostly covertly, notably the chairman of the constitutional committee who, at one point seemingly saw it as the solution to the problems of kith and kin, the **Béti**. Despite this, the EMIA–EMA constitutional proposals came up against the determined francophone majority, who refused to have a federal system of government. What is more, one of the architects of the constitution, Itoe, a minister and member of the **Cameroon People's Democratic Movement (CPDM)**, back-pedaled when the document, which initially had been meant for private circulation, was given the widest publicity. When a constitution was finally produced for Cameroon in 1996, the EMIA–EMA's recommendation for a federal structure was not adopted.

ENDELEY, EMMANUEL MBELLA LIFAFE (1916–1998). The first prime minister of British **Southern Cameroons**, Endeley was born on 10 April 1916, into a prestigious **Bakweri** family; he attended schools in **Buea**, Bonjongo, and Umahia (**Eastern Nigeria**). He specialized at the Nigerian School of Medicine in Yaba and served as assistant medical officer in **Nigeria** in 1942 and later as chief medical officer in Buea in 1945. He began his political activity as an organizer of **Cameroons Development Corporation (CDC)** workers in 1947, becoming general secretary of the union in 1948. Endeley was active in organizing strikes and in petitioning to visiting United Nations missions. As a result, he played a leading role in the formation of multiple political organizations to articulate the views of **British Cameroons**: the **Cameroon Youth League** (1939), the **Cameroons National Federation** (1949), and the Bakweri Improvement Union (1944).

He was elected to the Eastern Nigerian Assembly at Enugu in 1951. There he was a leading advocate for a separate regional status for Southern Cameroons and emerged as leader of government business in the first Southern Cameroon's Regional Assembly in 1954. Endeley led the break-away from the **National Council of Nigeria and the Cameroons (NCNC)** to form the **Kamerun National Congress (KNC)** with **John Ngu Foncha** and **Solomon Tandeng Muna** in 1953. He later came to espouse cooperation and to favor integration with Nigeria, a clear diversion from his earlier goals. This caused a major split in the KNC ranks, leading to the formation of the **Kamerun National Democratic Party (KNDP)** by Foncha in 1955. Endeley lost support and credibility in his attempt to work with the **Kamerun's People Party (KPP)**.

Following a narrow election win in 1957, Endeley was installed first **prime minister** of Southern Cameroons in 1958. He lost his post to Foncha in a January 1959 election. He formed the **Cameroons Peoples' National Convention (CPNC)** with the KPP in May 1960 to lead an effective opposition to the KNDP. Already branded as a pro-Nigerian advocate at a time of strong pan-**Kamerun** sentiments, Endeley's party lost the 1961 UN-administered **plebiscite**. Reduced to a leader of an opposition minority because of Foncha's popularity in a federal Cameroon, Endeley became an early cautious advocate for a one-party system in the country. Schism in the KNDP ranks gave Endeley the post of leader of government business in **West Cameroon** in 1965. He became a member of the **Cameroon National Union** Central Committee and was president of the Fako section from 1966 until 1985. Under the unitary system, Endeley became a member of the **National Assembly**.

ENGLISH. English is one of Cameroon's official languages according to Part 1, Article 3, of the **Constitution of 1996**. In reality, however, English is only a secondary language for most Cameroonians, who are more proficient in their various local languages. English is taught in schools and polished throughout the academic and professional career. *See also* ANGLOPHONE; BILINGUALISM; FRANCOPHONE; FRANGLAIS; FRENCH.

EQUATORIAL GUINEA. To the south of Cameroon lies the mainland portion of Equatorial Guinea. The mainland is referred to as Rio Muni and the main offshore island is now named Bioko (formerly Macias Nguema Biyogo and prior to that Fernando Po). The total area of the country is about 11,000 square miles. Until recently it has depended on plantation agriculture, mainly **cocoa**. **Coffee** and **timber** are also important, but petroleum provides much promise for the future. The population of 450,000 consists of several ethnic groups, but the **Fang** are the largest. The Fang also reside in Cameroon. Although it never was a colony of France, Equatorial Guinea has joined the **franc zone** and **Union Douanière Economique de l'Afrique Centrale (UDEAC)**. Spain was the country's colonial ruler.

ETEKY MBOUMOUA, WILLIAM-AURELIAN (1933–). The former minister and third secretary-general of the **Organization of African Unity** was born on 20 October 1933, in **Douala** into a wealthy family. He did primary and began secondary education in Cameroon before proceeding to France, where he passed his ***baccalauréat***. He studied law, graduating in 1953, and then enrolled in the famous Ecole Nationale de la France d' Outre-Mer. On completion in 1959, he returned home and was commissioned as deputy prefect in Yabassi and later as ***préfet*** of the very sensitive Sanana–Maritime Division. His skillful handling of the growing insurgency in the **Bassa** heartland opened to him the gates of higher duties. He was named minister of education, youth, and sports in June 1961; **Paul Biya** served in his ministry as secretary-general. The Federal **University of Yaoundé,** as well as the foundation of the education policy of Cameroon, were established during his tenure. Eteky-Mboumoua joined UNESCO briefly and served as president of UNESCO's General Conference. He was named special adviser to Pres. **Ahmadou Ahidjo** on return and following the resignation of **Nzo Ekangaki**, he became secretary-general of the **Organization of African Unity (OAU)** in 1974. He served in this capacity until 1980 when he resumed his duties as special adviser to the president.

Eteky Mboumoua was named minister in charge of missions at the Presidency in February 1984 and was moved to the Ministry of Foreign Affairs in July of that year. He served in this post until January 1987 when, because of a "*faute grave,*" he was relieved of his duties. Officially it was argued that Eteky-Mbouma opened high-level diplomatic engagements with Hungary without consulting the Head of State; other theories argue that there were previously alleged disagreements with President Biya over the reestablishment of diplomatic relations with Israel and his preference for a more activist stance toward the apartheid regime of South Africa. In 1995, Eteky Mboumoua was selected by the OAU to undertake a delicate diplomatic mission to the Comoro Islands to settle a political crisis. He is currently president of the National Red Cross Movement in Cameroon.

ETHNIC CONFLICT. Cameroon is a polyethnic society with over 300 ethnic groupings, presenting a complex and highly fragmented political structure. The population continues to identify primarily with subgroup loyalties rather than the symbols of the nation-state. Government **nation-building** policy has been to emphasize symbols of national unity and integration over those of ethnic belonging and solidarity. It has attempted to show the president as leader of all Cameroonians rather than his ethnic group. The membership of the **National Assembly**, the government, and the composition of a national soccer team or the ballet dance group are aimed at presenting the national image for common identification.

Conflict continues at several levels and hindered the establishment of a multiparty political system because of the assumption that membership would follow ethnic lines. The example of the head of state not blaming any particular region or ethnic group for the **coup attempt of 6 April 1984**, despite clear evidence to the contrary, was in line with the determination to preserve national unity and downplay ethnic conflict. Whereas **Ahmadou Ahidjo**'s policies appeared to aim at the eradication of ethnic identity as necessary to the formation of national identity, **Paul Biya** seems to recognize the possibility of the individual having a dual identity, ethnic and national.

In the 1990s, ethnicity became quite significant in the country's political life, in part due to Biya's heavy reliance on his ethnic group to fill positions in government and to otherwise favor his ethnic group. The opening of new political parties has seen the growth of many ethnically based organizations.

Violent conflicts between ethnic groups occur with unpleasant results. Recent examples include numerous clashes between Choa Arabs and Kotokas in the **Extreme North**, between Balikumbat and Bafanji in the **North West Province**, and Awing and Baligham also in the North West. Such conflicts are often caused by disputes over land. *See also* TOMBEL MASSACRE.

ETOUDI PALACE. *See* UNITY PALACE.

EUROPEAN ECONOMIC COMMUNITY (EEC). The EEC began as the European Coal and Steel Community in 1952 before becoming the European Economic Community in 1958 and later the European Union (EU) in 1967. The EC serves its members as a common market and has recently developed a common currency, the euro. The organization is a leading forum in the coordination of European trade relations, investment, and economic aid to African states. *See also* LOME AGREEMENTS; STABEX; SYSMIN; YAOUNDE AGREEMENTS.

EVOLUE. The *évolué* was the end product of the French **assimilation policy**, referring to any African who had fully assimilated French law, language, and customs. The *évolué* was the quintessential elite. He or she received wider political and economic opportunities than the indigenous masses. Consequently, the *évolué* was expected to admire French lifestyle and denigrate local mores.

EWONDO. Ewondo is the largest and most important group of the multifarious **Fang–Pahouin** conglomeration. Many authors simply refer to the entire Fang–Pahouins as Ewondo. The Ewondos are spread across the **Center**, **South,** and **East Provinces.** They also claim to be the indigenes of **Yaoundé**, the country's capital city that is locally referred to as "Ongola." More than 18 subethnicities have intermingled with other subgroupings of the Fang–Pahouin. However, the Ewondo language serves as the most popular language for the entire Fang–Pahouin conglomeration, especially in daily interaction and church fellowship. Ewondo was once proposed to serve as the national language. The most significant historic figures of the group include **Charles Atangana** and **Andre Fouda**.

EXTREME NORTH PROVINCE. This province covers a surface area of 31,984 square kilometers and consists of six divisions, 21 subdivisions, and nine districts. Its principal relief features are the **Mandara Mountains** in the west and the **Chad** Plain. It has a steppe vegetation and a dry tropical climate. About 1.7 million inhabitants live in the Extreme North Province. Animal breeding and agriculture are the major occupations of the local population. Millet and sorghum are essentially for subsistence, while **cotton** is the principal cash crop. Industrial activity is limited but tourism constitutes an important resource. **Maroua** (Diamare Division) is the provincial headquarters. Other important towns include Kaele (Kaele Division), Kousseri (Logone and Chari Division), Yagoua (Mayo–Danay Division), and Mora (Mayo–Sava Division and Mokolo (Mayo Tsanaga Division). The Extreme North Province was created on 23 August 1983.

EZA BOTO. *See* MONGO-BETI.

– F –

FANG–PAHOUIN. This ethnic group is distinguished by their territorial, demographic, and linguistic importance beyond the Cameroon boundaries. They are essentially **Bantu** and are affiliated to peoples in the neighboring countries of **Gabon**, Republic of **Congo,** and **Equatorial Guinea**. Historically, the Fang are the result of a migration from the northeast of Africa between the 17th and 18th centuries. Today, the Fang in Cameroon have settled in the **East**, **Center,** and **South Provinces** of the country and constitute a commanding cultural conglomeration of six ethnic groupings, including the **Ewondo**, the Banen, the **Bulu**, the Ntumu, the Mvae, and the actual Fangs. Pres. **Paul Biya** hails from this broad cultural grouping.

FAR NORTH PROVINCE. *See* EXTREME NORTH PROVINCE.

FEDERAL INSPECTORS OF ADMINISTRATION. Senior administrative officials were placed at the head of the six administrative regions of the federal republic in October 1961. They were the representatives of the federal government in each administrative region.

Of all the regions, it was the federal inspector of **West Cameroon** region who faced the greatest challenges. The duties of the federal inspector often conflicted with the prerogatives of, and quest for autonomy by, the **prime minister** of the federated state of West Cameroon. Federal inspectors performed civil and juridicial functions, executed federal rules and regulations, and coordinated federal activities in their various regions. With the advent of the unitary state in 1972, these federal inspectors of the administrative regions were replaced by **governors** of provinces. Some notable federal inspectors who later assumed other significant functions include Enoch Kwayeb, Enam Mba'a, Andze Tsoungui, Sabal Lecco, and Jean Marcel Mengueme.

FEDERAL NATIONAL ASSEMBLY. The legislative body of the former **Federal Republic of Cameroon** (1961–72) was a unicameral legislature elected for five years by universal suffrage. Representatives to the first Federal Assembly were selected by the state legislatures of **East** and **West Cameroon**. Direct elections to the Assembly were held in 1965 and 1970. Throughout its 11-year existence, the Federal National Assembly was composed of 50 deputies, 40 from East Cameroon and 10 from West Cameroon. *See also* NATIONAL ASSEMBLY.

FEDERAL REPUBLIC OF CAMEROON. French Cameroun became independent on 1 January 1960, and became the **République du Cameroun**. It was joined with **Southern Cameroons** on 1 October 1961, to form the Federal Republic of Cameroon. This federation consisted of two states. **West Cameroon**, the former Southern Cameroons, was by far the smaller of the two. This **anglophone** state had **Buea** as its capital. **East Cameroon**, the former French Cameroun, was larger with 80 percent of the population and **francophone**. Its capital was **Yaoundé**. As part of his policy of centralizing power in Yaoundé and in the presidency, **Ahmadou Ahidjo** ended the federation in 1972 to form the **United Republic of Cameroon**.

FEDERAL REPUBLIC OF GERMANY. *See* GERMANY.

FERNANDO PO. *See* EQUATORIAL GUINEA.

FERTILE CRESCENT. The relatively more productive area of the territory in which the French administration concentrated its economic activity covered only one-tenth of the **French Cameroun** territory, stretching as far north as **Foumban** and **Bafoussam** to the major cities of **Nkongsamba**, **Douala,** and **Yaoundé** as well as the deep south towns of **Kribi** and Ebolowa. This area coincided with the portions most served by the railroad and the most fertile zones in which major crops like **cocoa** and **coffee** are grown.

The semicircular shape of this exclusive economic zone had its center in Douala. Over 1.5 million people lived in this area during the French period in Cameroun. The Fertile Crescent is still the most economically active region in the country. In addition to its high concentration of substantial economic and human resources, many foreign enterprises are also located in the region. The spatial economic disequilibrium of independent Cameroun could partly be traced to this French project of accelerated modernization of the Fertile Crescent during the colonial area. *See also* BALANCED DEVELOPMENT.

FILM INDUSTRY. Cameroon's cinematographic industry is still developing. In its development, it has been influenced by values relating to the contact of two civilizations: the African and the European. This theme characterized early films of short duration produced by foreign artists. Between 1950 and 1960, scores of films were produced by foreign artists. During the same period, dozens and dozens of films were produced with an ethnohistoric basis, including *La Grande Case* (1951), *Oumarou* (1954), *Kalla* (1955), and *Connaissez-vous Ngaoundéré* (1957), among others.

After independence in 1960, the few Cameroonians enrolled in cinematographic institutes in France, and the creation of the **Cameroun Actualités** agency in 1962 changed the outlook of film production in the country. Major productions in this period included *Tam-Tam à Paris* by Therèse Sita-Bella and *Aventure en France* and *La Grande Case Bamiléké* by Jean-Paul Ngassa. These, as well as films by J. P. Dikonge

Pipa, Urbain Dia-Moukouri, and Daniel Kamwa graced the second phase of Cameroon's indigenous cinematographic experience.

Since the mid-1970s, Cameroonian artists have dwelt on the production of longer films to inaugurate a new era for the country's film industry. The major films of this era include popular successes such as *Mouna-Moto* (1974) by Dikonge Pipa and *Pousse-Pousse* (1975) by Daniel Kamwa. Both films deal with the theme of love and marriage in the face of traditional and modern influences.

The late 1980s and early 1990s heralded a new era in the Cameroonian film industry. This period witnessed a proliferation of Cameroonian films, some of which include *Quartier Mozart, Le Complot d'Artiste,* and *Have You Seen Franklin Roosevelt?*, all written by Jean-Pierre Bekolo. Other recently produced films include *Bikutsi Water Blues*, *Afrique, je te plumerai* (in which the author focuses on the violence that accompanied the prodemocracy movement in 1991), *La tête dans les nuages*, and *Clando*, all by Jean Marie Teno. The emphasis in these films has moved from love and marriage to sociopolitical problems in Cameroon. There are equally films on Cameroon music, the Nigerian–Biafra war, and the Angolan conflict produced by Cameroonians.

Despite the encouragement of the Ministry of Culture as well as the establishment of other institutions to promote indigenous film productions, Cameroon's film industry still faces severe monetary problems related to production costs and logistics of programming and distribution. Nevertheless, government strongly believes that a better-developed film industry could serve as an important instrument in the process of information and moral education in the country.

FIREWOOD. Wood is the main source of fuel for domestic energy in the traditional Cameroonian household. Firewood is obtained from the indiscriminate cutting down of trees, bushes, and forests in a bid to create new farmland. Generally, the search for firewood is a family activity, with **women** and children playing important roles. The search and sale of firewood has also become a prominent activity in the major towns and cities. Firewood production is one of the causes of deforestation in Cameroon.

FIRST SCHOOL LEAVING CERTIFICATE (FSLC). This certificate is awarded to successful schoolchildren after seven years of primary **education** in the English-speaking provinces of Cameroon. The examination is set by the Ministry of National Education and is administered toward the end of every school year. Successful performance in the FSLC is the key to admission into secondary or technical schools in **anglophone** Cameroon.

FLAG OF CAMEROON. The Cameroon flag, rectangular in shape, consists of three equal bands of green (top), red, and yellow with a yellow five-point star in the center of the red band. During the federal period, there were two stars in the upper left corner of the green band, one for each state in the federation.

FOCHIVE, JEAN (1931–1997). Fochive was head of Cameroon's intelligence service under the **Ahmadou Ahidjo** regime. From December 1961 until 1971, he served cumulatively as head of the Intelligence Department, director of the Service d'Etudes et de la Documentation (SEDOC), and chief of presidential security. As director of SEDOC, Fochive was at the head of Cameroon's most feared political institution. SEDOC was symbolic of the tight public security that prevailed under the Ahidjo regime. As director of presidential security, he was in charge of the Republican Guard and the military command post at the Presidential Palace. In 1971, Fochive was relieved of his duties as director of presidential security but maintained his position as director of SEDOC, now known as the Direction Générale d'Etudes et de la Documentation (DIRDOC). He served in this post until 1983 at the height of the **Ahidjo–Biya rupture** when he was appointed ambassador to China. In April 1989, Pres. **Paul Biya** returned Fochive to his post as Head of Cameroon's intelligence department, now known as the Centre National des Etudes et des Recherches (CENER). Fochive was later appointed as delegate-general for national security, a post he occupied until 1996.

FON (or NFON). This is the traditional designation for the highest authority within the traditional structures of the **Bali**, **Tikar**, **Bamiléké**, and **Bamoum** peoples of the Cameroon **Grassfield**. The fon is the powerful head of territorial, civil, and military authority within a given kingdom. His power emanates from a sacred kinship tying the living with the dead, and he rules over a kingdom from a palace adorned with royalty, independence, and respect. Under various colonial systems, only the British officially granted status to traditional authorities as part of their policy of **indirect rule,** while the Germans and French generally treated the *fons* with suspicion and disdain. Traditional systems that outlived the colonial era owe their survival to the voluntary allegiance of sub-*fons* as well as to the various councils and associations formed to provide support and legitimacy to indigenous rule. Since independence, the significance of traditional authority has shifted from the period of political coexistence in the era of a **West Cameroon House of Chiefs** to the present period of political integration of *fons* into the civil administrative machinery under the Ministry of Territorial Administration. The *fon* faces a dilemma in the **North West Province**. He owes his position to **Paul Biya** and the party in power, but his people support the **Social Democratic Front (SDF)**. *See also* CHIEFS.

FONCHA, JOHN NGU (1916–1999). The former **prime minister** of **West Cameroon** and vice president of the **Federal Republic of Cameroon** was born in Nkwen, **Bamenda,** in the **North West Province** on 21 June 1916. After early education in Bamenda and Buguma, **Nigeria,** he trained as a teacher and taught agriculture in Nigeria from 1941 to 1942. On his return to the **Southern Cameroons**, he took up teaching and was a headmaster in several Catholic schools in Bamenda. Simultaneously with his teaching profession, Foncha began an intensive and highly commendable political career. He was a founding member of the **Cameroons Youth League (CYL)**, the **Cameroons National Federation (CNF)**, and the **Kamerun National Congress (KNC)**. Between 1942 and 1945, he was secretary to the Bamenda Branch of the CYL. He also helped to establish the **Bamenda Improvement Association** in 1940, the Bamenda Catholic Teachers Union in 1944, a provincial branch of the **National Council of Nigeria and the Cameroons** in 1945, and the Bamenda branch of the CNF in 1949.

In 1951, Foncha was among the "Original Thirteen" elected in the Eastern House of Assembly in Enugu, Nigeria. Political disagreements over **reunification** led him to join the **Kamerun United National Congress (KUNC)**, and the KNC until he formed the **Kamerun National Democratic Party (KNDP)** in 1955. It was as general secretary of the KNDP, from 1955 to 1966, that Foncha gained political success and distinction as an advocate for reunification. In 1957, the KNDP made electoral gains by winning six seats, up from two seats in the Southern Cameroons House of Assembly, and in 1959 won the general elections. Foncha became prime minister of Southern Cameroons and in this position gradually cut off the territory from Nigerian politics with pro-unification campaigns before the British government in London and the United Nations in New York. A **plebiscite** to decide on reunification—

either remaining a region of **Nigeria** or joining an independent Cameroon—was agreed on. Foncha's KNDP won the 11 February 1961 plebiscite by a landslide majority in favor of reunification with **French Cameroun** and won the general election of 1959.

Having won the reunification battle, Foncha, as prime minister of West Cameroon, led the **anglophone** delegation to the **Foumban Conference**, while the **francophone** delegation was led by Pres. **Ahmadou Ahidjo**. The new federal **constitution of 1961** guaranteed Foncha the post of vice president of the **Federal Republic of Cameroon**, a post that he held from 1961 to 1970. Foncha remained prime minister of West Cameroon until 1965. When the **Cameroon National Union (CNU)** was formed in 1966, Foncha supported it because in his opinion, reunification did not "exclude the possibility of the formation of any other party." Foncha was later made first vice chairman of the CNU.

In 1970, Foncha was replaced by **Solomon Tandeng Muna** as vice president of the Federal Republic of Cameroon. Having lost the post of West Cameroon's prime minister to **Augustin N. Jua** in 1965, Foncha was constrained to retire from active politics in 1970. On 18 December 1979, however, Ahidjo appointed him to the largely ceremonial post of grand chancellor of national orders.

When in 1985 the **Cameroon People's Democratic Movement Party (CPDM)** rose from the ashes of the CNU, Foncha was made its first vice president. On 9 June 1990, Foncha resigned from this post because, in his view, he was used only as a window dressing and the CPDM leadership treated him as if he had become an irrelevant nuisance that had to be ignored and ridiculed. He was also reacting to the government's slaughter of innocent anglophones during a 26 May 1991 demonstration in Bamenda. On 19 July 1990, he was replaced as grand chancellor of national orders. In recent years, Foncha identified himself with those anglophone political leaders who advocate a return to the 1961 federation and became a leader of the **Southern Cameroons National Council (SCNC)**. He also was a leading figure and chairman of the board of the **Bamenda University of Science and Technology (BUST)**.

A man of multiple national and foreign honors, Foncha has received favorable reviews as an exemplary figure in early Cameroon politics. A more revisionist orientation in Cameroon scholarship and opinion, however, blames his performance at the Foumban Conference for the current marginalization of the minority **anglophone** population. Foncha died on 10 April 1999.

FONDS D'AIDE ET DE COOPERATION. *See* FONDS D'INVESTISSEMENT DU DEVELOPPEMENT ECONOMIQUE ET SOCIAL DES TERRITOIRES D'OUTRE MER (FIDES).

FONDS D'INVESTISSEMENT POUR LE DEVELOPPEMENT ECONOMIQUE ET SOCIAL DES TERRITOIRES D'OUTRE-MER (FIDES). The French National Assembly passed into law this investment fund for economic and social development of the overseas territories on 30 April 1946. FIDES was envisaged as a long-term and last-minute effort toward development by the contribution of the French government and the various distinct territories. In Cameroun, the funds were used to finance two economic plans from 1947 to 1953 and 1953 to 1957. On a comparative basis, Cameroun's quota from FIDES was far higher than all of **French Equatorial Africa**. This was partially due to Cameroun's special status as a **trust territory** of the newly formed United Nations Organization. The total fund of 80 billion French francs invested in Cameroun during the 10-year period supported local infrastructure, did less for indigenous welfare, and boosted the fortunes of European-owned firms operating in the territory. Toward independence, FIDES was renamed Fonds d'Aide et du Coopération (FAC).

FONLON, BERNARD NSOKIKA (1924–1986). This former minister and a renowned Cameroon intellectual was born on 24 November 1924 at Kimbo, Nso, in **North West Province**. He did early education at Njinikom and secondary school at Christ the King College in Nigeria. He entered the Bigard Memorial Seminary on completion, and after teaching at **St. Joseph's College**, Sasse, **Buea**, he gave up his quest for priesthood to plunge into scholarly education. He enrolled in the University of Ireland, the Sorbonne, and Oxford University, obtaining several degrees in literature. He served as secretary at the prime minister's office of **Southern Cameroon** in 1961; chargé de mission and translator/interpreter at the Presidency (1961–64); and as member of the Federal Parliament from 1964 to 1970 simultaneously with his cabinet post of deputy minister of foreign affairs. He became minister of transport and then minister of ports and telecommunication before heading the Ministry of Health and Social Welfare (1970–71). On leaving governmental duties, Fonlon moved to the **University of Yaoundé**, rising to the rank of professor and serving as head of the Department of Negro–African Literature. He remained in the university until his retirement in 1984 after having published 12 works on language, culture, philosophy, and politics. He was an ardent promoter of **bilingualism,** which he tried to make a national obligation. In 1962, he founded the scholarly journal ***Abbia:*** *Cameroon Cultural Review*, which brought together contributions of leading Cameroon intellectuals since the early postindependence era. Fonlon died in Canada in August 1986 while on one of his many lecture trips abroad. He remained a member of the Central Committee and Political Bureau of the **Cameroon National Union (CNU) and Cameroon Peoples' Democratic Movement (CPDM)** until his death.

FOOD SELF-SUFFICIENCY. Food self-sufficiency is a goal yet to be accomplished by many African countries, but a goal that Cameroon has attained or been close to for several years. The goal is to grow internally adequate food for the population or to have a balance between food imports and food exports. Cameroon's enviable record is the combination of natural, economic, and political factors. Policies such as the **Green Revolution** and the various institutions set up by the government have improved the level of food self-sufficiency. However, the government's desire to increase export crop production frequently conflicts with the desire for food self-sufficiency.

The export of food to neighboring African countries, especially **Gabon**, has also become a significant aspect of Cameroon's food policy. By doing so, the country seeks to become the granary of Central Africa. *See also* AGRICULTURAL POLICY; AGROINDUSTRY STRATEGY; AGROPASTORAL SHOW.

FOOTBALL. *See* INDOMITABLE LIONS.

FORCED LABOR. This hated policy of conscription for labor under duress and unbearable human conditions was practiced in the territory during the era of foreign domination. It was begun by the Germans in 1884 in the face of repeated local resistance to conscription and resultant labor shortage. In addition to poor working conditions, marginal health standards, and meager pay, the local inhabitants were sometimes forced to work rather than pay their taxes. It was through such means that the Germans carried out the vast construction of roads, railways, and other public projects.

The French **mandate** period continued this policy in their attempt to extend the German-built Mittelkamerun rail line and in the pursuit of economic exploitation. The labor force recruited from outlying and distant areas passed through harsh conditions that led to thousands of deaths. Thus, much of the primary development of the territory was made possible by the sweat and blood of the local population under forced labor. Many local inhabitants from **French Cameroun** took refuge in **British Cameroons** to escape forced labor conditions, especially during 1922–26. *See also* MISE EN VALEUR; PRESTATION.

FOREIGN POLICY. Cameroon's foreign policy is based on the establishment of relations with every country on the basis of equality, reciprocity, mutual respect of sovereignty, and noninterference. Such a policy is designed to contribute to harmonizing international relations and creating a truly and fully human international community. According to Pres. **Paul Biya**, this policy leads toward a more interdependent humankind, which ensures the autonomy of weak nations and protects their freedom through peaceful coexistence. In reality, Cameroon remains closely aligned with and dependent on **France**.

It is the head of state who determines the foreign policy of Cameroon. The implementation of this policy is done with the help of a Ministry of Foreign Affairs, headed by a minister. The ministry consists of six directorates based on geographic and issue areas. As part of its diplomacy of presence, participation, and expansion, Cameroon also maintains embassies in all continents and belongs to a variety of international organizations at the subregional, continental, and world levels. *See also* CENTRAL AFRICAN REPUBLIC; CHAD; COMMONWEALTH; COMMONWEALTH OF INDEPENDENT STATES; CONGO; EQUATORIAL GUINEA; GABON; GERMANY; GREAT BRITAIN; NIGERIA; UNITED STATES.

FOREIGN TRADE. Cameroon is dependent on foreign trade with neighboring African and major industrialized countries. Its subregional trade takes place within the **Union Douanière Economique de l'Afrique Centrale (UDEAC)** framework in which Cameroon dominates in its export of cigarettes, beverages, **sugar**, cement, and other locally produced materials. In its trade with other African countries, Cameroon has historically depended on the import of bauxite from Guinea, which is processed into **aluminum** in **Edea**. Cameroon also trades extensively with **Nigeria,** although **smuggling** has become rampant.

The bulk of Cameroon foreign trade is carried out with Western industrialized countries. In particular, **France** plays a preponderant role in Cameroon's foreign trade. In 1996, France was the source of 40 percent of Cameroon's imports. With the discovery and refinery of **petroleum** for export in Cameroon, the **United States** has emerged as an important trading partner as well as **Germany**, **Great Britain**, Italy, Spain, and Japan.

Until the exploitation of petroleum, the bulk of Cameroon's export to the industrialized countries was mainly in primary crops such as **cocoa**, **coffee**, **bananas**, **palm products**, and **timber,** while it imported manufactured products. Because of the low and declining prices of primary raw materials in the world market, Cameroon frequently experiences an unfavorable balance with many industrialized countries in its foreign trade. The case of France is particularly significant. Although Cameroon had a trade surplus with France in the early 1960s, the pattern of trade relations has developed into an alarming trade deficit for Cameroon since the mid-1970s. This unfavorable situation has remained a source of worry to Cameroon given the heavy dependence of its economy on France. In their regular summits with French leaders, both former president **Ahmadou Ahidjo** and his successor, **Paul Biya,** have emphasized this incongruence as a disturbing factor in their bilateral relationship. The government believes that the country's economic crisis is partly rooted in this unfavorable foreign trade picture. Part of its strategy to overcome the situation is in the diversification of its trade ties away from France. In 1996, exports from Cameroon were valued at $1.9 billion and imports at $1.5 billion.

FOUDA, ANDRE (1930–1980). A very influential mayor of **Yaoundé** and party bulwark of the postindependence era, Fouda was born in Djoungolo, near Yaoundé, into a rich, land-owning, aristocratic family. Fouda had a busy political career as legislator, minister, party patron, and municipal administrator. Although an early member of **Jeunesse Camerounaise Française (Jeucafra)** who turned conservative, Fouda's greatest political profile was achieved as mayor of Yaoundé and later as treasurer of the **Cameroon National Union (CNU)** until his death.

FOUDA, DOMINIQUE SIMA. *See* SIMA FOUDA, DOMINIQUE.

FOULAH. *See* FULANI.

FOULBE. *See* FULANI.

FOUMBAN. Foumban is headquarters of the Noun Division and seat of the sultan of **Bamoum**. Foumban is generally regarded as the capital of Cameroon's artisanal industry and tourism has served as the town's most significant activity. The streets are lined with modern and traditional houses, with the museum, the sultan's palace, and the artisan's shops being the most widely visited spots of the town.

FOUMBAN CONFERENCE. This was the official constitutional conference that lay the groundwork of the **Federal Republic of Cameroon**. It was held 17–21 July 1961, bringing together leaders of the **République du Cameroun** and representatives of **Southern Cameroons**. The 37 delegates (25 **anglophones** and 12 **francophones**) were to translate into practical reality the **plebiscite** decision of 11 February that was an overwhelming approval for **reunification**. Issues for debate dealt with federal jurisdiction versus state autonomy, nature of institutions, cultural blending, and the idea of a loose versus a highly centralized federation. Led by Pres. **Ahmadou Ahidjo**, the delegates from Cameroun envisaged a strong and ever growing centralized government, whereas under **John Ngu Foncha**, the Southern Cameroon's delegation anticipated a loose federation. These conflicting visions of the future federal republic were reflected in Ahidjo's proposed federal constitution and the proposals of the anglophone camp. Five days constituted hardly enough time for resolving such intricate propositions. Both sides again met in **Yaoundé** in August to finally hammer out their differences. In the end, the **Constitution of the Federal Republic** resembled the centralized pattern of Ahidjo more than it reflected the loose framework of Foncha. In recent years, anglophone political activists have portrayed the conference as a dismal defeat for anglophone interests and heaped much blame on those, like Foncha, who represented Southern Cameroons.

FRANC ZONE. This term applies to all of the countries and groupings of countries that have their currencies linked to the French franc. Most of the former colonies of **France** in Africa, as well as **Equatorial Guinea**, are members of the franc zone.

In this monetary union each state or group of states issues its own currency, but the value of that currency is always pegged to the value of the franc, now at the rate of one French franc to 100 local francs. In Africa these are generally known as **"CFA francs."** There are two major groupings of states in Africa in the franc zone: those of former French West Africa and those of **French Equatorial Africa** (plus Equatorial Guinea). In addition, the Comoros (Indian Ocean) and several Pacific island states are in the franc zone. The former French colonies of North Africa have left the franc zone. From time to time a state may leave the group or rejoin (e.g., Mali).

To issue currency and regulate their use, a number of institutions have been established. These include the West African Monetary Union, the Central Bank of West African States, and the West African Development Bank. In addition, there is the **Bank of Central African States** and the **Development Bank of Central African States**.

Advantages accrue to the smaller economies of francophone Africa in this franc zone arrangement, particularly in having a convertible currency that is easily exchanged in world trade. But there are also disadvantages, especially as France has control over decisions about revaluation and devaluation of the currencies. Many argue that the francophone African currencies have been too highly valued, making their goods more expensive on the world market than those of their competitors.

FRANCE. France was the **mandate** and **trust** authority of the **League of Nations** and the United Nations for the larger portion of Cameroon from 1916 to 1960. Consequently, both countries entertain a privileged relationship to the present time. The secret Franco–Cameroun accord of 25 December 1959 helped to boost France's continuous tie to independent Cameroun. Today, France is Cameroon's biggest commercial, military, political, and cultural partner. Cameroon's attempts at independent initiatives from France have not lessened the strength of their relations. Some problems that have recently emerged include the treatment of the large number of citizens in each other's country, the trade and balance of payment deficits adversely affecting Cameroon, and the suspicions surrounding the post-**Ahidjo** transition. The frequency of top-level contact between both countries has led to a pragmatic relationship based on a history of long-standing mutual interests. However, Cameroon's attempts to lessen its economic dependence on France have led to a reduction of France's role as purchaser of exports and provider of imports. *See also* DIPLOMACY; FOREIGN TRADE; SECRET AGREEMENTS; TILLIER AFFAIR.

FRANCO–AFRICAN SUMMIT. There are numerous strands that tie the former French colonies to each other, to **France**, and even to other French-speaking territories. Among these are the **franc zone**, the **Francophone Summit**, the Franco–African summit, and **La Francophonie**.

The first Franco–African Summit was held in Paris in November 1973. Ten former colonies of France and one of Britain, the bilingual Mauritius, attended. These have become annual events, usually preceded by a Conference of Foreign Ministers that sets the agenda. The venue shifts between France and Africa each year. Summit conferences provide an opportunity to discuss a variety of issues of interest to the members, to serve as a dialogue between the North and the South, and to take stands on major political and economic issues of world interest.

The Third Summit (Paris, 1976) established a solidarity fund to assist the poorest African countries, whether or not these are francophone. At the seventh meeting (Nice, 1980), an outline plan for a French commonwealth was drawn up.

FRANCOPHONE. This term refers to Cameroonians whose secondary medium of expression is the French language or to refer to that portion of the country previously ruled by **France**. Historically, the grouping corresponds to the population subjected to the French **mandate** and **trust territory** administration. Today, francophones in Cameroon live mostly in the **Littoral**, **Center**, **South**, **Extreme North**, **North**, **Adamawa**, **West,** and **East Provinces**, and they form the bulk of Cameroon's population.

FRANCOPHONE SUMMIT. This is one of several strands that bind the ex-colonies of **France**, other French-speaking territories, and France together. The **Franco–African Summit** is another, similar strand.

The first Francophone Summit, properly titled the Conference of Francophone Countries and Communities, was held in Paris in February 1986. The leaders of 39 French-speaking states and representatives of three regions from five continents took part. At the 1995 summit, **La Francophonie** was established.

LA FRANCOPHONIE. In many respects this 52-member organization is similar to the **Commonwealth**. Numerous organizations exist to tie French-speaking countries together for economic, cultural, political, and other purposes. One of these, the **Francophone Summit**, was the founding organization in 1995, although movement in this direction had taken place at earlier summits. The organization's first secretary-general, Boutros Boutros-Ghali, took office in 1997; in 1998, the name "Organisation Internationale de la Francophonie" was adopted. The organization's supreme body is the summit. There is the secretary-general, a permanent council, and a ministerial conference. Associated organizations include the Francophone University Agency, the Senghor University, the International Association of Francophone Mayors, and the Francophone Parliamentary Assembly.

The purposes of La Francophonie include the development of democracy, the maintenance of peace, and the development of solidarity through cooperation to provide for economic growth. It is also a means for France to exert influence in its former colonies. Cameroon is a member of La Francophonie. *See also* COMMONWEALTH.

FRANGLAIS. This new mode of speech and language in contemporary Cameroon society is sometimes termed *Camfranglais*. Developed since the mid-1970s, franglais became even more popular in the late 1990s. It is the direct consequence of the country's bilingual heritage. Franglais consists of a mixture of French, English, and Cameroon vocabulary in the construction of phrases for day-to-day expression. The new language variety is predominant in the more heavily populated and urbanized regions of the country, where **francophones** and **anglophones** frequently interact. It is believed that marketplaces and coastal areas as well as ports and sports stadiums are the likely places where franglais originated. Some music stars in the country have utilized this new parlance for their songs and gained national prominence. Franglais is clearly appropriate for the less educated Cameroonian or school dropout, for whom it serves as a shortcut to **bilingualism**. Educators and language experts express fears that franglais could reflect negatively on the written and spoken language of school-age Cameroonians. *See also* PIDGIN ENGLISH.

FRENCH. Part 1, Article 3, of the **constitution (1996)** makes French one of Cameroon's two official languages. In reality, however, French is only a secondary language for the majority of Cameroonians, who are mostly proficient in their various local languages. The French language is mostly studied in schools and polished throughout the academic and professional career. *See also* ANGLOPHONE; BILINGUALISM; ENGLISH; FRANCOPHONE; FRANGLAIS.

FRENCH CAMEROUN. French Cameroun existed as a **mandate** and **trust territory** of **France** from 1916 to 1945 and 1946 to 1960, respectively. Despite its special status, French Cameroun was ruled as part of **French Equatorial Africa** alongside **Gabon**, **Congo**, **Chad,** and the Oubangui-Shari (today's **Central African Republic**). French Cameroun was administered by a **commissioner** appointed from Paris, but many local indigenes assimilated to the French ideals. These ***évolué***s were allowed to serve at lower levels. In the post-1945 era, the territory was successively allowed parliamentary representation in the **Assemblée Territoriale du Cameroun (ATCAM)**, Assemblée Représentative du Cameroun (ARCAM), and **Assemblée Législative du Cameroun**

(ALCAM). Despite the democratic option, **Union des Populations du Cameroun (UPC)** candidates were denied opportunities to gain parliamentary seats, and the party was outlawed in 1955. In 1957, the first nonautonomous Cameroun government was formed under **André-Marie Mbida**. **Ahmadou Ahidjo** succeeded Mbida in 1958 and led the country to independence in 1960 and **reunification** in 1961.

FRENCH EQUATORIAL AFRICA. This is the geographic and administrative distinction for French colonies in the subregion (1916–60). The colonies of French Equatorial Africa (**Gabon**, **Congo**, **Chad,** and the Oubangi-Shari) were border territories to **French Cameroun**. The French managed to maintain an artificial distinction between French Equatorial Africa and French Cameroun even though the same policies were applicable to both territories. In the later periods, Cameroun political parties and parliamentary representatives insisted on the respect of the territory's special status under the **mandate** and **trusteeship systems**.

FRONT NATIONAL UNIFIE (FNU). The FNU was an anti–***parti unifié*** coalition formed in May 1962. The FNU rejected Pres. **Ahmadou Ahidjo**'s proposal for a unified national party. The FNU consisted of various small opposition parties in the **East Cameroon** Assembly. It was largely identified as a loose four-leader coalition consisting of **Charles Okala**, **Theodore Mayi-Matip**, **André-Marie Mbida**, and **Marcel Bebey-Eyidi**. They believed Ahidjo's proposal would culminate in a dictatorship. The leaders were imprisoned. The FNU opposition was the last significant hindrance faced by Ahidjo in his quest for a *parti unifié*.

FRONT OF ALLIES FOR CHANGE (FAC). The Front, sometimes translated as "Allied Front for Change," was formed in September 1994 by 13 opposition parties to present a unified front in elections. **John Fru Ndi** was its first chair. He was succeeded by **Samuel Eboua**.

FRONT POPULAIRE DE L'UNITE ET LA PAIX (FPUP). FPUP was an outgrowth of a disintegrating **Union des Populations du Cameroun (UPC)**. The FPUP was formed after the general elections of 1960 by **Bamiléké** remnants of the UPC who resented the electoral failures resulting from UPC extremism. Composed essentially of young, forward-looking elements from the presumed UPC stronghold of the western Bamiléké region, they aimed at preserving their self-interests within the national objectives defined by the **Ahidjo** government. The FPUP represented the loss of UPC influence and dominance among the Bamiléké.

Its leaders included Pierre Kamdem Ninyim, Wandji Nkuimy, Philippe Achinguy, and **Victor Kanga**, all of whom served in various cabinet positions for the **East Cameroon** or the federal governments. By July 1961, the FPUP had finally been absorbed in the party unification process undertaken by Ahidjo's **Union Camerounaise (UC)**.

FRU NDI, JOHN (1941–). Leader of the most populous and radical opposition party, Fru Ndi, fondly called "Ni" (a prefix that is added as a sign of respect to elders of the village and to outsiders) was born on 7 July 1941, at Baba II village in Santa Subdivision, in the **North West Province**. He began primary education in 1952 in Baforchu Basel Mission School, and in 1954, he moved to the Native Authority School in Santa, where he graduated in 1957 with the **First School Leaving Certificate**.

In 1960, Fru Ndi began secondary education in Nigeria, where he enrolled in the Lagos City College. Alongside his studies, he worked with the West Coast Fisheries and as a traffic officer at Ikeja Airport, Lagos. His efficient services earned him a scholarship from Accra contractors to study piloting at the Zaria Flying School in 1966. But the pogroms in the north, followed by the outbreak of civil war in Nigeria, thwarted his dreams of becoming a pilot.

Fru Ndi returned to Cameroon and took up trading, hawking items such as apples, **bananas**, sugarcane, and groundnuts, before setting up a vegetable society in the **Bamenda** main market. He later took to selling newspapers and magazines and then became sole agent for two local newspapers, ***Cameroon Times*** and ***Cameroon Outlook,*** in the North West Province. This became the forerunner for his entering the book business. It was in this position that his leadership qualities were demonstrated when Fru Ndi set up Ebibi Book Center. His position as manager of a bookshop enabled him to establish acquaintances and contacts. His leadership qualities were enhanced when he became president of a local football (soccer) team, PWD Football Club in Bamenda, a position to which he was reelected several times. He also served as president of a local traditional association of the people of Baba II. Between 1987 and 1988, he served as president of the Bamenda branch of the Lions Club International and, in 1985, attended the Lions Club convention in the **United States**. Though a Protestant, he is a member and patron of the Catholic Focolare Movement.

Fru Ndi's flirtation with politics began in 1988 when, following the introduction of the multiple list system in legislative and council elections, he contested in his attempt to enter Bamenda Urban Council. Having lost the election, he petitioned against electoral malpractice.

On 26 May 1990, Fru Ndi proved his mettle in politics by launching the **Social Democratic Front (SDF)** in Bamenda, despite the overwhelming presence of armed troops in town to prevent such an occurrence. Since then he has remained at the helm of the SDF as chairman.

In August 1992, in anticipation of presidential elections announced for October, the **Alliance for the Reconstruction of Cameroon through the Sovereign National Conference (ARC-SNC)**, a group of a dozen opposition parties, chose Fru Ndi as a single candidate for the opposition in the presidential elections. In addition, an extraordinary convention of the SDF held in **Douala** equally endorsed Fru Ndi as the party's presidential candidate. Expecting an easy victory in the elections, Fru Ndi declared 1992 a year of change. This was not to be, for amid abundant proof of electoral fraud, the results of the election ran against popular expectations. Nevertheless, the Union for Change, a group of hard-core opposition parties, declared him winner. The government reacted by placing him under house arrest for over a month. In the **elections for president (1997)**, Fru Ndi joined with several other opposition leaders in a boycott to protest the government's failure to ensure fair elections.

FUFU/COUSCOUS. This dish is a West African specialty derived from the boiling and pounding of major local foodstuffs such as **maize**, **cocoyam**, **cassava**, yams, or plantains. It is usually served individually or eaten in small groups and swallowed with a variety of tasteful traditional soups in different parts of the country. Generally, it is widely believed that the *fufu* or couscous is best eaten with the fingers rather than with cutlery. The use of the term *couscous* in this context should not be confused with its use in North African cooking, where couscous is quite a different food—a type of grain.

FULAH. *See* FULANI.

FULANI (FULAH, FOULAH, FOULBE, PEUHL). The Fulani are a distinctive, influential, and dominant ethnic group in northern Cameroon. There are various theses on the origin of this group. The Fulani are spread across West Africa and are basically pastoralists, though a second group long ago settled in cities and towns. Pastoralism allowed them to migrate and wander into the northern Cameroon habitat. Their conquest over the local population was largely achieved through the ***jihad*** led by

Uthman Dan Fodio and **Modibo Adama** in the 19th century. The Fulani administrative and political control faced severe challenges under various colonial regimes.

Fulani influence continued into the postcolonial period. They rallied behind **Ahmadou Ahidjo**'s **Union Camerounaise,** which led to their acquisition of political power. Many Fulanis have been successful in business and political endeavors. Apart from their common cultural traits, the Islamic religion (*see* ISLAM) is also a force for unity among the Fulanis. Their language, Fulfulde, is spoken by the nearly 500,000 Fulanis in the country. However, their social, economic, and political influence in society declined with the controversy and political changes following the Ahidjo resignation. Apart from the former president, other leading Fulani include **Sarkifada Moussa Yaya**, **Maigari Bello Bouba**, **Youssoufa Daouda,** and most other prominent personalities from the Northern provinces. A Fulani group, the Bororo, is also present in the **North West Province**.

– G –

GABON. The Gabonese Republic is one of three countries on Cameroon's southern border. The population consists of several ethnic groups, including the **Fang,** who also occupy parts of Cameroon. Gabon has a population of about 1 million and occupies 103,347 square miles. The country is well endowed with mineral resources and has the highest per capita income in Africa. Many Cameroonians find employment in Gabon, and the country is a good market for Cameroon food products. Gabon is a member of **Union Douanière Economique de l'Afrique Centrale (UDEAC)** and the **franc zone**.

GANTY, VINCENT (unknown). A political activist in the 1930s, Ganty was a non-Cameroonian African who served as a spokesperson for the **Duala** grievances in Paris. The Duala requested action against German land expropriation policy in Cameroon. Ganty became self-appointed leader of the Duala claims before the **League of Nations** Mandate Commission. He also helped to articulate newfound Duala criticism against the French administration. Although Ganty probably hailed from Guinea he regularly presented himself as future leader of an independent Cameroon. *See also* MANDATE SYSTEM.

GAROUA. This was the capital city of **Northern Cameroon,** which was reduced to three provinces in 1983. Since then, Garoua has been the headquarters of one of the three provinces, the **North**. Its original inhabitants have since disappeared, and only small traces of Fali presence remain. The **Fulani** invasion and hegemony in the area turned Garoua into the capital of a Fulani chiefdom, or *lamidat*.

Despite the presence of foreign trade in the early colonial period, Garoua continued to lag behind the other towns of the country due to its distance form the centers of authority. At independence, the policy of **balanced development**, enunciated by Pres. **Ahmadou Ahidjo**, who hailed from Garoua, enabled the city to grow into an industrial, communication, economic, and tourism center. From a population of about 30,000 in 1967, Garoua's population was 63,900 in 1976. The population has continued to rise due to the high level of migratory activity in the area.

It was in Garoua that President Ahidjo formed the **Union Camerounaise** in 1958 and held the first Congress of the **Cameroon National Union (CNU)** in 1969.

GARRI (TAPIOCA). *Garri* is the most widely consumed derivative of **cassava**. Harvested cassava is peeled, grated, and roasted to produce white or yellow flour, *garri*. Compared to other foodstuffs, it is relatively cheap and has been widely used in the urban areas by the working-class population as a substitute for more nutritious, more expensive food. *Garri* can be soaked in cold water and sweetened for a drink. It can also be boiled in hot water and eaten with any locally prepared sauce. Except for the migrant Nigerians in the country, no particular ethnic group considers *garri* as its staple; nonetheless, it has become a widespread favorite.

GENDARMERIE. This quasi-military command and security force is common in francophone Africa. Gendarmes are used to maintain general law and order and to conduct investigative operations required for sustaining the integrity of the territory. In this respect, the competence of the gendarmerie was more expansive than that of the police force. A French military official served as commandant of the gendarmerie from its inception until February 1966. During this period, the indigenes from **Ahmadou Ahidjo**'s **North Cameroon** constituted the bulk of uniformed gendarmes in the country. Gendarmes played a heavy-handed role in the suppression of public dissent and terrorist insurgency in the 1960s. The gendarmerie operated as a federal force. and its jurisdictional powers were more strongly resented in the **anglophone West Cameroon**. It is widely believed that **corruption** is rampant within the gendarmerie.

In February 1966, the General Delegation of the National Gendarmerie was created, with **Issa Bakary** as its first delegate-general. The delegation consisted of the gendarmerie high command, an administrative and technical center, a technical advisory, various gendarmerie legions, and the legion of the Republican Guard at the Presidency of the Republic. Following the foiled **coup attempt of 6 April 1984**, the Republican Guard was disbanded. The gendarmerie continues to play a significant role in national defense and internal security. This has led to serious conflict with the police force in the country. The continued dominance of indigenes from the North is reflected in the successive appointments of Northerners as delegate-generals of the institution. *See also* AMADOU ALI.

GENERAL CERTIFICATE OF EDUCATION (GCE). An examination is required for secondary and postsecondary graduates in **anglophone** Cameroon. At the secondary level it is known as the ordinary level, while at the postsecondary level it is known as the advanced level. The GCE was written, graded, and published by the University of London until January 1977. The examination consisted of various subject tests. In June 1977, Cameroon's Ministry of National Education organized the GCE examination for the first time at both levels.

Despite the growing disenchantment on the performance rate in the GCE, the anglophone population resisted government's reform and harmonization proposal in 1983. The proposals would have made the format of the GCE identical to that of the **francophone Brevet d'Etudes du Premier Cycle (BEPC)** and ***baccalauréat*** exams. Following anglophone protests and the establishment of a Commission of Inquiry under Professor Joseph Mboui, secretary-general at the Ministry of National Education, the GCE was allowed to continue to exist in its original form.

Following the poor management and organization of the GEC by the Ministry of National Education between 1992 and 1993, anglophones, through the Teacher's Association of Cameroon (TAC) and the Confederation of Anglophone Parents–Teachers Associations of Cameroon (CAPTAC), successfully demanded control of the management and organization of the exam. Consequently, in 1993, the government created the Cameroon General Certificate of Education (GCE) Board. Since its creation, the board has introduced a number of reforms. Performance has also improved. In the 1997 session, the advanced level pass stood at 49.45 percent, up from 41.95 percent in

1996, while the ordinary level pass results stood at 50.05 percent as against 44.22 percent in 1996. *See also* EDUCATION.

GEORGE, SAMPSON A. (1922–1959). One of the early politicians in **Southern Cameroons**, George was born in **Mamfe** on 20 November 1922, to a Nigerian father, Henry George, and a Cameroonian mother. George studied in Mamfe as well as Lagos and Port Harcourt, Nigeria. He served in the postal service before becoming a freelance journalist. He became interested in politics and was a prominent member of the Zikist Vanguard before emerging as an active trade unionist. He joined other political organizations, including the **Cameroons Youth League (CYL),** where he was secretary-general, and the Mamfe Town Native Authority. Under the Macpherson Constitution, George was one of the "Original Thirteen" Southern Cameroonians who was elected to the Eastern House of Assembly in Nigeria. He was also a member of the Nigerian House of Representatives in Lagos. He was a strong advocate of the **reunification** between British and **French Cameroun** and in 1956 outlined his ideas in his *Kamerun Unification: Being a Discussion of a 7-Point Solution of the Unification Problem*. George never lived to see his cherished ideals of independence and reunification materialize because he died in a London hospital on 10 October 1959.

GERMAN GOVERNORS OF KAMERUN (1884–1915).

Soden, Julius von: 26 May 1885–14 February 1891
Zimmerer, Eugen von: 15 April 1891–13 August 1895
Puttkamer, Jesko von: 13 August 1895–9 May 1907
Seitz, Dr. Theodor: 9 May 1907–27 August 1910
Gleim, Dr. Otto: 28 August 1910–29 January 1912
Ebermaier, Karl: 29 January 1912–1915

GERMANY. Because Germany was a former **protectorate** power in **Kamerun** (1884–1916), German–Cameroon relations have a lasting legacy in history. Despite the loss of **World War I**, the cravings of the pan-Germanists and the territorial quest of Hitler continued to bring the African continent to the spotlight. In Cameroon, many old people maintained an unflinching attachment to Germany through language. In more recent years, after an initial visit by **Ahmadou Ahidjo** in 1968, Pres. Heinrich Lubke visited Cameroon in 1975, and Cameroon's return visit came in 1986 by Pres. **Paul Biya**. German chancellor Helmut Kohl visited Cameroon in 1987 to seal a growing relationship between the two countries. Trade has become an important component of the Cameroon–German relationship, as evidenced in the first German trade fair in black Africa held in **Yaoundé** in October 1986. Prominent areas in the relationship include cultural exchange, construction and engineering, and electronics contracts, although these are still relatively low-level ties when compared to Cameroon's wide-ranging bonds with **France**. For the Germans, Cameroon serves as a response to a historic calling and a breakaway from French domination of much of Africa, while for Cameroon upgrading relations with Germany helps to reduce its dependence on France. *See also* FOREIGN POLICY.

GHOST TOWN OPERATIONS. The ghost town (*ville morte*) operation was the civil disobedience campaign that rocked Cameroon between May and December 1991. A brainchild of Mbua Massock, the campaign was launched by the National Coordination Committee of Opposition Parties (NCCOP), with the avowed aim of compelling the government to convene a sovereign national conference to lay down guidelines for future elections and governance in Cameroon. The methods adopted varied from nonviolent action to confrontation: taxis were grounded, together with all other commercial vehicles; shops and hospitals were closed; the population was advised not to pay taxes; official holidays (e.g. national day celebrations) were boycotted; people stayed away from their job sites under threat of being subjected to beatings; individuals who identified themselves with the government in power were either beaten or had their property burned. The main brewery company suffered losses and destruction of property because it was purported that some politicians owned shares in it. On 24 May 1991, the operation launched the so-called "**Yaoundé** Plan of Action," with the declared objective to starve the capital and bring the government to submission. People were advised to stockpile items and stay indoors.

Government's response came quick and fast. In an address to Parliament, Pres. **Paul Biya** categorically ruled out the convening of any national conference, lashed out at opposition parties for their policy of confrontation, and stated that they could only claim to speak for the Cameroon people after they had been elected to Parliament, banned the NCCOP, and proscribed all public meetings organized by NCCOP. The army was called in to restore calm, and seven of the 10 provinces were transformed into operational command regions, with operational commanders. The remaining three provinces that did not fall under this arrangement were the strongholds of the ruling party. In addition the government carried out mass arrests of protesters, and the media, both written and audiovisual, were heavily censored.

Biya's stand worsened the situation. The NCCOP urged Cameroonians to strengthen the Yaoundé Plan of Action. Worse still, the nation's economic nerve center, **Douala**, was paralyzed by strikes and sit-ins. In addition, opposition parties planned a march on the presidential residence in Yaoundé, and clashes with the forces of law and order multiplied. The government's firm stand seemed to have paid off for the ghost town operation, which, hitherto, ran for seven days a week and now was reduced to five days, with Saturdays and Sundays as days for replenishing. In addition, the planned march on Yaoundé was frustrated.

On the whole, the effects on the country were telling. Politically, instability became the order of the day. Economically, prices of foodstuffs and other articles skyrocketed, creating favorable conditions for black marketing; the communication system stopped functioning; the only commercial port in the country stopped functioning; many businesses could not operate for fear of being burned down.

As the economy went further downhill, Biya was forced to budge. Short of convening a sovereign national conference, which was the main demand of the initiators of the civil disobedience campaign, Biya invited leaders of all opposition parties to a conference, to lay down rules for the democratic process in Cameroon. This invitation led to the holding of the **Tripartite Conference** in Yaoundé in November 1991. Thereafter, the ghost town operations dwindled. At the Yaoundé Tripartite Conference, the opposition parties agreed to call off the ghost town operations. See also ALLIANCE FOR THE RECONSTRUCTION OF CAMEROON THROUGH THE SOVEREIGN NATIONAL CONFERENCE (ARC-SNC).

GLEIM, OTTO. Gleim was the fifth **German governor** in **Kamerun** (1910–12). He was widely remembered for his energetic support for the **Dualas** against a proposed German project to expropriate Duala property. The governor also opposed any bargain that involved the surrender of the Cameroon territory near **Chad** in exchange for parts of French Congo.

GONI WADAY. Goni Waday led a Mahdist uprising against German colonial rule in August 1907 in the northern areas of **Kamerun**. The Mahdist group was opposed to another Muslim group, the Usmanuya group, which collaborated with the Germans. A second Mahdist leader was **Hayatu ibn Sa'id**.

GOUVERNEMENTSRAT. *See* ADVISORY COUNCIL

GOVERNORS. Under the provincial system, governors serve as administrative heads of Cameroon's 10 provinces. The use of governors in postindependence Cameroon began in 1972 with the establishment of administrative provinces. They replaced the **federal inspectors of administration** who had served as direct representatives of the head of state in the previous federal structure of government. Governors supervise the activities of the ***préfets*** within their areas of jurisdiction. They are appointed by presidential decree and hold yearly meetings presided over by the minister of territorial administration. Unlike *préfets,* governors are not normally recruited from former National School of Administration and Magistry (ENAM) graduates. They are usually drawn from a pool of senior and competent officials of the country's civil service system. The position of governor apparently will be abandoned when the **constitution of 1996** regional system is operational.

GRAND DÉBAT. The Grand Débat idea was **Paul Biya**'s response to calls for a sovereign national conference. First announced on 23 March 1993, government proposed discussion of the **constitution of 1972**. Soon after, the government produced a draft constitution, apparently emanating from the earlier **Tripartite Conference**. Prepared by the secretary-general of the Presidency, **Joseph Owona**, this became known as the Owona constitution. Various organizations produced draft constitutions, but there was little opportunity for "Grand Débat" until late in 1994, when Biya invited party leaders to a Constitutional Consultative Committee. The government produced a revised draft of the Owona Constitution as the basis of discussion, but the document did little to meet opposition demands. The sessions of the committee made no progress and were essentially boycotted by most important opposition leaders. The next step was the government's decision to introduce a revised document for discussion and adoption in the November 1995 session of the **National Assembly**. On 18 January 1996, the new constitution was adopted. As opposed to the sovereign national conference concept, which envisaged open debate by all interested parties, the Grand Débat process had been dominated by the Biya government, and the resulting **constitution of 1996** was largely in keeping with Biya's desires—a strong president in a highly centralized system. See also ALLIANCE FOR THE RECONSTRUCTION OF CAMEROON THROUGH THE SOVEREIGN NATIONAL CONFERENCE (ARC-SNC).

GRASSFIELD/GRASSLAND. This open vegetational feature of land is characteristic of the interior areas between Widekum in the **South West Province,** through the **Bamenda** Plateau in the **North West,** into the savannah plains and highlands of the **Western Province** of Cameroon. The region is relatively fertile for agricultural production, and this characteristic has led to the development of peculiar cultural attributes. Linguistically, the people of the region are generally characterized as semi-Bantu, and they share similar political and social institutions. Inheritance in the social structure is essentially patrilineal, while the political system is centrally organized and headed by a powerful **chief** or a **fon**. The people of the Grassfield also excel in pottery, metalworks, sculpture, and other handicraft activities. This extreme diversity of techniques and skills are expressed in a rich culture that is jealously preserved despite the open assault by modernizing influences. It is this tenacity of history and tradition that sometimes accounts for the pejorative view of the Grassfield (Graffi) by Southern peoples who live along the coast.

GREAT BRITAIN. Great Britain was **mandate** and **trust** authority of the **League of Nations** and the United Nations of the smaller portion of Cameroon from 1916 until 1961. However, the British failed to exercise direct authority over the territory, neglecting their special status. For over 40 years, **British Cameroon** was administered as part of **Nigeria**. Furthermore, the separation between **Northern** and **Southern Cameroons** led to a troubling aftermath. In 1961, Northern Cameroons voted in a **plebiscite** to join independent **Nigeria,** while Southern Cameroons decided to forge its destinies with independent Cameroon.

In the 1990s, relations between the two countries became closer and more positive, symbolized most dramatically when in 1995 Cameroon became a member of the **Commonwealth**. *See also* NORTHERN CAMEROONS CASE.

GREEN REVOLUTION. This economic development strategy was designed to boost agricultural productivity. The Green Revolution was originally conceived for the specialized growth of **rice**, **wheat,** and **maize** in Latin America and Southeast Asian countries. Since then, the Green Revolution has been popularized across other developing countries as an effective model for higher agricultural yields through the intensive use of capital, chemical fertilizers, improved seeds, and other technological advances.

The Cameroon government launched this strategy for its agricultural development during the first national **agropastoral show** in **Buea** in

March 1973. The Green Revolution was geared toward eliminating archaic methods of production and various constraints on small farmer production. Although directly targeted at the farmer, the Green Revolution rhetoric broadly envisioned raising the awareness of the entire population toward respect for agriculture and optimum development of the soil.

The Green Revolution led to the creation of multiple agricultural institutions, including the **National Fund for Rural Development (FONADER)** and various **cooperatives**. The Green Revolution has endured as a popular slogan of governmental authorities and was credited for the high level of **food self-sufficiency** attained by Cameroon. However, these ambitious designs did not revolutionize the pattern of agriculture in the country. Alongside increasing mechanization techniques, agricultural practice is still largely dominated by rudimentary techniques of small rural farmers. *See also* AGROINDUSTRIAL STRATEGY; INDIVIDUAL CROPS.

GROUPE DE HUIT. This was a parliamentary coalition in the **Assemblée Législative du Cameroun (ALCAM)**. The coalition was composed of eight representatives from the **Mouvement d'Action Nationale du Cameroun (MANC)** party and consisted of **Betote Akwa**, **Charles Assale**, **Paul Soppo Priso**, Gaston Behle, Hans Dissake, Ekwabi Ewane, Aloys Ntonga, and François Obam. The Group de Huit was essentially southern politicians opposed to the growing dominance of the **Ahmadou Ahidjo** party, the **Union Camerounaise,** with strong roots in the North.

GROUPE DES PROGRESSISTES. This parliamentary coalition of 10 representatives in the **Assemblée Nationale du Cameroun (ANCAM)** between 1960 and 1961 consisted of the **Mouvement d'Action Nationale du Cameroun (MANC)** and the **Parti Socialiste du Cameroun (PSC),** which joined in a government coalition with **Ahmadou Ahidjo**'s **Union Camerounaise (UC)** in May 1960. Two of the group's prominent members, **Charles Assale** and **Charles Okala**, were appointed first prime minister and foreign minister of the **République du Cameroun,** respectively. In 1961, the Groupe des Progressistes dissolved and merged with the UC.

– H –

HAMADJODA ADJOUDJI (1937–). This longtime minister of livestock, fisheries, and animal industries was born in 1937 in Banyo, **Adamawa**

Province. He did his elementary education at the Rural School in Banyo and the Regional School in **Ngaoundéré** before proceeding for secondary and high school studies to the Collège Moderne in **Garoua** and later to the **Lycée Leclerc** in **Yaoundé**. In 1963, he passed the examinations into the French National Schools for Veterinary Sciences and studied successively in Alford and later at the Faculty of Medicine in Paris. In 1968, he graduated with a doctorate in veterinary sciences and a special diploma for veterinary services in tropical countries. On his return home in 1969, he worked in Ngaoundéré in various specialized functions until 1974, when he was appointed managing director of the Company for the Development and Exploitation of Animal Production (SODEPA). Adjoudji served in this function until his nomination to the cabinet on 7 July 1984, as minister of livestock, fisheries, and animal industries. He later served as secretary for youth affairs in the Central Committee of the **Cameroon People's Democratic Movement**. On 7 December 1997, Hamadjoda Adjoudji was reappointed to his post as minister of livestock, fisheries, and animal industries in Biya's 22d government.

HANNON. Hannon was a Phoenician explorer from Carthage. He sailed into the Bight of Biafra in the fifth century B.C. and recorded seeing eruptions of a large volcano that he called "The Chariot of the Gods." It was later widely believed that the volcano is the contemporary **Mount Cameroon**.

HARMONIZATION. This is an educational policy designed to provide similarity, congruence, and equivalence between the school systems of **anglophone** and **francophone** Cameroon. The process involves unifying the contents of courses, the length of various educational cycles, and the common use of teaching models in both systems. Harmonization also involves creating appropriate equivalences for various certificates and degrees earned at home and abroad. The quest for harmonization led to the creation of a Service of Equivalence in the Ministry of National Education. The term *harmonization* is frequently used to define the process of bringing together the French and British inheritances in other spheres of activity. *See also* EDUCATION.

HAYATU IBN SA'ID. Hayatu ibn Sa'id was a leader of the radical Mahdist group of Muslims that opposed the imposition of German colonial rule in northern **Kamerun** in the period around 1900. *See also* GONI WADAY.

HEWETT, EDWARD H. Hewett was the belatedly dispatched British itinerant consul who arrived "too late" on 19 July 1884, one week after the German annexation of **Kamerun** had taken place. Attempts by Hewett to open strong contacts with other Kamerun chiefs who did not sign the German treaty were unsuccessful. Nevertheless, Hewett managed to hold onto the Victoria (now **Limbe**) area as a vital British base until 21 April 1885, when this was ceded to German control.

HIGH COMMISSIONER. *See* COMMISSIONER.

HOLLONG, ETIENNE. A former member of the defunct Republican Guard, Hollong was a key figure in the **destabilization plot** against the state announced by Pres. **Paul Biya** on 22 August 1983. He was born at Toupouri in **North Cameroon** but never converted to **Islam**. He served in the reserved area of presidential security under Pres. **Ahmadou Ahidjo** and into the transition era. He had gained a reputation as the elite marksman in the ranks of the Republican Guard. In two meetings with his former bosses (Capt. Ahmadou Salatou and Cmdt. Ibrahim Oumharou) and Ahidjo loyalists, Hollong was charged to execute a secret and undisclosed mission. Hollong informed the new deputy director of presidential security, who arrested Salatou and Oumharou. Both men were detained, tried, and imprisoned while Hollong was decorated and promoted in 1984.

HOLT, JOHN (1842–1904). Holt was an influential English businessman. He took over the commercial activities of another English merchant, James Lynslager, following his death in 1864. In 1867, he founded the John Holt, Ltd., company in Liverpool and established an agency in Bimbia, along the Cameroon coast. During the British period in Cameroon, the John Holt company located in Victoria (**Limbe**) and became the most important trading store until the mid-1960s.

HOLY GHOST FATHERS. *See* CATHOLIC CHURCH.

HOUSE OF CHIEFS. *See* WEST CAMEROON HOUSE OF CHIEFS.

HUGHES, JEFFERY (1935–). In 1996, Jeffery Hughes, a 61-year-old Australian businessman, was convicted in Australia of plotting to overthrow the **Biya** government. For a period of time, he had been gathering weapons to supply an attempt to either overthrow Biya or establish an independent English-speaking country in the **anglophone** provinces. No information has been made available to link Hughes to any individual or group in Cameroon, although there are rumors of attempts to recruit anglophones resident in Europe and the **United States** to take part in a violent revolution to make anglophone Cameroon an independent state. *See also* ZERO OPTION.

HUMAN RIGHTS. Essentially, these are the inalienable rights of self-expression, representation, decent living conditions, and fair treatment under given circumstances. In the Cameroonian political lexicon, the government proclaims its adherence to the inalienable and sacred rights of the human being. It affirms its attachments to the fundamental freedoms embodied in the Universal Declaration of Human Rights. However, the government tends to elevate the "collective and sovereign will of the people" above individual human rights. For this reason, the country has been featured prominently in yearly issues of the Amnesty International reports. The concerns of the institution have ranged from judicial inadequacies, religious persecution, and political repression to cases of prisoners of conscience. Government authorities have persistently denied such reports. The **Ahmadou Ahidjo** regime was believed to be inflexible to appeals by Amnesty International, and the **Paul Biya** administration is also held accountable by the organization for identical rights abuses.

Under the Biya regime, however, efforts hove been made to give a face-lift to the country's poor human rights record. On 8 November 1990, decree 90/1459 created a National Commission on Human Rights and Freedoms. The commission is empowered to inspect penitentiary services—police stations, gendarmeries—and to submit a report to the authorities concerned. Dr. Solomon Nfor Gwei has been the chairman of this commission since its creation. However, almost no funding is provided for commission activities and so it has proven to be ineffective. Despite the creation of the commission, critics doubt its effectiveness, especially as the country's human rights record has not improved. The main detention centers still exist; they include the Tchollire Re-education Center, the Yoko Labour Camp, and Tignère in the **North;** Mantoum in the **Western Province;** and Loumie and Yokadouma in the Southeast. Various Cameroon groups have arisen to defend human rights; among the most significant is the Human Rights Defence Group, headed by **Albert Mukong** and based in **Bamenda**.

HUMAN RIGHTS DEFENCE GROUP. *See* HUMAN RIGHTS.

HYDROELECTRICITY. Cameroon has great hydroelectric potential (500,000 megawatts), and portions of this are being exploited. The three major dams at **Edea**, Lagdo, and Songboulou produced almost three million kilowatt hours of electricity in 1995, 95 percent of all electricity in the country. An additional dam, the Nachtigal project, is under construction. Cameroon's **aluminum** production is based on the provision of inexpensive electricity from the Edea Dam.

– I –

IBO. The Ibo are an ethnic group in the South and Eastern regions of neighboring **Nigeria**. Ibo flooded into **Southern Cameroons** throughout the period of British **mandate** and **trusteeship** rule. They engaged in and almost dominated petty commerce activity in Victoria (**Limbe**), **Tiko,** and **Kumba** and were active in agriculture. Since independence, they have also established in **Bamenda** and have moved into **Douala** and **Yaoundé** in the pursuit of trade opportunities. The Ibo presence and domination in petty trading and other sectors contributed to an anti-Ibo feeling in the preindependence era. Nevertheless, during the Nigerian Civil War (1967–70), many Ibos fled their country as refugees into **West Cameroon**.

IBRAHIM, SALLE (?–1984). Salle was commander of the Presidential Guard during the transition period between the **Ahmadou Ahidjo** and **Paul Biya** regimes. He was military leader of the **coup attempt of 6 April 1984.** He hailed from the North and was ostensibly closer to former president Ahidjo. Colonel Salle used the pretext of an impending transfer of the presidential guards to rally a few hundred of them with sophisticated military equipment to rebel against President Biya. After early successes, the mutiny was crushed by local forces. Salle was dismissed, court-martialed, and executed. The Republican Guard was disbanded following the coup attempt.

ID-UL-FITR. *See* RAMADAN.

INDIGENAT. This name refers to the entire range of rules and penalties generally utilized to administer the mass of local indigenes in **French Cameroun**. It consisted of a clearly defined legal regime that restricted the people's participation in various sociopolitical activities and benefits. The *indigénat* was specifically decreed in 1924 for French territories and later applied to the **mandate** territories such as Cameroon. It was abolished in 1946 following the **Brazzaville Conference**.

INDIRECT RULE. Indirect rule is the colonial system of administration in which African rulers were allowed to exercise authority on behalf of the European colonial power. The policy of indirect rule is largely identified with the British colonial system in Africa. It was established by Lord Frederick Lugard in the period in which he served in Northern **Nigeria**. Indirect rule was later applied in other African regions of the British empire. In the **Southern Cameroons** territory, the British sought cooperation with existing chiefs, especially in the Bamenda Division, and attempted to create more centralized systems of authority in other divisions where such power structures were absent. Indigenous and appointed **chiefs** were to perform the major functions of government, especially on matters of taxation, law, succession to leadership, and community boundaries. Divisional officers were to stay in close contact with the local leaders. Relations between British officials and local authorities were not particularly harmonious. Conflicts of interest prevailed, and many chiefs were deposed or sentenced to prison during the British period. Apart from the need to preserve cultural unity, the British were constrained to adopt indirect rule because of practical shortcomings such as meager material resources, the scarcity of personnel, and lack of popular legitimacy. The greatest irony of the indirect rule policy was that the British transferred power to the Western-educated African elites rather than the traditional authorities whom they had courted throughout their period in the territory. *See also* DIRECT RULE; RESIDENTS.

INDOMITABLE LIONS. This rather ostentatious title of the Cameroon national football (soccer) team was decreed on 31 October 1972 in the aftermath of the Eighth African Nations Cup debacle. After this, the team entered a period of severe crisis from 1972 to 1978 and failed to live up to the expectations of the authorities and its supporters. In 1979, the Indomitable Lions began making their presence felt across Africa and the outside world. They qualified for the 13th edition of the African Nations Cup in Libya and honorably represented Cameroon in the 1982 and 1990 World Cups. During the 1990 World Cup, they became the first African nation to qualify for the quarterfinals of the competition. They played in the 1984 Olympic Games in Los Angeles and won the African Nations Cup in 1984 and 1988. After the 1990 World Cup expedition, the team once again entered a period of severe crisis, reflected in its mediocre performances in the 1994 World Cup in the **United States** and the African Nations Cup in Burkina Faso in March 1998. This showing notwithstanding, the Lions qualified for the 1998 World Cup in France. The name, the Indomitable Lions, has always been a popular one for **sports** fans and a publicity symbol for the country.

Football is Cameroon's most popular sport, and its successes and failures have become a matter of national pride. The sense of Cameroon identity and pride probably has never been stronger than in the aftermath of the 1990 World Cup performance of the Indomitable Lions. Cameroon's national football hero is Roger Milla.

INSTITUT D'EMISSION DE L'AFRIQUE EQUATORIALE FRANÇAISE. *See* BANK OF CENTRAL AFRICAN STATES.

INTERMINISTERIAL COMMITTEE ON INTELLIGENCE. Created by presidential decree of December 1986, this committee was charged with making periodic assessments of information and intelligence concerning the internal and external security of the nation. Its secretariat is headed by the special chief of staff to the president. It meets once a month on summons by its chairman, who can call a meeting as often as he deems necessary.

INTERNATIONAL MONETARY FUND (IMF). The IMF was founded in July 1944 with the purposes of promoting international monetary cooperation, expanding world trade, assisting members with balance of payment problems, and providing technical assistance. In recent years, it has played a significant role in Africa in relation to the debt crisis. It often works closely with the **World Bank**. It is seen by many in Africa as a source of undesirable interference in the domestic economic affairs of sovereign African states. There is a board of governors, a board of directors, and a managing director. The headquarters is in Washington, D.C.

As Cameroon's economy went into severe decline in the 1980s and 1990s, the IMF, along with the World Bank and major aid-giving countries, played an increasingly important and powerful role in pressuring the Cameroon government to take steps to improve the economy. **Structural adjustment programs (SAPs)** were to bring about economic and political reforms.

INVESTMENT CODES. These consist of the various policy guidelines set by government to determine conditions for local and foreign investments in the country. Overall, investment codes are aimed at encouraging the participation of private foreign interests in the Cameroon economy. Underlying Cameroon's posture on investment is the policy of **planned liberalism**.

The first investment code was passed in June 1960 by Law 60/64 and has been renewed or changed over the years. In essence, Cameroon's investment codes have been particularly favorable to private investment. The turbulence and political uncertainty of the early independence period was a decisive factor in the determination to entice worried private economic interests to invest in the country. In response to the economic crisis and to pressure exerted via the **structural adjustment program (SAP)**, Cameroon's investment codes have been altered to provide more room for private investment, foreign and domestic, and less interference and involvement by the government. The current investment regulation was set up in 1990, and new tariff codes were introduced in 1994. The Investment Code approves and promotes investment. Foreign and local investors enjoy the same rights. New small and medium-size enterprises require 35 percent local equity; there is no restriction on larger companies. Reserved sectors include **petroleum**, water, telecommunications, **aluminum,** and **cotton** in which direct foreign investment is not allowed, but equipment and services may be provided to the parastatals. The Cameroon Investment Code, introduced in 1990 and amended in 1994, offers a package of incentives for investors.

ISLAM. The conversion of Cameroonians to Islam dates back to the early activities of traders and pastoralists in the North. The pacific mode of conversion was accelerated at the beginning of the 19th century through the holy war of conquest (the ***jihad***), led by a leading **Fulani** warrior, **Uthman Dan Fodio**. Proselytizing by Muslim teachers is still common in northern Cameroon. The major non-Muslim groupings in the North are the Massa, Mataka, Kapsiki, and Mofu. Generally, the non-Muslims in the area are referred to as ***Kirdi*** (which translates literally as "pagans").

Apart from the northern provinces, the **Bamoum** in the **Western Province** have adhered to the Islamic faith since the conversion of the 16th sultan. The actual number of Muslims in the country is not well established, but small fractions of adherents also exist among the **Tikar**, Wute, Gbaya, Fali, Nsaw, and **Bamiléké** groupings. Islamic schools and institutions are also located across the country. It is estimated that 20 percent of the population, or about 2,800,000 Cameroonians, follow the Islamic faith. *See also* MUSLIM POPULATIONS; RAMADAN.

ISSA BAKARY (1940–). A former delegate-general for the National **Gendarmerie**, Bakary was born in Lombo, near **Garoua** in the present-day **North Province** (Benue Division). After primary and secondary education, he entered the National School of Administration and Magistracy (ENAM) and the Institut des Hautes Etudes d'Outre Mer in France, where he graduated as a civil administrator. On his return home, he became the first Cameroonian to head the National Gendarmerie in 1970. He served in this post until November 1982, when he was removed in absentia (while on medical treatment in France) on the weekend of the Ahidjo–Biya transition. Thus, Issa Bakary was the first "unpolitical" casualty of the regime transition from **Ahmadou Ahidjo** to **Paul Biya**. With the introduction of multiparty politics in December 1990, he joined the **National Union for Democracy and Progress (UNDP)** and was instrumental in the drawing up of a platform of action between the **Cameroon People's Democratic Movement (CPDM)** and the UNDP that allowed the latter to join President Biya's 22d government of December 1997.

– J –

JAMOT, EUGENE (1879–1937). This French medical doctor is famed for his fight against sleeping sickness. Born on 14 November 1879, Jamot joined the military as a medical doctor. He served in **Chad** and **Congo** before his transfer to **French Cameroun** in 1922. He played an active role in the prevention, research, and treatment of sleeping sickness until his retirement in 1936.

JANTZEN UND THORMAHLEN. This Hamburg commercial and trading firm played a significant role in the German annexation of **Kamerun** in 1884. An agent of the firm, Johannes Voss, was present during the signing of the **protectorate** treaties. Following the annexation, Jantzen und Thormahlen concentrated in dock and rail activities and began exploration into the interior.

JEUNESSE CAMEROUNAISE FRANÇAISE (JEUCAFRA). An elite, quasi-political, sociocultural, and youth organization that is significant for bringing together a wide array of political figures of early Cameroon nationalism. Founded in 1939 under the initiative of Gov. Gen. Richard Brunot largely to oppose German demands for the return of Cameroon, Jeucafra was initially led by **Paul Soppo Priso** but also included key politicians of contrasting viewpoints such as the radical nationalist **Reuben Um Nyobe** and the conservative nationalist **André Fouda**. During **World War II**, Jeucafra remained tightly pro-French and fervently anti-German. Its attempt to protect nationalist aspirations following the war was contrary to its attachment to and inspiration from French authorities. However, much of Jeucafra demands were reduced to better treatment of the *fonctionnaires* and improvement of the economy to promote development of the territory and fairer chances for the indigenous population. In 1945 under Fouda and **Louis Paul Aujoulat**, Jeucafra became Unicafra, and a definitive split with other leading members followed. Um Nyobe founded the **Union des Populations du Cameroun (UPC)** in 1948.

JEUNESSE DEMOCRATIQUE CAMEROUNAISE (JDC). This subsidiary organization of the **Union des Populations du Cameroun (UPC)** was primarily designed for youths. Formed in 1952, the JDC developed into a petition-writing and propaganda agency of the UPC movement. Its leader, **Theodore Mayi-Matip**, later emerged as an influential UPC figure following the dissolution of the organization on 13 July 1955.

JIHAD. *Jihad* is an Arabic term meaning "a struggle." In terms of **Islam**, *jihad* refers to religious struggle in terms of both personal faith as well as warfare in defense of the faith. In Cameroon, an early 19th-century *jihad* spread across **Adamawa** as an integral part of **Uthman Dan Fodio**'s wars against Hausa chiefs in northern Nigeria. **Modibo Adama** was chosen in 1806 by Uthman Dan Fodio to lead the *jihad* in the region that today consists of northeastern **Nigeria** and northern Cameroon. Led mainly by the **Fulani**, numerous other ethnic groups also participated, including a number of Cameroon groups that joined the Fulani cause. When the *jihad* ended in 1901, the Fulani had successfully incorporated several non-Fulani groups into a political and social framework that was ruled under Muslim religious precepts. *See also* MUSLIM POPULATIONS.

JOINT PROCLAMATION. This historic event, which occurred on 22 April 1955, inaugurated the rebellion against French rule in Cameroun. The joint proclamation was issued by the militant **Union des Populations du Cameroun (UPC)** and other affiliated organizations declaring the termination of French **trusteeship** and calling for general elections. Thereafter, the UPC launched a series of riots and demonstrations that led to its banning in May 1955.

JUA, AUGUSTIN NGOM (1924–1979). A former prime minister of **West Cameroon** (1965–68) and one of the most admired and loved **anglophone** politicians, Augustin Ngom Jua was born in Kom, Wum, in 1924. After being educated locally at St. Anthony School, Njinikom, he took up teaching and in 1952 entered politics as a member of the Wum Divisional Native Authority Council. Two years later he was elected into the **Southern Cameroons** House of Assembly and in 1955 with the help of **John Ngu Foncha** and Anthony Ngunjoh formed the **Kamerun National Democratic Party (KNDP)**. In 1961, Jua served as minister of social services in the **West Cameroon** government. In 1965, he served as secretary of state for finance in the West Cameroon Government before being appointed **prime minister** of West Cameroon that same year. As prime minister, he was determined to secure the autonomy of the state of West Cameroon within the federation. Consequently, he ran into bitter conflict of principle with the **federal inspector of administration,** who was the direct representative of the president in the federal region. The result of this conflict was that Jua was abruptly dropped as prime minister of West Cameroon on 11 January 1968, in favor of **Solomon Tandeng Muna**. Before his death, Jua was a member of the **Cameroon National Union (CNU)** party and a parliamentarian.

JUDICIARY. There are a Supreme Court, a Court of Appeal, and tribunals, as defined in Part I of the **constitution of 1996.** Although the courts are defined as independent of the executive and legislative branches, judges are appointed by the president. There is also a **Court of Impeachment**.

– K –

KALE, P. M. (1910–1966). Kale was a leading politician of the preindependence era in **Southern Cameroons** and Speaker of the **West Cameroon** House of Assembly until his death in August 1966. He spent much of his life in the pursuit of Cameroon nationalism. Born on 20 March 1910 in **Buea**, Kale did his primary education in Buea before proceeding to Nigeria for his secondary education. In April 1935, he arrived in Lagos and was immediately caught in the whirlwind of militant activism. He became a founding member of the

Cameroon Welfare Union, joined the **National Council of Nigeria and the Cameroons (NCNC),** and cofounded the **Cameroon Youth League (CYL)** and the **Cameroons National Federation (CNF)**. He was also instrumental in the formation of the Bakweri Union and the **Bamenda Improvement Association**. As a member of the NCNC, Kale tried to project the Cameroonian personality in Nigeria and the outside world.

In 1953, Kale returned to the Southern Cameroons and together with **Nerius N. Mbile**, created the **Kamerun People's Party (KPP),** which merged with the **Kamerun National Congress (KNC)** to form the opposition coalition known as the **Cameroons Peoples' National Convention (CPNC)** in 1960. In 1959, he left the KPP and founded the **Kamerun United Party (KUP),** which advocated the independence of British Southern Cameroons as a separate political entity. After the 1961 plebiscite, he became speaker of the West Cameroon House of Assembly. His completed manuscript, *Political Evolution in the Cameroons*, was published posthumously in August 1967.

KAME, SAMUEL (1926–). Kame, a former permanent secretary for national defense at the Presidency, was a key figure of the **Ahidjo** presidency. Born on 24 December 1926, in Baham in the Mifi Division of the **Western Province**, Kame studied at the Ecole Supérieure d'Administration in **Yaoundé** before leaving for France. He successively attended the Lycée Carnot in Cannes, the Faculty of Law, and the Institut d'Etudes Politique at the University of Paris. In 1957, he graduated from the Ecole Nationale de la France d'Outre-Mer as an administrator.

Kame served in various administrative regions of the **Bamiléké** region from 1957 until 1959. In these capacities he was instrumental in breaking the **Union des Populations du Cameroun (UPC)** resistance of the Bamiléké ***maquis***. This pushed him into other vital national roles. He was a member of the Constitutional Committee of December 1959 and later served as inspector general of administrative affairs. His longest tenure was in the office of permanent secretary for national defense (1960–82). Throughout this period, he also played a significant role in party affairs. Kame was a member of the executive bureau of the **Union Camerounaise** (1962–65), provisional political secretary of the **Cameroon National Union (CNU)** (1966–75), and member of the Central Committee and the Political Bureau of the CNU party (1975–85). He was dropped from party duties at the **Bamenda "All-Party" Conference**.

KAMERUN. *Kamerun* is the German spelling for *Cameroon*. The territory was a German **protectorate** between 1884 and 1916. Consequently, this spelling is still often used specifically to identify the German epoch in Cameroon history. Kamerun was also used by preindependence movements such as the **Kamerun National Democratic Party (KNDP)**, **Kamerun National Congress (KNC),** Kamerun People's Party (KPP), **Kamerun United National Congress (KUNC),** and **One Kamerun Party (OK)** parties to symbolize their desire for **reunification** of **French** and **British Cameroons** during the **trusteeship** period.

KAMERUN NATIONAL CONGRESS (KNC). The party is significant for having brought together leading **British Cameroon** politicians—**Emmanuel Endeley**, **Solomon Tandeng Muna**, **John Ngu Foncha,** and **Sampson George**—under a single-party platform. The first phase in the formation of this party was the May 1949 Kumba Conference of 17 Cameroons groups, which led to the creation of the **Cameroons National Federation (CNF)** and made strong appeals for **reunification**. This was followed by contacts with **French Cameroons** associations, including the **Union des Populations du Cameroun (UPC)**, which led to the founding of the **Kamerun United National Congress (KUNC)**. The fusion of KUNC and CNF led to the formation of the Kamerun National Congress by the end of 1952.

The second phase saw emphasis on Cameroon autonomy vis-à-vis **Nigeria**. The Cameroons members of the **National Council of Nigeria and the Cameroons (NCNC)** waged a campaign in favor of separation from Nigeria, resulting in a legislative crisis in the Nigerian Eastern House of Assembly. By May 1953, Endeley had led key Cameroonian members to demand separate autonomy from the NCNC through the Kamerun National Congress. A minority faction, led by **Nerius Mbile**, **P. M. Kale**, and Motomby-Woleta, opposed this move and formed the Kamerun People's Party (KPP). As Endeley moved the Kamerun National Congress (KNC) toward closer integration with Nigeria in December 1953, Foncha organized a majority breakaway from the KNC to form the **Kamerun National Democratic Party (KNDP)** in 1955. Endeley's KNC allied with the KPP but gradually lost in successive elections to the KNDP. To check the KNDP's popularity, KNC and KPP merged to form the **Cameroons Peoples' National Convention (CPNC)** in 1960.

KAMERUN NATIONAL DEMOCRATIC PARTY (KNDP). This party was formed in March 1955 under the leadership of **John Ngu Foncha**.

The KNDP was virtually the governing party of **West Cameroon** from 1959 to 1966. It is widely assumed the party was formed to serve as the platform for the pursuit of Cameroon **reunification** after the **Kamerun National Congress (KNC)** (to which many leading Cameroon politicians belonged) failed to reach a consensus on the reunification issue. The KNDP's enthusiasm for reunification led to its short-lived collaboration with the outlawed **Union des Populations du Cameroun (UPC)** party of **French Cameroun**. However, the conservative nationalism of the former and the radical nationalism of the latter caused an early breakdown. Foncha organized a majority breakaway from the KNC in March 1955. By 1957, the newly formed KNDP had increased its parliamentary representation from two to five, and later in January 1959 it won over the government of **Southern Cameroons**. By gaining 14 seats in the Southern Cameroons House of Assembly, the KNDP had grown in four years from a splinter to a government party. The KNDP proreunification manifesto was presented to the United Nations in New York and the British Parliament in London. The 11 February 1961 **plebiscite** was a landslide victory for the party in favor of reunification.

In selling itself as a regional party, the KNDP was only partially successful. Most of its leadership (Foncha, **Solomon Tandeng Muna,** and **Augustin Jua**) hailed from the **Grassfield** areas. Although a government party, the KNDP had an uphill task gaining credibility in the coastal divisions. Its hegemony over **West Cameroon** politics was undisputed. The KNDP gained in successive elections at state and federal levels. Following reunification, it called for "loose federation" with the **Cameroon Republic**. This appeal was a slight drift from its earlier enthusiastic pursuit of reunification. In 1965, Muna split from the KNDP, forming the **Cameroon United Congress**, to seek greater unity and harmony with **East Cameroon** than was advocated by the KNDP. The "loose federation" idea caused the KNDP to stay out of the trend in Cameroon politics. In September 1966, party unification was achieved with the formation of the **Cameroon National Union**. In May 1972, government centralization led to the creation of the **United Republic of Cameroon**.

KAMERUN TIMES. *See CAMEROON TIMES.*

KAMERUN UNITED NATIONAL CONGRESS (KUNC). This political party, led by **R. J. K. Dibongue** and **Nerius N. Mbile,** was formed with the aim of promoting the unification of French and **British Cameroons**. Through its motto "Toward self-government or independence for a united **Kamerun**" and its objectives, the KUNC called for setting a target date for independence and the cancellation of customs and fiscal barriers to facilitate the free movement of persons and goods between the two **trust territories**. The KUNC attracted a large following, especially from petty traders who depended on smuggled goods from **French Cameroun**. The party merged with the **Cameroons National Federation** to form the **Kamerun National Congress** under **Emmanuel M. L. Endeley** in 1953.

KAMERUN UNITED PARTY (KUP). The Kamerun United Party was created in 1959 by **P. M. Kale** and was dedicated to vote for independence even though this was not an alternative in the United Nations **plebiscite**. Kale and the KUP insisted on a third option which was very popular among the traditional rulers of **Southern Cameroons**. He went on to inform the UN that the KUP would boycott the plebiscite if a third alternative was not included. As a sign of protest, he urged his sympathizers to tear their ballots in half when a third alternative was not included. After **reunification**, the party withered away.

KANGA, VICTOR (1931–). Kanga, a former minister in the Federal Republic of Cameroon, is a polished intellectual disgraced and imprisoned by the **Ahmadou Ahidjo** regime. Kanga earned a doctorate in law in 1956 and trained as a customs expert before returning home in 1957. He was elected to the **National Assembly** and became the rising star of **Bamiléké** and Cameroonian youths. He served as justice minister in 1960, minister of national economy in 1961, minister of finance in 1964, and minister of information and tourism in July 1966. He was arrested in November 1966 to serve a jail term for alleged publication of antigovernment rumors. He remained in jail and house arrest throughout the remainder of the Ahidjo era. Pres. **Paul Biya** finally granted Kanga his release and appointed him chairman of the governing board of the International Telecommunications Company of Cameroon (INTELCAM). Kanga was replaced in 1991 by **Victor Mukete**.

KINGUE, ABEL (1923–1964). A revolutionary opponent of the **Ahmadou Ahidjo** regime, Kingue joined the **Union des Populations du Cameroun (UPC)** in 1948 and made unsuccessful bids for a parliamentary seat in the 1949, 1951, and 1952 legislative elections. In 1954, he became vice president of the UPC and leader of the resistance committee until the UPC was banned in 1955. Between 1955 and 1959, he moved with the exiled UPC to **British Cameroons**, Cairo, and finally to Conakry in Guinea, where he died on 16 June 1964.

KINGUE, MICHAEL DOO. *See* DOO KINGUE, MICHAEL.

KIRDI. *Kirdi* is used to denote non-Christian, non-**Muslim** Sudano–Nigritic and Chadic peoples inhabiting north Cameroon. During the ***jihad*** of the 19th century, some of the indigenous population sided with the **Fulani**, eventually assimilating and becoming virtually indistinguishable. The remainder opposed the Fulani and took refuge on mountains and hilltops in the area from which they put up a fierce resistance. The few Kirdi who remain in close contact with the Fulani generally serve as slaves in large Fulani families, although there have been varying degrees of assimilation between the Fulani and the Kirdi. Kirdi constitute the majority of the population in the North but have never constituted a strong political voting bloc. Desirous of their votes, the Fulani, who have historically despised the Kirdi, courted the isolated Kirdi clan groups to boost the electoral chances of the **Union Camerounaise (UC)**.

The Kirdi are not truly a unified group and are in reality a number of different cultures that have been grouped together under this single term, which literally means "pagan," in opposition to the Muslim Fulani. Included under this umbrella term are such groups as the Massa, Matakam, Kapsiki, Guiziga, Fali, and many others too numerous to name. Most of these groups have settled in the **Mandara Mountains**. Major personalities to emerge from the Kirdi include **Luc Ayang** and **Etienne Hollong**. In recent years these groups have tended to support minority parties in the North in opposition to the Fulani-dominated **National Union for Democracy and Progress (UNDP)**.

KOME, ALBERT NGOME. *See* NGOME KOME, ALBERT.

KORUP NATIONAL PARK. Korup, in the southwest bordering **Nigeria**, is an area of ancient rain forest that Cameroon has determined to preserve. Various nongovernmental organizations are assisting in the project. More than 20 villages exist inside the Korup reserve, and numerous experiments are under way to allow the inhabitants of the villages to coexist and prosper with the plants and animals of the reserve. Researchers discovered a vine, *Ancistrocladus korupensis,* that shows promise in the fight against **AIDS-HIV**.

KOTOKO. Kotoko was the successor in the 15th century to the **Sao** civilization in north Cameroon. It consisted of various small kingdoms like Makari, Mara, Kousseri, and Logone-Birni. These were organized within the Kotoko state, ruled by a king. By the mid-15th century, the Kotoko state included major portions of today's northern Nigeria and Cameroon. It became part of the Bornu empire in the 19th century. Kotoko was divided between north and south for administrative purposes and converted to **Islam** by outside conquerors or Muslim missionaries. Until the advent of colonial rule in the late 19th century, the Logone-Birni kingdom remained the most significant kingdom of the Kotoko peoples. The Kotoko have recently been involved in **ethnic conflicts** with their neighbors, the Choa Arabs.

KPE. *See* BAKWERI.

KRIBI. This major touristic center and headquarters of the Ocean Division is in the **South Province**. Originally, Kribi was inhabited by the Batangas. The town was particularly important during the period of German scientific expeditions into the Cameroon interior. Since independence, Kribi's coastal location allows it to serve both as an important touristic center and as a minor port. All year many European and Cameroonian tourists are entertained in Kribi. In addition, the port is now valuable for the export of **cocoa** and **timber**. Plans are under way to further develop the port facilities of the town as well as the industrial potential. A plywood factory exists here, and proposals for a liquid natural gas plant and an iron-and-steel complex have been considered. The new petroleum **pipeline** from **Chad** will end here, raising fears that an environmental disaster will spoil the miles of white sand beaches, varied wildlife, and natural vegetation.

KUMBA. Kumba is the largest town and serves as administrative headquarters of Meme Division in the **South West Province**. It is essentially inhabited by the Bafaws but has also been the center of large settlements by the **Ibo** from **Nigeria** and North Westerners. It played an important role as host town of several nationalist meetings of various political parties such as the Cameroons National Federation in 1949 and the **Kamerun United National Congress (KUNC)** in 1951. After 1955, Kumba became the provisional headquarters of the underground **Union des Populations du Cameroun (UPC)** movement following its expulsion from **French Cameroon**. The strong anti-Nigerian feeling that developed in the town helped the **Kamerun National Democratic Party (KNDP)** and the **One Kamerun Party (OK)** to make their most significant gains here. After independence, the railway linking **Douala (East Cameroon**) and Kumba **(West Cameroon)** became an important avenue for communication. Today, the town continues to grow as a center for the production of major agricultural foodstuffs, **cocoa**, and commerce.

KUO, FELIX SENGAT. *See* SENGAT-KUO, FELIX.

– L –

LABARANG, MOHAMADOU (1956–). The youngest cabinet member in Cameroon's political history, Mohamadou Labarang served as minister-delegate for General State Inspection and Administrative Reforms from August 1985 to May 1988. Born on 1 January 1956 in **Ngaoundéré**, **Adamawa Province**, he did his primary and secondary education at the Ecole Principale and Collège Mazenod. He later studied at the **University of Yaoundé,** the University of Paris at Nanterre, and the National School of Administration and Magistracy (ENAM). On completion he served as assistant divisional officer in Mokolo before being called for duties at the Presidency of the Republic. In **Ahmadou Ahidjo**'s government, he worked successively as attaché and chargé de mission in the Office of the President. In February 1984, Pres. **Paul Biya** appointed him assistant secretary-general at the Presidency with rank of minister. He later became minister-delegate for General State Inspection and Administrative Reforms. During the **Bamenda Congress** in 1985, he was voted into the Central Committee of the **Cameroon People's Democratic Movement (CPDM)** as an alternate member. He worked as chairman of the board of directors of the National Social Insurance Fund before being appointed Cameroon's ambassador to Saudi Arabia and the Sultanate of Oman.

LAKE CHAD. This lake is shared by Cameroon, **Chad**, Niger, and **Nigeria**. Fed by the **Logone** and **Chari Rivers**, its size varies depending on the season. In most places it is shallow, even swampy, and thus has been of little use for transport purposes. It does support an important fishing industry.

LAKE CHAD BASIN COMMISSION (LCBC)/COMMISSION DU BASSIN DU LAC TCHAD (CBLT). This body was established on

22 May 1964, with major alterations to the original agreement in 1972. The purpose is to encourage cooperation in the use and development of the resources of the Chad Basin and to ensure that no state takes action that would adversely affect the lake's water level or flow. However, considering the length of its existence, not much has been accomplished. Several studies were undertaken in early years on water supplies and use, agriculture, and livestock. Fishery centers were established in **Nigeria** and **Chad**, free movement for fishermen was agreed on, and in January 1973 a Development Fund was established. Projects were contracted in 1976, but activity could not be undertaken because of fighting in Chad. No meetings of the commission were conducted between 1978 and 1982 for the same reason. And, by 1984, there were reports of conflicts between the member states leading to suspicion and trouble within the commission. Charges of unapproved diversion of lake water by member states were made.

In 1985, the members agreed to undertake a campaign against rinderpest, a cattle disease. Improvements in road and rail communications, health campaigns, and drought and antidesertification activities have all been suggested. Recent activities have included the restoration of the depleted waters of the lake. A proposal for a joint security force to fight banditry in the lake region is under consideration.

The LCBC is the commission and a secretariat. Cameroon, Chad, Niger, and Nigeria are the original members. In 1994, the **Central African Republic** became a member. The headquarters are in N'Djamena, Chad, although this was moved temporarily to **Maroua**, Cameroon, during the Chad crisis.

LAKE MONOUN. *See* LAKE NYOS DISASTER.

LAKE NYOS DISASTER. Cameroon's worst natural disaster was an unusual tragedy in which 1,700 people died following suffocation from toxic gas released from Lake Nyos near Wum in the **North West Province** on 21 August 1986. Most of the victims were villagers sleeping in their homes. In addition, hundreds of others had severe wounds and burns from the incident and lost their cattle. International assistance for the incident, from industrialized and African countries as well as private donors, was swift and generous. Previously, in August 1984, a similar incident at Lake Monoun near **Foumban** had led to a death toll of 37 people.

Explanations for the cause of the disaster have been extremely varied, complex, and confusing. Two international conferences organized by the

Cameroon government and UNESCO have been inconclusive on the actual cause of the gas explosion except for their assertion that "Cameroon is bisected by a linear zone of crustal weakness." Local interpretation of the disaster holds that supernatural forces were involved and the incident was a sign of the anger of the gods and ancestors of the tribe. This man-made cause is popular among laymen. A rumor spread widely that the U.S. Central Intelligence Agency (CIA) had conducted nuclear experiments at the lake.

Although it is considered impossible to exclude the possibility of a further disastrous event or to predict its occurrence, the suggestions of degassing the bottom water of this and several similar lakes appear very costly for the Cameroon government. The government is developing a policy to remove villages situated in situations similar to the Lake Nyos disasters. Recent studies indicate a new threat at Lake Nyos. One of the crater walls surrounding the lake has worn thin and may soon collapse. Subsequent flooding would cause serious damage in Cameroon and Nigeria.

LAMIDO (pl. LAMIBE). The *lamido* is the **Fulani** chief at the head of a cultural-administrative unit known as the *lamidat*. There are over 21 *lamidats* in the northern Fulani area. Among the Cameroonian Fulanis, there are six kingdoms (*lamidats*) in the **Ngaoundéré** zone of **Adamawa**, 11 in the **Garoua** zone of the **Benue River,** and four around **Maroua** in the Diamare Division.

The *lamibe* at the head of these kingdoms possess substantial religious, social, judicial, and political power. They constitute a separate class, characterized by conservative tendencies. After periods of initial cooperation, they began to resist the accommodative and progressive stance of a new class of Northern elites, championed by **Ahmadou Ahidjo** and his closest collaborators. This created some degree of friction between the Fulani postcolonial leadership of the country and the religious constituency in the interior. The Ahidjo government sought to limit the influence of the *lamibe* to the mosque and to dilute their political influence. This became largely successful as the destruction of traditional power became a national assignment that affected the former **West Cameroon House of Chiefs** as well.

A typical *lamido* functions with a government consisting of a *fada* (council) of 12 members serving as ministers. The *lamidat,* however, is a highly hierarchical society consisting of freemen (*rimbe*) and the slaves (*matchoube*). Following the crisis with the Adhijo government, the *lamibe* lost their usual traditional privileges of imposing tributes through taxes and the flagrant use of the police force in nonreligious assignments. The oldest *lamidat* is that of Rey Bouba, founded in 1804, while those of Ngaoundéré (1836) and Garoua (1839) have emerged as the most significant. In the multiparty era, the *lamido* faces a dilemma. He is dependent on the central government, dominated by Biya and his party, but his followers generally support **Maigari Bello Bouba** and his party and pressure the *lamido* to do the same.

LEAGUE OF NATIONS (1919–1946). The League of Nations was the first major international organization of the 20th century, created in 1920 by the victorious powers of **World War I**. It assumed legal and political control of the former German colonies through a **mandate system** of administration. European powers were allowed to administer the territories of the defeated powers under the supervision of the League of Nations. **French Cameroun** and the **British Cameroons** were mandated territories until 1946 when the organization ceased to exist. These became **trust territories** under the United Nations system.

LECCO, FELIX SABAL. *See* SABAL LECCO, FELIX.

LECLERC, PHILIPPE (1902–1947). Leclerc, a French army general, led a group of 24 Free French partisans who landed in **Douala** on 26–27 August 1940 during **World War II**. Leclerc took control of **French Cameroun** for General de Gaulle and later became Free French **commissioner** of the territory until 1943. In honor of General Leclerc's conquest a high school, the **Lycée Leclerc**, was named after him.

LIBERALISME COMMUNAL. *See* COMMUNAL LIBERALISM.

LIMBE (FORMERLY VICTORIA). Limbe was once the leading cosmopolitan town of **anglophone** Cameroon. Originally known as Fho by the **Bakweris**, the town was christened Victoria in 1858 by British missionaries led by **Alfred Saker**. It remained a virtual British possession following its annexation by Consul **Edward H. Hewett** on 19 July 1884. The British gave up the Victoria settlement to the German **protectorate** in 1887.

The Germans developed Victoria into an agricultural metropole with expansive plantations and schools as well as a **botanical garden**. In addition to its coastal location, port facilities, and commercial significance, the town remained more renowned although **Buea** was the capital of the territory. The slump of Victoria gradually began with the **reunification** of 1961 and accelerated under the unitary system prevalent since 1972. Many business establishments fled from Victoria to **Douala** to take advantage of port facilities and comparatively better fiscal incentives. Therefore, for much of the 1970s, Victoria was referred to as a "ghost town." The inauguration of the National Oil Refinery Company (SONARA) in 1981 on the outskirts of the town did not lead to the expected uplift of Victoria. The name of the town was suddenly changed from the Anglo-Saxon Victoria to the more indigenous-sounding Limbe in 1982. The town is still the divisional headquarters of Fako Division in the **South West Province**. During the British period, the term *Victoria* was also used to denote one of the four divisions of the *Cameroons Province.*

LITTORAL PROVINCE. The Littoral Province covers a surface area of 20,200 square kilometers and consists of four divisions and 19 subdivisions. The province is divided into three relief zones: the plains of the South, the plateaus, and the mountains of the North. The climate is tropical with two seasons: the dry season (November–March) and the rainy season (April–October). Much of the population is concentrated in the provincial capital, **Douala** (Wouri Division). About 90 percent of the country's industrial activity is concentrated in the Littoral Province; commercial, transport, and hotel activities are very highly developed. Its coastal location and port facilities make Douala the gate of entry to the country. Modern agricultural activities are equally on the rise. Other important towns include **Nkongsamba** (Mungo Division), Yabassi (Nkam Division), and **Edea** (Sanaga Maritime Division). The Littoral Province has existed in its present form since 1972.

LOCK PRISO, CHIEF. This fanatical pro-British **Duala** chief of Hickory Town on the Cameroon River refused to sign the German **protectorate** treaty in 1884. He quarreled with the pro-German King Bell and resisted German attempts to disband the **Court of Equity**. In December 1884, German marines were called in to suppress the uprising and demolish the small coastal town ruled by Lock Priso.

LOGONE AND CHARI RIVERS. These are important tributaries of **Lake Chad**. The Logone actually flows into the Chari and includes other rivers such as the Winna and Mbere. Politically, the Logone serves as the divide between Cameroon and **Chad**.

LOI CADRE. The Loi Cadre was passed by the French National Assembly on 23 June 1956 to provide an institutional framework for the gradual evolution of overseas territories toward self-rule. Thanks to the Loi Cadre, the French accelerated reforms and allowed various territories to adapt to their particular circumstances in the quest for independence. In Cameroun, elections to the **Assemblée Territoriale du Cameroun (ATCAM)** were introduced based on universal suffrage. A local political movement, **Courant d'Union Nationale,** was formed by **Paul Soppo Priso** to reject the terms of the Loi Cadre because of its outright disregard for Cameron's juridical distinctiveness as a **trust territory**. The Mollet–Defferre government later conceded to the insufficiency of the Loi Cadre provisions for **Cameroun**.

LOME AGREEMENTS. The Lomé Convention, actually a series of four agreements between the **European Economic Community (EEC)** and the African, Caribbean, and Pacific (ACP) states, covers issues of aid, investment, and trade between the two groups. The first Lomé Convention, Lomé I, replaced the **Yaoundé Convention** in 1975 and established a new framework for cooperation. It provided for EEC aid to the ACP and earmarked approximately 99 percent of the latter's primary commodity exports for duty-free entry into the former. Lomé I also created **STABEX** to stabilize the price fluctuations in agricultural products being exported to the EC from the ACP. In 1981, Lomé II covered the same areas of cooperation and introduced the **SYSMIN** program designed to stabilize the price fluctuations for minerals. Lomé III, in 1985, expanded EC aid and placed an emphasis on the rehabilitation of existing ACP industries. Lomé IV, signed in 1989 and designed to last 10 years, addressed the debt crisis as well as aid and commodity price fluctuations.

LOST WAX METHOD. *See* CIRE PERDUE CASTING.

LOTIN, EBOA (1942–1997). This important Cameroonian musician was born Emmanuel Eboa Lotin in Banamouti-Douala in 1942. He recorded his first single, "Mulema Mwam, Elimba Dikalo," in 1962. He later became known as a master of the **makossa** style. Lotin played guitar, harmonica, bass, and keyboards in his music and also had interests in literature, theater, and cinema. He died in November 1997.

LUC, AYANG. *See* AYANG, LUC.

LUTHERAN MISSION. This Protestant doctrinal group draws inspiration from the writings of Martin Luther. Cameroon Lutherans are essentially under the dual influence of American and Norwegian Lutherans. Together, they have made significant inroads into the Muslim-dominated north Cameroon and various parts of the **East Province**. Lutherans have a bible school in Meiganga and a printing station and a hospital in Kaele; the seat of the Lutheran Church in Cameroon is **Ngaoundéré**. The Norwegian and American missions fused to form a national church.

LYCEE LECLERC. This was **French Cameroun**'s most prestigious high school. Located in **Yaoundé**, it was established as a government institution for the training of first-rate students in secondary education. Students in the institution generally take the **Brevet d'Etudes du Premier Cycle (BEPC)** or ***baccalauréat*** examinations on completion. For a long time after independence, the principal of this institution in the nation's capital was considered superior to other supervisors of secondary education across the country. Many Cameroon elites—including Ayissi Mvodo, Bidias a Ngon, Ndam Njoya, Ngongang Ouandji, **Youssoufa Daouda**, Pres. **Paul Biya**, and Ze Nguele—attended this renowned institution. *See* Leclerc, Philippe

– M –

MAIMO, HERMAN (1944–1999). Maimo was an economist and former minister of equipment. Born in Nso, Bui Division, of the **North West Province** on 7 April 1944, he was educated successively in Catholic School, Bota, in the **South West Province** (1954–60) and the Sacred Heart College, Mankon in the North West. He pursued his university education in Washington, D.C., at the Catholic University of America and Howard University, obtaining B.A., M.A., and Ph.D. degrees. On returning home, he served as regional chief of service for the **National Produce Marketing Board** in **Limbe** until his nomination in 1984 to replace **Issa Adoum** as director of the **National Fund for Rural Development (FONADER)**.

Maimo was appointed minister of equipment in 1985 and remained in that post until May 1988. He also served as an alternate member of the Central Committee of the **Cameroon People's Democratic Movement (CPDM)**.

MAIZE (ZEA MAYS). Maize, or corn, is a cereal crop cultivated throughout Cameroon, especially in the **North West**, **West**, **Littoral**, **South,** and **North Provinces**. When freshly harvested, maize is boiled, roasted, or grated into several varieties. Foodstuffs such as **fufu**corn, kokicorn, cornbread, cornchaff (with beans), or a beverage known as cornbeer are all made with maize. Corn juice is also used to make a favorite breakfast hot drink popularly known as "pap."

MAKOSSA. Makossa is Cameroon's most popular **music**. It is originally traced to the **Dualas**, who inhabit the **Littoral Province**, but its popularity now extends across the country and through much of the African continent. The word literally translates into "make me dance" from the Duala. It is a generally smooth and lively sound that irresistibly drives the listener to the floor. Most makossa musicians sing in the Duala language, sometimes interspersed with **French** or **pidgin English**. However, it is not only Dualas who compose the makossa. The makossa has been used by many other Cameroonian artists and non-Cameroonians from Burkina Faso and Benin.

Because of the popularity of the music across Africa in recent times, artists spring up every day. Two of the most recent stars are Petit-Pays and Papillon. More classic artists include **Manu Dibango**, **Francis Bebey**, and **Eboa Lottin,** as well as Nelle Eyoum, Ebanda Manfred and Villa Vienne, Ekambi Brillant, Dina Bell, Toto Guillaume, Pierre de Moussy, Prince Ndedi Eyango, Misse Ngoh François, Emile Kangue, Marcel Tjahe, Nkotti François, Jackie Ndoumbe, Joe Mboue, Penda Dalle, and Charlotte Mbango.

MAMFE. This Cameroonian town bordering **Nigeria** is the headquarters of the Manyu Division in the **South West Province**. Under the Germans, the administrative region was originally known as Ossidinge and was later named Mamfe Division by the British. On 11 August 1959, the British convened the **Mamfe Conference** on the future of **Southern Cameroons** in which they warned of the dire financial, economic, and administrative consequences of its separation from Nigeria. The importance of Mamfe as a bustling commercial and communication town declined with Cameroon's independence and **reunification** in 1961. The town itself has been largely deserted by indigenes of Mamfe, the **Bayangi**, who now live in crowded quarters in other major cities along the coast such as **Limbe** and **Douala**. This has also contributed to the slow development in the town and in Manyu Division in general.

MAMFE CONFERENCE. This was an all-party conference held in 1959 in the **Southern Cameroons** border town of **Mamfe** to decide on various issues concerning the future of the **British Cameroons** territories. Participants sought to take a common stand on becoming an integral part of **Nigeria** or joining **French Cameroun** before an important **trusteeship** council session on the issue. Among participant parties was the **North Kamerun Democratic Party** from the **Northern Cameroons**. No consensus was reached at the end of the conference.

MANDARA MOUNTAINS. One of the most significant mountain structures in north Cameroon, the Mandara Mountains are located north of the **Benue River**. The most significant peak rises to over 1,450 meters and is known as the Zelediba mountain. The people of the area are known as the Mandara and were Islamized in 1715. They became particularly successful during the reign of Boukar Guiana (1773–1828). The Mandara even challenged the **Fulani** hegemony until they were defeated by the Bornu leader, **Rabah**, in 1895.

MANDATE SYSTEM (1922–1946). The international system of administration set up at the Versailles Peace Conference of 1919 was embodied in Article 22 of the Covenant of the **League of Nations**. It sought to ensure the moral and material well-being of the peoples in the mandated territories, including the former German colonies. Although the laws of the administering European power were applied to each territory, a permanent Mandates Commission supervised the activities of the mandatory authorities through the receipt of annual reports. The Franco–British mandates over the separate Cameroon territories were signed in London on 10 July 1919, with France receiving four-fifths of the old **Kamerun** and Britain receiving two separate areas known as the British **Northern Cameroons** and **Southern Cameroons**. After **World War II,** the mandates became **trust territories** under the United Nations.

MANGA BELL, DOUALA RUDOLF (1873–1914). This is the son of the famous King Bell (1838–1898), whom he later succeeded in 1910. Born in 1873 in **Douala** and educated at home and in Germany, he attacked the ruthlessness of the German colonial system when he became king in 1910. His anticolonial sentiments and willingness to defend indigenous rights led to his deposition, arrest, and condemnation on 14 August 1913 for "treason against the Kaiser and the Empire." He was hanged in 1914, exactly six days after the outbreak of **World War I**, at the age of 41. As an early nationalist, Rudolf Douala Manga Bell was long forgotten by his people and only vaguely mentioned in history books. In March 1985, he gained an overdue public appreciation when the government christened a graduating group of the Ecole Militaire Inter-Armes cadet officers in his honor. *See also* AKWA.

MANIOC. *See* CASSAVA.

MANU DIBANGO. *See* DIBANGO, MANU.

MAQUIS. This French term is used to describe insurgency fighting by underground **Union des Populations du Cameroun (UPC)** elements against government forces. The *maquis* movement was operated from the deep equatorial forests of the **Bassa** countryside and later engulfed the **Bamiléké Grassfield.** Travel to and across areas of heavy *maquis* activity was discouraged, and a state of emergency was in force in these areas. Although the colonial and postcolonial administrations described its opponents as bandits, the UPC exalted the *maquis* as "a form of militantism on a secret seal." The *maquis* was a constant scare in Cameroon politics between 1956 and 1971. The death of **Reuben Um Nyobe** in 1958, the assassination of Osende Afana in Boumba-Ngoko in the east in 1966, and the execution of the UPC leaders implicated in the **Ndongmo affair** in 1971 all contributed to the collapse of the Cameroon *maquis* movement.

MAROUA. Maroua has been the capital of the **Extreme North Province** since its creation in 1983, and it was previously the headquarters of Diamare Division. Throughout its history, Maroua has played the role of an unfortunate rival of **Garoua**. By 1930, Maroua was the second city in **French Cameroun** after **Douala**. Its decline today is largely the result of political forces. Former president **Ahmadou Ahidjo** hailed from Garoua, and under his regime that city experienced an unparalleled development in contrast to Maroua. By 1980, Maroua only possessed a corn oil mill, a secondary school, and a prefecture. It had been reduced to an average city with an exceptional **Fulani** charm reserved for old historic cities. Its population of 67,000 at the time of the 1976 census made it the fourth largest city in the country. Maroua now serves as a zone of attraction for investments and migrants. Its new status as a provincial capital as well as the hosting of an **agropastoral show** has added to its development.

MATAGA, PHILIPPE (1938–). Mataga is currently the minister of foreign affairs. Born in Edea on 3 March 1938 of parents who actually hailed from Ndom around the Eastern Bambibi area in the Sanaga–

Maritime Division, he attended the Catholic Mission school in **Edea** (1946–51), the Junior Seminary in Edea and Akona (1951–54), and the **Lycée Leclerc** in **Yaoundé** from 1954, obtaining a ***baccalauréat*** in philosophy in 1958. He left for university education the same year, studying in Bordeaux but finally obtaining his history degree from the University of Grenoble in 1962 and a postgraduate diploma (D.E.S.) from the Sorbonne in 1963. He did a one-year diplomatic specialization at the Institut des Hautes Etudes d'Outre-Mer, obtaining a diploma in 1964.

Mataga was employed in the Ministry of Foreign Affairs from January 1965 serving in Yaoundé and as adviser in the embassy in Paris and at the Cameroon Mission to the United Nations in New York until 1971. He continued to serve at the ministry until 1972 when he was appointed director of the African Regional Center for Labor Administration (Cradat). From 1975 to 1978 he was director of cultural affairs in the Ministry of Information and Culture until his return to Foreign Affairs. He became deputy director of international organizations from 1978 to 1980 and rose to the rank of secretary-general in the Ministry of Foreign Affairs from September 1980 to January 1983.

Mataga was called to the Presidency of the Republic as technical adviser from January 1983 and gained a junior cabinet position as deputy director of the Civil Cabinet of the President in March of the same year. From November 1986, he served as minister of labor and social insurance until he was appointed as foreign minister to replace the veteran **William-Aurelian Eteky Mboumoua** on 23 January 1987. Widely regarded as a strong confidant of the head of state, Mataga is a leading personality of the **Biya** era. In 1990, he became ambassador to Israel.

MAYI-MATIP, THEODORE (1927–). An early rebel politician who turned parliamentarian and party loyalist in the postcolonial state, Mayi-Matip was born on 2 June 1927 in Eseka, near **Edea**. After elementary and secondary education, he continued to study independently and emerged as a student of **Bassa** history and culture as well as the needs of the Cameroon masses.

Mayi-Matip was cofounder of the **Union des Populations du Cameroun (UPC)** in 1948 and served alongside **Reuben Um Nyobe** as the movement's theoretician, strategist, fortune teller, and griot. His official tile, however, was head of the youth wing of the UPC. He joined the French colonial administration but was suspended in 1950 because of his UPC militancy. He became the administrative secretary of the UPC, and when the UPC was outlawed in 1955, Mayi-Matip was imprisoned in

Maroua and Mokolo. After his release, he rejoined the UPC. It is believed that he fumbled or conspired with enemies when he predicted that 13 September 1958, the day Um Nyobe was murdered, would be a fine day. After the assassination of Um Nyobe, Mayi-Matip offered his services to the **Ahmadou Ahidjo** government and created the legal wing of the UPC. He immediately won elections and gained a seat in the Cameroon Assembly. As a member of the opposition, he joined **Rene-Guy Okala**, **André-Marie Mbida,** and **Marcel Bebey-Eyid**i and founded the **Front National Unifié (FNU)**, which criticized Ahidjo's attempt to create a single party. They were arrested under Decree 62-0F-18 of 12 March 1962, tried, and imprisoned. After two and a half years in jail, Mayi-Matip was released on the understanding that he would collaborate in the dissolution of the UPC as a political force. This measure facilitated the creation of the one-party structure, the **Cameroon National Union (CNU)**. Henceforth, he joined the CNU and became an influential member in the highest organ of the party. From 1973 Mayi-Matip served as vice president of the National Assembly until 1988, when he was defeated in the legislative elections. In 1990, he was removed from the Central Committee and Bureau of the **Cameroon People's Democratic Union (CPDU)**. He later rejoined the UPC when multiparty politics was reintroduced in December 1990.

MBAPPE, ROBERT MBELLA. *See* MBELLA MBAPPE, ROBERT.

MBELLA MBAPPE, ROBERT (1937–). A former director of the Office of the President of the Republic, Mbella Mbappe is an accomplished scholar, magistrate, and administrator. Born on 21 October 1937 in Ebone in the Mungo Division, **Littoral Province**, he did primary education successively in Ebone, Ndoungue, and **Douala** from 1943 until 1950. He was in **Lycée Leclerc**, **Yaoundé,** from 1950 to 1957 before earning a scholarship to study law in Bordeaux, France. He obtained law certificates in 1959, 1960, and 1961 and went on for graduate work. In 1963, he earned the *diplôme d'études supérieures* in private law and successfully defended his *doctorat d'état* in June 1969. In addition to his academic background, he trained professionally as a magistrate on a Cameroon government scholarship from October 1961 to 1964.

Mbella Mbappe later occupied important posts in the Ministry of Justice, including vice president of the Yaoundé Court of Appeal (1964–66). He served as prosecutor of the Republic in the Yaoundé Court of First Instance (1966–67); prosecutor-general in the **Garoua** Court of Appeal

(1967–70); and director of judicial affairs and secretary-general in the Ministry of Justice (1970–73). His longest post was in university administration when he served as chancellor of the **University of Yaoundé** from 1973 until 1980. Despite his controversial years as chancellor of the university, Mbella Mbappe continued to rise in the country's administration. In 1980, he returned to the Ministry of Justice to serve as prosecutor-general at the Supreme Court of Cameroon until June 1983, when he was made a member of Pres. **Paul Biya**'s government. Between July 1983 and July 1984, he served as minister of posts and telecommunications and then minister of national education between July 1984 and November 1984. He was then moved to the post of director of cabinet at the Presidency of the Republic and in 1985 was nominated to the Central Committee of the **Cameroon People's Democratic Movement (CPDM),** where he served as deputy for organization. He remained in that post until 26 November 1992, when he was appointed to head the Ministry of National Education. In December 1997, he was dropped from government but returned to service as chairman of the board of the Telecommunications Regulatory Agency on 17 December 1998.

MBIDA, ANDRE-MARIE (1917–1980). Cameroon's first preindependence **prime minister**, Mbida was born in Edingding near **Yaoundé**, in the Nyong-et-Sanaga District. He did his primary education there at a Roman Catholic seminary. Between 1945 and 1950, he worked in the French service as legal secretary. In 1957, he opened his own business in Ebolowa. By 1952, he had become so popular that he defeated political heavyweights such as **Louis Paul Aujoulat** to gain a seat in the **Assemblée Territoriale du Cameroun (ATCAM);** between 1953 and 1956, he served as councilor in the French Union. In 1956, he was elected as a deputy to the French National Assembly.

It was to Mbida's credit that many Cameroonians, not strictly adhering to the **Union des Populations du Cameroon (UPC)**, began expressing hostility against the French administration. He eventually became the national hero for a country still in search of independence and nationhood. His big legislative following in the Assemblée Territoriale led to the request for him to form the first Cameroun government in 1957. Mbida needed a coalition to make the preindependence government a reality, and this was achieved by the formation of the so-called Nationalist Front. However, despite his strong opposition to the French, Mbida later espoused a program that placed him at odds with other early nationalist leaders, denying the concept of nation in Cameroun and expressing a desire to delay independence until a strong local economy was in place.

Mbida's coalition gradually fell apart as the French showed increased readiness to oust the Cameroon prime minister. In a well-orchestrated political machination, Mbida was removed as prime minister in favor of his deputy, **Ahmadou Ahidjo**, in February 1958. Apart from his dislike of the French, Mbida was allegedly intolerant to minority interests, remained inflexible over the terrorist situation, and prescribed harsh penalties to deal with the **Bassa** insurgency. Consequently, Mbida not only alienated the French but antagonized factions of the Cameroonian population. He went into voluntary exile after his forceful removal from office in 1958 and joined the exile wing of the UPC in Conakry, Guinea.

In 1960, Mbida returned to Cameroun under the cover of a government amnesty to contest the local elections. His political platform was embodied in the goals of the **Parti des Démocrates Camerounais (PDC)**, which grouped together various **Fang** groupings of the Yaoundé area. Although his party performed well and entered the ruling coalition with Ahidjo's **Union Camerounaise (UC)**, Mbida was not given any prominent political office. While in the Parliament, he was arrested for an alleged conspiracy against the government and jailed for three years. In 1965, he was released from prison and later developed eye problems. However, he succeeded to settle on good terms with Ahidjo and live a secluded life out of public view. He died in October 1980.

MBILE, NERIUS NAMASO (1923–). Mbile was an important figure in Southern and **West Cameroon** politics. Born in Lipenja near **Kumba** on 4 April 1923, Mbile attended primary school in Kumba before proceeding to **Eastern Nigeria** for his postsecondary education. He became identified with the quest for nationalism, joined the **National Council of Nigeria and the Cameroons (NCNC),** and served as secretary-general of the **CDC Workers Union** (1949–51) and later its president (1949–51). He allied closely with **Emmanuel Endeley** in the formation of political pressure groups and parties. He became secretary-general of the **Kamerun United National Congress (KUNC)**. In 1951, he was one of the "Original Thirteen" to be elected from Southern Cameroons to the Eastern Regional House of Assembly, Nigeria.

When a coalition was effected with Endeley's **Kamerun National Congress (KNC)** in 1957, Mbile was appointed minister of transport in the first ministerial government in **Southern Cameroons**. He became deputy leader of the **Cameroons Peoples' National Convention**

(CPNC) and campaigned for Southern Cameroon's association with **Nigeria**. A renowned parliamentarian, Mbile served in the Eastern Regional House of Assembly in Enugu, the House of Representatives in Lagos, the Southern Cameroons House of Assembly, and the West Cameroon House of Assembly. He also served in West Cameroon as minister of works (1965–67), minister of lands and surveys in 1968 and secretary of state for primary education (1969–72). After the formation of a unitary state in 1972, he retired to become a businessman until 6 November 1992, when he was appointed chairman of the **Cameroon Development Corporation (CDC)**.

MBOG, FELIX TONYE. *See* TONYE MBOG, FELIX.

MBOUMOUA, WILLIAM-AURELIAN ETEKY. *See* ETEKY MBOUMOUA, WILLIAM-AURELIAN.

MBWE-MBWE. The 10th ruler of the **Bamoum** dynasty reigned during the 18th century. He extended his political control across the Noun River through a conquest of 48 chiefdoms. After an initial **Fulani** invasion of the Bamoum Kingdom, Mbwe-Mbwe erected fortifications around the town of **Foumban** to defend and save the entire kingdom.

MERRICK, JOSEPH (1808–1849). This Jamaican Baptist missionary of African origin was the pioneer missionary on the Cameroon coast. He reached Fernando Po in 1843 before establishing the Cameroon mission in Bell Town and Bimbia in 1844. By his multifarious activities as an explorer, teacher, minister, and craftsman, he laid the groundwork on which **Alfred Saker** built and expanded the Baptist Missionary activity in Cameroon. Merrick translated the Bible into Isubu (the Bimbia dialect), published a textbook for elementary teaching in the language, set up a printing press, developed a machine for making local materials such as bricks, climbed **Mount Cameroon,** and paid the first non-African visit to the Bakoko people. He died in 1849 on a voyage to England for a vacation. Although Joseph Merrick's legacy was overshadowed by the later activity of Alfred Saker, a boys' secondary school, the Joseph Merrick Baptist College in Ndu in the **North West Province**, was established to honor his achievements. *See also* BAPTIST MISSION; NATIVE BAPTIST CHURCH.

LE MESSAGER. This newspaper was founded in 1979 by Pius Njawe, who is now its editor. The newspaper has become one of the most popular in the country as it has taken courageous and often radical stands against the government and its policies. Although *Le Messager* is not affiliated with any political party, it must be considered as part of the opposition press. It is renowned for its campaigns for democracy and **human rights** and for its frequent disclosures of scandals in the government. As a result, Pius Njawe is frequently arrested—as are those who write for the newspaper—and has spent much time in jail. See also *CAMEROON OUTLOOK; CAMEROON TIMES; CAMEROON TRIBUNE; L'EFFORT CAMEROUNAISE.*

MESSMER, PIERRE (1916–). He served as high **commissioner** to Cameroun (1956–58) following bloody riots in **Douala**. He tried to develop a more conciliatory leadership in the handling of the burning sociopolitical and economic issues inherited in his tenure. The Messmer administration exercised skillful politics, especially in the treatment of the National Union Movement of **Paul Soppo Priso,** and helped to reduce the popularity of the movement's program and appeal.

MEY, OUSMAN. This senior public administrator served as **governor** of the **North Province** for over a decade. Appointed in 1972, Governor Mey was removed from office on 22 August 1983 under the **Biya** presidency. During his long years as governor, he held other important posts at various administrative boards of parapublic corporations. After 1983, Mey was replaced by Fosi Yakum Ntaw as governor and relegated to a noninfluential post in the Ministry of Territorial Administration. He is presently chairman of the National Social Insurance Fund (CNPS).

MILL HILL FATHERS. *See* CATHOLIC CHURCH.

MINISTER OF STATE. This term denoted Cameroon's highest-ranked minister in the national government. A minister of state was presumed to possess special prerogatives over and above an ordinary government minister. The criterion for selection was never known, but practice suggested that a Northerner, an **Ewondo** of the **Center South**, a personality from the **Bamiléké** region of the **Western Province,** and a leading **anglophone** were usually adorned with the title of minister of state throughout the **Ahmadou Ahidjo** era.

MINISTRY OF WOMEN'S AFFAIRS. The ministry, created on 4 February 1984 by Pres. **Paul Biya**, is charged with coordinating, researching, and monitoring all aspects of **women**'s affairs in the country. The aim is to promote the interest of women in the economic, political, social, and cultural spheres of the state to ensure their total integration in the society. Generally, the typical Cameroonian traditional culture is male oriented. This ministry attempts to contribute toward greater understanding and realism in the position of women as well as to provide avenues for change in social mentalities in the Cameroon society. In addition to the creation of a Ministry of Women's affairs, a wing of the ruling party, the **Cameroon People's Democratic Movement (CPDM),** caters to women's matters. In May 1988, the functions of the Ministry of Women's Affairs were fused with those of the Ministry of Women's and Social Affairs. In December 1997, this ministry was once more split into two separate ministries: the Ministry of Women's Affairs under **Yaou Aissatsu**, and the Ministry of Social Affairs under Magdalene Fouda. The Minister of Women's Affairs is also the head of the women's wing of the CPDM.

MISE EN VALEUR. This term refers to an ostentatious French colonial policy of promoting planned economic development in previously unexploited areas. Originally elaborated in 1923 by Colonial Minister Albert Sarraut, the idea has been used to demonstrate **France**'s commitment to development of its territories. It was also conceived as an integral part of the new **association policy**, which emphasized the use of indigenous labor and material.

The view that the *mise en valeur* was particularly successful in **Cameroun** is erroneous because it is based principally on economic indicators of trade and exchange rather than on impact on the masses. The local population suffered social and economic disintegration of indigenous structures, unemployment rose, and hardship was a bitter characteristic of the labor system. Most road and railway construction still operated under the use of the *corvée* and ***indigénat*** system.

Furthermore, the idea of planned development was limited by the fact that the French concentrated their projects in the **"Fertile Crescent"** region leaving the greater part of the territory in substandard condition. This relative imbalance in terms of economic growth and development characterized the territory's economy into the independence epoch. While a few ethnic groups, such as the **Bamiléké**, gained materially from the *mise en valeur,* others, such as the **Bassa**, suffered from it. The numerous French citizens in Cameroun at the time were its main beneficiaries. *See also* FORCED LABOR.

MONETARY UNION OF EQUATORIAL AFRICA AND CAMEROON/ UNION MONETAIRE DE L'AFRIQUE EQUATORIALE ET CAMEROUN (UMAEC). Founded in 1962 to determine monetary policy for the member states (the former colonies of **French Equatorial Africa** plus Cameroon) acting as a single entity with a common currency, the UMAEC was very similar to the West African Monetary Union. The Bank of Central African States issued the currency of the Union. The UMAEC is reported to be inactive and replaced by the **Central African Monetary Union**.

MONGA, CELESTIN. A Cameroonian banker, Monga became a celebrity between 1990 and 1993 due to his activity in the prodemocracy movement. In the 27 December 1990 edition of ***Le Messager***, Monga wrote an open letter to Pres. **Paul Biya**, accusing him of being indifferent to the social and economic plight of Cameroonians. In consequence of this letter, he was arrested, tried, and given a three-year suspended sentence. Less than three years after, Monga conducted an interview with the controversial ex–finance minister, Robert Messi Messi, in which the latter exposed massive misappropriation of funds in a local bank, **Société Camerounaise de Banque (SCB),** by the president's wife, Jeanne Irene Biya, during his tenure as general manager of the bank. The implication was that the collapse of the bank was linked to the presidential couple. These two episodes undoubtedly made Monga popular, especially given the sociopolitical-economic atmosphere in Cameroon in the early 1990s. Thus, in May 1992, as rumors spread of the impending arrest of Monga on his return from abroad, a large crowd invaded the **Douala** international airport to prevent his arrest.

Monga published *The Anthropology of Anger*, a significant contribution to the study of democratization in Africa.

MONGO-BETI (ALEXANDRE BIYIDI) (1930–). This famous Cameroon author lived in exile for several years. Alexandre Biyidi was born in 1930 in the **Center Province**. He attended primary school in a Catholic mission school before entering **Lycée Leclerc** in **Yaoundé**. He completed his ***baccalauréat*** at age 19 before leaving for France in 1951, where he studied at Aix-en-Provence and later at the Sorbonne, earning a doctorate to become a professor of modern literature.

Prior to his accumulation of academic honors, Biyidi gained popularity as an author. It was at this stage that his use of a pen name began. Under the name Eza Boto he published his first novel, *Ville Cruelle*, in

1954. He later used the pen name Mongo-Beti to publish his more popular works, such as *The Poor Christ of Bomba* (1956), *Mission to Kala* (1957), and *King Lazarus* (1958), which all were powerful attacks on the mission mentality in dominated African societies. His other works, published after the independence of colonial entities in Africa, include *Perpetua and the Habit of Unhappiness* (1974) and *Remember Ruben* (1974), this last an unmistakable dedication to **Reuben Um Nyobe** and Cameroon's forgotten nationalist era. His fearless attacks on the postcolonial structures led to the banning of all his publications in Cameroon. This act has only helped to intensify his disgust, and he maintains a vigorous stance against the fragile regimes of independent Africa. Biyidi returned to Cameroon in 1992.

MONSIEUR SANS OBJET. In a 1991 speech denying the need for a sovereign national conference, Pres. **Paul Biya** stated that "la conférence nationale est sans objet pour le Cameroun." The opposition immediately began to refer to Biya as "Monsieur sans objet."

MOUMIE, FELIX-ROLAND (1926–1960). Moumie is one of the heroes of Cameroon nationalism. A radical nationalist and convinced marxist, he resorted to guerrilla warfare to advance the political claims of the **Union des Populations du Cameroun (UPC).** He was killed on 3 November 1960 by French security agents, presumably on orders of the Cameroun government, in Geneva, Switzerland. Born in **Foumban**, Moumie was educated in Cameroon and later earned a medical degree at the Ecole Normale William Ponty, near Dakar, Senegal, in 1950. He was a founding member of the UPC and rose to the level of copresident of the organization by 1952. He served in **Maroua** as a local physician before becoming UPC president.

Widely feared and discredited by the French administration because of its marxist convictions, the UPC was outlawed after 1955, which forced Moumie to go into exile living successively in **British Cameroons**, Cairo, Conakry, and Accra. As a leader of the UPC, he was usually at loggerheads with **Reuben Um Nyobe** over the manner of pursuing their vital interests. Moumie considered Um's tactical approach as too moderate and diplomatic and largely unsuited to the crushing colonial challenges. Moumie had grandiose designs for the UPC that could be summarized in the economic, theological, and political levels as marxist. It was this that brought him close to the radical nationalist leaders of Africa such as Nkrumah, Sekou Toure, and Nasser who sympathized with his cause after 1958. Although a fierce militant, Moumie was largely in charge of mobilizing outside sympathy and finance for the UPC, especially in support of the fighting guerrillas (***maquis***) in the **Bassa** and **Bamiléké** countryside. *See also* ALLIANCE FOR THE RECONSTRUCTION OF CAMEROON THROUGH THE SOVEREIGN NATIONAL CONFERENCE (ARC-SNC).

MOUNT CAMEROON. The highest mountain in West Africa rises to over 4,070 meters (13,350 feet) and interrupts the low-lying region of the Cameroon coast. The mountain has remained an active volcano with irregular eruptions, most recently in 1999. The mountain is located in the **Buea** area and known by the local inhabitants as "Fako." It is the source of livelihood and employment for many **Bakweri**. Tourists and explorers have also taken high interest and adventure on the mountain. There are three stages to the summits, popularly known as Huts I, II, and III. The climb to the mountain top is no longer a simple touristic attraction. Beginning in 1973, the Guinness Company has sponsored an annual Mount Cameroon race held every February. New trails also have been opened to offer the hiker a several-day trek to various locations on this huge structure.

MOUNTAIN CHAIN OF THE WEST. It originates from the volcanic islands of the Gulf of Guinea, Bioko (formerly Fernando Po), and Sao Tomé and extends for about 1,800 kilometers into the north east. The mountainous chain rises in the **Littoral** and **South West** and **West Provinces** and reaches to Mora in the North. It is interrupted by the **Benue** basin near **Garoua**. This mountainous chain includes **Mount Cameroon** (4,070 meters), the Menengouba (2,050 meters), the Bamboutos (2,680 meters), the **Bamiléké** Plateau (2,100 meters), the Bamoum massive, as well as the Mandara and **Atlantika Mountains**. The mountainous chain gradually diminishes into the **Lake Chad** basin.

MOUSSA YAYA, SARKIFADA (1926–). Although he was never a government minister, Moussa Yaya was a political potentate par excellence from 1958 until 1982. In January 1983, he suffered the worst humiliation in the country's political history when he was stripped of all his posts by former president **Ahmadou Ahidjo**. Born in **Garoua** on 3 April 1926, he attended the Ecole Principale de Garoua and did technical training in **Maroua**. His only nonpolitical duty was as head of the Benue subsector for animal breeding. He later became an indispensable confidant of President Ahidjo, who selected him for the **Assemblée Territoriale du Cameroun (ATCAM)** following the death of a Northern incumbent in 1956. He was secretary-general and political secretary of the **Union Camerounaise (UC)** (1958–66); secretary of social affairs for the **Cameroon National Union (CNU)**; and member of the Political Bureau (1966–83). His party duties were exercised alongside his role as member of Parliament to which he was successively reelected and served as deputy speaker, but virtually the de facto head, from August 1959 until January 1983. In parliament he was president of the first Commission of Constitutional Law, General Administration, Justice and the Armed Forces, and, least known to the public, he was president of the High Court of Cameroon (1964–83). He participated actively in the Executive Committee of the Inter-Parliamentary Union and was a member of multiple Cameroon permanent delegations to the United Nations and a member of the Cameroon Delegation to The Hague on the referendum issue with **Great Britain** at the International Court of Justice.

The public apparently knew Moussa Yaya most in his range of corporate duties. He was chairman, vice chairman, or board member of at least 10 of the most highly funded state corporations, including that for electricity (Société Nationale d'Electricité du Cameroun, SONEL), water **(National Water Corporation of Cameroon, SNEC)**, investment **(National Investment Company, SNI)**, hydrocarbons **(Société Nationale des Hydrocarbures, SNH)**, and air transport (Cameroon Airlines, CAMAIR). For this remarkable accumulation of functions, Moussa Yaya had the widest clientele and constituency of any politician in Cameroon history.

That his powerful role ended on 10 January 1983 could simply be taken as coincidental with the end of the Ahidjo era. However, the irony of Moussa Yaya's political misfortune was that it was inflicted by one who had been his mentor all along, former president Ahidjo. Still serving as chairman of the Cameroon National Union after his resignation as head of state, Ahidjo accused Moussa Yaya and four others of engaging in subversive maneuvers aimed at creating confusion in party ranks that could endanger national unity. Ahidjo believed the overly ambitious Moussa Yaya could be a threat to his constitutional successor. Critics of the former president later argued that Moussa Yaya was only eliminated because he detested Ahidjo's active presence in the nation's affairs and was ready to reveal the former president's insincerity to the country. Moussa Yaya was readmitted into the **Cameroon People's Democratic Movement**, at his request, by Pres. **Paul Biya** in 1987. He does not hold any official party post and continues to live a private life as founder-director of the Walde Sarkifada Ranch in Malombo in the **Adamawa Province**.

MOUVEMENT D'ACTION NATIONALE DU CAMEROUN (MANC). This alliance party was created from a coalition of the **Ngondo** establishment (led by **Paul Soppo Priso**) and the Association Traditionelle Bantu Efoula-Meyong (led by **Charles Assale**) in March 1956. The MANC sought to bring about the integration of all political forces in the country around a "common minimal program." French authorities considered it as a **Union des Populations du Cameroun (UPC)** movement in disguise. In the Legislative Assembly elections, MANC gained eight seats to form the **Groupe de Huit** opposed to the **André-Marie Mbida** government in 1957. It joined **Ahmadou Ahidjo's** coalition government of 1958–60.

MOUVEMENT POUR LA DÉFENCE DE LA REPUBLIQUE/MOVEMENT FOR THE DEFENCE OF THE REPUBLIC (MDR). This small party gets its support in the **Extreme North Province**. To a large extent its support is based on anti-**Fulani**, anti-**Islam**, anti–**National Union for Democracy and Progress (UNDP)** sentiment. As such, the MDR apparently has received support and encouragement from the **Cameroon People's Democratic Movement (CPDM).** In the **elections for the National Assembly (1992),** the MDR won six seats. As the CPDM failed to win a majority of seats, the CPDM and MDR formed a coalition government. In return, the MDR was given four cabinet positions. In the **elections for the National Assembly (1997),** the MDR won only one seat, the one contested by MDR leader Dakolé Daïssala. The CPDM won a majority and no longer had any need for a coalition with the MDR.

MOVEMENT FOR DEMOCRACY AND PROGRESS (MDP). *See* NATIONAL UNION FOR DEMOCRACY AND PROGRESS (NUDP/UNDP).

MUKETE, VICTOR E. (1918–). Mukete was the first Cameroonian chairman of the **Cameroon Development Corporation (CDC)**. He is the traditional head (*fon*) of the Bafaw, member of the **Economic and Social Council,** and a member of the Central Committee of the **Cameroon People's Democratic Movement (CPDM)** party. Born on 15 November 1918 in **Kumba**, **South West Province**, he attended the government school there before pursuing his education in Umuahia and the Yaba Higher College of Agriculture in Nigeria. He also studied in Ibadan and at the University of Manchester, graduating with a degree in botany in 1951. After a year at Cambridge University, he returned to work as an agricultural officer in the Nigerian Civil Service and assumed other political roles. He later became general secretary of the **Kamerun National Congress (KNC)** and member of the Federal House of Representatives in Lagos. He was a federal minister without portfolio and served as Nigerian federal minister for research and information from 1951 until 1959. Mukete played an important role in the early politics of transition in **Southern Cameroons** and has served in different capacities, including vice president of the Chamber of Commerce, Industry and Mines and member of the National Council of Credit in post**reunification** Cameroon. Fon Mukete's lasting legacy was in the post as first Cameroon chairman of the CDC (1960–81). Since then he has fully engaged in a vast private agricultural enterprise and assumed active party political functions and as a leading member of the country's Economic and Social Council. He is currently chairman of the Société des Telecommunications Internationales du Cameroun (INTELCAM).

MUKONG, ALBERT WOMAH. A **human rights** activist, author, and politician, Mukong is currently executive director of the Human Rights Defence Group (HRDG) based in **Bamenda**, **North West Province**. He has been detained and imprisoned several times by the **Ahmadou Ahidjo** and **Paul Biya** governments because of his strident demands for democracy, human rights, and the rule of law. In the 1990s, he was also active in demands for **anglophone** rights, the return of federal government, and the possible independence of **Southern Cameroons**. Among his numerous publications, *My Stewardship in the Cameroon Struggle* (1992) and *Prisoner without a Crime* (1989) are quite important.

MUNA, SOLOMON TANDENG (1912–). Muna is a longtime leading figure in Cameroon politics. Former president of the **National Assembly**, vice president of the **Federal Republic,** and prime minister of **West Cameroon,** he was born in 1912 in Ngyen-Mbo, Momo Division, in the **North West Province**. He received primary education at the Local Authority School in Bali (1916–26) and the Government School in **Bamenda** (1926–31). He entered the Government Teacher's Training College in Kake, near **Kumba**, in the **South West Province** (1934–36), graduating with a Grade III certificate in 1936; he earned a Grade II certificate in 1942 and a Grade I certificate in 1947. He obtained a diploma from the Institute of Education of the University of London in 1959, specializing in school administration and teacher training. He served as headmaster, head tutor, and supervisor of schools (1937–54).

Thereafter, Muna's life was embroiled in the politics of the quest for independence in **British Cameroons** and **reunification** with **French Cameroun**. He was deputy leader of the **Kamerun National Congress (KNC)**, which led to his successive ministerial positions. He was minister of works for Eastern Nigeria (1951–53) and Executive Council member for National Resources for Southern Cameroons (1954–57). Muna broke away from the KNC in 1957 along with other "reunificationists" to form the **Kamerun National Democratic Party (KNDP)**, led by **John Ngu Foncha**. It was thanks to the successive wins of the KNDP in the general elections that Muna owed his posts of minister of works (1959) and minister of commerce and industry (1959) in the Southern Cameroons government. At independence in 1960, Muna served as minister of finance. He was among the few **anglophone** ministers in the federal government of Cameroon, where he served as minister of transport, mines, posts and telecommunications from 1961 until 1968.

In the interim, Muna led the breakaway from the KNDP to form the **Cameroon United Congress** in 1965. In 1966, he served in the Central Committee and the Political Bureau of the **Cameroon National Union (CNU)** party. In 1967, he was appointed **prime minister** of **West Cameroon** and from 1970 until 1972 he served as vice president of the **Federal Republic of Cameroon**. He was a minister of state in the first unitary government of the country until he was elected president of the National Assembly in 1973.

Consequently, Muna became the leading figure for anglophone Cameroonians and the second personality in the country after Pres. **Ahmadou Ahidjo**. Rightly or wrongly, many anglophones tended to blame him for the strains inherent in the system. His constitutional prerogative as successor to the head of state was lost in a constitutional amendment of June 1979. Nevertheless, as speaker of the National Assembly, Muna played multiple international roles, including vice president of the ACP–EEC Consultative Assembly (1976–77), copresident of the same body (1978–82) and leader of the Cameroon parliamentary group to the Inter-Parliamentary Union and the Union of African Parliaments. He also exhibited wide-ranging interests in his role in the scout movement, serving as chief scout in West Cameroon (1968–72), chief scout of Cameroon (1973–79), chairman of the Africa Regional Scout Committee (1972–76), and a member of the World Scout Committee.

Muna survived the post-Ahidjo transition and even attempted an unsuccessful peace shuttle in 1983 between **Yaoundé–Garoua**–Yaoundé and Paris to seek reconciliation in the growing feud between Pres. **Paul Biya** and former president Ahidjo. Muna was reelected to the Central Committee and Political Bureau of the **Cameroon People's Democratic Movement (CPDM)** in March 1985 but resigned in April 1988, just prior to the first competitive legislative election in Cameroon's postindependence history. Throughout his long political career, Muna personally met with over 100 foreign leaders and received medals from many foreign countries.

MUNGO RIVER. This important drainage feature flows across the Loum, Mbanga, and **Nkongsamba** area. The Mungo is politically important. The bridge at Bekoko over the Mungo River was widely used for political demarcation between former **West** and **East Cameroon** until 1972. Cameroonians from both ends of the Mungo bridge needed a *laissez-passer* (travel pass) to cross over to the other federated state.

MUSIC. In addition to makossa and bikutsi, the two most popular styles across the country, other varieties of Cameroon music include the tsamassi of the **Bamiléké**, which was popularized by André-Marie Tala; the mangambou of the Bangangté, made known by Pierre Diddy Tchakounte; the assiko traditional musical rhythm of the **Bassa**, propagated by Jean Bikoko; and the typical sound of the coastal peoples, ambas-i-bay, revived by Salle John.

Cameroon has other musicians who have made a name in a particular way. Jo Biso and Vicky Edimo are making strides in the world of jazz, Tim and Foty excelled in vocal acrobatics, the Nigerian-based Prince Nico Mbarga sent a sensation across all Africa with his superhit "Sweet Mother," and Arbo Gaste Mbella specializes in religious music and gospel songs from his longtime base in France. More recently, a softer, more poetic style of music is gaining popularity due to the talents of such artists as Henri Dikongué and Sally Nyolo. It is thanks to these personalities that Cameroon music is fast competing with Cameroon football as the most distinctive factor with which a majority of Africans have come to identify the country. *See also* DIBANGO, MANU.

MUSLIM HOLY WAR. *See* JIHAD.

MUSLIM POPULATIONS. A conglomeration of ethnic groupings in today's northern provinces have adopted the Islamic faith. These groupings consist of large entities such as the **Fulani**. Although a common universal belief ties them together, they still retain their unique sociocultural attributes. The Muslim population of the northern provinces is not a unified or coherent ensemble.

The Mandara were organized in a weak kingdom in the northern portions of the mountainous chains and Islamized by the Choa Arabs at the beginning of the 18th century. Islamic influence was strongest with the **chief** and his entourage and only gradually reached the local populations. Political, fiscal, and religious authority is vested in the *tixe* (sultan), who symbolized political centralization. The Mandara population was stratified socially into freemen and slaves, and commerce grew out of trade with the powerful Bornu Kingdom.

The Fulani are the largest of the Islamic peoples in northern Cameroon. Their settlement is the result of successive migrations in the late 18th century. Today they constitute a distinctive grouping based largely on their ethnic features and their glorification of **Islam**. Learning in Fulani society is highly regarded, particularly in Islamic teachings. The teacher is known as the Modibo, and their role in Fulani society is revealed in the leadership of **Modibo Adama**. Besides learned men, the preponderant role of the warrior is exemplified in the conquest of **Uthman Dan Fodio**. Contemporary Fulani Muslims are grouped in collectivities headed by a "commander of believers" known as the ***lamido.***

It was the fervent belief in religion that led to the declaration of the holy war (***jihad***) against their neighbors and the establishment of Fulani hegemony centered in Yola, **Nigeria**. Ardent pastoralists, nomadism is a major occupation of the masses in the complex and highly stratified society. Islamic populations also exist in **anglophone** Cameroon, where the **Bororo**, a Fulani group, have settled in the **North West Province**. In the **Western Province**, the **Bamoum** are also Muslims.

MUSONGE, PETER MAFANY (1942–). Musonge was born 3 November 1942 at Muea near **Buea** in Fako Division, **South West Province**. He attended primary school in Muea and secondary school in **St. Joseph's College**, Sasse, 1956–61, where he graduated with a West African School Certificate. He proceeded to the United States to the Drexel Institute of Technology, Philadelphia, from where he graduated with a B.S. in civil engineering in 1967; the next year he completed his master's degree. In March 1969, he was recruited into the **West Cameroon** Department of Public Works in Victoria (**Limbe**) as an engineer in charge of the laboratory. He was later posted to serve as the assistant area engineer in

Bamenda, until November 1970 when he was appointed to the post of engineer at the Directorate of Roads and Bridges in the Ministry of Transport, **Yaoundé**. Between September 1972 and October 1973, Peter Musonge held several top engineering positions in the government.

In 1976, Musonge returned to the United States to attend a course at the **World Bank** Institute for Economic Development in Washington, D.C. On his return, he served as deputy director of roads up to 1980, when he was appointed General Manager of the Civil Engineering Laboratory (LABOGENIE) in Yaoundé, a post he led until April 1984. In 1981, Musonge attended the Paris-based Institute for Higher Commercial Studies. Between April 1984 and August 1988, he headed the Civil Engineering Equipment Pool (MATGENIE), before being appointed general manager of the **Cameroon Development Corporation (CDC)**. His tenure as general manager of the CDC salvaged that corporation from economic collapse. In fact, his tenure as general manager of the CDC confirmed his possession of rare managerial skills.

Musonge has many academic and national honors to his credit. He was decorated with the Commander of the Order of Valour, one of the highest awards in Cameroon. He is also a fellow of the Cameroon Society of Engineers and president of the African Natural Rubber Producers' Association (ACNA). He was at once chairman of the University of **Buea** Development Fund Management Committee and member of its council. On 19 September 1996, Musonge was appointed prime minister, the second anglophone to be appointed to that post since the introduction of multiparty politics in 1990. He was reappointed to that position in December 1997.

MVENG, ENGELBERT, S. J. (1930–1994). Mveng was an historian, author, artist, and Catholic priest. Born on 9 May 1930 in Enam-Ngal in the Ntem Division, Reverend Father Mveng was an accomplished scholar. He attended mission and diocesan schools in Ebolowa and **Yaoundé** between 1936 and 1948 and later taught and attended the seminary in Akono and Otele. Between 1951 and 1953, he trained as a Jesuit novitiate in the then Belgian Congo before leaving for Europe in 1954 for studies in three licenses in theology, letters, and philosophy as well as a doctorate in philology from the University of Paris in 1964.

Mveng returned home in 1965 and lectured in the Department of History at the **University of Yaoundé,** rising to the level of head of department on several occasions. He also served as the country's director of cultural affairs and won several prizes for his scholarly and artistic works. His various manuals and texts, such as *L'Histoire du Cameroun,* have been revised several times since 1963. The latest edition in the series on Cameroon history was published in 1984. Father Mveng was murdered in 1994 under mysterious circumstances. No solution to the crime has been determined.

– N –

NACHTIGAL, GUSTAV (1834–1884). Nachtigal, a German explorer, was a military physician who led expeditions across the African continent. He was appointed German imperial consul-general in Tunis in 1884. From Tunis, Nachtigal traveled to establish German territories along the coast, including the German **Kamerun protectorate**, 12 July 1884. Nachtigal was the key German personality present during the hoisting of the German flag over **Douala**. He died on his return trip to **Germany** in 1884.

NATION BUILDING. Nation building is the process of creating a national identity to overcome the centrifugal forces of subnationalities prevalent in many postcolonial societies. Nation-building symbols consist of every act or object that reflects the very essence of state over a region or an ethnic group. Cameroon faces more than a fair share of the nation-building problem. It not only struggles with multifarious ethnic groupings but also faces problems of regional divisiveness (**Grassfield** vs. coast, North vs. South), language differences (**francophones** vs. **anglophones**), and religious divisiveness (**Muslim** vs. **Christian**). These problems were crucial in the decision leading to the formation of a unitary state and the continuance of a centralized system of administration thereafter. *See also* BILINGUALISM; ETHNIC CONFLICT; TOMBEL MASSACRE.

NATIONAL ANTHEM. *See* CAMEROON NATIONAL ANTHEM.

NATIONAL ARMY OF KAMERUN LIBERATION/ARMEE DE LIBERATION NATIONALE DU KAMERUN (ALNK). This is the official name of the guerrilla forces of the **Union des Populations du Cameroun (UPC)** that organized the underground insurgency against government troops between 1955 and 1962. Its activities were most effective in the West, East, and South regions of the country. A triumvirate of **Felix-Roland Moumie**, **Ernest Ouandie,** and **Abel Kingue** comprised the Comité Directeur, which had bases in radical African countries like Guinea, Egypt, Ghana, and Congo. Local leadership of the ALNK was controlled by various individuals, including **Osende Afana**.

NATIONAL ASSEMBLY. The Cameroon National Assembly is the country's legislative body and a historical successor to the **Federal National Assembly,** which was dissolved in 1972. The current assembly began existing in its present form in May 1973. It originally consisted of 120 members selected from various provinces on a demographic basis. They are elected by direct and universal suffrage for a five-year term. The Assembly meets in plenary and ordinary sessions of 30 days each and consists of various committees presided over by an internally elected chairman. Members of the Assembly can be called into an extraordinary session by the head of state or a two-thirds majority of parliamentarians. They elect their own members of the National Assembly Bureau. Prior to the drawing up of a new constitution for Cameroon in 1996, the president (speaker) of the Assembly was the provisional successor to the Head of State. Between 1973 and 1988, members to the National Assembly were preselected by the party and presented to the electorate for approval. Generally, the electorate unanimously approved the party's single list. No member of Parliament has tabled a bill on the floor, and the head of state has exercised this prerogative almost single-handedly.

In July 1983, a constitutional amendment increased the number of parliamentarians from 120 to 180. After the November 1987 session, the Assembly was dissolved in favor of a new democratic option. For the first time, the party selected competitive lists of party members for various regions of the country in the parliamentary election of April 1988. Eighty-four percent of incumbent parliamentarians lost their seats. The 15-year speaker of the National Assembly, **Solomon Tandeng Muna**, resigned prior to the elections in March 1988. He was replaced by another **anglophone**, Lawrence F. Shang, in June 1988.

The advent of multiparty democracy in December 1990 brought further changes in the Assembly. For the first time since its creation, election was conducted on a multiparty basis. The legislative elections of March 1992 were thus won by four parties: the **Cameroon People's Democratic Movement (CPDM)** won 88 seats, the **National Union for Democracy and Progress (UNDP)** won 68 seats, the **Union des Populations du Cameroon (UPC)** won 18 seats, and the **Movement pour la Défence de la République (MDR)** won six seats. Despite this, the Assembly remained a CPDM-dominated one, especially as the MDR allied itself with it. Alongside this development was the change in the Assembly's president. For the first time since the formation of a unitary state, a **francophone**, Cavayé Yegué Gibril, became president of the Assembly, taking over from Lawrence F. Shang.

The **constitution of 1996** creates a two-chamber legislature with a Senate and the National Assembly. The president of the Senate or his vice president becomes the interim successor of the head of state should the country's president be incapacitated or die. The second multiparty elections to the Assembly were held in May 1997, with seven parties winning the following number of seats: the CPDM, 116; the **Social Democratic Front (SDF),** 43; the UNDP, 13; the Cameroon Democratic Union, five; the MDR, one; the UPC, one; and the Mouvement Pour la Libération Jeunesse Camerounaise (MLJC), one. Another change in the Assembly concerned the introduction of the question-and-answer session during the March 1998 ordinary session of Parliament.

NATIONAL ASSEMBLY OF CAMEROUN/ASSEMBLEE NATIONALE DU CAMEROUN (ANCAM). ANCAM was the legislative body of the **République du Cameroun** from April 1960 until October 1961. The historic successor of the **Assemblée Législative du Cameroun (ALCAM)**, it came into existence following the general election of 10 April 1960, with the **Union Camerounaise** as the dominant party. Following his investiture as the first president of the République du Cameroun, on 5 May 1960, **Ahmadou Ahidjo** began the process leading toward the eventual dissolution of parliamentary opposition and the formation of the unified party, the Union Camerounaise and the **Union Nationale du Cameroun (UNC),** in September 1966. The ANCAM was a unicameral legislature and had legislative powers over persons and property rights; political, administrative, judicial, and security matters; as well as socioeconomic and financial policies.

NATIONAL CENTRE FOR ADMINISTRATION AND MAGISTRACY/CENTRE NATIONAL D'ADMINISTRATION ET DE MAGISTRATURE (CENAM). CENAM is the institutional successor to the National School of Administration and Magistracy/Ecole Nationale d'Administration et de Magistrature (ENAM). Created in 1979, ENAM was designed to train elite Cameroonian officials for the dispensation of justice and the execution of administrative functions. The cream of Cameroonian elites graduated from ENAM. However, ENAM was largely considered an institution for Northerners, the region of the former head of state. This placed Northerners at a variety of important posts within governmental and parapublic structures. In a postresignation interview, former president **Ahmadou Ahidjo** denied such allegations. On 27 September 1985, a presidential decree created CENAM to provide the administrative hierarchy with capable cadres and the ability to respond to the challenges of change and development. Unlike ENAM, CENAM is aimed to respond to Pres. **Paul Biya**'s vision of the country. It is designed to serve as a symbol of the **New Deal** by making administrative reform and new techniques an important factor in the training.

NATIONAL CIVIC SERVICE FOR PARTICIPATION IN DEVELOPMENT. *See* NATIONAL OFFICE FOR PARTICIPATION IN DEVELOPMENT (ONPD).

NATIONAL COORDINATION COMMITTEE OF OPPOSITION PARTIES (NCCOP). *See* GHOST TOWN OPERATIONS.

NATIONAL COUNCIL OF NIGERIA AND THE CAMEROONS (NCNC). This political party was founded by nationalist leaders of **Nigeria** and **British Cameroons** to exert pressure on **Great Britain** to hasten the political development of the two territories. It was formed in August 1944 and led by the Nigerian, Dr. Nnamdi Azikiwe. Key Cameroonian members in the NCNC included **Emmanuel M. L. Endeley**. The major organizations from British Cameroons affiliated to the NCNC were the Cameroon Youth League, the **Bamenda Improvement Association,** and the Bakweri Union.

The party collapsed in 1953 as a result of a prolonged governmental crisis in the Eastern Regional House of Assembly in Nigeria and the quest for a separate autonomy by a significant faction of the Cameroonian membership. The **Kamerun National Congress** and the Kamerun Peoples' Party were formed out of this split within the NCNC. Despite its short-lived existence, the NCNC was the closest political partnership linking the destinies of Nigeria and Cameroon in the preindependence period.

NATIONAL FOOTBALL TEAM. *See* INDOMITABLE LIONS.

NATIONAL FUND FOR RURAL DEVELOPMENT/FOND NATIONAL DE DEVELOPPEMENT RURAL (FONADER). FONADER was one of the major institutions charged with the implementation of the **Green Revolution**. It was established in 1973 as part of government preoccupation with agriculture, which remains the base of the country's economy. It was designed to display a particular bias in favor of the rural dweller, who constitutes the bulk of the country's population. FONADER activities covered areas such as agriculture, animal husbandry, silviculture, art- and craftwork, and rural habitation. Aid was granted to well-defined projects approved by the administrative board of FONADER. These loans were repayable but did not carry any interest.

In its years of operation, the apparently simple procedures of an application for credit and technical study and justification for assistance have turned out to be overly complicated and bureaucratic. This scared off the aspiring rural dweller whom FONADER was mandated to serve. FONADER became the tool of the wealthy urban Cameroonian who is well versed in the corrupt practices of the system. Cut off from the services of FONADER as well were youths trained in the **National Office for Participation in Development**, who required credit and assistance to enable their establishment as agriculturalists. For these reasons, and in the wake of a crushing **economic crisis**, FONADER was reorganized in 1987 with a better-oriented **Crédit Foncier** to cater to the objectives previously assigned to FONADER. In 1990, the Cameroon Agricultural Bank opened and took over most of FONADER's activities.

NATIONAL INVESTMENT COMPANY/SOCIETE NATIONALE D'INVESTISSEMENT (SNI). The SNI was created in 1964 by the government as an institution to foster the dynamic role of the private sector in stimulating the growth of industries and the construction of major development projects. To perform this task, the SNI serves as the principal institution for mobilizing and orienting national savings toward economic, social, agricultural, commercial, and financial development through creating major projects, undertaking all significant studies and financial operations, buying or selling investment capital of companies, and contributing to the financial management of major companies. As a result, the SNI is considered a catalyst of development. The **economic crisis** has led to pressure for SNI to divest itself of numerous holdings through closure and **privatization**.

NATIONAL LANGUAGES. These include the languages of the 300 ethnic groupings in the country. National languages are distinct from official languages, which in Cameroon are **French** and **English**. Consequently, national languages have a lower priority in the country although some have been widely developed to script level. Early Christian missionaries translated the Bible and song books in **Duala**, Mungaka, **Ewondo,** and others. Sultan **Njoya** had invented an original script for the **Bamoum** language. Currently, national languages receive only minimal programming in radio broadcasts. A recent study advocated the use of various languages on a regional basis to facilitate communication. According to this study, **Fulani** would serve for the northern provinces; Ewondo for the **Center**, **South,** and **East;** and **pidgin English** for the rest of the country. Today, numerous languages are being reduced to writing by the members of the Summer Institute for Languages, a Christian missionary organization. Several national languages are on the verge of becoming extinct. *See also* BILINGUALISM; FRANGLAIS; NATION BUILDING; PIDGIN ENGLISH.

NATIONAL OFFICE FOR PARTICIPATION IN DEVELOPMENT/ OFFICE NATIONAL DE PARTICIPATION AU DEVELOPPEMENT (ONPD). Created in 1974 as part of a broad program designed to dynamize Cameroon's development objectives and to integrate youths into the process, it was then known as the National Civic Service for Participation in Development and was attached to the Ministry of Youth and Sports. Reorganized in 1979, the National Civic Service took on its present title and has since been attached to the Ministry of Agriculture. However, because of its wide-ranging objectives of civic training and moral, professional, and military preparation, as well as the need to encourage interest in agriculture and the settlement of youths in rural areas, various other ministries participate in ONPD activities.

The ONPD could largely be seen as a mechanism designed to ward off the alarming threat of **rural exodus**. The main undoing of this strategy is the failure to provide youths with the necessary incentives and resources to facilitate their establishment in the rural areas. Its greatest accomplishment was the "Sahel-Vert" project of the mid-1970s, which aimed at arresting the gradual desertification in northern regions of the country by planting trees.

NATIONAL PORTS AUTHORITY (NPA). This is a public corporation of an industrial and commercial character under the control of the Ministry of Transport. The NPA has financial autonomy. Its mission is to equip, manage, and develop the ports of the country, the major of which are **Douala**, **Kribi**, and **Limbe**/Tiko. It is also mandated to study ways toward the establishment of new ports. The corporation attempts to match Cameroon port equipment and installation to modern exigencies, to provide better management methods, and to train adequate personnel for the execution of technical services. Much of the authority's activity has been concentrated in the Douala port, where the company also has its headquarters. While the Douala port clearly handles both national and international needs of neighboring countries, this concentration has led to the slump of the ports of Limbe and Tiko in the **South West Province**. Kribi has increased in significance in recent years. On completion of the Chad–Kribi **pipeline**, it will become a very important port.

Apart from its tendency toward differential development of the country's natural resources, the port system is also the target of public outrage because of the prevalence of fraud, clandestine activities, and the considerably high import duties. The National Ports Authority and its adjoining custom services became easy targets of the **Paul Biya** slogan of "**rigor and moralization**." Due to widespread corruption and mismanagement, major sectors of NPA responsibility have been taken over by part of the **privatization** process that has resulted from the **economic crisis**.

NATIONAL PRODUCE MARKETING BOARD (NPMB)/OFFICE NATIONAL DE COMMERCIALISATION DES PRODUITS DE BASE (ONCPB). The board was created by law on 9 September 1972 but was finally established by presidential decree in 1978. The decree specified its structure and functioning, as well as defined its duties: to regulate prices for raw materials to farmers, to seek equity between producers' guaranteed prices and export sale prices, to organize and control the sale of agricultural products in domestic and international markets, and to take necessary measures to improve the quality and quantity of agricultural production. The NPMB also represented Cameroon in all international organizations dealing with raw materials issues, which made it a member of multiple organizations. An equally important part of its domestic activity included granting subventions to various parastatal institutions to permit them to carry out their specific programs. Its most significant task included fixing prices for the produce of a majority of the country's population. In 1984, the NPMB began with an ostentatious price policy that substantially raised the income of the local populations in net value.

The NPMB was particularly active in the buying and marketing of **cocoa**, **coffee**, **cotton**, groundnuts, and **palm** kernels, which are essential to Cameroon's agricultural prosperity. The establishment of the NPMB eliminated the Caisse de Stabilisation de Prix in former **East Cameroon** and the Produce Marketing Organization in the former **West Cameroon**. The NPMB worked in close collaboration with subsidiary personalities or institutions, such as the Licenced Buying Agents in the **anglophone** provinces and the *exportateurs agrées* in the **francophone** regions, both of which served as middlemen in the relations between farmers and the NPMB. Mismanagement and the economic recession that set in around 1987 led to the dissolution of the NPMB and the liquidation of its assets in 1991. The NPMB's functions have been taken over by the National Cocoa and Coffee Board, which is in charge of buying and marketing of cocoa and coffee. *See also* AGRICULTURAL POLICY.

NATIONAL REHABILITATION CENTER FOR THE HANDICAPPED. Created in 1972 in Etoug-Ebe at the outskirts of **Yaoundé**, the center is charged with the main objective of integrating people with disabilities into the lifestream of society. The center is simultaneously under the Ministries of Public Health and Social Affairs, causing questions of jurisdiction, competence, and coordination to emerge. Since its conception, the Etouge-Ebe Center has fulfilled an international vocation involving the care of people with disabilities from neighboring countries including the **Central African Republic, Chad, Congo,** and **Gabon**. In general, the center has very limited resources to attain an appreciable degree of efficacy.

NATIONAL SCHOOL FOR ADMINISTRATION AND MAGISTRACY (ENAM). *See* NATIONAL CENTRE FOR ADMINISTRATION AND MAGISTRACY (CENAM).

NATIONAL UNION OF CAMEROON WORKERS (NUCW). This union was formed in 1972 out of an amalgamation of postindependence professional groups and worker's unions from **West** and **East Cameroon**. It was believed that these unions served the designs of various political parties. Between 30 October and 13 November 1971, three major trade unions—the Union des Syndicats Croyant du Cameroun (USCC), the Fédération des Syndicats du Cameroun (FSC), and the West Cameroon Trade Union Congress (WCTUC)—were dissolved. It is from the ruins of these unions that the Union of Cameroon Workers was born in 1969. In 1972, the union was renamed the National Union of Cameroon Workers (NUCW) for the sake of **nation building**. The NUCW became affiliated to the national party and followed the political options defined by the **Cameroon National Union (CNU)**. The first president of the NUCW was Moise Satougle Defith (1972–75). He was replaced by Jerome Abondo, who served as president until 1985. The president of the NUCW was an official member of the Central Committee of the CNU.

NATIONAL UNION FOR DEMOCRACY AND PROGRESS (NUDP)/ UNION NATIONAL POUR LA DEMOCRATIE ET LE PROGRES (UNDP). **Maigari Bello Bouba** had been a significant figure in the **Ahmadou Ahidjo** administration, and many expected him to succeed Ahidjo as president. However, **Paul Biya** became the next president, and as relations between Biya and Ahidjo deteriorated, Bello Bouba went into exile in **Nigeria**. As the multiparty era dawned, from exile he declared the formation of a new party, the National Union for Democracy and Progress (NUDP). The NUDP was legalized in 1991 under the leadership of **Samuel Eboua**, another strong Ahidjoist. Bello Bouba returned from exile, and a struggle immediately began between him and Eboua for leadership of the party. In 1992, the struggle was won by Bello Bouba, and Eboua left the NUDP to found the Movement for Democracy and Progress (MDP).

The NUDP has been built on the Ahidjo inheritance. Its main strength is in the northern provinces, especially among the **Fulani** and **Muslim populations**. In the **elections for the National Assembly (1992),** the NUDP won 68 seats to become the largest opposition party. It showed strength in the **anglophone** areas, but only because the **Social Democratic Front (SDF)** of **John Fru Ndi** boycotted the election. In the **elections for the National Assembly (1997),** the SDF participated and the NUDP lost its anglophone support. In 1997, Bello Bouba accepted a ministerial position in the Biya cabinet.

While the NUDP is a significant opposition party, it has a more conservative orientation than the more radical SDF. Its leaders are more willing to work with the Biya government. As an ethnic and regional party, it will be difficult for the NUDP to broaden its appeal beyond its present areas of strength.

NATIONAL WATER CORPORATION OF CAMEROON/SOCIETE NATIONALE DES EAUX DU CAMEROUN (SNEC). It was created in 1967 to handle the management of water supply installations, and the transportation, storage, and distribution of water in the rural and urban agglomerations of the country. Popularly associated by its French acronym, SNEC, the corporation is a mixed enterprise operating on the basis of concessions. It operated principally in the former **East Cameroon**, while the Public Works Department (PWD) controlled water supply in the former **West Cameroon**. Following the political and structural centralization of 1972, SNEC began operating nationally, taking over functions formerly assigned to the PWD. Only a small proportion of the population receive piped water in their houses. Many localities have no safe water supply. In addition to the lack of geographic breadth of its services, a damaging critique against SNEC is the high charges levied for the use of a basic necessity like water. SNEC is scheduled for **privatization** under the **structural adjustment program (SAP)** set up to meet the **economic crisis**.

NATIVE AUTHORITIES. These were indigenous representatives of various ethnic groups, recognized or created by the British administration in **Southern Cameroons**. This system of administration was known as **indirect rule**. It was the result of practical necessity by the British rather than any trust or interest in the native authorities. Throughout the period of British rule, the administration suffered from a chronic lack of funds and personnel to carry out policy. Native authorities became an inescapable alternative.

The predominance of an indirect rule policy was tainted by reported British disrespect, arrest, and imprisonment of local **chiefs** in the early periods of the administration. The official proclamation of an indirect rule policy was made in April 1921 by **resident** Maj. F. H. Ruxton. Native Authorities were of three different categories: the well-established hereditary traditional leadership of the ***fons*** in the **Bamenda Grassfield** area, the village or district head appointed by the British or accepted by the population, and a council of elders in areas where authoritative leadership could not be imposed. Native authorities handled taxation, criminal offenses, health development, and road construction. They could keep half of the revenues obtained through taxation and court fines. The entire system of **indirect rule** in Africa was the brainchild of a leading British official, Lord Lugard, who also served in **Nigeria**.

NATIVE BAPTIST CHURCH (NBC). This important religious institution in colonial and preindependence Cameroon brought together 3,000 members by 1955 and remained an edifice of Christian nationalism and combative leadership. Native Baptists were formed by the English Baptists prior to German rule. They were given much independence and self-government in their religious organization. Although this initially worried the Germans, they quickly developed good relations. The major Native Baptist Churches were in the coastal towns of **Douala**, Victoria (**Limbe**), and Hickory.

Leadership was a crucial determinant in the NBC's existence. In Victoria during the German epoch, native Pastor Wilson worked closely with the Germans and ably retained the quasi-autonomy of his church. In Douala, it was the German pastor Bender who ordained **Lotin Same** in 1908. Lotin Same later became president of the NBC in 1915, and a troubling relationship ensued with the French authorities. Despite French determination to make missionaries defend its colonial vision, the NBC refused to be aligned as a subsidiary of the Society of Evangelical Missions of Paris. This made the NBC an autonomous religious institution of the first order. The church stressed Christian indigenization and religious coexistence. These claims embarrassed the French, who regarded the NBC as a "ferment of anarchy" and branded its members as "German Baptists." The NBC still exists today in Douala, **Yaoundé,** and other localities. *See also* BAPTIST MISSION.

NDAM NJOYA, ADAMOU (1942–). Professional diplomat, professor, former minister, and author, Ndam Njoya was born in Njika-Foumban, **Western Province,** on 8 May 1942. He did his early education in **Foumban**, **Nkongsamba,** and **Yaoundé** before embarking on an extraordinary academic career in France. He successively obtained a degree, postgraduate diploma, and *doctorat d'état* in public law from Panthéon, with a dissertation published as *Le Cameroun dans les relations internationales.* He later entered the Institut des Hautes Etudes d'Outre-Mer and the Institut International d'Administration Publique in Paris, obtaining a diploma in administration and diplomacy. Ndam Njoya also participated in courses on related issues in Corsica, Geneva, The Hague, and London.

Since returning home in 1969, he has served in the Ministry of Foreign Affairs and lectured in the Law Faculty of the **University of Yaoundé**. He was the founding director of the International Relations Institute of Cameroon (IRIC) (1972–75) before his appointment as vice minister of foreign affairs in 1975. From December 1977 until July 1980, Ndam Njoya left an indelible mark as minister of national education. He was the precursor of the **rigor and moralization** slogan that became popular under the **Paul Biya** presidency, at a time Ndam Njoya had left office. Among other things, he introduced stringency to the educational system, limited the **francophone** *probatoire* and ***baccalauréat*** to one-session exams, and implemented the early stages of the Cameroon **Gen-**

eral Certificate of Education (GCE) that was no longer administered by the University of London. In addition, during his tenure as education minister, an age ceiling was set for admission into the university.

Although well intentioned, Ndam Njoya was criticized particularly as his measures affected a broad section of the population, including the ruling class that had been accustomed to corrupt practices in determining the success of children at primary and postprimary institutions. He was transferred to the largely insignificant office of minister-delegate at the General Inspection of State and Administrative Reforms in July 1980 and was dropped from government in January 1982.

Ndam Njoya has also engaged in multiple sociocultural, international, and literary activities. Within Cameroon he served as chairman of the Executive Committee for the Service of the Handicapped, as editor in chief of the journal *Cameroun-Littéraire,* as founder-president of the Institute of Islamic and Religious Studies of Cameroon, and as publisher of the Islamic Cultural review *Al-Houda*. Outside Cameroon, he served as consultant to UNITAR in 1983 and in October 1985 was elected a member of the UNESCO Executive Council. Concomitant with many other transnational functions with relevance to religion, he was a member of the UN Group of Intergovernmental Experts from January 1986 to December 1987.

Ndam Njoya made a comeback into Cameroon politics when multiparty politics was reintroduced in the country. He founded the **Cameroon Democratic Union (CDU),** which received government recognition in June 1991. Ndam was instrumental in attempts at easing the tense sociopolitical and economic situation in the country. Consequently in November 1991 he led a delegation of opposition parties to, and took part in, the **Tripartite Conference**, which resulted in the Yaoundé Tripartite Declaration. In 1992, he contested the presidential elections and emerged fourth. In January 1996, he was elected mayor of the **Foumban** Urban Council but boycotted the 12 October 1997 presidential elections.

He has always been an advocate of the philosophy of new ethics. He is currently the president of the World Conference of Religions and Peace, as well as performing multiple other transnational functions of relevance to religion. He is also an accomplished author and writer in law, political science, history, international relations, and political ideas. In addition, he composes theatrical pieces, poems, and fiction.

NDEH, NTUMAZAH. *See* NTUMAZAH NDEH.

NDOLE. A popular Cameroonian vegetable dish, originally identified with the **Duala** but rapidly gaining popular taste among other ethnic groups, *ndolé* is prepared with special leaves, similar to spinach, mixed in oil, and ground peanuts. It is seasoned with salt, pepper, and onions and generally highly spiced. With smoked fish or meat as well as dried crayfish added to it, *ndolé* can be eaten with a variety of Cameroonian foodstuffs, especially plantain and yams. It is now widely used and may be considered as a national food.

NDONGMO AFFAIR. In August 1970, the bishop of **Nkongsamba**, Albert Ndongmo, was arrested by the government for aiding underground leaders of the **Union des Populations du Cameroun (UPC)**. These leaders (**Ernest Ouandie**, Wambo le Courant, and Celestin Takala) were tried and sentenced to death in 1971, while the bishop received a life sentence. Although Bishop Ndongmo was actually critical of government's exploitative policies vis-à-vis the poor and had close ties with the UPC, he was accused as the ring leader in the plot to overthrow Pres. **Ahmadou Ahidjo**. Many foreign leaders—including the French socialist François Mitterrand and Pope Paul VI—called for clemency especially on Bishop Ndongmo's behalf. The three UPC leaders were executed by a firing squad in **Bafoussam** in 1971, while Bishop Ndongmo was released and sent out of the country in 1975. The Ndongmo affair led to the collapse of the UPC insurgency in the Western Bamiléké countryside. All the personalities implicated in the Ndongmo affair were **Bamiléké**.

NEUKAMERUN. *See* NEW KAMERUN.

NEW DEAL. The New Deal (*politique de renouveau*) refers to Pres. **Paul Biya**'s vision of Cameroon. The New Deal aims at building a political society in which the economy is at the service of man and social justice serves as the guiding rule in the distribution of the fruits of production. The New Deal also strives toward the creation of a perfect nationhood of integration and the building of a truly humane democracy based on **communal liberalism**.

The essence of the New Deal was to distinguish the new Cameroon polity under President Biya from that of the **Ahmadou Ahidjo** years. The New Deal was an expression of the renewed aspiration in the average Cameroonian toward a more participatory society. Previously excluded political groupings have maximized their demands on the system based on greater openness and adherence to democratic ideals.

The major political landmarks of the New Deal have been the introduction of competitive lists in the legislative election process and the voluntary return of some former Cameroonian exiles from abroad. While Biya has moved with great hesitation toward a more transparent and multiparty system, the movement toward democracy can be considered an achievement of the New Deal. The New Deal has also been hit by shortcomings. Activities by nonestablishment political figures, such as Joseph Sende and Gordji Dinka, have been utilized by government to illustrate the limits of the New Deal experiment. *See also* BAMENDA CONGRESS; RIGOR AND MORALIZATION.

NEW KAMERUN (NEUKAMERUN). A territorial exchange between **France** and **Germany** in 1911 allowed Germany to obtain a considerable piece of territory from French Congo in compensation for surrendering its existing rights over Morocco to France. The acquisition of part of the French Congo territory increased Kamerun's territorial size from 465,000 to 760,000 square kilometers. There was considerable debate on the rationale for such territorial exchange, which did not provide any potential for commercial exploitation or economic value for Germany. The German colonial secretary was forced to resign over the issue. The New Kamerun territory remained part of German **Kamerun** until 1916. Following the defeat of the Germans in the Kamerun Campaign of **World War I**, the territory was returned to France as part of French Equatorial Africa.

NFON. *See* FON.

NGANGO, GEORGES (1932–1998). This elite economist and leading governmental figure in the **Paul Biya** administration served as minister of national education until April 1989. He was born in Elongnango in the Sanaga-Maritime Division of the **Littoral Province** on 17 June 1932 and attended Catholic institutions in Marienberg and **Edea** before entering the seminaries in Edea, Akono, and Mvaa for secondary education. His higher education was in the Universities of Strasbourg, Bordeaux, and Lyon where he successfully obtained bachelor's degrees in economics and sociology and a *doctorat d'état* in economic sciences. On his return to Cameroon, he served as professor in the faculty of law and economics of the **University of Yaoundé** and as the dean of faculty. He was also appointed director-general of the University Center of **Douala** prior to his ministerial function.

Professor Ngango gained political prominence under the Biya presidency, where he was a fervent advocate of an open political system with pluralist participation, including multiparties and multiple candidates for election. His ministerial functions included minister in charge of missions at the Presidency (1983–85), minister of information and culture (1985–86), and minister of national education (1987–89). He was also a member of the Central Committee of the **Cameroon People's Democratic Movement (CPDM)**, in which he served as first assistant in charge of administrative and financial inspection. Before his death in May 1998, Ngango was chairman of Crédit-Foncier, successor to the **National Fund for Rural Development (FONADER)**.

NGAOUNDERE. Ngaoundéré has been capital of the **Adamawa Province** since 1983. It is a rapidly growing tourist center, especially since 1974, with the construction of a Trans-Cameroon railway terminus in the city. In the 1976 census, the city's population was 39,000.

Ngaoundéré is not simply a meeting point of Cameroon's northern and southern regions; it is also considered a transition zone between West and Central Africa, a division designated by the **Adamawa** plateau. The city's altitude provides a very comfortable climate that serves to attract tourists. The granitic and volcanic aspects of its physical milieu have also led to increased scholarly research in the area. However, its greatest all-around attraction is its vast adornment of flora and fauna. For all these reasons, the infrastructure of the city has been developed considerably through the provision of highways and hotel services. In addition, Ngaoundéré hosted several national events in recent times, including the national **agropastoral show** and the national schools and university sports competition, which have contributed to the city's growth and development. The University Center for Applied Industrial Sciences has also been a significant boost to the city. This has now become the University of Ngaoundéré, serving all of the northern provinces.

NGBE (EKPE). This Leopard Cult of the **Cross River region** is thought to have originated among the Ejagham. This cult is a governing gerontocratic brotherhood/association in which membership can be purchased and it has spread throughout the Cross River region over time through this means. Successive grades within Ngbe are purchased by the member. Each grade gains further initiation into the secret knowledge of the cult. This knowledge is publicly represented through ***nsibidi***, a symbolic language that can be represented graphically or through dance. The name of the cult denotes the derivation of its power from the spirit of the leopard.

NGHAKY, NZO EKHAH. *See* EKANGAKI, NZO.

NGOME KOME, ALBERT (1939–). A former minister of transport and director-general of the **National Fund for Rural Development (FONADER)**, he was born on 18 October 1939 in Mpako, Meme Division in the **South West Province**. He attended N. A. School, Nyasoso (1947–54); Cameroon Protestant College, Bali (1955–59); and Cameroon College of Arts, Science, and Technology in Bambili (1962–64). He pursued university education at Hamilton College in New York (1965–68), obtaining a bachelor's degree in government, and at the University of Lancaster, England, where he earned a master's degree in politics (1968–69). He was appointed deputy director of credit (1973–77) and became director thereafter until his appointment as minister of transport in 1979. He served in this capacity until he was dropped from government in February 1984. In 1985, he was appointed chairman of the board of directors of FONADER, and in 1986, he became director-general of FONADER. He was removed as director in 1991 and since then has retired to private business.

NGONDO. Ngondo is a highly significant cultural assembly of the **Duala**. It served as the **Council of Notables** and had the potential for an activist political role in the nationalist period. Like the Kumsze for the **Bamiléké**, Ngondo was initially close to the radical stance of the **Union des Populations du Cameroun (UPC)** against colonial rule. Many traditional associations turned against colonial authorities that denied participation and exercise of indigenous culture. However, the effort of French authorities to divest the UPC of popular support led to a cooling-off of the relationship between the UPC and the Ngondo government. After independence, Ngondo's relations with the new leaders of the country remained uncordial, leading to the banning of its festival for some time. Such a stormy evolution has contributed to Ngondo's gradual loss of popular appeal. This mood notwithstanding, Ngondo was revived with the advent of political liberalization in the early 1990s. Today Ngondo is not limited to the Dualas but embraces all people of coastal origin in its annual festivals. Political figures who gained their renown through the Ngondo establishment include **Betote Akwa** and **Paul Soppo Priso**.

NGU, VICTOR ANOMAH (1926–). This renowned surgeon, imminent scholar, and former minister of public health was born in **Buea** on 19 February 1926. He actually hails from the **North West Province**. After primary education in **Bamenda**, secondary school in **St. Joseph's College**, Sasse, **Buea**, and Government College Ibadan, Nigeria, Anomah Ngu attended medical school of the University of London from 1951 until 1954. Thereafter, he began a successful career as house surgeon, medical officer of the **Cameroon Development Corporation (CDC)**, and registrar, senior registrar, lecturer, senior lecturer, professor, and head of the Department of Surgery in the University of Ibadan, Nigeria, until 1972. On his return home, he became professor of the University Center for Health Sciences until September 1974, when he was appointed vice chancellor of the **University of Yaoundé**. In July 1982, he became delegate-general for scientific and technical research and was named minister of public health in February 1984.

Multiple national, international, and academic honors have accompanied this brilliant professional career, in particular the Albert Lasker Medical Research Award in Clinical Cancer Chemotherapy in 1972 and president of the Association of African Universities from 1980 to 1982. His party functions include former youth secretary of the National Party, assistant secretary for **women**'s affairs, and member of the Central Committee of the **Cameroon People's Democratic Movement (CPDM)**. Professor Ngu is presently prochancellor of the University of **Buea**.

NGUELE, ROSE ZANG. *See* ZANG NGUELE, ROSE.

NIGER BASIN AUTHORITY (NBA)/AUTHORITE DU BASSIN DU NIGER (ABN). In 1980, the NBA replaced the Niger River Basin Commission, begun in 1963, which had accomplished little in its years of existence. Integrated development of the Niger Basin through the cooperation of the riverine states via the mechanism of the NBA was the main purpose of the organization. Among the various activities are research and data collection, infrastructure development, maintenance and facilitation of navigation, meteorological and environmental studies and reporting, and agropastoral development projects. A major task is attracting external funds to support these activities.

The members of the Niger Basin Authority are Benin, Burkina Faso, Cameroon, **Chad**, Ivory Coast, Guinea, Mali, Niger, and **Nigeria**. The structures include a Summit of Heads of State and Government, a Council of Ministers, an Executive Secretariat, and technical committees. The headquarters is in Niamey, Niger. The NBA maintains a Fonds de Développement du Bassin du Niger, a development fund. In 1987, a joint meeting of the Authority and the **Lake Chad Basin Commission (LCBC)** was held in N'Djamena, Chad. To this time, NBA activities have been largely limited to research and planning rather than implementation of projects. Because a major tributary of the Niger River, the **Benue River**, flows in Cameroon, Cameroon has joined the NBA.

NIGERIA. Africa's most populous country and Cameroon's most significant neighbor, Nigeria borders Cameroon to the west. Both countries have maintained good relations, with occasional periods of strain over the years. Historically, there is a cultural affinity between the people of the two countries. Moreover, through the joint administration of Nigeria and the adjoining British **Southern Cameroons**, there was a constant flow of persons across their common borders. Many Nigerians worked and settled in Cameroon, while a host of **anglophone** Cameroonians studied there and intermarried with Nigerians.

This common identification led to the formation in 1944 of the **National Council of Nigeria and the Cameroons (NCNC)**, designed as a nationalist platform for both territories. However, prior to independence, strong anti-Nigerian sentiments developed as an integral part of Cameroon nationalism. Out of the 1961 **plebiscite** came a short period of tense relations when British **Northern Cameroons** became part of Nigeria. In addition, the **border conflicts** between both countries have led to frequent accusations and consultations between the governments. This border management diplomacy failed on 18 May 1981, when Cameroon border patrol guards killed five Nigerian soldiers. Cameroon apologized and paid compensation to the families affected by the fatal event. In 1983, over 10,000 Cameroonians were expelled from Nigeria. Many Nigerians continue to live in Cameroon and are widely engaged in trade, farming, and domestic activities. Despite this, incidents continue to occur along the border.

In December 1993, relations became strained once again when Nigerian troops attacked and occupied the **Bakassi** Peninsula, an oil-rich area along the maritime border claimed by both countries. Other conflicts have emerged along northern borders and with the construction of the Lagdo Dam in Cameroon, which reduced river flow into Nigeria. Apart from border conflicts, the **smuggling** of goods and products across their mutual borders is also a major cause for concern. There are embassies in both capitals as well as consulates in **Buea** and **Douala**, and Calabar,

Nigeria, to handle complex issues affecting Nigerian-Cameroon relations. *See also* NORTHERN CAMEROONS CASE.

NJANGI. *See* TONTINE/NJANGI.

NJAWE, PIUS. *See* LE MESSAGER.

NJEUMA, DOROTHY LIMUNGA (1943–). The former vice minister of national education was born in **Buea** on 26 June 1943 and attended the local government school (1948–55). She left for the Queen's School, Enugu, **Nigeria** (1955–62), for secondary education. Her university studies were at Brown University in the **United States** (1962–66), from which she obtained a bachelor's degree in biology, and at the University College, London (1966–70), where she earned a Ph.D. in zoology.

On return home, she lectured at the Faculty of Science of the **University of Yaoundé** and rose to the rank of associate professor before appointment as vice minister in 1975. She served in this post for 10 years and as chairperson of the Administrative Board of the Centre for the Publication of School Textbooks (CEPER) (1977–85). She is one of few **women** to hold the rank of minister. She was replaced by Catherine Ngomba-Edo. Njeuma later served as technical adviser in the Ministry of Higher Education and Scientific Research, before her appointment as director of the Buea University Centre. When the center was upgraded to a university in 1993, she was made vice chancellor.

NJOYA (SULTAN) (1876–1933). He was the 16th sultan of the **Bamoum** dynasty and an important figure in early Cameroon history in political, religious, and intellectual terms. Njoya was too young to assume power personally when his father, Sultan Nsangou, died in 1888. In his place, Njoya's mother served as regent for two years. In 1890, at the age of 15, Njoya became sultan. Although the Bamoum were close to the British prior to German annexation, they came to accept German rule, and Njoya received high regard as an imperial official. This attachment to the Germans was to ruin his political career with the advent of the French administration. In 1923, Njoya was deposed and his Bamoum territory carved into 17 chieftancies. Exiled to **Yaoundé** in 1931, he died in the capital on 30 May 1933.

Apart from his political significance, Njoya's renown is symbolized by his high sense of achievement as an intellectual and sociocultural innovator. He developed an original alphabet of 83 letters and 10 numbers called ***shu mom,*** which he used to write the *History of the Customs and Laws of the Bamoums.* Under the strong influence of a German missionary, Njoya turned to Christianity, although he spent time trying to create his own Christian–animist religion. By 1916, he had converted to **Islam**, the predominant religion of most Bamoum today. The **Foumban** palace constructed under his reign still attracts hundreds of tourists and foreign dignitaries. It has been restored by UNESCO and now houses a museum of Bamoum culture. He is widely remembered as well for his multiple sociocultural innovations: drawing the map of Bamoum, compiling Bamoum legends and tales, preparing pharmaceutical compilations, establishing a museum for the preservation of art, and constructing a mechanical mill to grind corn. Postcolonial authorities have still not granted Njoya the historic recognition commensurate with his multiple accomplishments. Nonetheless, the leading elites from Bamoum have invariably hailed from the Njoya family.

NJOYA, ADAMOU NDAM. *See* NDAM NJOYA, ADAMOU.

NJOYA, SEIDOU NJIMOLUH (1904–1992). One-time sultan of the Bamoum and local spiritual head of the Islamic faith, Seidou was born in 1904 of royal parents. He was the 18th king of the Bamoum and was highly schooled in ***shu mom*** (the writing of his father) as well as in **French** and **English**. He was enthroned in June 1933 following the exile and death of his father, remaining in power for almost 60 years. Apart from his royal functions, Njimoluh Njoya also served for 20 years as a member of the legislative and national assemblies of Cameroon. Consequently, he was considered a link between the Bamoum and both colonial and postcolonial authorities. Before his death in 1992, he remained the principal link between his people and government authorities. He was succeeded by his son, Ibrahim Mbombo Njoya. *See also* NJOYA (SULTAN).

NKONGSAMBA. This city is headquarters of the Mungo Division and the third most populated city in the country. In the 1976 census, over 71,000 people were recorded in Nkongsamba. It was originally inhabited by the Mbo, but it took on a more cosmopolitan outlook during the colonial period. The French policy of intensive economic exploitation of a productive region known as the **Fertile Crescent** largely accounted for its economic vitality.

Farming and cultivation of major cash crops, as well as the establishment of various tertiary sector activities, continue to dominate life and activity in Nkongsamba. Although the town is merely a divisional headquarters, it has a high-ranking mayor, officially known as the government delegate of the municipality. Only three other cities (**Yaoundé**, **Douala**, and **Bamenda**) have such a status.

The biggest population grouping in Nkongsamba recently is not the indigenous Mbo but the migrant **Bamiléké**. They command the production and commercialization of **cocoa**, **coffee**, **bananas,** and other cash crops.

NKUETE, JEAN (1944–). Secretary-general of the government, an economist, and a monetary expert, Nkuete was born in Balessing in the Menoua Division of the **Western Province**. He is one of the country's rising stars. He did primary education in Penja and Dschang before pursuing secondary education in **Nkongsamba** from 1956 obtaining his ***baccalauréat*** in 1963. He went overseas for university studies at the Catholic University in Milan and the School of Economic Development in Rome. He earned a graduate degree and a diploma from both institutions.

Nkuete served in the Ministry of Economic Planning in 1969 when he returned to Cameroon both in **Yaoundé** and in the **Littoral Province**. He was deputy director of planning before he was moved to the Office of the **Prime Minister**. He served first as director of economic affairs and later as technical adviser to the prime minister until his appointment as deputy director of the Paribas–Cameroon bank.

On 12 April 1983, Nkuete joined the government as assistant secretary-general at the Presidency of the Republic. He served in this capacity until his major appointment as secretary-general of the government on 21 November 1986. This post is particularly significant under the **Paul Biya** presidency, coordinating interministerial affairs, approving decisions that were previously reserved for the head of state, and preparing the agenda for cabinet meetings. He left this post on 16 May 1988. From government Nkuete moved on to serve as director of the **Douala** branch of the **Bank of Central African States (BEAC)** and then as executive secretary of the Economic and Monetary Union of Central Africa. Prior to assuming his high office, Jean Nkuete taught in the Faculty of Laws and Economics and a host of other higher institutions of learning.

NORTH KAMERUN DEMOCRATIC PARTY. This **Northern Cameroons** party participated in the **Mamfe Conference** of 1959. It advocated the union of **Northern** and **Southern Cameroons** and eventual **reunification** with **French Cameroun**.

NORTH PROVINCE. It covers a surface area of 65,160 square kilometers and consists of four divisions, 10 subdivisions, and one district. Its relief features comprise the Benue Plain and the **Atlantika Mountains**. The two main vegetational types of the province are the wooded savannah and the steppe vegetation. The North has the tropical climate of two seasons: the dry and rainy seasons. Most of the population is engaged in animal breeding and agriculture. Agroindustrial projects have been established, and tourism plays an important role in the economy of the province. **Garoua** (Benoue Division) is the headquarters of the province. Other important towns include Poli (Faro Division), Guider (Mayo–Louti Division), and Tchollire (Mayo–Ray Division). The present administrative unit of North Province came into existence on 23 August 1983.

NORTH WEST PROVINCE. It covers a surface area of 18,100 square kilometers and has a population of about 1,190,000 inhabitants. It consists of seven divisions, 10 subdivisions, and three districts. The North West Province has a mountainous relief system and a rather temperate climate. The population is engaged in economic activities, especially agriculture, animal breeding, and handicrafts. The economic productivity of the province is high, and traditional culture continues to be a vital part of political and social organization. The provincial headquarters is in **Bamenda** (Mezam Division), a town that is more developed than the other towns of the province. In 1996, two more divisions were created bringing the total number of divisions in the province to seven. The principal towns include Fundong (Boyo Division), Kumbo (Bui Division), Ndop (Ngoketunjia Division), Nkambe (Donga–Mantung Division), Wum (Menchum Division), and Mbengwi (Momo Division). The province was established in 1972. In the 1990s, the North West was the stronghold of political opposition to the **Paul Biya** government and the center of **anglophone** discontent.

NORTHERN CAMEROONS. This designation indicates the British territories located in the northern portion of **British Cameroons**. In reality, the British had more than one distinct territory in the north. The **Atlantika Mountains** separated the various parts of Northern Cameroons at the **Benue River**. Administered as parts of **Nigeria**, Northern Cameroons consisted of the Tigon–Ndoro–Kentu area in the Benue Province; the Southern and Northern **Adamawa** Districts in the **Adamawa Province**, and the Dikwa Division in the Bornu Province. No administrative links existed between Northern and **Southern**

Cameroons, and both regions developed separate identities. This led to the **plebiscite** outcome in which North Cameroons voted for integration with Nigeria as opposed to **reunification** with the **République du Cameroun**. Only 97,659 people voted for reunification, while 146,296 voted for integration with **Nigeria**. Diplomatic and international legal pressures by the Cameroun government to contest the alleged irregularities of the outcome were unsuccessful. Northern Cameroons officially became part of the Federation of Nigeria on 1 June 1961. *See also* NORTHERN CAMEROONS CASE.

NORTHERN CAMEROONS CASE (CAMEROON VS. THE UNITED KINGDOM). In a United Nations **plebiscite** of 1961, inhabitants of the Northern Cameroons voted to integrate with Northern **Nigeria** and become part of the Federation of Nigeria. In reality, this was a logical outcome of the nature of British administration since 1916.

The Cameroon government accused **Great Britain** of complicity, first before the UN, where it failed to gain sufficient support, and later to the International Court of Justice (ICJ) at The Hague. In 1963, the court ruled in favor of abiding by the decision of the UN. Cameroon accepted the ICJ's ruling but relations with Great Britain suffered a temporary chill under the outspoken and flamboyant foreign minister, **Charles Okala**.

Apart from the multiple voting irregularities Cameroonian officials detected in the Northern vote, it was Vice President **John Ngu Foncha** who sought to iron out the differences, realizing deteriorating relations with Britain would have adverse effects on **West Cameroon**. Cameroonian leader **Ahmadou Ahidjo** came out with a more prophetic declaration when he argued that "history will judge on this issue." He also argued that a combination of both the Southern and Northern Cameroons vote (rather than the isolated counts of distinct regions) would have shown an overwhelming choice in favor of **reunification** with the **République du Cameroun**. The loss of British Northern Cameroon was politically disturbing for Ahidjo, given that the population of the area would probably have aligned with his major area of support, the **Northern Province** of the **Republic of Cameroon**, and boosted his base of support in the early period of independence.

NORTHERN MASSACRE. On 21–22 October 1979, in Dolle and the Makari area in the Logone and Chari Divisions of **North Cameroon**, government paracommandos from **Maroua** massacred 200 people, including **women** and children, who protested the failure of the administration to open a village school despite local contributions toward its construction. The villagers turned their rage on security officers on a cleanup campaign killing 14 police officers and seriously wounding three. Reinforcements from Maroua led to the massacre and razing of the village. The Cameroon government denied the gravity of the situation and put forward the thesis of a quack Chadian marabout resisting arrest as the center of the story. The Northern Massacre of 1979 was the first serious domestic security embarrassment to the government since its crushing of the **Union des Populations du Cameroun (UPC)** rebellion in the early years of independence. Occurring in the North, it was a severe blow to then president **Ahmadou Ahidjo,** who hailed from the region. *See also* ETHNIC CONFLICT.

NORTHERN PROVINCE. Established in 1972, the Northern Province covered the entire stretch of territory from the **Adamawa** highlands to **Lake Chad**. This extensive administrative entity gained added significance because of the largely **Muslim population**, the relative underdevelopment of the region, and the leadership bonus in Pres. **Ahmadou Ahidjo**, who hailed from there. It was widely believed in the Ahidjo era that behind the slogan of "**balanced development**," the province was largely favored in various development projects like industries, schools and colleges, tourist facilities, airport and road facilities, as well as sports infrastructure. A single **governor**, **Usman Mey,** served in the province for 11 years until 1983. In the wake of the **Ahidjo–Biya rupture,** it was feared in **Yaoundé** that the mammoth province could secede from the rest of the country. In August 1983, Pres. **Paul Biya** divided the Northern Province into three new provinces: **Adamawa**, **North,** and **Extreme North**. The **Center–South Province** was also divided into the **Center** and **South Provinces**, partly to quell suspicion that the reorganization of the provinces was solely designed against the former Northern Province.

NSHARE. Nshare is the presumed founder of the **Bamoum** people in the 17th century. Nshare was the son of a **Tikar** chief who absconded from his ethnic group with a group of loyal supporters heading south. He crossed the Mbam River and settled in Nji-Mom against heavy opposition from people around the Mbam area, 30 kilometers north of **Foumbam**. Nshare could only survive at the cost of opposition and conflicts with neighboring groupings and their rulers. Nonetheless, he skillfully brought 17 chiefs under his control to become paramount **chief** of the Pa-Mbam, from which the name Bamoum is derived. Thereafter the kingdom extended even farther to include Mfom-Ben, from which the name Foumban is derived. It was this dynasty that continued to reign through the legendary Sultan **Njoya** to the present incumbent sultan of the Bamoum people. A set of traditional and popular songs have been composed in honor of Nshare.

NSIBIDI. This system of pictographic signs and danced motions is used as a form of communication among members of the **Ngbe** (Ekpe) cult in the **Cross River region** of southwestern Cameroon and southeastern **Nigeria**.

NTARINKON PALACE. This refers to the private residence of **John Fru Ndi**. His **Social Democratic Front (SDF)**, one of the major opposition parties, was launched on 26 May 1990 at Ntarinkon Park in **Bamenda**. Police and military attacks on SDF supporters left six civilians dead. Ntarinkon Park is very near Ndi's residence.

NTAW FOSI YAKUM. *See* YAKUM-NTAW, FOSI.

NTUMAZAH NDEH (1926–). A militant politician of the pre**reunification** era, founder of the **One Kamerun Party (OK)** and radical opponent of the postcolonial regimes in Cameroon, Ntumazah was born in Mankon, **Bamenda,** and educated there until 1944. He moved to **Douala** thereafter and was exposed to the wave of **Union des Populations du Cameroun (UPC)** ideology before returning to Bamenda. He became notorious for participation in various local disputes. When the UPC took refuge in **Southern Cameroons** in 1955, Ntumazah emerged as a principal collaborator. In 1957, he formed the One Kamerun Party (OK) in Southern Cameroons following the departure of the UPC. Under his leadership the One Kamerun Party became a strong advocate of reunification and democratic institutions. In his appearances before the United Nations in 1957, 1958, and 1959, Ntumazah gained high marks for his polished style and the fierceness and depth of his convictions. Apart from his leadership position in the OK, Ntumazah Ndeh neither won a local election nor held any political office in Cameroon. He left the country for exile at independence and lived mainly in London, but he continued to maintain close ties with the UPC in France. Following the political liberalization that came in the wake of the legalization of multiparty politics, Ntumazah returned from his exile in 1991 and became the national president of the UPC.

NYOBE, REUBEN UM. *See* UM NYOBE, REUBEN.

– O –

OFFICE CAMEROUNAIS DE BANANES. *See* BANANA.

OFFICE NATIONAL DE COMMERCIALISATION DES PRODUITS DE BASE (ONCPB). *See* NATIONAL PRODUCE MARKETING BOARD.

OFFICIAL LANGUAGES. According to Paragraph 3 of Part I of the **constitution of 1996,** "The official languages of Cameroon shall be **English** and **French**, both languages having the same status. The State shall guarantee the promotion of bilingualism throughout the country." Consequently, business in governmental offices and lectures in schools, colleges, and institutions of higher learning, as well as public texts and presidential decrees, are published in both official languages. *See also* BILINGUALISM; FRANGLAIS; NATIONAL LANGUAGES; PIDGIN ENGLISH.

OKALA, RENE-GUY CHARLES (1910–). Okala was independent Cameroon's first foreign minister, and his rather outspoken and daring stance on diplomatic issues apparently contributed to the eventual reduction of the status and prestige of the post.

Okala was born on 19 October 1910 at Bilome in the Mbam Division of the **Center Province,** and he did primary education in a Catholic seminary in **Yaoundé** and later served as a teacher. His employment by a British firm polished his bilingual competence and led to his civil service function as an interpreter in 1938. In later years, he became more renowned for his political activities: founder of the **Jeunesse Camerounaise Française** (1939), elected and reelected to the Representative Assembly in the 1940s and 1950s, and senator to the French Council of the Republic. Okala held various ministerial offices prior to formal independence in 1960. In the first **Ahmadou Ahidjo** independent government, he was named foreign minister (1960–61). He was a bitter critic of **Great Britain** and **Nigeria** for the outcome of the 1961 **plebiscite** that led to the loss of British **Northern Cameroon**.

Dismissed as minister in 1961, Okala was arrested in June 1962 for domestic political reasons. Along with other opposition leaders he was tried and convicted of conspiracy and sentenced to four years imprisonment. Okala was released from jail in 1965 in a deal that led to the dissolution of the Cameroon Socialist Party in which he had served as a leading member since its founding in 1959. He was later co-opted into the **Union Camerounaise (UC)** and **Cameroun National Union (CNU)** parties and was named roving ambassador to the president in 1968. He again fell out of grace in the period that led to the formation of the unitary state in 1972. *See also* NORTHERN CAMEROONS CASE.

ONANA AWANA, CHARLES (1923–1999). Cameroon's veteran finance minister in the **Ahmadou Ahidjo** era was born in 1923 in Ngoulemekong. He occupied important administrative functions as principal secretary to the deputy prime minister, Ahmadou Ahidjo. In 1960, he was named federal minister of finance; in 1961, minister delegate at the Presidency for Territorial Administration; and again minister of finance in 1963. He was first secretary-general of the **Union Douanière Economique de l'Afrique Centrale (UDEAC)** in 1964 and returned to government as minister of planning and territorial development 1970 until 1972. Under the unitary state in 1972, he was again named minister of finance until his eviction from government in 1975. Onana Awana was reputed to have been a close adviser to Pres. **Paul Biya** in the 1980s and 1990s. He died 10 January 1999 in Paris.

ONE KAMERUN PARTY (OK). This was the remnant of the short-lived **Union des Populations du Cameron (UPC)–Kamerun National Democratic Party (KNDP)** collaboration from 1955 until 1957. The UPC fostered interterritorial links with the **British Cameroons** in the late 1940s and took temporary shelter there following repression and banning in **French Cameroun**. The One Kamerun Party emerged from this contact in 1957. Its leader, **Ntumazah Ndeh**, originally hailed from British Cameroons and contributed to popularizing the party in the area. He was a former member of the UPC directorate. Although not very popular or successful, the OK Party gained a constituency among the labor force, **cooperatives** members, and urban employees as well as university students abroad and local intellectuals with its appeal for radical nationalism. The OK Party advocated **reunification** as its primary goal and faded out of existence when this goal was achieved in 1961.

ORGANIZATION OF AFRICAN UNITY (OAU). The OAU is an international governmental organization of independent countries in Africa. Cameroon was a founding member of the OAU on 25 May 1963 in Addis Ababa, Ethiopia. Former president **Ahmadou Ahidjo** participated in all summits of the organization held during his long tenure in office. In

1969, he served as chairman of the organization and presented the Lusaka Manifesto before the United Nations concerning the conflict in Southern Africa. However, the country's most symbolic commitment to the organization has been the roles of **Nzo Ekangaki** and **William-Aurelian Eteky Mboumoua** as secretaries-general of the OAU from 1972 to 1974 and 1974 to 1978, respectively. Between 1996 and 1997, Cameroon's head of state, Pres. **Paul Biya**, who until then had participated only once (1984) in the annual OAU summits since he came to power, served as chairman of the organization.

OSENDE AFANA. *See* AFANA, OSENDE.

OUANDIE, ERNEST (1924–1971). A revolutionary leader of guerrilla forces in the **Western Province** of the country, Ouandie was born in 1924 in the then **Bamiléké** Division. He was educated locally before embarking on a teaching profession at the age of 16. However, it was politics that later determined his life as he joined the Cameroon chapter of the French left-leaning Confederation General du Travail (CGT) in 1944. It was this wing that eventually emerged in the postwar era to form the first authentic Cameroonian political movement, the **Union des Populations du Cameroun (UPC)** in 1948.

Following the outlawing of the party in 1955, he left the French territory and took refuge in **Bamenda**, **British Cameroons**. He later moved on to Egypt and Ghana, where the UPC had established as a community of political exiles. He returned to the country in early 1962 to clandestinely run the guerrilla operation now in full force in the Bamiléké countryside against government and French troops loyal to Pres. **Ahmadou Ahidjo**. He was caught in August 1970 and arraigned in the conspiracy trial with Wambo le Courant, Celestin Takala, and Bishop Albert Ndongmo. Following detention in Mbanga, he was court martialed and sentenced to death. The execution took place on 15 January 1971. *See also* NDONGMO AFFAIR.

OUMAROU, AMINOU. *See* AMINOU, OUMAROU.

OWONA CONSTITUTION. *See* GRAND DEBAT.

OWONA, JOSEPH (1945–). A prominent jurist and scholar, Owona was born on 23 January 1945 in Akom Bikoe in the Ocean Division. He attended primary school in Mbalmayo (1953–58) and secondary school at College Vogt in **Yaoundé**. He entered the **University of Yaoundé** and earned a *licence en droit* before proceeding to Paris to obtain a *diplôme d'études supérieures* in political science in 1970. Thereafter, he served as assistant lecturer at the University of Paris I Sorbonne-Panthéon until 1972, when he returned home. Simultaneously with his doctoral research, Owona lectured in the Faculty of Law and Economics, the School of Journalism, and the Higher Police College in Yaoundé. From 1973 until 1976, he served as chief of service for teaching and research at the University of Yaoundé.

In 1976, he obtained his *doctorat d'état* and the title of *agrégé de droit public et science politiques.* He was named director of the International Relations Institute of Cameroun (IRIC) in September 1976 simultaneously with his post as head of the Department of Public Law in the University of Yaoundé. In 1983, Owona became chancellor of the university for a brief period before joining the cabinet in 1985 as assistant secretary-general at the Presidency with the rank of minister. Following the reorganization of the Presidency in November 1986, he was appointed to the post of assistant secretary-general of government. He remained in this position until 1988 when he was appointed minister of higher education and scientific research. Owona was later moved to the Presidency in April 1992 as secretary-general, a post he occupied until 1994 when he became minister of public health. Following the second presidential elections under the multiparty system, Owona was appointed minister of youth and sports on 7 December 1997.

As a scholar, Professor Owona is a figure of international renown having lectured in the University of Brazzaville, University of Bordeaux, Marien Ngouabi University, and the African Institute in Moscow in various capacities until 1983. He has published extensively on public and constitutional law, political science, **human rights**, and disarmament in various scientific journals and has served as consultant for international organizations, multinational corporations, and foreign governments.

OYONO, FERDINAND-LEOPOLD (1929–). A longtime diplomat and leading African writer, Oyono was born on 14 September 1929 in Ngoulemakong in the Ntem Division of the **Center Province**. After secondary education in France where he successfully obtained his ***baccalauréat,*** Oyono studied law at the University of Paris (Sorbonne-Panthéon). He graduated with a *licence* (L.L.B.) and later enrolled in the diplomatic section of the Ecole Nationale d'Administration in Paris. In 1958, he served in the French foreign service as chargé de mission and later in the French embassy in Italy until the independence of Cameroon in 1960.

Oyono was appointed Cameroon's ambassador to France and recalled home in 1961 as legal consultant in charge of studies. In 1962, he served as Cameroon's minister plenipotentiary to the **European Economic Community (EEC)** in Brussels and from 1963 to 1965 as ambassador to Liberia. He returned to Brussels as ambassador to the Benelux countries and the EEC from 1965 to 1968. Thereafter, he served as ambassador to Paris until 1974 when he became Cameroon's permanent representative to the United Nations in New York. During his long tenure at the United Nations, Oyono presided over sessions of the Security Council and was vice president of the General Assembly. He was moved to Algeria as ambassador in 1982 and later to **Great Britain** in the same capacity in September 1984. He was appointed to the high cabinet function of secretary-general at the Presidency of the Republic in 1985, a post that he held until he became minister of housing and town planning in November 1986. He remained at this post until 1993, when he was appointed minister of external relations. In December 1997, Oyono was once more moved to become **minister of state** in charge of culture. A minister of state is indicative of very senior status in the cabinet.

Apart from his wide-ranging diplomatic experience and ministerial duties, Ferdinand Oyono is most renowned to the outside world as a leading African writer. His numerous publications include *Houseboy* and *The Old Man and the Medal*.

– P –

PAGAN GROUPING (SOCIETES PAIENNES). This term is frequently used to denote non-Islamized populations of the northern regions of Cameroon. They existed prior to the establishment of **Fulani** hegemony and resisted all attempts at Islamization. Their present settlement pattern was influenced by the construction and development of other states of the Sudan belt and the Chadian basin. They were obliged to migrate as Fulani pressure and conquest increased. The major groups today include the Massa, the Matakam, the Kapsiki, and the Guiziga. Numerically, the Matakam are the largest of these groupings that took up early settlement in the **Mandara Mountains** to escape Islamic persecution. They have survived despite the lack of a centralized political structure. Major personalities to emerge from these populations include **Luc Ayang** and **Etiénne Hollong**.

These people are called "pagan" because of their nonsubscription to **Islam**. Christian missionaries have been very active and successful with these groups in recent years. Politicians opposed to Fulani domination in northern politics, especially the **National Union of Democracy and Progress (UNDP)**, have also been successful with these groups.

PAHOUIN. *See* FANG-PAHOUIN.

PAÏENNES. *See* PAGAN GROUPINGS.

PALLOTINE MISSION. *See* CATHOLIC CHURCH.

PALM PRODUCTS. These include palm wine and kernel and palm oil produced from a variety of palm trees growing across the West African coast. Peasant and plantation production are both significant. While export considerations have been important, domestic use of palm products for consumption (especially as palm oil and palm wine) is very significant.

Despite efforts by the colonial administrations to encourage individual palm exploitation, plantations were more predominant in palm production. The **Cameroon Development Corporation (CDC)** plays a leading role in the production and industrial processing of palm products, especially in the **South West Province** of the country. Other palm product initiatives exist in the French-speaking areas of the country under the auspices of SOCAPALM (Cameroon Palm Grove Company). Palm oil is far less significant as an export today than in the immediate postindependence period. However, domestic consumption remains popular among the local population despite large-scale importations of other vegetable oils.

PARTI DES DEMOCRATES CAMEROUNAIS (PDC). This organization was founded in 1958 as a party with strong religious and ethnic participation. Occasionally it is referred to as the Démocrates Camerounais, and, at its founding, the name Parti des Démocrates Chrétiens was suggested. Roman Catholic and **Ewondo**, **Bulu,** and Eton support provided most of the PDC's followers. In the 1960 elections, PDC candidates won 63 percent of the vote in the Nyong et Sanaga Province.

The period of its formation and the areas of its electoral support identify the PDC with **André-Marie Mbida**, preindependent Cameroun's first **prime minister**. Removed from office in 1958, Mbida went into exile in Conakry, Guinea. But the PDC continued with support from **Louis Aujolat** and the Ad Lucem group and with assistance from **Charles Atangana** and **André Fouda**. However, the PDC did not prosper, and by the mid-1960s, it had ceased activity.

PARTI SOCIALISTE CAMEROUNAISE (PSC). This minority political grouping was formed in November 1959 under the leadership of **Charles Okala**. In June 1962, the party formed a loose coalition, the **Front Nationale Unifié (FNU),** opposed to **Ahmadou Ahidjo**'s idea of ***parti unifié***. The party fell into oblivion following the arrest and imprisonment of Okala in July 1963. The PSC later fused with other parties to form the **Cameroon National Union (CNU)** in September 1966.

PARTI TRAVAILLISTE CAMEROUNAIS. This minority political party in **East Cameroon** was formed by **Marcel Bebey-Eyidi** in March 1962. The party lost its political existence following the arrest and imprisonment of its leaders. Its opposition to **Ahmadou Ahidjo**'s ***parti unifié*** option was unsuccessful.

PARTI UNIFIE. This political concept was developed by **Ahmadou Ahidjo** in 1960. It was designed to create a common ground of operation among feuding political parties. The *parti unifié* signified that parties could voluntarily dismantle their artificial differences and work together in unison within a one-party structure. It was through the *parti unifié* idea that former President Ahidjo consolidated his governing **Union Camerounaise (UC)** into a one-party structure, the **Union National Camerounaise (UNC)**.

The unified party idea was put forward in opposition to the idea of single party, which implied constraint and obligation. Many other politicians or political parties opposed to the idea of a monolithic national party as the high point of dictatorship fell into political disfavor or disbanded.

PEACE CORPS. On 1 March 1961, Pres. John F. Kennedy established the Peace Corps, an organization designed to assist in Third World development through the use of volunteers from the **United States**. On 23 July 1962, an agreement was reached between the governments of Cameroon and the United States to begin Peace Corps activity in Cameroon. The first volunteers, assigned only to **West Cameroon**, the English-speaking part of the country, arrived in September 1962 to begin teaching in secondary schools. Over the years the program has expanded to all regions of Cameroon. Volunteers have worked in various levels of education; public health; credit union and **cooperatives** development; agriculture, forestry, and fisheries programs; and community development projects. Several other countries have developed similar programs in Cameroon, most significantly the Dutch, Germans, and British.

PEACE-WORK-FATHERLAND. This is the official motto of Cameroon as denoted in the **constitution of 1996**, Part 1, Paragraph 7.

PEOPLE'S REPUBLIC OF CHINA (RELATIONS WITH). One of Cameroon's most remarkable foreign policy decisions was the early recognition of the People's Republic of China (PRC) in 1971 despite opposition from **France**. Because the PRC supported one of the militant **Union des Populations du Cameroun (UPC)** factions, **Yaoundé**'s rapprochement with Peking led to the weakening of the UPC's insurgency. This trade-off was a boost to Cameroon's diplomacy and a catalyst in its quest for national unity. Since the early days of mutual suspicions, relations have grown in the fields of agricultural technology, health assistance, and training with the opening of a Chinese hospital in Mbalmayo, energy production with the construction of a **hydroelectric** dam in Lagdo, **North Province**, cultural cooperation with the construction of the magnificent Palais de Congrès in Yaoundé, and military assistance.

PETROLEUM. This has been Cameroon's most significant export since the 1980s. Petroleum deposits were known to exist in Cameroon as early as the 1950s, but this was rarely officially confirmed by the postindependence federal government. Following the creation of the **United Republic of Cameroon** in 1972, the government followed up with a definite petroleum policy. Permits are granted to foreign companies, who bear the total cost of exploration while government receives 60 percent of the royalties. Over 15 foreign petroleum companies from **France**, the Netherlands, Norway, Canada, and the **United States** participated in the country's early petroleum exploration bid in **Limbe**.

Following these early stages, the government maintained a cloud of secrecy over production and export of Cameroon's petroleum. It is widely believed that Cameroon's exploitation and export of petroleum began in December 1977 with an estimated output of 13,000 barrels per day. The price of Cameroon's petroleum per barrel remained an equally guarded secret in the early period, but the bulk of the exports went to the United States. The **Ahmadou Ahidjo** government also did not disclose the destination of petroleum revenues, which were not included in the national budget. This tactic is known as "***compte hors budget***." The typical Ahidjo strategy was not to base the nation's economy entirely on its petroleum. According to Ahidjo, agriculture was the mainstay of

Cameroon's economy because "before petroleum there was agriculture and after petroleum there will be agriculture."

On 16 May 1981, Ahidjo inaugurated the National Oil Refinery in Victoria (**Limbe**), although the refinery company, SONARA, had existed on paper since 1976. The export and management of Cameroon's petroleum improved its balance of trade with many foreign countries. It allowed government to engage in important long-term development infrastructure and boost its creditability in economic management in various international circles. However, for the average Cameroonian, the home production of petroleum was no panacea for high gasoline prices. In the wake of the worldwide slump in oil sales, the price of Cameroon's petroleum dropped from $29 per barrel in 1984 to $26 in 1985 and reached an all-time low of $10 in 1986. The precipitate drop of Cameroon's petroleum price is projected by the government as one of the main causes of the country's **economic crisis**. As the economy continued to decline and government became even more desperate for income, "forward oil deals" came into play. The government sells oil at reduced price in advance of production to get immediate income. In the long term, such a policy is harmful. *See also* FOREIGN TRADE; PIPELINE; SOCIETE NATIONALE D'HYDROCARBURES.

PEUHL. *See* FULANI.

PIDGIN ENGLISH. This lingua franca in contemporary Cameroon results from historical and cultural circumstances. It is a mixture of native dialects with an unorthodox but convenient use of mostly English words. Many of the early traders on the Cameroonian coasts prior to German annexation in 1884 were the British, and there were British missionaries, too. Local inhabitants were largely unschooled but eager to work and develop relations with early traders. Pidgin English arose to serve the transactions between the two sets of actors.

Pidgin English is still widely used in the country, and its use continues to spread. It serves as the lingua franca between **anglophones** and **francophones**. Indigenous languages and French have an influence on pidgin English in certain parts of the country. *See also* BILINGUALISM; FRANGLAIS.

PIPELINE. Chad, a land-locked country, has major oil deposits in the Doba Basin. However, these are of value only if a means to export the valuable liquid can be found. Cameroon and Chad agreed to construct a pipeline from the oil fields through Cameroon to the port at **Kribi**. In January 1994, agreement was reached with Exxon, Shell, and Elf Aquitian oil companies to build the pipeline, and construction was under way in early 2000. The project was the largest investment in Sub-Saharan Africa at that time at a cost of $2.5 billion. Cameroon is expected to earn at least $500 million from the project, and for several years many Cameroonians will be employed in the construction of the pipeline, 1,050 kilometers in length. There is considerable concern about the effects of the project on the environment. The Cameroon Oil Transportation Company (COTCO) will represent Cameroon's interest in this project. *See also* PETROLEUM.

PLANNED LIBERALISM. Planned liberalism was the key concept in Cameroon's economic development philosophy. The main poles of this concept were double: the encouragement of private initiative and reliance on market forces as well as government regulation of investment and the judicious allocation of resources. Major actors in the execution of this philosophy were the private individuals and foreign companies, on the one hand, and parastatal enterprises and the national government, on the other. Conceived in 1965 following the abandonment of **African socialism**, planned liberalism was a deliberate attempt at ideological neutrality. It sought to integrate the best elements of capitalism and socialism in respect to private initiative and national sovereignty. The state therefore entered into partnership with private foreign enterprises to execute certain highly prized economic ventures. Economic misfortunes since the mid-1980s have led to criticism of the planned liberalism philosophy due to poor governmental judgment at guiding private foreign investment, the pervasive **corruption** paralyzing bureaucratic structures, and the overheated process of industrialization. There is now considerable pressure for the government to **privatize** the parastatals, turning them over to private enterprise. *See also* ECONOMIC CRISIS; STRUCTURAL ADJUSTMENT PROGRAM.

PLEBISCITE (1961). The United Nations organized and supervised a plebiscite on 11–12 February 1961 to determine the future of the British territories in Cameroon. **Great Britain** ruled its Northern and Southern territories separately. It also developed a strong identity between the Cameroons territories and **Nigeria**. The populations of the Cameroon territories were to decide between integration with the Nigerian federation or **reunification** with the **République du Cameroun**. Overwhelmingly, the **Southern Cameroons** voted for reunification with Cameroun (233,571 for reunification and 97,741 against). **Northern Cameroon** voted for inclusion in Nigeria (146,296 for Nigeria and 97,659 for Cameroon). *See also* NORTHERN CAMEROONS CASE.

POLITIQUE DE RENOUVEAU. *See* NEW DEAL.

PONDI, PAUL (1928–). Cameroon's ambassador to the **United States** and formerly first delegate-general for national security, Pondi was born on 10 February 1928 in Ngog-Bassong, Nyong and Kéllé Division of **Center Province**. After completing elementary education in Eseka in 1947 and the famous Evangelical Mission Institute of Libamba at Makak in 1950, he passed the ***baccalauréat*** from **Lycée Leclerc** in 1955. For five years he served as regional controller of finance and climbed to the rank of civil servant (*functionnaire*). In 1960, Pondi was appointed delegate-general for national security and in this capacity played a crucial role in quelling the **Union des Populations du Cameroun (UPC)** rebellion and insurrection that was rife in the early days of Cameroon's independence. This contributed to the stabilization of the new republic and the **Ahmadou Ahidjo** regime. Between 1972 and 1977, he was ambassador to Zaire and, from 1977 to 1981, ambassador to **Great Britain**, before being appointed Cameroon's ambassador to the United States in January 1982. He retired in 1997.

POPULATION EXPLOSION. This term is used to explain and account for the rapid increase of population in a given area over a period of time. Cameroon's population was estimated at barely five million in 1960. By 1976, when the most ambitious census drive was held, the official accounts placed the country's population at 7.802 million inhabitants. By 1982, Cameroon had over eight million inhabitants. In 1998, the population was estimated to be 15 million, with a growth rate of 2.81 percent per year. Life expectancy is 51 years.

There is assumed to be a relationship between economic development and population growth. It is widely, though not universally, thought that rapid population growth is a detriment to economic development, especially if the rate of population growth is greater than the rate of growth of the gross national product (GNP). Consequently, the previous pronationalistic slogan "operation 10 million inhabitants" is now being replaced by the president's warning that while procreation is a human and natural right, it must be brought under control. Cameroon is moving from a pro-population growth view to a population control attitude.

Much of Cameroon's population is essentially young, since most Cameroonians have only been born since independence. In 1998, it was estimated that 46 percent of the population was 14 or younger, but only 3 percent was over 65.

PRÉ, ROLAND. Pré was appointed high **commissioner** of **Cameroun** in November 1954. He had gained wide-ranging experience in the colonial service in Gabon, Guinea, and Upper Volta. He was considered progressive but tough and a ready answer to the growing radicalism in Cameroon politics represented by the **Union des Populations du Cameroun (UPC)**. Consequently, he began an anti-UPC campaign by forming various local councils to offset the growing strength of the movement. He called for the integration of many planters, traders, and workers into newly formed traditional institutions that were opposed to the UPC. However, some of his measures also alienated moderates, especially his decision to control the powers and activity of the **Assemblée Territoriale du Cameroun (ATCAM)**. Pré personally declared an all-out war to "crush communist activity" in February 1955 at a time of unrest and economic malaise in **French Cameroun**. He also took economic decisions that alienated the white *colons* (settlers) in Cameroun. All these measures gave rise to intermittent strikes organized in **Douala** by various labor groups. Between 22 and 30 May 1955, major bloody riots engulfed Cameroun affecting the towns of Douala, **Yaoundé**, **Nkongsamba,** and Mbanga. The French administration estimated the loss of 26 lives, including two Europeans. Before he was replaced in April 1956, Pré took the ultimate political decision by banning the UPC from legal existence.

PREFET (SENIOR DIVISIONAL OFFICER). The *préfet* is the head of administrative units in the country. These administrative units are known as *départements* in French and as *divisions* in English. The division is the subunit of the province. The *préfet* is appointed by presidential decree and has various subordinates, including the first and second assistant divisional officers, the subdivisional officer, and the district head, below him. Since independence, most *préfets* have been graduates of the **National Center for Administration and Magistracy (CENAM)**, formally known as ENAM. Various Cameroonian personalities have risen from prefectorial ranks into cabinet portfolios. These include **William-Aurelian Eteky Mboumoua**, Enoch Kwayeb, and Jean-Marcel Mengueme.

PRESBYTERIAN CHURCH. *See* AMERICAN PRESBYTERIAN MISSION; BASEL MISSION SOCIETY.

PRESTATION. In this system of **forced labor** applied by the French in **Cameroun**, males performed a 10-day free labor service to government. It was only imposed on Camerounians of the *sujet* status. French authorities accepted financial contributions from the *sujet* in lieu of the required prestation. Local **chiefs** collaborated with French administrators for the operation of this exploitative policy.

PRIME MINISTER. A position with this title has appeared and disappeared in both state (during the federal period) and central governments of Cameroon. Its most recent appearance is in the **constitution of 1996**. The prime minister is the head of government (the president is the head of state). The prime minister cannot be a member of either house of Parliament. The prime minister is appointed by the president, but the **National Assembly** may pass a vote of no confidence or a motion of censure, forcing the prime minister to resign.

PRISO, CHIEF LOCK. *See* LOCK PRISO, CHIEF.

PRISO, PAUL SOPPO. *See* SOPPO PRISO, PAUL.

PRIVATIZATION. Many African states have played a major role in investment in a wide range of companies as part of their effort to encourage economic development. These parastatals have frequently become economic disasters. With the **economic crisis** of the 1980s and the intervention of the **International Monetary Fund (IMF)**, the **World Bank**, and various donor nations, there has been pressure on African governments to turn these parastatals over to private ownership, a process termed *privatization*. Many parastatals were badly managed, poorly planned, overstaffed, and the focus of corrupt practice. It is assumed that private ownership will lead to rational management and profitability. Too, the sale of government shares will provide revenue to assist the government to pay off its debts.

Cameroon's government has invested in numerous parastatals, ranging from pulp and paper companies (**Cellulose du Cameroun/CELLUCAM)** to banks (**Société Camerounaise de Banque**) to utilities, transportation, and so forth. Pressure to divest began to grow in the mid-1980s, and the first sale took place in 1990. The list of planned divestments includes most of the well-known companies in the country—Camair (the airline), Camship, and Regifercam (the railroad) in transport; Hevecam, Sodecoton, Socopalm, **Cameroon Development Corporation**, and Camsuco in agriculture; SONEL, Intelcam, **National Water Corporation of Cameroon (SNEC)**, and SOTUC in public utilities; and the Port of **Douala** are among those frequently mentioned. Some 60 to 70 companies are to be liquidated and 25 or more sold.

In general, government has moved slowly with this process. The parastatals have been an excellent source of patronage, and many officials have become very rich from the management positions they have received in them. Moreover, the reductions in staff associated with economic rationalization have been politically unpopular and are an important factor in the massive unemployment problem the country faces in the late 1990s. Also, the sales of the parastatals have not been as beneficial as expected. The least successful companies have been the most difficult to sell. In some instances buyers have been willing to take profitable parts of companies and to leave the government stuck with the unprofitable parts. Prices received have been lower than hoped, and more often than desired, foreigners (especially French) have been the purchasers rather than Cameroonians.

PROTECTORATE. This is the official German title of the **Kamerun** territory between 1884 and 1916. The particular notion of the protectorate entailed German supervision over the affairs conducted by native Kamerun rulers.

PROTESTANTISM. Protestant Christian missionaries have strongly influenced Cameroon history, beginning with the English **Baptist** missionaries on the Cameroon coast. In later periods, various other mission groups—including the American, French, and Swiss **Presbyterians**; the American Baptists; the French Protestant missions; the Norwegian and American **Lutheran missions** as well as the Adventists, Baha'is, and Jehovah's Witnesses—have established bases in Cameroon. *See also* BASEL MISSION; CHRISTIANITY.

PROVINCES. *See* REGIONS.

PUTTKAMER, JESKO VON. The third German governor in **Kamerun** (1895–1907) was a strong advocate of penetration into the interior and instrumental in expanding the plantation economy. Under his tenure, the design for a railway project was established. Consequently, he was the champion of **forced labor** and was characteristically harsh vis-à-vis the local population. Puttkamer had a particular dislike of the **Duala,** defending the rights of whites and soldiers over indigenous **women**. For these reasons, he was constantly in conflict with various missionary establishments throughout his tenure. Puttkamer was dismissed as governor for his uncomely behavior toward the local population.

PYGMIES. A distinctive population grouping, pygmies are widely considered as the oldest inhabitants of the southern primary forest of the country. Their numbers have been consistently reduced with the retreat of the primary forest. Today they number only about 6,500 and are mostly found in the small villages of the **East Province** bordering the Republics of **Congo** and **Gabon**. Despite their diminishing numbers, pygmies have retained their cultural and occupational skills. Their monogamous family patterns, religious attachment, and presumed magical prowess have attracted many studies of their society by anthropologists.

– R –

RABAH. Rabah was an influential Bornu ruler in the late 19th century. During his reign, Kanembu and the Mandara people in north Cameroun were conquered in 1895. Rabah later fell to French invaders in 1900.

RADIO TROTTOIR. This phrase (literally "sidewalk radio") refers to the circulation of sensational rumors by unofficial sources in Cameroon. Under the **Ahmadou Ahidjo** regime, strict news censorship occurred; occasionally, foreign press coverage of Cameroon's affairs was seized. There is more freedom under the **Paul Biya** regime, but journalists within the country have restricted opportunities to be creative. Because explanations are not given to various national issues, this information is "fabricated" as a means to satisfy the population's curiosity. Usually Radio Trottoir stories are not unfounded. They contain some germ of truth, but the facts are usually inflated well beyond their true proportions. Such rumors are mostly prevalent in periods of national crisis, public suspicion, and questioning. In the aftermath of the **coup attempt of 6 April 1984**, President Biya cautioned the population that the truth comes from above while untruth circulates from below. This notwithstanding, Radio Trottoir continues to gain ground as a popular institution.

RALLIEMENT. This term was used to signify the campaign by the **Ahmadou Ahidjo** government to entice and rally declared opponents of the political system to the national cause. The *ralliement* strategy was particularly in operation between 1958 and 1960. Various **Union des Populations du Cameroun (UPC)** rebels, including **Theodore Mayi-Matip** and Kamdem-Ninyim, were given official status and allowed to maintain a legal opposition, the *raillé* UPC, in the **Assemblée Législative du Cameroun (ALCAM)**. The *ralliement* strategy helped to weaken the underground insurgency and strengthened Ahidjo's control of the country.

RAMADAN. The ninth month of the Muslim year is a period of fasting from sunrise to sunset. Feasting often occurs after sunset. However, during the day the lack of food and drink can have a very tiring effect, with negative effects on daily activities. Ramadan is one of the five basic duties ("pillars") of the Islamic faith. On the day after Ramadan, a feast is held, Id-ul-Fitr. This is a national holiday in Cameroon. *See also* ISLAM.

RAMADIER, JEAN. Ramadier served as French high **commissioner** in **Cameroun** in 1958. He played a crucial role in engineering the process by which the unpredictable **André-Marie Mbida** government lost parliamentary and popular support. This led to Mbida's forced resignation in 1958 and facilitated his replacement by Vice Premier **Ahmadou Ahidjo** on 18 February 1958. Ramadier was removed from office in May 1958 after completing this task.

RASSEMBLEMENT CAMEROUNAIS (RACAM). RACAM was a fervent nationalist political party formed in April 1947, following a split within the ranks of **Union Camerounaise Française (Unicafra)**. It was formed by trade unionists and established a constitution intended to be the charter of an independent **Cameroun**. The charter stressed the indigenous will of the population based on the collective responsibility of a united and indivisible people. RACAM's populist and radical stance led it to serve as the crucible for the birth of the **Union des Populations du Cameroun (UPC)** in 1948. Compared to predecessor movements, it was no tool of the French designed to suppress pro-German sentiments. In relation to post-1945 movements, RACAM became the prototype of an organization formed to assault colonialism wherever and however it was manifested. Banned by the French because of its unabashed radicalism, its banner was taken up by the UPC, whose key leader, **Reuben Um Nyobe**, was among the nine founding members of RACAM.

RASSEMBLEMENT DEMOCRATIQUE AFRICAIN (RDA). This pan-**francophone** African political movement grouped leading parties from French territories to provide an avenue to demand broader civil and political rights for French-speaking Africans. Formed in 1946, it won seats in the French National Assembly in the same year. It entered into a close alliance with the French Communist Party until 1955. The **Union des Populations du Cameroun (UPC)** became a member of the RDA from 1948 in a bid to develop and broaden African bases of support.

RASSEMBLEMENT DEMOCRATIQUE DU PEUPLE CAMEROUNAIS. *See* CAMEROON PEOPLE'S DEMOCRATIC MOVEMENT.

RASSEMBLEMENT DU PEUPLE CAMEROUNAIS (RAPECA). This party bearing the same name as the **Rassemblement du Peuple Camerounais (RPC)** (see following entry) emerged in 1959. However, it was distinguished from the RPC by its more popular acronym RAPECA. Formed by **André Fouda** in **Yaoundé,** it aimed to be an allied party to the Démocrates Camerounais led by **Paul Soppo Priso**. RAPECA became significant in its own right when it participated in the Round Table for reconciliation of French Camerounian parties.

RASSEMBLEMENT DU PEUPLE CAMEROUNAIS (RPC). This was one of the many political movements in the French trust territory of **Cameroun** organized in the postwar period. It became particularly prominent in the **Bamiléké** region as an anti–**Union des Populations du Cameroun (UPC)** forum. Its leadership was recruited among the traditional conservative Bamiléké chiefs who on three occasions in April 1955 prevented the UPC from holding meetings in the area. The movement became less active after violent confrontations with the UPC.

REGIONS. Until 1996 the country had been divided into 10 administrative provinces. These were directly administered from **Yaoundé** by appointed officials led by an appointed **governor**. According to the **constitution of 1996**, the 10 provinces are now to be known as regions, and their governance is substantially altered. The regions have jurisdiction in economic, social, health, educational, cultural, and sports development. A Regional Council and its president are the administering authorities. The council will consist of divisional delegates indirectly elected and representatives of traditional rulers elected by their peers. Local members of Parliament will serve as advisers to the council. The council elects the regional president from among its members. An administrator appointed by the president of the Republic retains substantial power over the council. The president of the Republic may suspend or dissolve a council and its president. Additionally, the president of the Republic may change the names and boundaries of a region and create additional regions.

These provisions were established to meet public demands for decentralization of government and to placate those demanding a return to a federal system. The latter group was not satisfied, and many in the former group argued that this was only a façade, not true decentralization.

As of early 2000, provinces were still in place and regional structures had not been established.

RENAISSANCE CAMEROUNAISE (RENAICAM). RENAICAM was formed in December 1948 in Abongmbang as another anti–**Union des Populations du Cameroun (UPC)** political grouping by elite indigenes from the eastern part of the territory. RENAICAM was largely formed with the help of the French administration, determined to weaken the influence of the UPC across the territory. The movement disappeared in 1957. It was principally composed of the **Ewondo-**Maka people. *See also* RASSEMBLEMENT DU PEUPLE CAMEROUNAIS (RPC).

REPUBLIC OF CAMEROON. This has been the official English-language name of the country at two points in time: when the French **trust territory** had become independent (1 January 1960) until **reunification** (when it became the **Federal Republic of Cameroon**) and from 1984 to the present. *See also* REPUBLIQUE DU CAMEROUN.

REPUBLIQUE DU CAMEROUN. This was the official name of French **Cameroun** when it became independent on 1 January 1960. The new country was headed by a president and a unicameral legislature. The new political entity faced domestic and international challenges. Its domestic challenge was the insurgency of the **Union des Populations du Cameroun (UPC)** against the government of Pres. **Ahmadou Ahidjo**. Its international challenge was the critical attitude of radical African leaders because of the republic's close alliance to **France**. The République du Cameroun was a short political experiment. It ceased to exist with the **reunification,** which gave birth to the **Federal Republic of Cameroon**. The term *La République du Cameroun* was popular in the 1990s among **anglophones** who use it to signify their desire to return to a federal status or to become an independent state. The term suggests the illegitimacy of the 1972 formation of a unitary government and the perceived inferior, dominated position of anglophones in that system. *See also* REPUBLIC OF CAMEROON.

RESIDENTS. Leading administrative and political officers when British **Southern Cameroons** was the **Cameroons Province** (1916–49) were titled "residents." The province consisted of four divisions: Victoria (**Limbe**), **Kumba**, **Mamfe,** and **Bamenda**. After 1949, Bamenda was made a separate province, relieving the strain and neglect in the British administrative setup.

Residents were responsible for the efficiency of the public service in the province. Because of the lack of personnel prevalent in the British system of the time, they ended up performing multiple fiscal, technical, political, and administrative functions. Residents were not all-powerful. They received orders from the lieutenant governor in Enugu, **Nigeria**, and the governor-general in Lagos. They never stayed in office long enough to grasp the needs and peculiarities of the province. The resident's office was in **Buea** and, after 1949, also in Bamenda. Some of the most remembered residents include P. V. Young, Maj. F. H. Ruxton, E. J. Arnett, G. H. Findlay, A. E. F. Murray, and A. F. Bridges. *See also* INDIRECT RULE.

List of Serving Residents of the Cameroons Province, 1916–1949

All were substantive appointments, except those noted with an asterisk. Abbreviations are as follows: Ag., acting; DO, district officer; Res., resident; SDO, senior district officer; Snr., senior.

K. V. Elphinstone	1916
E. C. Duff (Res.)	1916–17
P. V. Young (Res.)	1917–19
Capt. W. G. Ambrose	1919
Dr. J. C. Maxwell (Res.)	1919
J. Davidson (Res.)	
Capt. G. Anderson	1919–25
N. C. Duncan (DO)	
Major F. H. Ruxton (Res.)	
R. W. M. Dundast	1921–25
W. E. Hunt (DO)	
E. J. Arnett (Res.)	1925–28

Capt. Buchanan Smith	
H. J. Aveling (Ag. Res.)	1928–29
E. J. Arnett (Res.)	
M. Greggor (DO)	
G. S. Browne (Snr. Res.)	1929–32
F. B. Carr* (DO)	
J. W. C. Rutherford (Res.)	1933–34
D. W. Firth (Snr. Res.)	
G. H. Findlay (Snr. Res.)	1935–38
K. V. Hanistch* (Deputy Res.)	
A. E. F. Murray (Res.)	
N. C. Denton	1939–42
Please (first name unknown)	
Major Sealy-King	
P. G. Harris (Snr. Res.)	
J. Macrae Simpson* (DO)	1943–45
Capt. A. Leeming* (SDO)	20 March 1945–10 October 1945
A. F. B. Bridges (Res.)	
N. A. P. G. Mackenzie* (SDO)	14 February 1946–4 August 1949
G. S. Osborn* (DO)	5 August 1949–31 December 1949
D. A. F. Shute* (Snr. Res.)	25 August 1949–31 December 1949

REUNIFICATION. This is the process by which Cameroonian peoples forged a common political unity following the demise of the dual **mandate** and **trusteeship** administrations in the territory. The reunification objective was to return Cameroon to its 1914 composition as it existed under the German **protectorate**.

Proreunification sentiments were first expressed in radical nationalist platforms such as the **Union des Populations du Cameroun (UPC)** and in party names that spelled Cameroon with a *K,* such as the **Kamerun National Democratic Party (KNDP)** or the **One Kamerun Party (OK)**. Such a trend mirrored elite nostalgia for the territory's past and its aspiration for the future. In the end, partial geographic reunification was achieved through a United Nations–supervised **plebiscite** and a series of constitutional conferences. However, in a highly controversial outcome, British **Northern Cameroons** voted to join the Nigerian Federation rather than the **République du Cameroun**. For this reason, the Cameroon reunification was an incomplete process. Only **Southern Cameroons** opted for reunification to form the **Federal Republic of Cameroon** with the République du Cameroun on 1 October 1961.

Despite the long quest for reunification, critics believed that in the constitutional conferences **Ahmadou Ahidjo** manipulated **anglophone** politicians to establish a strongly centralized presidential system in which he easily prevailed. In addition, the creation of the one-party structure in 1966 and the unitary structure in 1972 are seen as attempts at consolidating personal power as well as promoting the reunification process. Apart from the political reality of reunification, Cameroon's reunification is also identified in multiple symbols such as road and stadium names, the dual official languages, and the tensions of coexistence between two contrasting communities of peoples. In 1970, the celebration of 1 October as reunification day was discontinued; 11 February, the date of the reunification **plebiscite**, continues to be celebrated as Cameroon Youth Day. *See also* BILINGUALISM; FOUMBAM CONFERENCE; NATION BUILDING; NORTHERN CAMEROONS CASE.

REVOLUTION VERTE. *See* GREEN REVOLUTION.

RICE. Although it was not a commonly used food in precolonial Cameroon, German experiments found Cameroonian soils fertile for the growing of rice. This was the case in areas of Yagoua, Nanga Eboko, and Doume. No extensive growth of rice existed prior to 1971, and the local market survived through imports. But in recent years demand has grown considerably. As a result, the state initiated the **Société d'Expansion et de Modernisation de la Riziculture de Yagoua (SEMRY),** a rice project aimed at enhancing agricultural revenue in the isolated areas of growth and to limit large-scale imports. Like most agroindustrial ventures, SEMRY was established at heavy capital cost that made the price of its rice, when compared to imported rice, prohibitive. For this reason, imported rice has remained popular despite the government's attempts to push for the consumption of local rice. In all, 96,000 tons of rice were produced locally in 1986, but only 36,000 tons were marketed. Cheaper imports took the remainder of the market. Rice is a widely consumed food all across the country. In recent years, Cameroon production of rice has averaged 55,000 tons per year, but 200,000 tons are imported per year. *See also* AGRICULTURAL POLICY; FOOD SELF-SUFFICIENCY.

RIGOR AND MORALIZATION. This has been the key slogan of the **Paul Biya** presidency. It is based on the idea that the Cameroonians could attain higher goals and objectives with greater sense of purpose and dedication. According to the head of state, "rigor and moralization" signifies the struggle against tribalism, sectarianism, clientelism, provocation, and intoxication with continuous efficacy. Consequently, moralization becomes a permanent endeavor against laxity, fraud, diversion of public resources, **corruption**, favoritism, and arbitrary action. The slogan was immensely popular in the early stages of the Biya presidency. It was applied in multiple practical cases, mentioned in all public speeches at all levels in the country, and served as the demarcation line between the **Ahmadou Ahidjo** and Biya regimes. Over time, the public has become very cynical with respect to the "rigor and moralization" concept as the Biya regime has become known as even more corrupt than its predecessor. *See also* NEW DEAL.

ROSICRUCIAN ORDER. In the early 1600s in Germany, occult powers were claimed by a Christian Rosenkreutz in pamphlets that spread across Europe. From this have sprung various groups claiming Rosicrucian origins. Pres. **Paul Biya** and many of his closest associates are members of a Rosicrucian Order. Some argue that membership is a stepping stone to power in Cameroon. Although the Rosicrucian Order is in many ways a secret society, the names of members do slip out from time to time. **Titus Edzoa** is among those reputed to be a member.

RUBBER. During the German epoch, rubber was the single most important export of **Kamerun**. Initially, rubber was gathered from wild trees, but later it was cultivated in large plantations in the southwest and southeast regions of the country. The predominance of rubber was later overtaken by **cocoa**, **coffee,** and **palm products** as principal export crops.

While the **Cameroon Development Corporation (CDC)** accounts for production in the **South West Province**, Hévéa-Cameroun (HEVECAM) was created in 1975 in response to the sudden increase of rubber prices. Like most parastatals in Cameroon, HEVECAM has faced severe problems of structural and financial nature. **Privatization** is expected. Cameroon's natural rubber faces increasing competition from the less expensive synthetic rubber and other natural rubber producers.

RURAL EXODUS. It is a widespread tendency for the local population to leave the rural areas in favor of the urban parts of the country. This rural exodus is largely the result of the absence of socioeconomic amenities in the rural areas, which tends to push the population away from villages, and the comparatively better amenities in the urban centers, which tends to pull the deprived folk into the major cities. It is the sum total of these push and pull factors that creates the conditions for rural exodus. The desire for a larger income and the relative low earning capacity in rural areas are significant factors in this equation.

Government attempts to overcome this trend by improving conditions in the rural areas and providing adequate facilities in the urban areas to cater for the influx of rural migrants. All villages in the country have been particularly hard hit by the rural exodus, while the cities have grown tremendously as a result of this phenomenon. Attempts to improve conditions in smaller, provincial urban centers have been made in an effort to slow the exodus to **Yaoundé** and **Douala**. *See also* POPULATION EXPLOSION; SOCIÉTÉ DU DÉVELOPPEMENT DU NKAM; URBANIZATION.

RUSSIA. *See* COMMONWEALTH OF INDEPENDENT STATES.

– S –

SABAL LECCO, FELIX (1920–). The former president of the **Economic and Social Council** was born in 1920 in Lena, near Bertoua in the **Eastern Province**. He attended primary school at Bertoua and Doume. He later earned a diploma from the **Yaoundé** School of Administration and worked as a teacher and chief of examination in the Education Service (1948–57). In 1957, he became chief of cabinet to the minister of works and social welfare. In 1960, he was appointed assistant divisional officer of Lom and Kadei Division. Sabal Lecco later participated in a two-year course on administration in Paris and was appointed to several posts on return. He served as ***préfet*** (senior divisional officer) of the Dja and Lobo Division (1963–64) and in the same capacity for Mungo Division (1964–65). From September 1965 to September 1969, he served simultaneously as **federal inspector of administration** for the **Littoral Province** and senior divisional officer for the Wouri Division. After a short tenure in the **East Cameroon** government as secretary of state for rural development, Sabal Lecco joined the federal cabinet as minister of justice in June 1970. From 1972 until 1974, he was the minister of public service. When the first **Economic and Social Council** of the **United Republic of Cameroon** was formed in 1974, Sabal Lecco became its chairman. He also held important posts in the Central Committee of the **Cameroon National Union (CNU)**, including the powerful office of political secretary. He remained a key political figure until his replacement in 1984, when he was dropped from his party duties and named ambassador to Italy. He was later replaced by Michael Tabong Kima.

SADOU DAOUDOU. *See* DAOUDOU, SADOU.

ST. JOSEPH'S COLLEGE. This is the oldest and most prestigious secondary school in **anglophone** Cameroon. Much of the male anglophone elite received its education at this institution, located at Sasse, near Bonjongo and **Buea**. **Catholic** missionaries opened a primary school at this site in 1912, but the secondary school accepted its first students in 1939.

SAKER, ALFRED (1814–1880). This English Baptist missionary served in Jamaica and Fernando Po (1843–45) before establishing a Christian mission on the Cameroon coast on 22 June 1845 in **Douala**. His entire missionary activity benefited from the early knowledge and experience of **Joseph Merrick**. In 1849, he performed the first conversion and baptism of indigenous Cameroonians from his permanent station in Bimbia. He learned the **Duala** language for the Duala versions of the Bible. This facilitated missionary activity among the Duala and led to the opening of new stations in Deido and Bonaberi. Saker is equally remembered for discovering and making Victoria (today's **Limbe**) the first permanent English settlement on the Cameroon coast in 1858. He remained in Cameroon for 30 years before returning to England in 1876. The expansion of the Baptist church in Cameroon is largely owed to him. An outstanding secondary school for girls in Limbe, Saker Baptist College, and a mission secondary school in Douala, Collège Alfred Saker, have been named after him. *See also* BAPTIST MISSION.

SALATOU, AHMADOU (1946–). Salatou was a gendarme officer, aide-de-camp of former president **Ahmadou Ahidjo**. Together with **Ibrahim Oumharou,** he fomented the plot to assassinate Pres. **Paul Biya**. Salatou was arrested, tried, and condemned to death on 28 February 1984. President Biya later commuted the death sentence. *See also* DESTABILIZATION PLOT.

SAMBA, MARTIN-PAUL (1875–1914). Originally known as Mebenga m'Ebobo, Samba was born in Metoutoe-Engong, near Ebolowa, in the contemporary **South Province**. He grew up in **Kribi** and became close to the Germans who settled there. He served under the German explorer Kurt von Morgan, who sent him to **Germany** for education and military training. Samba later served as a lieutenant in the German Imperial Army and rose to the rank of captain.

On his return home in 1895, he participated in the various explorations by Germans in the **Kamerun** hinterland. In this role, Samba was widely considered a traitor by the local population. In 1910, he turned to his folk and was enthroned as traditional **chief** in Ebolowa. He became the strategist of the local resistance against the German invaders rather than an accomplice of the German imperial dream. At the outbreak of **World War I**, Samba publicity declared his intention to take action against the Germans in a letter to French authorities in Brazzaville. The Germans intercepted the communication and immediately considered Samba a public enemy. He was arrested, charged with high treason, and executed by a firing squad on 8 August 1914. Samba has been hailed as a nationalist and hero in the same category as **Douala Rudolf Manga Bell**.

SAME, LOTIN (1882–1946). Same was president of the **Native Baptist Church (NBC)** during the French administration of **Cameroun**. Born in **Douala** in 1882, he grew up as an intelligent youth under German clergymen. He was ordained into the clergy in 1908. His ardor and hard work led to his nomination in 1915 as president of the Conference of Baptist Churches in **Kamerun** and president of the NBC. Same developed a strong attachment to the Germans, which led to increased friction with the succeeding French authorities. The French, who were determined to put religious leaders in the service of their colonial vision, experienced a showdown with the NBC because of the determination and combativeness of Lotin Same. From 1930 until 1945, the French denied recognition to the NBC and opposed Same's use of the title "president" of the NBC as subversive. Short of an arrest, the French tried to entice him into the **Jeunesse Camerounaise Française (Jeucafra)**. Same's heroism lies in his independence and conviction that one could be a Christian without being French. He died in 1946; the NBC was officially recognized by the French in 1949.

SANAGA RIVER. Cameroon's longest river extends 918 kilometers and originates from the tumultuous descent of the **Adamawa** plateau before turning into a large river fed by tributary streams. Important rivers serving as tributaries to the Sanaga include the Lom, Vina, Meng, Mbam, and Noun. The Sanaga basin also includes the **Wouri**, **Mungo**, Nyong, Ntem, and Campo Rivers. The Sanaga is not navigable because of the many rapids and waterfalls around the north of **Yaoundé** and around **Edea**, but these features do create great hydroelectric potential. Some of this potential has been put to use.

SANGHA RIVER. The Sangha is an important tributary of the Congo River. The Sangha River also serves as the frontier between Cameroon and the Republic of **Congo**. The major affluents of Sangha consist of Kadei, Boumbe, Ngoko, and Dja Rivers, which are all located in the **East Province**.

SAO. The Sao was a civilization well developed by A.D. 500, which reached its height between the ninth and 15th centuries. Located to the south of **Lake Chad** and near the Chari River, Sao is known to us today mainly through oral history and archaeological discovery. Sao was eventually displaced by **Kotoko** in the 15th century.

SECOND EXTRAORDINARY CONGRESS OF CAMEROON NATIONAL UNION. The historic congress of 14 September 1983 was the result of the political rupture between the head of state, Pres. **Paul Biya,** and party chairman, **Ahmadou Ahidjo**. Ahidjo stepped down from the party leadership on 27 August 1983 with a provocative declaration from Paris. His resignation was proof of the unworkability of political dualism in the Cameroon system. The congress also ended the political primacy of Ahidjo in Cameroon politics. The Central Committee of the party met on 7 September under President Biya's chairmanship, approving the holding of an extraordinary congress for 14 September 1983. Various options were open for the 14 September congress. Moderate reformers argued for a simple reorganization of the Central Committee, while radical reformers called for new elections and a revision of the **constitution of 1972**. In the end, the congress only discussed the election of a new party chairman. President Biya was unanimously elected to the post at the end of the one-day event. In his closing speech, Biya introduced his policy slogan of the **New Deal**. *See also* AHIDJO–BIYA RUPTURE.

SECRET AGREEMENTS. A set of entangling agreements between **France** and its former territories in Africa was signed prior to the attainment of sovereignty by the African territories. According to international law, such agreements between two unequal partners are questionable. The Secret Agreements between France and Cameroun were signed on 31 December 1958 and included agreements in the following fields: military and financial cooperation, cultural affairs, administrative relations, civil aviation and aeronautics, military assistance, and a consular and legal convention. The various agreements provided France with an absolute privilege and advantage in the conduct of the affairs of the new **République du Cameroun**. These secret agreements led several countries to question the sovereignty and independence of Cameroun. *See also* FOREIGN POLICY.

SECRETARIAT-GENERAL AT THE PRESIDENCY. Cameroon's most powerful ministerial institution at the present time (2000) is the very foundation of political centralization and administrative bureaucracy. The Secretariat-General was a creation of Pres. **Ahmadou Ahidjo** in the 1960s, which gradually accumulated political functions. It held a determinant role in the governmental mechanism and individual realities. To gain a government contract, open a law firm, or begin a pharmacy, approval had to come from the Secretariat-General. The personalities serving in this capacity have all been important figures: Mongo Soo, Christian Tobie Kuoh, **Paul Biya**, **Samuel Eboua**, **Sadou Daoudou,** surrounded by able assistants, **Felix Sengat-Kuo**, Ayissi Mvodo, and **Maigari Bello Bouba**.

The personality of the office gradually weakened under the Biya presidency with Abouem A Tchoyi and **Ferdinand Oyono,** who left the presidency to assume less powerful posts. In a reorganization of government on 22 November 1986, Biya abolished the Secretariat-General at the Presidency in favor of the Secretariat-General of Government. The president later resumed the old practice with the re-creation of the Secretariat-General at the Presidency on 15 May 1988.

SEITZ, DR. THEODOR (1863–1949). Seitz was the fourth German governor of **Kamerun** (1907–10). Compared to his predecessors, Seitz was a remarkable humanitarian who showed great interest in the welfare of the local population. He called for the end of domestic slavery and favored the increase of indigenous representatives in local councils. He began the negotiations with **France,** which led to the German acquisition of a large part of French Congo in 1911 in exchange for Morocco. This new territory was known as **New Kamerun (Neukamerun)**.

SELF-RELIANT DEVELOPMENT (DEVELOPPEMENT AUTO-CENTRE). This is an economic policy aimed at integrated national development through effective control of the main factors of production by the government and the people. As defined in 1975, self-reliant development is development for the people, by the people. It subordinates Cameroon's international economic relations to the objectives of domestic development, depending principally on local efforts and labor. A self-reliant policy is based on the following options: a production policy more sensitive to domestic demand, a greater mobilization of financial and monetary policy toward internal savings, and an enhanced wage and employment policy. Since its enunciation, self-reliance has served the designs of the agricultural sector. This has been directed toward increased productivity and self-sufficiency in food and the encouragement of cash crop production, along with constant increases in the prices of these crops. Increases in total public investment in agriculture since the third Five-Year Development Plan and the establishment of the **National Fund for Rural Development (FONADER)** are aimed toward the self-reliant objective. By encouraging small-scale farmer projects and youth participation, the self-reliant doctrine aspired to make Cameroon the food supplier of Central Africa. *See also* AGRICULTURAL POLICY.

SEMENGUE, PIERRE (1933–). Semengue is commander-general of Cameroon Armed Forces and a highly revered and admired officer. Born in Lolodorf, in the Ocean Division, he attended primary school and later enrolled in **Lycée Leclerc** in 1949, from where he graduated with high marks in 1956. He entered the Hanson-de-Sailly academy to prepare for admission into the famous Saint-Cyr Military School, which he completed in 1959. He did a year of training in the Ecole d'Application d'Artillerie before returning to Cameroon.

Semengue renounced his title of French officer and joined the Cameroon army, commanding forces in the critical zones of conflict of the postindependence era: **Edea**, Dschang, and **Bafoussam** (1960–64). He returned to Paris to the Ecole d'Etat Major of the Ecole Supérieure de Guerre and obtained a diploma in 1965. This moved him to the rank of lieutenant colonel and the post of commander of ground forces. He was promoted to colonel in 1969 and brigadier general in 1973 and was made inspector general of the armed forces, a function with no power, command, or authority. Under Pres. **Ahmadou Ahidjo**, it was widely believed the post was created to eclipse the general's popularity and to blunt his ability to seek political office. Semengue was appointed divisional general and chief of staff in June 1983 by Pres. **Paul Biya**.

Although his home was surrounded in the early hours of the **coup attempt of 6 April 1984** and he was a key target of the rebel troops of the Republican Guard, Semengue managed a miraculous escape to take control of the counteroffensive that crushed the mutiny. The identification of Semengue as a confidant of Biya is right but unrevealing. Semengue has upheld constitutional authority through competence, abnegation, and loyalty as head of the military since independence. It is to him that Cameroon owes its envied luck of a country that has never succumbed to military rule in the turbulence so characteristic of African politics.

SENATE. The **constitution of 1996** provides for a two-house legislature, a **National Assembly** and a Senate. As of April 2000, the Senate had not become operational. Chapter II of the constitution defines the Senate as having 10 senators from each of the regions, previously known as provinces. Seven are elected by indirect universal suffrage and three are appointed by the president to serve a five-year term. To become law, bills must be approved by both houses.

SENGAT-KUO, FELIX (1931–1997). A former minister of information and culture and current political secretary of the **Cameroon People's Democratic Movement**, Sengat-Kuo was born in **Douala** on 4 August 1931. He did primary education there before proceeding to **Yaoundé** for secondary school. He studied law in Paris and served in essentially diplomatic posts from 1960 until 1966, as cultural adviser in the Cameroon Embassy in Paris in 1960; director of cabinet in the Foreign Ministry in 1961; technical adviser in 1962; minister plenipotentiary and permanent secretary of the Union Africaine et Malgache (UAM) at the United Nations in 1963; and permanent representative at the UN in 1964.

In 1967, Sengat-Kuo was recalled home to serve as minister in charge of missions at the Presidency. He served as assistant secretary-general at the Presidency in 1968 and rose to the rank of vice minister in 1969 and that of minister from 1970 until 1979. Prior to **Ahmadou Ahidjo**'s resignation, Sengat-Kuo had been stripped of his governmental and party functions although he was the principal architect of the **constitution of 1972.** In the difficult moment of crisis with Pres. **Paul Biya**, Ahidjo turned to Sengat-Kuo as political adviser. Sengat-Kuo's animosity for Ahidjo and his stronger personal ties to President Biya led to his reentry into government as minister of information and culture from 1983 until 1986. In 1983, he also became a member of the Central Committee and the Political Bureau, and political secretary of the national party. When the **Cameroon People's Democratic Movement (CPDM)** was created in March 1985, he was appointed secretary-general of the party. He was also president of the board of directors of the Palm Groves Company (SOCAPALM).

After his removal from President Biya's government, Sengat-Kuo left the CPDM (1992) and moved to the opposition, identifying himself with the group of hard-core opposition parties, particularly the **Social Democratic Front (SDF),** which called for the organization of a sovereign national conference in Cameroon as a solution to the country's political crisis. He was secretary-general for the **Alliance for the Reconstruction of**

Cameroon through the Sovereign National Conference (ARC-SNC). Before his death in 1997, he was vice president of the Union for Change, which advocates the creation of a federal state for Cameroon.

SENIOR DIVISIONAL OFFICER. *See* PREFET.

SERVICE D'ETUDES ET DE LA DOCUMENTATION. *See* FOCHIVE, JEAN.

SERVICE D'EQUIVALENCE. *See* HARMONIZATION.

SHU MOM. This is the official alphabet of 83 letters and 10 numbers developed by the Sultan **Njoya**, the 16th sultan of the **Bamoum**.

SIMA FOUDA, DOMINIQUE (1934–). Sima Fouda, a former president of the now defunct **Cameroon Trade Union Congress (CTUC),** was born in Ngomedzap in the Nyong and So Division of the **Center Province**. After primary and secondary education in Akono, he enrolled in the School of Journalism in Lille, France. He returned home on completion to serve as secretary-general of the Chamber of Agriculture and later became editor in chief of ***L'Effort Camerounais*** (1965–71). He joined the Cameroon News Agency, where he served as chief of service for foreign news and president of the Union of Journalists of the Private Press and Mass Media Workers. It was from this last capacity that he was unanimously elected president of the newly formed Cameroon Trade Union Congress in December 1985. When the latter was dissolved in June 1992 and replaced by the Confederation of Cameroon Trade Unions, Sima Fouda was replaced as president by Etame Ndedi Emmanuel.

SLAVE TRADE. Cameroon served as a supply zone for the export of African slaves to the New World after the Portuguese exploration on the Cameroon coast. Cameroon slaves were generally sold to the Fernando Po collection center. Between the 1750s and 1820s, the **Duala** served as "slave trading middlemen" in these transactions. Most slaves traded from the Cameroon coast are believed to have come from inland as well as from the neighboring Batangas and the **Bassa**. Another major source area was the **Bamenda Grassfield**. Slaves from here were exported via the **Cross River** to Calabar. Disagreements between the Duala middlemen and the European merchants as well as the successive abolition of slavery by various European governments led to the decline of this inhuman commerce. Later in the 19th century, trade in ivory and **palm** oil on the Cameroon coast gradually replaced the slave trade.

SMUGGLING. Smuggling is the illegal importation or exportation of goods across international borders. Although smuggling occurs in every country, in Cameroon in the 1980s and 1990s it assumed such large proportions that the government's financial basis was threatened. Government derives much of its revenue from import–export duties. Many local businesses were also threatened as cheaper goods flooded in from neighboring states, especially **Nigeria**, and undersold Cameroon-made goods. One of the most dramatic instances was gasoline. Nigerian gasoline was smuggled into Cameroon by the truckload and sold from large glass bottles along highways throughout Cameroon. Many gasoline stations went out of business. Textiles, sugar, beer, cement, matches, and soap are other frequently smuggled goods. Once inside Cameroon, Nigerian goods spread throughout the countries of the **Union Douanière de l'Afrique Centrale (UDEAC)**.

SOCIAL DEMOCRATIC FRONT (SDF). In the 1990s, the SDF was the most radical opposition party in Cameroon. The SDF was formally launched at **Ntarinkon Palace** in **Bamenda**, **North West Province**, on 26 May 1990 amid a massive military presence. Considering the circumstances under which it was born, including the killing of six innocent youths by security forces, a constitutional proviso allowing the existence of political parties, and the party's ideology, the SDF has maintained a policy of confrontation with the government for the better part of its existence. The party remains the most radical and popular of all opposition parties in Cameroon.

It took the lead in the prodemocracy movement in Cameroon and, under the leadership of **John Fru Ndi**, played a preponderant role in the **ghost town operations** that rocked Cameroon between May and December 1991. The SDF strongly advocated a sovereign national conference as the logical take-off point for the transition from a one-party to a multiparty system.

In November 1991, the SDF refused to sign the final communiqué at the **Tripartite Conference,** which, among other things, required the opposition parties to call off the ghost town operations. The SDF therefore continued to uphold the policy of confrontation in its relations with government, but it was forced to concede in 1996, when an attempt to protest the appointment of government delegates to councils won by the party did not produce the desired results. Thereafter, the party adopted the policy of noncooperation as an alternative to confrontation. Nevertheless, the 1996 elections were a landmark in the life of the party because, for the first time, the party officially won elections.

In March 1992, the SDF had boycotted the **elections for the National Assembly**, a decision that raised controversy over whether the party should have participated in those elections. However, at the party's first convention held in Bamenda on 21–28 May1992, it was decided that henceforth the party would participate in elections. Consequently, the party participated in the **elections for president** of 11 October 1992, expecting a landslide victory against the governing **Cameroon People's Democratic Movement (CPDM)** party and to eventually change Cameroon. These expectations were dashed when the fraudulent results of the elections gave victory to the CPDM (39.97 percent) instead of the SDF (35.96 percent). This heralded a period of disillusionment, and problems of discipline began to emerge and preoccupy the party.

In the process, prominent party officials were shown the way out. Some of them included Barrister Ben Muna, the party's campaign manager; Dr. Siga Asanga, founding member and secretary-general of the party; and other members of the National Executive Committee, the policy-making organ of the party. These expulsions shook the foundations of the SDF, as rumors became the stock-in-trade of party officials, and witch-hunting became the ideal weapon frequently used by some position-seeking individuals to guard their interests.

What is more, SDF sympathizers accused the **Paul Biya** government of having rigged the elections, thereby depriving the party of victory. Party militants and sympathizers went on a rampage throughout the country, leading to the loss of life and property. Government's reaction was to place the entire North West Province, the political base of the SDF, under a state of emergency, and arrest and detain several officials and sympathizers of the party.

The party seemed to have recovered from its tribulations when it won the 1996 council elections. At its fourth convention held in **Buea** on 11–13 December 1996, the SDF launched a constitution, an economic program, and a Truth and Reconciliation Commission, to enable dismissed party officials to rejoin the party. Constitutionally, the party advocates a decentralization of the administration though the creation of a federal structure for Cameroon. The constitution advocates a four-state federation—namely, Adamawa-Mandara, Fako-Kilum, Nyong-Ngoko, and Wouri-Batié. In addition, a federal capital territory shall be the seat of the federal government.

Economically, as a solution to Cameroon's economic problems, the SDF advocates a policy of social economic liberalism. This policy includes, among other things, the elimination of monopolies in the economy, the creation of independent trade union organizations to protect workers' interests, a drastic reduction in the size of government, the complete elimination of government interference in the conduct of business, and the **privatization** of state-owned enterprises to attract foreign investors. The party's economic policy is contained in its National Economic Salvation Programme (NESPROG).

The SDF contested the **elections for the National Assembly and for the president of 1997,** winning 43 of the seats. Attempts to get the party to participate in a broad-based government failed. Thus, the party remained the only party represented in Parliament but absent from the government. *See also* ALLIANCE FOR THE RECONSTRUCTION OF CAMEROON THROUGH THE SOVEREIGN NATIONAL CONFERENCE (ARC-SNC).

SOCIAL JUSTICE. This is considered the first duty and governing idea of the Cameroon state. At the microlevel, the policy consists of giving all citizens an equal chance to develop their personalities through **education**, job opportunities, health care, and decent housing. These amenities enable the individual to "enjoy life, love himself and his neighbors, be assured of his security and know he is needed at all times." At the macrolevel, social justice consists of attempts by government to balance opportunities of various social classes, ethnic groupings, and geopolitical regions through equitable resource allocation. Whereas former Pres. **Ahmadou Ahidjo** denied the existence of social classes or disadvantaged regions in the country, Pres. **Paul Biya** envisaged the creation of a new society of social transformation in which the exorbitant privileges of the few and the impoverishment of the masses would be eliminated, for a political society of equity, harmony, and interdependence. Despite these pronouncements, Cameroon society is still characterized by marked, disturbing inequalities and latent disharmony at the micro- and macrolevels.

SOCIETE CAMEROUNAISE DE BANQUE (SCB) SCANDAL. In an article published in May 1992 in *Jeune Afrique Economie*, **Celestin Monga** described an interview with Robert Messi Messi, former director-general of SCB, a government-owned bank that had become bankrupt and was closed in August 1989. Messi claimed that a major factor in the bank's demise had been the frequent withdrawals of bank funds without repayment by Irene Biya, wife of Pres. **Paul Biya**. Messi claimed that Mrs. Biya and other top officials had taken more than five billion CFA francs, without repayment. *See also* BANK CRISIS.

SOCIETE CAMEROUNAISE DES TABACS (SCT). *See* TOBACCO.

SOCIETE DE DEVELOPPEMENT DE LA RIZICULTURE DANS LE PLAINE DE MBO (SODERIM). This **rice** development company was created in May 1977 to cultivate over 2,000 hectares of rice and other products as well as to create channels for their commercialization. SODERIM depends largely on the exploitation of the Nkam valley area. The headquarters of the company is in Santchou near Dschang in the **West Province**. *See also* AGRICULTRAL POLICY; SOCIETE D'EXPANSION ET DE MODERNISATION DE LA RIZICULTURE DE YAGOUA.

SOCIETE D'EXPANSION ET DE MODERNISATION DE LA RIZICULTURE DE YAGOUA (SEMRY). This development company was created in 1954 for the cultivation and processing of **rice** in northern Cameroon. By 1972, the company produced over 6,000 tons annually. Its productive capacity was extended and improved with loans from foreign institutions such as the **World Bank** and the Fonds d'Aide et de Coopération (FAC). Despite the ambitious project, SEMRY has not prevented the large-scale consumption of imported rice from overseas across the country. Semry was reorganized in February 1971 and charged with irrigated production using the paddy variety. In 1989, it was reorganized, the number of laborers was reduced, and SEMRY activities were narrowed to the production of rice. Production and other activities were no longer to be handled by SEMRY. Insufficient management and high costs have prevented SEMRY from producing an economically viable product. The company is now being restricted in the scope of its activities and some portions are to be **privatized**. *See also* AGRICULTURE POLICY; SOCIETE DE DEVELOPPEMENT DE LA RIZICULTURE DANS LE PLAINE DE MBO (SODERIM).

SOCIETE DU DEVELOPPEMENT DU NKAM (SODENKAM). A regional land settlement and integrated rural development scheme, the project; begun in 1966, aimed at integrating development of pioneer villages in a sparsely populated region of 120,000 hectares in the **Littoral**

Province. It sought to provide technical and cooperative marketing support for major cash crop production and also promote social development. It was financed solely by the government of Cameroon and envisaged the settlement of 18,000 to 22,500 inhabitants by 1981. *See also* RURAL EXODUS.

SOCIETE FINANCIERE DE RECOUVREMENT. *See* BANK CRISIS.

SOCIETE NATIONALE DES EAUX DU CAMEROUN (SNEC). *See* NATIONAL WATER CORPORATION OF CAMEROUN.

SOCIETE NATIONALE DES HYDROCARBURES (SNH). SNH was created by presidential decree of 13 March 1981 as an industrial and commercial company for the promotion of hydrocarbon exploration and guarantor of the state's interest in this domain. According to Article 4 of the statute, the National Hydrocarbon Company conducts all studies, collects all information, supervises the execution of contracts between the state and foreign oil companies, and undertakes the training of Cameroonian personnel relative to the **petroleum** industry. The company is headed by a director-general responsible to a board of administrators who are all appointed by the head of state. The level of autonomy of the company is further limited by various other companies such as the National Refinery Company (SONARA) and the company for the Study and Exploitation of Cameroon's Natural Gas (SEGAZCAM). In addition, apart from a slim ministerial control by the Ministry of Mines and Power, the direct supervision of the functioning of the SNH is maintained by the **Secretariat-General at the Presidency**. The headquarters of the company is located near the presidency in **Yaoundé**. In a related development, the Cameroon Oil Transportation Company (COTCO) was established to oversee the **Chad–Kribi pipeline**.

SOCIETE NATIONALE D'INVESTISSEMENT. *See* NATIONAL INVESTMENT COMPANY.

SOCIETES COOPERATIVES DE DEVELOPMENT RURAL (SOCOODER). *See* COOPERATIVES.

SODEBELE. *See* WHEAT.

SODECOTON. *See* COTTON.

SODEN, JULIUS VON (1846–1921). Kamerun's first **German governor** (1885–91) was an advocate of joint partnership between government and economic enterprises in the exploitation of the territory. He made **Buea** the capital of the territory, began an experimental **botanical garden** project in Victoria (**Limbe**), opposed the purchase of indigenous **women** by white officials, and consolidated German rule on the Kamerun coastal regions with the help of various Christian missions.

SOPPO PRISO, PAUL (1913–1996). An early Cameroon politician and postindependence business magnate, Soppo Priso was born in **Douala** on 19 July 1913. He was educated by French Protestants locally to rise as a dependable elite and *assimilé*. He was instrumental in the anti-German movement of the interwar period and later emerged as president of the **Jeunesse Camerounaise Française (Jeucafra)** created by the French to rally anti-German sentiments. This position served as the base for Soppo Priso's political career. After **World War II,** he became a prosperous contractor for public works and buildings. Between 1947 and 1952, he was a deputy in the **Assemblée Législative du Cameroun (ALCAM)** and from 1952 to 1955 served as the president of the **Assemblée Territoriale du Cameroun (ATCAM)**. He was equally a deputy in the Legislative Assembly from 1956 to 1960 prior to independence.

Soppo Priso was a cofounder of the **Mouvement d'Action Nationale Camerounaise** in 1956, which was suspected of pro–**Union des Populations du Cameroun (UPC)** leanings by the French. In the 1955 legislative elections, the UPC declined to present alternative candidates and backed Soppo Priso. He was widely considered the compromise candidate for **prime minister** following his proposition of a common "minimum program," which advocated **reunification** of the Cameroons and a general amnesty for the outlawed UPC. His **Courant d'Union National (CUN),** formed on 6 June 1956, was supported widely by various politicians of the time and served as the platform for a nationalist program toward self-rule, independence, national reconciliation, and independence. The collapse of the CUN in November 1956 also began the gradual disappearance of Soppo Priso from the political scene. In April 1960, he lost his parliamentary seat to Prince **Douala Manga Bell**. Thereafter, Soppo Priso retired from political life to become an independent contractor. He was widely believed to have been Cameroon's first millionaire, and continued to maintain this level of success until his death in May 1996.

SOSUCAM. *See* SUGAR.

SOUCADAUX, ANDRE. A French **governor** or high **commissioner** in Cameroun (1949–54), he established the various postwar administrations by favoring *lamibe* in the North and creating artificial chiefdoms in the South. Economically he practiced laissez-faire vis-à-vis the European employers in Cameroun but was not very friendly to the trade union. Soucadaux was replaced in 1954 with the fear that he was unable to handle the upsurge of **Union des Populations du Cameroun (UPC)** radicalism.

SOUTH PROVINCE. This province covers a surface area of 47,059 square kilometers and consists of three divisions, 14 subdivisions, and five districts. The relief features are the coastal plain and the plateau of about 300 meters' elevation. Primary forest is the major vegetational feature. It has an equatorial climate with two seasons, dry and rainy. Over half a million people (500,200 inhabitants) live in the South Province. Agriculture, in food and cash crops, is the main activity of the population. Other activities include fishing, forestry, and small animal breeding. **Kribi** (Ocean Division) is the province's most important touristic location, but Ebolowa (Ntem Divison) is the provincial headquarters. The only other important town is Sangmelima in the Dja and Lobo Division. The South Province was created on 23 August 1983.

SOUTH WEST PROVINCE. It covers a surface area of 27,520 square kilometers and consists of six divisions, 17 subdivisions, and two districts. Its major relief feature is **Mount Cameroun,** locally known as "Fako." The province has a hot and humid climate of four seasons: two dry and two rainy. The population is estimated at 756,800 inhabitants. Agriculture in the province dominates the economy with modern plantations for the cultivation of **tea**, **cocoa**, **rubber,** and **palm products**. The country's most important industrial project, the SONARA oil refinery, is located there. **Buea**, in Fako Division, is the provincial headquarters. In 1996, two more divisions were created in the South West Province, thereby bringing the total to six. The important towns include Bangem (Kupe–Manenguba Division), Fontem (Lebialem Division,) **Limbe** (Fako Division), **Kumba** (Manyu Division), **Mamfe** (Manyu Division), and Mundemba (Ndian Division). The South West Province was established in 1972.

SOUTHERN CAMEROONS. The Southern Cameroons was one of two British territories in **British Cameroons** from 1916 to 1961. Southern

Cameroons corresponded to the Victoria (**Limbe**), **Mamfe**, **Kumba,** and **Bamenda** Divisions. It was initially attached to the Southern Provinces and later to the Eastern Provinces of **Nigeria**. It was supervised by a British **resident** who received orders from the lieutenant **governor** in Enugu. Officially, the British named Southern Cameroons as the "**Cameroons Province**." Southern Cameroons gained self-government in 1958 under its premier, **Emmanuel M. L. Endeley**. It was Southern Cameroons that voted for **reunification** with **French Cameroun** in the **plebiscite** of 11 and 12 February 1961. Reunification of French Cameroun and the Southern Cameroons was finalized on 1 October 1961. *See also* NORTHERN CAMEROONS.

SOUTHERN CAMEROONS NATIONAL COUNCIL (SCNC). The SCNC is one of the many pressure groups that supported the so-called "**zero option**" or secession of **anglophone** Cameroon. The use of the name **Southern Cameroons** was orchestrated by the argument by some anglophone Cameroonian leaders that the **francophone**-led Cameroon leadership was ruling the country without constitutional basis. This conclusion was drawn from the premise that **Ahmadou Ahidjo** had neglected the provision in the constitution for the enactment and amendment of the federal **constitution of the Federal Republic of Cameroon (1961)**. This group of anglophone Cameroonians therefore considered that anglophone Cameroon had not yet achieved independence, thus their use of the appellation Southern Cameroons, an appellation used for that territory in the period prior to **reunification**.

Even though it adopts an extremist stand as far as the anglophone course is concerned, the SCNC advocates a peaceful approach to attaining independence for anglophone Cameroon. This is reflected in its motto: "force of argument and not the argument of force." To achieve its objectives, the SCNC, through the Anglophone Standing Committee, strives to sensitize the international community on the anglophone course. It communicates with the United Nations, the International Court of Justice, the **Commonwealth** Secretariat, and governments outside Cameroon.

In June 1993, when the secretary-general of the Commonwealth visited Cameroon to examine whether the country had fulfilled the conditions for admission, the SCNC unsuccessfully tried to convince him to admit anglophone Cameroon, and not the Republic of Cameroon, as a member of the Commonwealth. In spite of this, and to the embarrassment of SCNC members, Cameroon was admitted to the Commonwealth in November 1995. At the Commonwealth summit in New Zealand, in which Cameroon gained its admission, the SCNC requested the organization of a Quebec-styled independence referendum for Southern Cameroons and repeated its call for a separate anglophone Cameroon membership of the Commonwealth. A similar memo was given to the high commissioner of the **Organization of African Unity (OAU)** Commission on Human and People's Rights in September 1998.

In 1995, shortly after the second **All Anglophone Conference** (AAC II) in **Bamenda**, the SCNC sent a delegation to the UN, composed of prominent anglophone Cameroonians such as **John Ngu Foncha**, **Solomon Tandeng Muna,** and **Albert Mukong** to plead anglophone Cameroon's course. While there, the delegation presented a formal petition against the annexation and independence of anglophone Cameroon. On the way home, it stopped in London and issued the London communiqué that stated that 1997 was a turning point in the struggle. On returning home, it organized a tour of administrative capitals in the two anglophone provinces and presented a UN flag to anglophone Cameroonians as proof of the fact that the UN had agreed to reopen the Southern Cameroons file. The leader of the SCNC is Prince Essola Ndoki Mukete.

Other pressure groups that support the zero option include the Free West Cameroon Movement (FWCM) and the **Ambazonia** Movement of Fon Gorji Dinka.

SOVIET UNION. *See* COMMONWEALTH OF INDEPENDENT STATES.

SPORTS. Sports are important aspect of national policy, considered a physical and moral imperative. For this reason, a government department, the Ministry of Youth and Sports, exists to cater to sports needs. Various traditional sports such as wrestling and canoe racing have given way to modern sports disciplines such as football (soccer) and cycling. Initially, modern sports are widely transmitted and practiced at primary and secondary school levels. The Office of Schools and University Sports Competition (OSUSC) organized games at local, divisional, provincial, and national levels every school year. It was replaced in 1992 by the National Federation for College and University Sports (Fédération National des Sports Scolaire et Universitaire, FENASCO), which took over the functions of OSUSC. In addition, the new federation organizes sports activities for the primary schools at the provincial level, for the secondary schools at the national level, and university games. Although nonscholastic sports is essentially amateur, it is hotly contested at all levels. Various teams in the **francophone** parts of the country were initially established on an ethnic basis, while sports teams in **anglophone** provinces have departmental or corporation names. Intense rivalry and violence in domestic sports are a drawback to the cherished ideal of national unity. Victories in international sports competitions generally strengthen national cohesion and are a source of pride and prestige.

Apart from the Ministry of Youth and Sports, the Cameroon Olympic Committee propagates the need for total commitment to the sports ethic. Various sports federations such as the Cameroon football federation (FECAFOOT) work closely with the sports ministry and the national Olympic committee. A score of other federations—for instance, the Cameroon Handball Federation (FECAHAND), the Cameroon Boxing Federation (FECABOXE), and the Cameroon Volleyball Federation (FECAVOLLEY)—organize sports competitions for their disciplines. A national sports institute is in **Yaoundé,** and other sports centers have been established across the country for the training of cadres and coaches. Private economic enterprises also contribute to the promotion of national and international sports. For instance, the Cameroon Brewery Company opened and currently runs a football school in **Douala**. The most memorable achievements of Cameroon sports have been in football, including an honorable participation in the World Cup in 1982 and 1990, impressive victories in the African Nations' Cup competition, and numerous victories in the various Continental Club competitions. *See also* INDOMITABLE LIONS.

STABEX (STABILIZATION OF EXPORT EARNINGS). This is the agreement between the **European Economic Community (EEC)** and its associated states that provides payments to agricultural product exporting countries when the price for their product falls below established limits. It is an attempt to stabilize prices. STABEX was established in the Lomé I Convention. It is similar to **SYSMIN**. *See also* LOME AGREEMENTS.

STATUT DU CAMEROUN. This law was passed by the French National Assembly to implement the recommendations of the **Loi Cadre** in 1956. It was ratified by the **Assemblée Législative du Cameroun (ALCAM)** on 22 February 1957. The statute provided the framework for Cameroun's self-rule and independence.

STRUCTURAL ADJUSTMENT PROGRAMS (SAP). SAPs are primarily a tool of the **International Monetary Fund (IMF)**, the **World**

Bank, and the major industrial states to bring about economic reforms in the developing countries of the world, including Cameroon. As the **economic crisis** of the 1980s and 1990s became widespread, many such countries faced severe **debt** problems. They turned to the IMF and other institutions for assistance. However, that assistance was given with strings attached—the SAP. In general, the SAP aims at bringing the recipient country into the free market economy, reducing government involvement in the economy, and reducing **corruption** and mismanagement. In recent years, political strings have been added to the SAP with demands for democratization, transparency in government, and multiparty systems.

To qualify for debt relief and new loans, and to attract new foreign investment, debtor countries accept the often stringent rules of a SAP, a concept referred to as *conditionality*. Among the most frequent requirements are devaluation of the currency, reduction of government spending and efforts to balance the budget, liberalization of **foreign trade**, **privatization** of government-owned businesses, reduction of wages, and promotion of export products.

Cameroon has undertaken steps to meet these requirements, although often with hesitancy. On several occasions loans have been withheld by the IMF and donor nations to force Cameroon to proceed. Among the most dramatic steps are the very large reductions in wages and benefits—as well as reduction in total employment—of the civil service; privatization; reduction of regulations and interference in free trade; changes in **investment codes**; devaluation of the currency and restrictions on the export of currency; cutbacks in development spending; reductions in spending on health care and **education**; and debt reductions negotiated with the Paris Club and bilaterally.

These programs may prove to have long-term positive effects, but in the short run they are associated with a serious reduction in the quality and longevity of life in Cameroon. Domestically and internationally, the SAP concept has come under political attack due to the often harsh and brutal effects of the SAP on many of the people in the countries involved. It is the lower and middle classes that are most seriously harmed.

SUGAR. Sugar is a significant product processed out of sugarcane grown across the rain forest zone of Cameroon. The Germans played a very small role in the development of sugar production, and French and British administrations only allowed for local cultivation and sale of sugarcane. The Cameroon government regarded sugar production as important for economic development. The SOSUCAM (1976) and CAMSUCO (1980) sugar companies were established with heavy foreign investment. A second sugar company was justified by the need to satisfy indigenous demand given persistent shortages and high prices. The export of Cameroon sugar suffered from the protectionist measures imposed by the **European Economic Community (EEC)** in reaction to world overproduction in the sugar market. In 1998, Cameroon produced 1,350,000 tons of sugarcane, down from 1,500,000 tons in 1988. *See also* AGRICULTURAL POLICY.

SULTAN. *See* NJOYA, SEIDOU NJIMOLUH; NJOYA (SULTAN).

SYSMIN. This is the agreement between the **European Economic Community (EEC)** and its associated states in the developing world to attempt to stabilize mineral export prices. It also provides loans for development purposes. SYSMIN was established in the Lomé II Convention. It is similar to the **STABEX** agreement. See also LOME AGREEMENTS.

– T –

TAKUMBENG (TAKEMBENG). In recent use, it is the name given to a group of **women** in their sixties and seventies who gathered around the home of **John Fru Ndi** to protect him after his house arrest after the **elections for the president of 1992**. Earlier, Takumbeng had appeared at **Social Democratic Front (SDF)** rallies. Using their power of age and maternity, these women use shame to keep police and soldiers from misbehaving. On occasion, they are a powerful force in the **North West Province**. Some observers suggest that the Takumbeng concept is derived from the earlier **ANLU**.

TANKEU, ELIZABETH (1944–). Currently minister of planning and regional development, she was born on 29 February 1944 in Yabassi. She hails from the **Western Province**. She did primary education in Bangangté (1951–58) and attended **Lycée Leclerc** (1958–65) for secondary education. She went to France thereafter and engaged in advanced commercial studies for two years before enrolling in the Faculty of Law and Economics in the University of Paris, where she majored in econometrics. On completion in 1971, she served in the Ministry of Planning and later as chargé d'études for economic and financial analysis. From 1976 to 1979, she was deputy director of planning. She became director in 1980 and served in this position until her appointment as vice minister of planning and industry on 12 April 1983. In May 1988, she was appointed minister of planning and regional development, a post she held until April 1991, when she was dropped from government.

TAPIOCA. *See* GARRI.

TATAW, JAMES TABE (1933–). Tataw was one of the four generals and army chiefs of staff. General Tataw was born in **Mamfe** in the **South West Province** on 9 May 1933 and did primary education in Besongabang before entering the Cameroon Protestant college (then known as Basel Mission College) from 1949 until 1953. He later studied in Ghana before his admission into the Royal Military Academy in Aldershot, England. There he obtained the Queen's combatant commission as a second lieutenant. He later attended the University of Sorbonne and did summer courses in Strasbourg, France. As a lieutenant colonel, he attended the famous Ecole de Guerre in Paris (1973–74) and in 1980 attended the French Institute of National Defense.

His military training was done alongside professional duties first in the Nigerian army, prior to independence, and later in Cameroon. In Cameroon he has held multiple posts, including platoon commander, company commander, battalion commander, and military sector commander. In 1981, following Cameroon's border conflict with **Nigeria**, he was named commander of the National Army. In 1983, following the severe threat to state security during the **Ahidjo–Biya rupture,** he was made general. He now serves as army chief of staff and has played important roles in developing better relations with Nigeria, particularly on the **border conflicts**.

TCHINAYE, VROUMSIA (1932–1982). Tchinaye was a long-serving minister and controversial figure under the **Ahmadou Ahidjo** presidency. Born in October 1932 in Guiseye, Mayo Danai, he did primary education in Yagoua, **Maroua,** and **Garoua** to obtain his **Brevet d'Etudes du Premier Cycle (BEPC)** in 1946. In 1947, he was selected into a course that allowed him to enter the renowned Public High School of Bongor in **Chad**. On return to Garoua, he obtained a metropolitan scholarship to France in 1953 for studies in Reims and Marne. He later specialized in veterinary sciences but also earned a degree in natural sciences in 1959. He was director of the Ecole Normale

Supérieure in **Yaoundé** until 1961, when he gained appointment to higher governmental position.

In 1962, he was appointed general **commissioner** for youth, sports, and popular education. He served as secretary of state for rural development in 1964 and as secretary of state for finance in 1965. He became a member of the federal government in 1970, serving as minister of information and culture until 1974 and as minister of civil service from 1974 to 1978. Tchinaye was reputed for his highly critical mind that led to declarations and public speeches that were usually an embarrassment to government authorities. He was relieved of his ministerial post in May 1978 but was returned to a high position in December 1979, as delegate-general for scientific and technical research. He remained at this post until his death in 1982.

TCHOUNGUI, SIMON PIERRE (1916–1998). Former **prime minister** of **East Cameroon,** Tchoungui was born on 28 October 1916 at Nkolmending in Mefou Division. He went to school there and served as a medical aid in **Yaoundé** and Mbalmayo prior to **World War II**. He was a World War II Free French soldier (1942–45). He studied at the Dakar Medical School, returning home in 1947 as a surgeon. From 1950 to 1956, he trained in the University of Paris, obtaining a doctorate in medicine. In 1960, Tchoungui was medical superintendent of the Yaoundé Hospital before becoming minister of public health in 1961. He was minister of national economy in 1964, then a minister without portfolio (1965) before becoming prime minister of East Cameroon in October 1965. He held onto his post until the declaration of the **United Republic of Cameroon** on 20 May 1972. Since the 1960s, he served in the honorary position of president of the Cameroon Red Cross and played leading roles in the **Cameroon National Union** and the **Cameroon People's Democratic Movement**. Dr. Tchoungui died in April 1998.

TEA. The Germans experimented with growing tea in the **botanical garden** of Victoria (**Limbe**) and at the site of the present-day Tole Tea Estate, finding it to be highly successful. The British later contributed to the extensive production of the crop in its **Southern Cameroons** territory. Major tea plantations exist in Tole and Ndu under auspices of the **Cameroon Development Corporation (CDC)**. The takeover of Ndu Tea from Estates and Agency Ltd. in 1977 was significant in leading to the expansion of the CDC to the **Grassfield** of the **North West Province**. In 1979, the CDC acquired land at Djuttitsa near Dschang for an important tea project in the **Western Province**. In 1998, Cameroon produced 4,000 tons of tea. Although tea is widely consumed locally, only Tole tea has attained an international reputation for export, mainly to **Chad**. *See also* AGRICULTURAL POLICY.

TEACHERS ASSOCIATION OF CAMEROON. *See* CAMEROON ANGLOPHONE MOVEMENT.

TERRITORIAL ASSEMBLY OF CAMEROUN. *See* ASSEMBLEE TERRITORIALE DU CAMEROUN (ATCAM).

TESSA, PAUL (1938–). One-time secretary-general at the Presidency, Tessa hails from the **Western Province**. His active governmental duties began as chargé de mission at the Presidency in 1969 and later as minister of equipment, housing, and lands (1972–75). Removed from government, Tessa remained in relative obscurity until his appointment in 1986 as general manager of the Press and Editing Company of Cameroon (SOPECAM). He became the biggest beneficiary of the 1988 post-election government when he was elevated from SOPECAM to become secretary-general at the Presidency. In 1989, he was transferred to the Ministry of Transport and Public Works. He remained in this post until April 1992 when he was dropped from government.

THEATER. Theater is one of the more underdeveloped art forms in Cameroon. The performing arts in Cameroon have generally received little government support and have historically been subject to extensive censorship, particularly during the **Ahmadou Ahidjo** era. One may consider two major branches of drama within the country. The first is indigenous drama and dance occasions, which continue to thrive and hold an important place in the lives of many Cameroonians. The second consists of the more syncretic merging of European-style with Cameroonian dramatic traditions. The latter consists largely of either comic theater or theater based on indigenous religious and legendary material.

The one troupe that does receive government support is L'Ensemble National des Dances Traditionelles du Cameroun (Cameroon National Traditional Dance Ensemble), formed in 1963. It has performed its repertoire of Cameroon's various music and dances internationally. However, support for this troupe waned during the 1990s. Other drama troupes include the Théâtre Universitaire at the **University of Yaoundé**, founded in 1975 as the Club d'Art Dramatique. The Yaoundé University Theatre was founded soon afterward. As with L'Ensemble National, these two troupes ran into difficulties surviving during the 1990s. Other supporters of the performing arts largely consist of foreign cultural centers.

The most famous Cameroonian dramatist today is **Nicole Werewere-Liking**. Other well-known dramatists include Guillaume Oyono-Mbia, who no longer writes for the stage, Sankie Maimo, Victor Musinga, and Bole Butake. There are degree-granting programs in the Performing Arts at the University of Yaoundé, University of Yaoundé I, and the University of **Buea**.

THONG LIKENG, JOHANNES (1914–1953). Thong Likeng was an indigenous prophet and founder of the Nyambe–**Bantu** religion, an unrecognized precursor of Cameroon's cultural renovation. Born in Lipombe near Eseka in the Nyong and Kelle Division, Thong Likeng went to school in Makak, Eseka, and **Yaoundé** but was expelled and never graduated with a primary school certificate. Nevertheless, he was a mass servant for the **Catholic Church** during the few years spent in school. In 1930, he escaped to **Gabon** en route to Dakar in Senegal, where he associated with magicians and went to graveyards regularly. He joined the French navy as a means to facilitate his entry to France. On arrival in France in 1938, Thong left the navy and engaged in the sale of perfumes and beauty products in markets and public places. In July 1943, he gained authorization from the occupying German administration to form his association, L'Oeuvre d'Entraide Africaine, popularly known as "Mission du Soleil." It was designed to assist Africans and others in their material, moral, and spiritual needs.

His religion, the Nyambe-Bantu (Creator of the Superior Race), was to serve as a vehicle for African emancipation. The Nyambe-Bantu emphasized the belief in religious laws and customs that were rooted in the experience and tradition of ancestors. Thong Likeng received a diploma in occult science by correspondence studies and was widely known as "Professor" by a cross-section of the educated African population in France.

He returned to Cameroon on 30 June 1945 and began practices designed to provide for greater cultural restoration. He opened a school where only the indigenous **Bassa** language was taught; he established a church in which **Christianity** was denigrated as a white man's religion; and he set up a clinic where **women**, children, and men were treated with the use of traditional herbs and at very minimal costs. In 1948, Thong Likeng was imprisoned in **Edea** for illegal practice of medicine and exiled to Tibati in **Northern Cameroons**. Following his release in April 1949, Thong Likeng settled in **Douala**, where his popularity and occult prowess grew rapidly among the youths and downtrodden in society. He was known to heal incurable illnesses, to turn water into wine, to shield people from danger and accidents, as well as to provide luck and success for struggling workers and students. He was also known to have malevolent powers.

In 1951, Thong Likeng attempted to turn this wide appeal to political advantage. He was a candidate in the 17 June 1951 elections to the Metropolitan French National Assembly. His political platform envisaged the creation of a corporative-independent state based on reform, equality, and protection of cultural values. Thong Likeng lost in the election and later formed the Organisation Animiste Camerounaise (OAC), popularly known as the "Eglise Liyomba."

His last public appearance was on 12 April 1953. Thong Likeng is believed to have disappeared when another dead body was found on his bed on 31 May 1953. A territory-wide search for his body was undertaken, with no definite clue to the circumstances of his disappearance.

Thong Likeng's legacy in Cameroun is controversial. His prophetic and religious activity qualify his mission as messianic and syncretic. He could also be considered a protonationalist in his fervent belief for liberation and cultural renovation based on tradition and custom. However, his message and activity neither acquired national recognition nor received the backing of the indigenous elites of the preindependence era in Cameroun.

TIKAR/TIKARI. Tikar is a general classification referring to the major ethnic groupings of the **Bamenda** highland. These are highly centralized and densely populated settlements that moved into their present locations from somewhere to the northeast. They broke up into separate but nearly identical entities made up of several ethnic groups, including the **Bafut**, Kom, Ndop, and Nso peoples. These entities are organized into chiefdoms constituting a state system of marked hierarchy and authority. Power and authority reflect the rich tradition and spiritual aura surrounding the role of the **Fon** at the head each of the major Tikar groupings. There are traces of the Tikar system prevalent in many societies of the **Western Province** of the country, particularly in terms of their patrilineality and political structure. Only the Wum and Kom groups are matrilineal. The Tikars, along with the Chamba and the Widekum, are generally referred to as **Grassfield** in view of the major vegetational feature of the region.

TIKO. Tiko, a commercial town in the **South West Province** located near the coast, had played a prominent role in commercial relations with Europeans in the 19th century, which led the Germans to convert it into a port. Under the British administration, an air strip was constructed to serve the entire territory. Since independence, Tiko has been redesigned to serve as the link between former **East** and **West Cameroon**, leading to the construction of a subport and the reunification road connecting Tiko to **Douala** in April 1969. These governmental measures as well as its new administrative status as a subdivision have not improved the chances of this town in relation to **Limbe**, **Kumba**, or Douala. On the contrary, a slump has characterized development in Tiko despite the presence of **Cameroon Development Corporation** facilities. Originally inhabited by the **Bakweri,** the town is largely dominated today by Nigerian (**Ibo** and Yoruba), Benin (Elaje), and predominantly **Bamiléké** interests.

TILLIER AFFAIR. This scandal involving the Cameroon government and a French journalist, Jacques Tillier, in mid-1986 led to a showdown between the French press and the Cameroon public. While public image strategies are undertaken by all governments worldwide, the Tillier affair is particularly significant for an understanding of the post-**Ahidjo** strains of the Cameroon government. The government employed Tillier, a writer for *Journal du Dimanche*, on a salary of 10 million CFA francs every three months, to improve Cameroon's image abroad and to spy on the activities of former president Ahmadou Ahidjo, who lived in the south of **France**.

Tillier, who was also a former secret service agent, allegedly spied on Ahidjo in France and abroad. Cameroon's main news organs gave extensive coverage to the controversy, which they considered an attempt at destabilization and machination. At nonofficial levels, Cameroon–French relations were hurt by this incident. The government apparently broke off with Tillier following the revelation and scandal.

TIMBER. Despite its considerable transportation costs, timber has been a prominent Cameroon export to Europe and recently to Asia. In 1905, the Germans began the exploitation of timber resources in **Kamerun** with an unrestricted land concession to a forestry company. This same policy was followed by the French and British administrations after **World War I**. Many sawmills and plywood mills are in service, and Cameroon's timber reserves have been considerably depleted since independence. There is extensive local use of wood, especially for cooking fires and house construction, but timber is essentially an export product. Despite decreasing reserves, the fear of deforestation and desertification, as well as growing warnings against wanton exploitation of natural resources, the government has failed to take serious steps toward restraint and rationalization in timber exploration. In 1995, it was estimated that 555 million cubic feet of timber was cut. In June 1999, it became against the law to export timber. The intention is not to decrease the export of wood products but to increase the export of finished goods such as lumber and plywood. This will increase the value of the exports and provide employment for Cameroonians. Nonetheless, Cameroon still has large forest reserves, the second largest in Africa. *See also* FIREWOOD.

TOBACCO. Cameroon produces tobacco through the services of the Société Camerounaise des Tabacs (SCT), which is widely spread across the **Eastern Province** in Bertoua, Batouri, and Betareoya. Over 10,000 planters are employed by the SCT. Tobacco production is also common in the **Western Province**, especially in **Bafoussam** and Foumbot, as well as in **Bamenda** in the **North West Province**. These production chains in the western highlands are controlled by the SACTA company, an affiliate of the subregional Bastos company of Central Africa. Much of Cameroonian tobacco is made into various cigarette brands by the Basto company. Cameroon also produces tobacco for cigar wrapping. *See also* AGRICULTURAL POLICY.

TOMBEL MASSACRE. This bloody slaughter of **Bamiléké** by an indignant **Bakossi** mob in the predominantly Bakossi town of Tombel took place on 31 December 1967. The Tombel massacre was a classical case of a **nation-building** problem whereby Bamiléké from what was then **East Cameroon**, who had migrated and taken up important commercial stakes in the Bakossi area, were viewed with suspicion and animosity. Although the Tombel massacre was aimed as an immediate retaliation to the Christmas robbery and murder of four Bakossi purportedly by the Bamiléké, the underlying cause was Bakossi frustration at the loss of their land and commerce to the Bamiléké migrants. There is a deep-seated animosity between the two ethnic groups. Over 230 Bamiléké were reportedly killed in the massacre, and a military tribunal sentenced 140 Bakossi to various prison terms in a bid to quell the disorder. It is believed that many Bakossi died as a result of government violence. *See also* ETHNIC CONFLICT.

TONTINE/NJANGI. A variety of informal savings groups are widespread in Cameroon. In essence, these rotating credit associations are a means for individuals to accumulate capital for large expenditures. In its simplest form, an *njangi* (**anglophone**) or *tontine* (**francophone**) might have anywhere from five to 20 members. The group meets on a regular basis, often on or after pay day, and each member contributes a set amount of money, all of which is given to one member. At the next meeting, the same process occurs, with a different member taking the accumulated sum. This rotation continues until each member has received the payout. There are numerous variations of this plan: the number of members can be very large, huge amounts of money may be involved, and there are numerous ways to determine which member will receive the payout.

TONYE MBOG, FELIX (1934–). This former minister of foreign affairs was born on 14 May 1934 in Ṣo-Dibanga. After primary and secondary education, he enrolled in the Faculty of Law of the **University of Yaoundé** and later completed training at the National School of Administration and Magistracy (ENAM), Yaoundé. He also earned a diploma from the famous Institut des Hautes Etudes d'Outre-Mer in Paris. Thereafter, he served in the Presidency for five years (1964–69) and as secretary-general in the Ministry of Labour (1969–72). On joining the first government of the **United Republic of Cameroon**, he remained as minister until 1985, occupying five posts. He was minister of youth and sport from 1972 until 1979 with the task of rebuilding confidence following Cameroon's defeat in the eighth African Nations Cup played in **Yaoundé**. From 1979 until 1982, he was minister of agriculture; then minister of labor and social insurance (1982–83); and during the difficult period of transition from **Ahmadou Ahidjo** to **Paul Biya** and the attempted coup, he served as minister of foreign affairs (1983–84). His last ministerial duty was as minister of post and telecommunications (1984–85). Since 1986, he has served as general manager of the Cocoa Development Corporation (SODECAO).

TORRE, XAVIER. Torre was the last French high **commissioner** in Cameroun. His tenure coincided with the advent of the relatively pro-French self-government of Prime Minister **Ahmadou Ahidjo** to power. Torre initiated the last phase of the French presence in Cameroun and was instrumental in the transition period as well as the signing of the preindependence **secret agreements** with France.

TRANS-CAMEROON RAILWAY. This important development project was completed in 1975. The rail line links the administrative capital, **Yaoundé**, in the south to the provincial city of **Ngaoundéré** in the northern **Adamawa Province**, covering a distance of 930 kilometers. The project is of both political and developmental significance. Politically, it ties together the otherwise isolated northern and southern geographic regions of the country, which contributes to the much needed sense of community through integration. Unfortunately, the expectation of extending the rail line northward into the **Chad** basin and eastward to the **Central African Republic** as part of an overall **Union Douanière Economique de l'Afrique Centrale (UDEAC)** scheme of economic integration has not been fulfilled. In terms of development, the railway serves as a possible instrument for the exploitation of large bauxite deposits found in the Martrap–Tibati areas in the north and the shipment of products in the area for distribution and export. It is an important part of the railroad–highway link between Chad and **Douala**.

The Trans-Cameroon railway project was financed by an international consortium of French, American, and **European Economic Community (EEC)** sources at over $80 million. It prolonged a preexisting network concentrated in the south connecting Yaoundé, Douala, **Kumba**, and **Nkongsamba** areas. The Cameroon National Railway Authority (REGIFERCAM), which handled the railway infrastructure, was the largest transport corporation in the country. It faced severe competition from highway transporters due to the newly constructed Douala–Yaoundé road. As part of the **privatization** program, REGIFERCAM has been sold. A Franco–South African company, SAGA-COMAZAR, has now taken over under the name Cameroon Railways (Camrail).

TRIPARTITE CONFERENCE. Held between 30 October and 13 November 1991, the talks were convened by Pres. **Paul Biya** in response to repeated calls for a sovereign national conference. Its aim was to diffuse sociopolitical tension that had been building up in the country ever since the legalization of multiparty activity in September 1990. The conference was to prepare preliminary drafts for an electoral code and to define conditions for access to public media by all parties. Invited to attend the talks was a cross-section of Cameroonian society, including all political parties, independent personalities, elder statesmen, and representatives of public authorities. Opposition parties grouped themselves into the Coordination Committee of Opposition Parties with **Samuel Eboua**, president of the **National Union for Democracy and Progress**, as chairman.

Prime Minister Sadou Hayatou chaired the talks. The conference opened in a stormy atmosphere as bitter arguments ensued between the ruling **Cameroon People's Democratic Movement (CPDM)** party and opposition politicians over the agenda of the meeting, the latter pointing out that the government-proposed, two-point agenda was largely insufficient. Unable to resolve differences over what to include and what not to include on the agenda, 20 opposition parties staged a walkout. When they returned on 5 November 1991, they criticized the conference chairman, Hayatou, for not being the right person to chair the meeting and for attempting to pressure participants to endorse a prearranged agenda. The opposition walked out again after reiterating their demand for a sovereign national conference and accusing the chairman of ignoring most of the preconditions that they had proposed. The persistent walking in and out of the conference deliberations was condemned by the chairman. However, in an attempt to pacify the opposition parties, he added a third point on other matters to the agenda.

On 3 October 1991, the deadlock was overcome when the opposition parties, which had walked out of the deliberations, returned after the intervention of eminent personalities such as **John Ngu Foncha** and **Felix Sengat-Kuo**. Despite their return, the hard-core opposition parties, feeling that the prime minister would not be impartial in his position as chairman, called on him to step down and asked that his place be taken by a neutral person. Here again, the participants split over who should chair the meeting. Some participants felt that the prime minister was the right person to chair the meeting, taking into consideration protocol and the fact that he was appointed by the president. To overcome the impasse, Cardinal **Christian Tumi** proposed the appointment of two vice chairmen.

One burning issue in the deliberations centered on the creation of an independent electoral commission, which was demanded by the hard-core opposition. The demand for such a commission came up because of the opposition's fears that the government could not be neutral in the organization of elections. On the contrary, progovernment participants wanted the minister of territorial administration to continue with the organization of elections in the country. Meanwhile, the opposition parties set up a team under the **Cameroon Democratic Union's (CDU)** Dr. **Adamu Ndam Njoya**, to discuss a deal with government. The heckling and bickering notwithstanding, conference participants reached a consensus and on 13 November 1991, signed a declaration, dubbed the Yaoundé Declaration, in which they agreed on the following points:

withdrawal of operational military commanders who had been appointed by government in response to the opposition's launching of the **ghost town operations**; release of people illegally detained for political reasons; a tax moratorium for people, including businessmen, severely hit by ghost town operations; a calling off by opposition political leaders of ghost town operations; and a lifting of the ban on political rallies by the government. The radical opposition party, the **Social Democratic Front (SDF),** and several other groups refused to sign the declaration, pointing out that they doubted government's commitment to enforce the declaration's recommendations.

Before the conference wound up on 18 November 1991, it produced a draft electoral code and another accessible to the audiovisual media by political parties, but it failed to agree on the form of government to be established. While some (especially **anglophones**) spoke in favor of a federal system of government, others (mostly **francophones**) intimated that federation would amount to questioning national integration. Furthermore, it was decided that in a future constitution, presidential power would be separated and the term of office limited. Many agreed that there should be decentralization of powers and that a Senate, Constitutional Court, and a House of Chiefs should be created. They argued that a future constitution should clearly separate the powers between the three arms of government: the executive, legislative, and judicial. Finally, they established a Tripartite Committee on Constitutional Matters to draft proposals for a new or revised constitution. *See also* ALLIANCE FOR THE RECONSTRUCTION OF CAMEROON THROUGH THE SOVEREIGN NATIONAL CONFERENCE (ARC-SNC).

TRUST TERRITORIES. Both **French** and **British Cameroons** became trust territories of the United Nations **trusteeship system** in 1945, following the demise of the **League of Nations** under the UN Charter. Trust territories were to be granted proportionate devolution of control and power, eventually leading to self-government and independence. This was a clearer responsibility than the weak stipulations for the earlier **mandate** territories. The existence of a political option for the trust territories spurred the rise of nationalist movements in both territories. Consequently, the French and British authorities were forced to hasten the pace of transition to self-government and independence. Supervision of these efforts was carried out by the UN Trusteeship Council through visiting missions, questionnaires, and nationalists' petitions to the council. French Cameroun ceased to be a territory on 1 January 1960 and British

Cameroons on 1 October 1961, at which time French Cameroun joined Southern Cameroons to become the **Federal Republic of Cameroon**. British **Northern Cameroons** became part of the Federal Republic of **Nigeria**. *See also* NORTHERN CAMEROONS CASE.

TRUSTEESHIP SYSTEM. The trusteeship system was established under the Charter of the United Nations as a qualitative improvement to and a historic successor of the **mandate system** of the **League of Nations**. Cameroon became British and French **trust territories** under the United Nations Organization. The trusteeship regime was to promote the political, economic, social, and educational advancement of the inhabitants of the trust territories and their progressive development toward self-government and independence.

Consequently, the postwar order provided a more efficient supervisory mechanism through visiting missions and their periodic on-the-spot investigations, the establishment of annual reports on conditions in the territory, and the participation of local political groupings and figures to present grievances and set demands before the world body. The Trusteeship Council eventually set the stage for political emancipation in Cameroon by calling for a **plebiscite** in **British Cameroons**, determining the status of the various parts of the territory until the attainment of independence in January 1960 and **reunification** in October 1961. *See also* ADMINISTERING AUTHORITIES.

TSANGA, DELPHINE (1935–). Cameroon's first female minister, Tsanga was born in Lomié, in the Upper Nyong Division. She was enrolled for primary school in **Douala**, Yokadouma, and **Yaoundé** at various times before entering the Collège de Jeune Filles in Douala for secondary education. On completion in 1955, she was admitted to Lycée Jos in Douala and then received a scholarship to study in France. She trained as a professional nurse at the Catholic Institute and at the School of Nursing and the Red Cross in Toulouse.

Tsanga returned to Cameroon in 1960, serving in various capacities in the Yaoundé and **Garoua** hospitals. Apart from her professional duties, she also became involved in politics. In 1964, she was named president of the National Council of Women in Cameroon. In 1965, she was elected into the Legislative Assembly and reelected in 1970. Prior to that she was elected president of the **women**'s wing (WCNU) of the unified party, the **Cameroon National Union (CNU),** in 1969.

In July 1970, Tsanga was appointed vice minister of health and public welfare, and on 30 June 1975, she became minister of social affairs. She served in this capacity and as president of the WCNU until the end of the **Ahmadou Ahidjo** regime.

Throughout her long years in public life, Tsanga was instrumental in mobilizing women's sympathies in favor of President Ahidjo's stay in power. She was believed to have continued to exhibit strong sympathies for Ahidjo, which apparently contributed to her removal as minister in July 1984 and as president of the women's wing of the party in March 1985.

TSOUNGUI, GILBERT ANDZE. *See* ANDZE TSOUNGUI, GILBERT.

TUMI, CHRISTIAN WIYGHAN (1930–). Born on 15 October 1930 in the village of Kikaikelaki, he studied in Nigeria, France, and Switzerland. In December 1979, he became the first bishop of Yagoua diocese and in November 1982 archbishop of **Garoua**. On 28 June 1988, he became a cardinal. He presently serves as archbishop of **Douala**.

– U –

UM NYOBE, REUBEN (1913–1958). Um Nyobe was a nationalist leader and the main spiritual figure of the **Union des Populations du Cameroun (UPC)**. He was born of humble parentage in Boumnyebel, the heartland of the **Bassa** country, in the Sanaga Maritime Division. After primary school in the region, he enrolled in the influential Teacher Training College in Foulassi, near Sangmelima. He dropped the training prematurely after one year for allegedly coming into conflict with the teachers of the **American Presbyterian Mission** in 1932. He educated himself and succeeded in an examination to join the lower ranks of the civil service. He served in the government finance office in **Douala** and as a court clerk in **Yaoundé** and **Edea**. His political outlook was to change over the years. He joined other early nationalists in the pro-French **Jeunesse Camerounaise Française (Jeucafra)**, which was used to stem German propaganda in the territory. From 1944, his leading role in the formation of a local branch of the French Confédération Générale du Travail (CGT) was well marked. He officially joined the movement of trade unionists in 1947 and was instrumental in transforming broad nationalist sentiments into the formation of the UPC in April 1948. The party became a branch of the interterritorial party of French Africa, the **Rassemblement Démocratique Africain (RDA)**. Um Nyobe rose to be one of the RDA's vice presidents in 1949, before the UPC broke away from the Rassemblement.

Um Nyobe played a more influential role in the UPC movement, where he served as secretary-general and upstaged many other party adherents by his fierce debate and oratorical genius. He represented the UPC at the United Nations, taking a consistently radical nationalist stance. This led the French to block his attempts to gain electoral victories. Although Um Nyobe was exposed to marxist thought in his early trade union days, he so perfectly internalized his marxism that the rationality and persuasiveness of his thought clearly surpassed ideological labels.

Um Nyobe stood unequivocally for immediate independence from the French, **reunification** with **British Cameroons**, and the cultural renaissance of the Cameroonian mind. As a leading political force by 1955, he engineered an insurrection that was crushed by the French and led to the banning of the movement. It was in the wake of this setback that Um Nyobe exercised his politics from the underground in hiding, among the ***maquis***.

Um Nyobe's political existence in the *maquis* was the crucial stage of his life. His immediate followers had been reduced to essentially Bassa elements. This led to the virtual dislocation of the UPC high command of **Felix-Roland Moumie** and Um Nyobe. However, his existence in the *maquis* was in sharp contradiction to his opposition to a purely military solution to the crisis. Nonetheless, an organizational mechanism had been created around him as the *grand maquis,* consisting of his close associates such as Um Ngo, Josué Bassogo, and **Theodore Mayi-Matip**. The band stayed in close collaboration, study, and meditation despite constant attempts at infiltration by government forces. It was in hiding, on 13 September 1958, a day Mayi-Matip declared all would be fine, that Um Nyobe was assassinated by a government gendarme, Paul Abdoulaye.

Um Nyobe's death was a great triumph for the **Ahmadou Ahidjo** regime and a heavy tragedy for Cameroon nationalism. His name was taboo for two decades in Cameroonian schools, colleges, and universities, but following the departure of Ahidjo in 1982, his most ardent followers continued to interpret his predictions and await his return for an eventual liberation, or *kunde,* in the Bassa parlance.

UNION CAMEROUNAISE (UC). The UC was the leading political party of the **République du Cameroun**. It eventually became the government party and the ***parti unifié*** of **East Cameroon** under the federal structure. The UC was formed in May 1958 in **Garoua** to provide the political base of support and legitimacy for the **Ahmadou Ahidjo** premiership. It was organized around a northern-based parliamentary group in the **Assemblée Législative du Cameroun (ALCAM)**. For this reason, the UC was originally considered a regional, Muslim, and essentially **Fulani** organization. Various northern traditional rulers, the *lamibe*, supported the movement. To boost its electoral chances, the UC leadership also courted the northern **Kirdi** for support and votes.

The UC emerged into a quasi-national party through a combination of co-optation politics, office distribution, and sheer political intimidation orchestrated by its leader, Ahmadou Ahidjo. As head of state, President Ahidjo enticed former opponents to denounce their political convictions in exchange for enhanced political office and membership in the UC. Various members of the opposition parties opposed to his idea of a *parti unifié* were arrested and imprisoned.

In various legislative elections between 1960 and 1965, the UC consolidated its primacy in politics to emerge as the single political party in East Cameroon. From this position of strength, Ahidjo later entered into negotiations with political parties of West Cameroon—the **Kamerun National Democratic Party (KNDP), Cameroons Peoples' National Convention (CPNC)**, and **Cameroon United Congress (CUC)**—to gain consent for dissolution in favor of a national one-party structure, the **Cameroon National Union**. *See also* FRONT NATIONAL UNIFIE.

UNION DES POPULATIONS DU CAMEROUN (UPC). An outstanding political party formed in **French Cameroun** in April 1948, the UPC represented a brand of militant nationalism that was unique in its time. The UPC was affiliated with the interterritorial party of French Africa, the **Rassemblement Démocratique Africain (RDA),** and was closely aligned to the French trade union movement and the French Communist Party. Because of its domestic activism and ideological alignments, the UPC fell prey to colonial repression and banning orders. In the 1951 and 1952 national and territorial assembly elections, UPC candidates were defeated with the blessing of the French authorities. In July 1955, the organization was banned for organizing the bloody **Douala** riots. Underlying the attitude of French colonial authorities was the perceived threat in the UPC political platform.

Unlike other parties, the UPC first called for an end to French rule, defended the need for rapid improvement in the living standards of the population, denied the incorporation of Cameroun into the French Union, and advocated the immediate **reunification** of French and **British**

Cameroons as a condition for independence. After it was outlawed in the post-1955 period, the UPC took refuge in **Kumba** in British Cameroons. However, despite its populist and nationalist agenda, the UPC did not emerge as a truly national party. Its membership and much of its leadership and operation were largely reduced to the **Bassa** and **Bamiléké** areas. Other local parties such as the Union Bamiléké, Evolution Sociale Camerounaise (ESOCAM), and **Renaissance Camerounaise (RENAICAM)** were established as anti-UPC groups. Moreover, the structural organization of the UPC was loose and dominated by two contrasting personalities: **Reuben Um Nyobe** and **Felix-Roland Moumie**. Nevertheless, the UPC was allowed to participate in United Nations debates of the **Trusteeship** Council, where it elaborated grievances against French rule and presented its strategy of decolonization.

After its condemnation to an illegal status in 1955, the UPC existed as an underground and an exile movement. It engaged in guerrilla action against French and Cameroon troops. These clandestine operations began in the Bassa countryside and culminated in the assassination of UPC leader Um Nyobe on 13 September 1958. Thereafter, the insurgency in the Bassa region disintegrated with the ***ralliement*** of **Theodore Mayi-Matip** to the **Ahmadou Ahidjo** government. Between 1960 and 1963, a legal UPC opposition had representatives in the **East Cameroon** Assembly. Clandestine insurgent activity, popularly known as the ***maquis***, later spread to the Bamiléké regions of the country. This insurgency was crushed with the arrest and execution of UPC figures such as Celestin Takala, Wambo le Courant, and **Ernest Ouandie** in 1971.

The exile wing of the UPC party operated in the early 1960s from Conakry, Cairo, and Accra. The UPC also had varying support from the Soviet Union and the **People's Republic of China**. On 3 November 1960, the leader of the UPC exile wing, Felix-Roland Moumie, was poisoned by French security agents in Geneva. From that time, the UPC operated from its headquarters in Paris and had a wide membership that included intellectuals and students. The UPC was headed by a Central Committee consisting of Wougly Massaga, Siméon Kuissu, and Elenga Mbuyinga. Critical studies on various aspects of Cameroonian politics, economy, and diplomatic performance were regularly published by the organization. The UPC was also a strong advocate of multiparty politics and respect for **human rights** in Cameroon.

During the transition of leadership in 1982, the UPC expressed great enthusiasm for the **Paul Biya** presidency but has since increased its criticism and disenchantment with the regime, especially after the abortive

coup attempt of 6 April 1984. This notwithstanding, the Biya regime allowed the return of former UPC exiles to Cameroon, among whom was **Ntumazah Ndeh**. Many were, however, later arrested for political disturbances before being released. Moreover, in a Supreme Court decision of August 1986, it was ruled that the UPC had lost its legal status as a political party. A private medical practitioner, Joseph Sende, had reprimanded the government for failing to recognize the UPC's right to existence on the basis of Cameroon's constitutional prescription.

The situation changed with the rebirth of multiparty democracy in the country in 1990. Following the president's decision to accept pluralist democracy, the UPC was legalized in 1991. The party has, however, lost much of its clout and popularity. Political infighting and factionalism within the party have effectively prevented it from making any significant headway in the country's political landscape. Its representation has largely been peripheral, in both the government and the legislature.

UNION DOUANIERE ECONOMIQUE DE L'AFRIQUE CENTRALE (UDEAC)/CENTRAL AFRICAN CUSTOMS AND ECONOMIC UNION (CACEU). This successor to the Union Douanière Equatoriale (UDE) was established on 8 December 1964, with headquarters in Bangui, **Central African Republic (CAR)**. The membership has varied over the years as the result of political disputes between the members and attempts by competing organizations to pull members into their orbit. The current membership consists of Cameroon, CAR, **Chad, Congo, Equatorial Guinea,** and **Gabon**. The Portuguese-speaking island country of Sao Tomé–Principe may join. The purposes of the union are to promote commerce among the members, to stimulate harmonious development, and to establish a common market. Eventually, this is to lead to economic union.

UDEAC organs are a Council of Heads of State, a Conference of Ministers of Agriculture and Animal Husbandry, a Management Committee, and a General Secretariat with a secretary-general. Subsidiary organizations include the **Bank of Central African States (BEAC),** the **Development Bank of Central African States (BDEAC),** and the Transequatorial Communications Agency. A meat and livestock community (Communauté Economique de Bétail de la Viande et des Ressources Halieutique), a reinsurance company (Société Communautaire de Réassurance), a pharmaceutical company (Société Communautaire des Produits Pharmaceutiques en Centrafrique), and a joint satellite project have been proposed. Studies were undertaken for a unified development of railways, including the construction of a rail link between the Atlantic coast and the CAR.

The UDEAC's main problem is the fair distribution of benefits to all of its members. Gabon and Cameroon are economically far ahead of Chad, CAR, and Equatorial Guinea. Cameroon is not simply an ordinary member of UDEAC. About half of the population of UDEAC is Cameroonian. Cameroon also serves as the port of entry for landlocked members such as Chad and CAR. There are attempts in the UDEAC treaty to equalize the disequilibrium among member states. These consist of a common taxing policy, the *tax unique;* the process of group consensus in the distribution of new industries; and the creation of a solidarity fund for financial assistance to disadvantaged countries. However, these measures have not reduced Cameroon's dominance in UDEAC. Since its inception, mostly Cameroonians have served as secretary-general, although the headquarters is in Bangui, CAR. The Secretariat carries out day-to-day activities of the organization. The policy-making function is reserved for the summit of the heads of states, which meets yearly in December.

A more recent problem is posed by the integration of Equatorial Guinea, which joined in 1983. Not only a latecomer, it is the only member not a former colony of **France**. Spanish-speaking in a French-speaking group, a member of a different monetary bloc, it is economically far behind the other members. The promise of **petroleum** exploitation on a large scale in Equatorial Guinea may alter this situation. *See also* ECONOMIC COMMUNITY OF THE STATES OF CENTRAL AFRICA; FOREIGN POLICY.

UNION FOR CHANGE. *See* ALLIANCE FOR THE RECONSTRUCTION OF CAMEROON THROUGH THE SOVEREIGN NATIONAL COUNCIL (ARC-SNC).

UNITED REPUBLIC OF CAMEROON. Upon the **reunification** of the **République du Cameroun** and **Southern Cameroons**, the **Federal Republic of Cameroon** came into existence. It had a short life, for in 1972 the federal system was replaced with a unitary, highly centralized system of government. The name of the county became the United Republic of Cameroon. Pres. **Ahmadou Ahidjo** followed policies to centralize all power in **Yaoundé** and in the presidency. One step was the formation of a single political party, the **Cameroon National Union**. A second step was the ending of the federation. However, this determination to end the federation has another explanation. A strong central unitary government is a French tradition, a tradition passed on to **francophone** Africa during the colonial era. The concept of federation is much more common in the **anglophone** experience, and this tradition is frequently employed in areas previously ruled by **Great Britain**. This difference in tradition is visible in Cameroon politics today, with widespread support for a return to the federal system among anglophones, but with little or no support among francophones.

In 1984, the country's name was changed again, to the **Republic of Cameroon.**

UNITED STATES OF AMERICA. Cameroon earned quick recognition from the United States at independence in 1960. However, attempts by the Cameroon government, in the heat of the cold war, to receive material and logistic support in crushing the **Union des Populations du Cameroun (UPC)** insurrection failed. Relations between the two countries improved with **Peace Corps** assistance, foreign aid, and growing trade in raw materials. Cultural ties grew substantially as young Cameroonians turned to the United States for their university studies. The Jimmy Carter administration's leaning toward Africa was particularly beneficial for Cameroon. In the late 1970s, U.S. banking and industrial interests became significant in the Cameroon economy, coincident with the growing export of **petroleum** to the United States. The United States is now one of Cameroon's largest trading partners (*see* FOREIGN TRADE). Both countries currently strive to upgrade their already growing relations for identical reasons: Cameroon seeks to diversify its alliances away from narrow dependence on **France**, while the United States aims to break France's monopolizing hold on **francophone** Africa and expand its ties. However, relations turned downward in the 1990s as the U.S. government condemned Cameroon for its poor **human rights** record and failure to become democratic. In the mid-1990s, agreement was reached between American oil companies and Cameroon on the construction of the **Chad-Kribi pipeline**, a major project. Since then, U.S.-Cameroon relations have improved.

UNITY PALACE. Unity Palace is the official residence in **Yaoundé** of the president. Construction began in the **Ahmadou Ahidjo** era, but the structure was completed under **Paul Biya**'s reign. The structure is also called the "Etoudi Palace," based on the name of the neighborhood in which it is located.

UNIVERSITY OF YAOUNDE. The University of Yaoundé was built and opened with French supervision and technical assistance in 1962. Originally known as the Federal University of Yaoundé, it became the University of Yaoundé when the **Federal Republic of Cameroon** became the **United Republic of Cameroon** in 1972. For 31 years, the institution was the epitome of Cameroon's **bilingual** initiative, bringing together students and professors of **francophone** and **anglophone** training. There are three major faculties: Law and Economics, Natural Sciences, and Letters and Human Sciences. Deans are appointed by the head of state, but the head of department is generally appointed on the advice of the faculty members.

Most French technical assistance agents who took up duties in the early period were eventually replaced by Cameroon scholars and administrators. The university particularly encouraged the recruitment of former students into the faculty staff ranks.

The highest authority within the university was the chancellor, who was a political appointee and who concentrated on administrative issues. Many former chancellors were promoted to become ministers in government: **Robert Mbella Mbappe**, Foumane Akame, **Joseph Owona**, Laurent Esso, and Peter Agbor Tabi. Vice chancellors were usually highly respected academicians. Among the office holders, **Victor Anomah Ngu** later became a minister. The secretary-general was also crucial in this administrative chain. As a team, these officials supervised over 13,000 students, the majority of whom were enrolled in the Faculty of Law.

Before 1993, the University of Yaoundé was an umbrella institution for other professional institutions (*grandes écoles*) attached to the university. The Advanced School of Mass Communication (ASMAC); the School of Medicine (CUSS); the School of Technology, Polytechnique; the International Relations Institute of Cameroon (IRIC); and the Advanced Teachers College, Ecole Normale Supérieure, were all attached to the University of Yaoundé. In addition, university centers were opened in **Douala** (business), Dschang (agronomy), **Ngaoundéré** (industrial services), and **Buea** (translation).

In April 1992, the government decided to decongest the University of Yaoundé and to improve on the quality of university education in the country. Consequently, the University of Yaoundé was split in two: University of Yaoundé I and University of Yaoundé II. University of Yaoundé I is composed of the Faculty of Natural Sciences and the Faculty of the Arts. Affiliated to it are also the professional institutions, except the school of translation in Buea. The University of Yaoundé II is made up of the Faculty of Law and Political Science and the Faculty of Economic Sciences. A further innovation was the transformation of the four university centers in Douala, Buea, Dschang, and Ngaoundéré into full universities.

Administrative responsibility in the universities of Ngaoundéré, Dschang, Douala, and Yaoundé I and II is in the hands of the rector and his vice, while in the University of Buea such responsibilities are handled by the vice chancellor and the registrar. Even though the professional schools are attached to universities, entry into them depends on a competitive entry examination, while entry into the faculties is based on success in the ***baccalauréat*** or the **General Certificate of Education (GCE)** Advanced Level.

URBANIZATION. The tendency for people to move from rural areas to urban centers and for government policies to promote the establishment of industries and infrastructure in the major cities is known as *urbanization*. Although urbanization has long been considered a demonstration of a country's modernization and development, it now provides alarming signals of a country's unequal development and underdevelopment.

The main cities of **Yaoundé** and **Douala** are the areas most affected by the urbanization trend, in part due to the government's deliberate policy of centralization of services and opportunities in the capital (Yaoundé) and the preference of indigenous and foreign companies of locating in the economic center, Douala.

In 1985, it was estimated that only 30 to 35 percent of the population lived in urban areas. The yearly 7 percent increase will mean that about 80 percent of the population will be concentrated in the urban areas by the year 2000. This creates substantial problems of education, lodging, sanitation, and security in these areas. The heavy budget of the Ministry of National Education, the separate Ministry of Urbanization, and the increased efforts to reduce city crime and violence by public security officials are examples of government attempts to triumph over a complex phenomenon. *See also* RURAL EXODUS.

UTHMAN DAN FODIO (1754–1817). The **Fulani** founder of the Sokoto Empire was born in Marafa near Gobir in present-day **Nigeria**. After studies in Agades, Uthman was employed by the king to serve as governor of royal princes but was dismissed in 1802 by a new king who detested growing Fulani influence in state affairs.

Uthman later studied and taught Islamic religion to emerge as a *modibo* (expert in Islamic sciences). Many Fulanis organized around him to reject the dictates and perverse practices of the king. In the ensuing four-year war, Uthman also set out to convert the dominant Hausa from paganism through the Holy War (***jihad***). Uthman's religious fervor led to the Fulani victory and the creation of a vast empire from Masina in the Upper Niger to the **Adamawa**. The empire disintegrated and was divided after his death in 1817.

– V –

VERDZEKOV, PAUL (1931–). Monseigneur Verdzekov is the first **anglophone** Cameroonian bishop, archbishop, and metropolitan of **Bamenda**. He was born on 22 January 1931 in Shisong, Bui Division, in the **North West Province**. He received primary education in Sacred Heart School, Shisong, from 1937 to 1944 and a two-year teacher training in Bambui from 1948 to 1950. From 1952 to 1954, he was enrolled in **St. Joseph's College**, Sasse, **Buea,** in the **South West Province**. He later pursued university education in the Pontifical Urban University of Rome (1958–62 and 1967–69). He obtained a licentiate in theology and a Ph.D. in social sciences from these institutions.

Under Pope Paul VI, he was appointed bishop of the newly created diocese of Bamenda and the first ever anglophone Cameroonian bishop. On 18 March 1982, Pope John Paul II raised Bamenda to an archdiocese, with Paul Verdzekov as its archbishop. Since his consecration, he has held two significant offices: president of the Cameroon National Episcopal Conference (1976–82) and member of the Sacred Congregation for the Doctrine of the Faith (appointed in 1984).

VICTORIA. *See* LIMBE.

VILLES MORTES. *See* GHOST TOWN OPERATIONS.

VOLLARBE. The Vollarbe is the second of the two large **Fulani** family groupings most prominent in northern politics. Compared to the **Yillaga**, the Vollarbe have a less significant warrior tradition. Nevertheless, they have preserved their peculiar cultural features and natural physical qualities through the centuries. The Vollarbe are found mostly in **Maroua**, **Ngaoundéré,** and Banyo.

– W –

WAZA NATIONAL PARK. This 17,000-hectare reserve is one of the most exciting to visit in West and Central Africa. Sixty kilometers north of **Maroua**, it contains numerous herds of elephants, ostrich, giraffes, lions, and a wide variety of birds and mammals. Several nongovernmental organizations are assisting Cameroon in developing the park and providing a better interface between the animals and the people who inhabit the area. The tourist and camping facilities were **privatized** in 1994. An Italian company, Ecaway, took over from Société Camerounaise du Tourisme (SOCATOUR), a government corporation. Other important parks in Cameroon include the National Benue Park, the Bouba Ndjidah National Park, and the **Korup National Park**.

WEREWERE-LIKING, NICOLE (1950–). Cameroon's best-known contemporary dramatist, Wéréwéré-Liking moved to Abidjan, Ivory Coast, in the late 1970s, where she later founded the Ki Yi Mbok Theatre in 1984. Her plays incorporate various rituals from Cameroon, usually concerned with society initiation, death, and healing, for cathartic effects. Her work with the Ki Yi Mbok Theatre also often uses marionettes.

WEST CAMEROON. The former British **Southern Cameroons** became West Cameroon when it existed as one of the two federated states of the **Federal Republic of Cameroon**. West Cameroon became a political reality on 1 October 1961. It ceased to exist following the referendum that gave birth to the **United Republic of Cameroon** on 20 May 1972. As a political entity, West Cameroon was headed by a government led by the **prime minister** and a bicameral House of Assembly and the **West Cameroon House of Chiefs.** Various West Cameroon prime ministers included **John Ngu Foncha**, **Augustin N. Jua,** and **Solomon Tandeng Muna**. *See also* WEST PROVINCE.

WEST CAMEROON HOUSE OF CHIEFS (1961–1972). This was a political institution in the bicameral **West Cameroon** legislature. Democracy in the House of Chiefs was limited by the nonelective nature of seats. Membership was open only to leaders of the most important chiefdoms and these were usually paramount **chiefs**. Their number varied over time but remained around 22 to 26. Although the institution of the House of Chiefs was a constitutional guarantee with paid members and regular sessions, it was not a powerful institution. It could only advise, deliberate, and handle limited issues of local administration. Because its consent was necessary for certain measures, the House of Chiefs could paralyze the process on some quasi-legislative issues. The need for greater political efficiency and reduction of unnecessary costs led to the demise of the House of Chiefs, and other embodiments of the federal structure, in May 1972.

WEST PROVINCE. This province covers an area of 15,960 square kilometers and consists of six divisions, 24 subdivisions, and two districts. It has two principal relief features: the plains and the high plateaus and mountainous chains of the west. Its tropical climate consists of four seasons, two dry and two rainy, with an average temperature of 22°C. Its vegetation consists of the savannah in the south and north and a forest gallery along internal lakes. Over 1.3 million inhabitants live in the province, and agriculture is very widely practiced. Commerce and trading are predominant in the domestic economy, which produces domestic and cash crops. **Bafoussam** (Mifi Division) is the provincial headquarters. Other important towns include Mbouda (Bamboutos Division), Bafang (Upper Nkam Division), Dschang (Menoua Division), Bangangté (Nde Division), and **Foumban** (Noun Division). The West Province was established in 1972. The West Province, which is **francophone** and inhabited mainly by **Bamiléké,** should not be confused with **West Cameroon**, which was an **anglophone** entity.

WHEAT. Local cultivation dates back to the early 20th century in the fertile lowlands across the **Logone and Chari Rivers**. Wheat-growing possibilities have not produced excellent results in Cameroon. Government stepped up interest in wheat with the establishment of Société de Développement pour la Culture et la Transformation du Blé (SODEBLE) in 1975. Wheat production under this initiative has been poor and frustrating. It is about the least popular crop among the masses and was designed with a very optimistic vision.

The SODEBLE project was virtually disbanded by government after 1981 in favor of a greater diversification through the production of **maize** and soya. Wheat, however, remains a major import as the taste for European-style bread has become widespread.

WILLIAMS, JOHANNES MANGA (?–1959). Chief Johannes Manga Williams worked with German and British administrations in the **Bakweri** area. His powers and the extent of his rule expanded greatly as a result. Williams, along with **Fon** Galega II of Bali, represented **Southern Cameroons** in the Eastern Nigerian House of Assembly under the 1947 Richards Constitution. Their experience was to be a factor in the later development of the **West Cameroon House of Chiefs**.

WORLD BANK. Also known as the International Bank for Reconstruction and Development (IBRD), the World Bank was established after **World War II** to assist in European recovery. Much of its attention is directed today to the Third World, and it is presently a major source of finance in Africa. Loans can be made to member governments or to private enterprises in member countries. The International Development Association (IDA), the International Finance Corporation (IFC), and the Multilateral Investment Guarantee Agency (MIGA) are affiliated. Membership in the **International Monetary Fund** is required before joining the IRBD. The **United States** dominates decision making in the bank. Bank offices are located in Abidjan, Ivory Coast, and Nairobi, Kenya. *See also* ECONOMIC CRISIS; PRIVATIZATION; STRUCTURAL ADJUSTMENT PROGRAM.

WORLD WAR I (KAMERUN CAMPAIGNS). From 5 August 1914 until 29 February 1916, **Kamerun** was a battleground for World War I, which had begun in Europe two days earlier. Allied forces (French, British, Belgian) launched a series of campaigns against German Kamerun after successfully encircling the territory. The northern campaigns penetrated from **Chad** under French command and from northern **Nigeria** under the British. In the South, French troops struck from **Gabon** and received reinforcement from Belgian militia. The Allied contingent on the Kamerun coast was a Franco–British creation of indigenous African soldiers from Nigeria, Gold Coast (later Ghana), and Sierra Leone as well as elite French troops from Dakar, Senegal.

The German forces were eventually overwhelmed by the numbers and coordination of the Allied command. They lost control of their political capital (**Yaoundé**) on 9 January and the stronghold of Mora on 20 February 1916. By that time, the remainder of German forces had fled to the island of Fernando Po in defeat. Allied forces were stationed in a fashion that determined the political division of postwar Cameroon. The French occupied much of the South and heartland regions of the territory; the British remained in the fringe areas bordering Nigeria. The later partition of the territory reflected these realities. *See also* DOBELL, CHARLES M.

WORLD WAR II (CAMEROON PARTICIPATION). Hitler's swift overrun of **France** and the imposition of the puppet Vichy regime had significant implications for **French Cameroun**. The recovery of France needed both the cooperation of Allies and the participation of the colonies. From London, Gen. Charles de Gaulle made a passionate broadcast to the French empire to "win the war after losing the battle." General **Philippe Leclerc** was to accomplish this mission in French Africa. He landed in **Douala** on 27 August 1940, and stripped civilian and military powers from Gov. Richard Brunof, who was more sympathetic to the Vichy regime. Leclerc also commanded an attack to cut off **Gabon** from its Vichy attachment and lobbied for **Chad**'s return to de Gaulle's "Free French Africa." The landing of de Gaulle in **Douala** in 1944 en route to Brazzaville was a great boost to African troops. Thousands of Cameroonians enlisted under General Leclerc in military campaigns to fight across North Africa, France, and **Germany**.

In **British Cameroons**, enlistment was done through the services of the **residents** in the province. Able-bodied Cameroonians were integrated into the **Nigerian** forces and had experience in expeditions across East Africa, the Middle East, India, and Burma. Wartime participation widened the horizons of many Cameroonians and accelerated the growth of nationalism. A special cemetery in the **botanical gardens** is dedicated to **anglophone** troops killed in the war.

WOMEN. Research on the situation of women in Cameroon is in the very early stages. However, it is clear that their role and position have varied from the precolonial to the colonial and independence periods and that their situation varies from one ethnic group to another, one region to another, and one religion to another. While the traditional view has been that women have been in a subordinate position to men throughout history, increasing evidence suggests that this has been overstated for the precolonial period but that a powerful effect of colonial rule was the deterioration of women's position in society. While there has been a struggle to rectify this situation in the independence era, women in many respects still do not receive equal status or treatment in Cameroon today. *See also* AISSATSU, YAOU; ANLU; BASSONG, ISABELLE; EKO, CATHERINE; MINISTRY FOR WOMEN'S AFFAIRS; NJEUMA, DOROTHY LIMUNGA; TAKUMBENG; TANKEU, ELIZABETH; TSANGA, DELPHINE; WEREWERE-LIKING, NICOLE; ZANG NGUELE, ROSE.

WOURI RIVER. The Wouri is an important drainage feature near the Cameroon coast. It was named the Cameroon River and christened Rios dos Camaroes (Rivers of Prawns) by the Portuguese in 1472. The Wouri is 246 kilometers long and draws on lakes from the interior. The entire Wouri stretch is characterized by swamps and sandbars, necessitating expensive measures to maintain navigation. The bridge over the Wouri River into **Douala** was completed by the French in 1955. A toll was paid for passage over the bridge until the mid-1970s.

– Y –

YAKUM-NTAW, FOSI (FON) (1933–). Traditional **chief**, criminal lawyer, former **governor** of the **North Province**, he was born on 12 October 1933 in Bambalang, Ndop, **North West Province**. He attended the government primary school there from 1942 to 1949 before proceeding to the Cameroon Protestant College, Bali, from February 1950 to December 1954. He later pursued law at the University of London and Inns of Court from 1965 to 1968, obtaining the bachelor of laws and barrister at law degrees.

He joined the police department on return home as head of the **Bamenda** service (1968–69) and chief of criminal investigation in **Buea** (1969–72). In 1972, he moved to **Yaoundé** as head of criminal investigation for the country and director of general administration for national security (1973–74). For nine years, he served as governor of the **South West Province** in Buea until 22 August 1983.

In the wake of the **destabilization plot** announced by Pres. **Paul Biya**, he was appointed governor of the North Province, a rather sensitive post at a very trying moment during the **Ahidjo–Biya rupture** in August 1983. Yakum-Ntaw was the first non-**Fulani** governor of the province. His strong personality and long experience were vital in the situation of crisis and fear leading to the foiled **coup attempt of 6 April 1984**. He retired in 1994.

Yakum Ntaw is a figure of no mean significance in traditional political circles. As a traditional ***fon*** of the Ndop tribe, by succession since 28 March 1968, he is the head of over 150,000 people in the North West Province.

YAOUNDE. Yaoundé is capital of the republic, a rapidly growing city and headquarters of the **Center Province**. It was founded in 1888 by the German explorer Georg August Zenker, who led a scientific exploration into the **Kamerun** interior following initial settlement on the coasts. Zenker lived in Yaoundé for almost three years without any direct contact with the indigenous people of the area. It was the German soldier and administrator Hans Dominik who encouraged the transformation of this hilly area. Since then, Yaoundé was inherited by the French and later maintained by postcolonial administrations as the country's capital.

Yaoundé is essentially in **Ewondo** country, with various subgroupings who occupy the many hills of the town on which their villages are established: Mvog-Ada, Mvolye-Mvog, **Beti,** and Effoulan. In original indigenous parlance, Yaoundé is known as "Ngolla" (hill), reflecting the hilly nature of the city.

Administrative offices are the essential hallmark of the city and received a substantive boost in 1972 under the unitary structure that brought about increased bureaucratic centralization. Civil servants all over the country make long pilgrimages to the capital to follow up the progression of the documents in various ministries.

Yaoundé's growing importance is also enhanced by the establishment of universities, including the **University of Yaoundé**, and multiple subsidiary professional institutions for medicine, diplomacy, journalism, education, and engineering, popularly known as the "*grandes écoles*." Additional educational institutions are also located here.

The population of the capital, counted at 314,000 in the 1976 census, has grown far beyond the narrow dimensions of an Ewondo settlement. In 1994, it was estimated to be 800,000. The country's major ethnic and linguistic groupings have taken up residence: the **Fulani** in **Briqueterie**, the **Bamiléké** in the Mokolo area, as well as scattered pockets of **anglophones** who came in as civil servants. A large international community serves the diplomatic needs of the country, with about 40 resident ambassadors in the city.

Until the **economic crisis**, government and municipal authorities spared no efforts to give Yaoundé a look and character deserving of a national capital and an international center. Construction projects became a permanent feature in the city in the mid-1970s. With the crisis, numerous projects, often half-completed, were abandoned. By the mid-1990s, the city had a tired, rundown appearance. Crime had become omnipresent, and at times uncollected trash and garbage were piled up on the main streets.

YAOUNDE AGREEMENTS. Various international agreements on association between the **European Economic Community (EEC)** and

18 newly independent countries of Africa were signed in the 1960s. The agreements were signed in the Cameroon capital of **Yaoundé** and were composed of various articles on trade, preferential treatment, aid and financial cooperation. The Yaoundé I Agreement was signed in 1963 and after prolonged negotiations renewed in 1969. In 1975, the Yaoundé Agreements were replaced by the **Lomé Agreements**.

YAOUNDE PLAN OF ACTION. *See* GHOST TOWN OPERATIONS.

YAYA, SARKIFADA MOUSSA. *See* MOUSSA YAYA, SARKIFADA.

YILLAGA. This is the largest of two family groupings of the **Fulani**. The Yillaga have a long-dating warrior tradition exhibited in extensive conquest of neighboring groupings of north Cameroon. Their main rival for dominance in the North is the **Vollarbe**. Component subgroups of the Yillaga include the *lamidat* of Rei-Bouba, Mindif, Bibemi, and Bindiri.

– Z –

ZAMBO COMMISSION. This was a high-powered commission of government and party officials charged to solicit ideas and suggestions on the realization of Pres. **Paul Biya**'s projected **New Deal** society of **rigor and moralization.** The members were appointed by the head of state in 1983. A one-time presidential adviser who later became a minister in the Biya presidency, Joseph Zambo, headed the commission.

ZANG NGUELE, ROSE (1947–). She was Cameroon's minister of social affairs from 1984 to 1988. Born in **Yaoundé** on 12 May 1947, she did primary education in Abong-Mbang and Lomie, in the **Eastern Province**, before returning to the capital for secondary education at Collège de la Retraite and **Lycée Leclerc** (1961–68). She later enrolled in the **University of Yaoundé**, graduating with a *licence* and a *diplome d' études approfondies* in modern languages in 1974. In July 1984, she became minister of social affairs. Prior to entering the government as minister, Zang Nguele had been active in party affairs. From 1976 to 1981, she served as secretary of the **women**'s wing of the **Cameroon National Union (CNU)** in Mfoundi Division, and later she became president of the same section (1981–85). She has served as vice president of the National Bureau of the **Cameroon People's Democratic Movement**

(CPDM). In March 1992, she was elected to the National Assembly, where she served until March 1997.

ZERO OPTION. The various strands of **anglophone** political thought range from inclusion and cooperation with the existing governmental structures to separation and independence. There is equal variation in method and approach. *Zero option* is the term used by those who propose independence for the anglophone areas through armed struggle. *See also* ALL ANGLOPHONE CONFERENCES; ANGLOPHONE PROBLEM; CAMEROON ANGLOPHONE MOVEMENT (CAM); SOUTHERN CAMEROONS NATIONAL COUNCIL (SCNC).

ZIMMERER, EUGEN VON (unknown). The second German **governor** of **Kamerun** (1891–95), he began a ruthless penetration into the Kamerun interior and faced resistance from local populations including the **Bakweri**, **Bassa,** and **Bulu**. Many of the plantations were established under his tenure, and he laid down the principles guiding land policy despite heavy opposition from the indigenous population and the **Basel Mission**.

ZINTGRAFF, EUGENE (1858–1897). This German explorer played an important role in the exploration into the **Kamerun** interior, especially during the governorships of **Julius von Soden** and **Eugen von Zimmerer**. He made a detailed study of his exploratory missions, which were generally considered too costly by the German administration. After initial explorations around the coast between the Cameroon River and the Rio del Rey, Zintgraff traveled north into the **Tikar**, **Bamiléké**, **Bali,** and **Fulani** areas. He developed more amicable relations with his new hosts after each conquest. He died in December 1897 in the Canary Islands on his way home on sick leave.

ZOA, JEAN (1924–1998). A former archbishop of **Yaoundé**, Zoa was a powerful political figure because of his religious following. He was born in Saa and educated by missionaries for much of his life, first at the parish school in Efok, then the Petit Séminaire at Akono, the Grand Séminaire at Muolye, and the Collegium de Propaganda file, Rome. Ordained a priest in 1950, he served in various posts as vicar in Ombessa until 1957, as parish priest in **Yaoundé** (1957–58), and as director of operations for the Archdiosese of Yaoundé (1958–61), until he was named archbishop of Yaoundé in 1961. Beginning then, Monseigneur Zoa became an important figure in Cameroon politics, particularly under the reign of **Ahmadou Ahidjo**, who was a Muslim. Despite the relative fairness of Ahidjo's stance, Christians looked on Zoa as a symbol of their religious dissatisfaction. He was implicated in some of the many conspiracies against the government. The state–church relationship suffered a severe strain in the heated 1970–71 trial of opponents of government, which included a Catholic bishop.

Under the **Paul Biya** presidency, the archbishop was still very significant and even more powerful. He was alleged to have initiated the drive to create a wedge between Ahidjo and his successor by calling ethnic meetings in his residence in the guise of Christian gatherings. Zoa's period of greatest celebrity was in 1986 during the long-awaited visit of Pope John Paul II to Cameroon. By making government incur heavy expenses for the visit, the **Catholic Church** was sending a strong message across the country. As leader of the biggest single religious bloc in Cameroon under the presidency of Biya, a former Catholic seminarist, Jean Zoa's profile remained at the peak of glory until the time that a junior archbishop, **Christian Tumi**, was appointed Cameroon's first cardinal in May 1988. Zoa died on 20 March 1998 in Yaoundé.

ZONE DE PACIFICATION (ZOPAC). This was a critical zone of the **Union des Populations du Cameroun (UPC)** insurgency between **Douala** and **Yaoundé**. The **André-Marie Mbida** government used a strategy of population resettlement to isolate the UPC from the shelter provided by the local masses. The resettled population received weapons and various signals to inform government troops of insurgent activity. The ZOPAC operation began in 1957 and was commanded by a French colonel, Jean Lamberton. By 1958, the strategy forced hundreds of UPC guerrilla fighters to take refuge in the forests and begin the ***maquis***. The ZOPAC strategy was operated in the **Edea** area of the Sanaga–Maritime Division and later in the **Bamiléké** countryside.

ZONES D'ACTION PRIORITAIRES INTEGREES (ZAPI). This regional integrated rural development project of seven selected areas of the **East**, **South,** and **Center Provinces** was implemented in 1967, under nongovernmental independent companies charged with boosting farmer organizations and providing extension and credit and opportunities for social development. Participants in the scheme could own land to grow cash and food crops and enjoy the ready availability of a good road network, water supply, electricity, health facilities, and other infrastructure for leisure activities. The various ZAPI projects included approximately

175,000 people and were financed by the Fonds d'Aide et de Coopération and the Cameroon government. Integrated rural development was the fad of the late 1960s onward that aimed at providing a modicum sum of economic and social amenities to a population grouping in an effort to increase agricultural production and slow the large-scale movement of rural dwellers to urban areas. Several integrated rural development regions now operating in Cameroon are based on lessons from the ZAPI effort. *See also* RURAL EXODUS.

Bibliography

CONTENTS

Introduction 288
- I. General 292
  - 1. Bibliographies and Dictionaries 292
  - 2. Guidebooks, Travel, and Description 293
- II. History 294
  - 1. General 294
  - 2. Precolonial 295
  - 3. Colonial 298
    - a. General 298
    - b. German Rule 300
    - c. French Rule 300
    - d. British Rule 302
  - 4. Postindependence 304
- III. Politics 304
  - 1. Domestic 304
  - 2. Foreign Relations 312
  - 3. Law 313
- IV. Economy 316
  - 1. General 316
  - 2. Agriculture and Pastoralism 318
  - 3. Finance, Credit, and Banking 321
  - 4. Foreign Aid, Trade, and Investment 322
  - 5. Mining, Industry, Commerce, and Communication 323
- V. Society 325
  - 1. Anthropology 325
    - a. General 325
    - b. Bamiléké and Related 326
    - c. Central South 327
    - d. Coastal and Southern 328

e. North 328
f. Northwest 330
2. Education 331
3. Religion 333
4. Sociology 335
5. Women 337
VI. Culture 340
1. Archaeology and Prehistory 340
2. Architecture 341
3. Arts, Artisanry, and Music 342
4. Language 345
5. Literature and Folklore 346
6. Media and Publishing 350
VII. Science 351
1. Geography, Geology, and Meteorology 351
2. Health, Medicine, and Demography 354
3. Flora and Fauna 356

INTRODUCTION

The number of publications on Cameroon has increased greatly in recent years. Readers can use the annual *Africa Bibliography* published by the International African Institute under the direction of Hector Blackhurst for up-to-date listing of articles. The *African Book Publishing Record* is the best source for items published in Cameroon. *African Studies Abstracts* (Leiden: African Studies Centre, quarterly) is an excellent source. The abstracts are well prepared and very helpful. Older materials are well covered in the standard Mark and Virginia DeLancey, A *Bibliography of Cameroon*. For German-language publications, see Max F. Dippold, *Une bibliographie du Cameroun.* Annotated references to recent works are found in Mark W. DeLancey and Mark D. DeLancey *Cameroon.* Previous editions of the *Historical Dictionary of the Republic of Cameroon* also contain many references not included here.

Regular coverage of events in Cameroon is difficult to find, but the magazines *West Africa* and *Jeune Afrique* are helpful. Annual surveys of political and economic events are available in Colin Legum, *Africa Contemporary Record* (New York: Africana, annual) and *Africa South of the Sahara* (London: Europa, annual). The monthly editions of *Africa Research Bulletin* are good sources. This comes in two editions, one for economic matters and one for political and social affairs.

The classic work on Cameroon history is Englebert Mveng, *Histoire du Cameroun*. Important general works on the precolonial era are rare, but Adamawa is well covered in Martin Njeuma, *Fulani Hegemony in Yola*; Salad Abubakar, *The Lamibe of Fombina*; and Anthony Kirk-Greene, *Adamawa, Past and Present*. The numerous works of Eldridge Mohammodou based on intensive study of oral history are significant for earlier periods. German rule is analyzed in Karen Hausen, *Deutsche Kolonialherrschaft in Afrika*, and the various volumes by Helmuth Stoecker. The classic work in English is Harry Rudin, *Germans in the Cameroons*. Also refer to Lewis H. Gann and Peter Duignan, *The Rulers of German Africa*.

Official versions of French rule include Pierre Chaleur, *L'oeuvre de la France au Cameroun,* and Victor Chazelas, *Territoires africains sous mandat de la France*. A very different view is expressed in Dieudonné Oyono, *Colonie ou mandat? La politique française au Cameroun de 1919 à 1946*. William B. Cohen, *Rulers of Empire* and Robert Delavignette, *Freedom and Authority in French West Africa,* present analysis of and a theory for French administration. More critical of that administration is the brilliant work by Richard Joseph, *Radical Nationalism in Cameroun*, and J. Achille Mbembe, *Ruben Um Nyobe*, which analyze the Union des Populations du Cameroun (UPC). British rule is less thoroughly studied, though David Gardinier's essay, "The British in the Cameroon's," P. M. Kale's *Political Evolution in the Cameroons*, and Alexandre Marc, *La politique économique*, are important contributions. Kale's book is difficult to obtain. The volume by Victor Ngoh, *Cameroon, 1884–1985,* provides valuable information, particularly on the British sector, but is worthwhile for both sectors. Martin Njeuma, *Introduction to the History of Cameroon in the Nineteenth and Twentieth Centuries,* brings together good material from several sources.

The annual reports to the League of Nations and the United Nations produced by the French and the British are important, although biased, sources on this period. Victor Levine, *The Cameroon from Mandate to Independence*, is an excellent overall view of the political history of the period from 1916 to 1961. A Cameroon perspective is available in Victor Ngoh, *Constitutional Developments in Southern Cameroons 1946–1961*. Analysis of more recent political events is found in the various works of Jean-François Bayart, most of which are in French. In English, see Mark W. DeLancey, *Cameroon, Dependence and Independence*, and his essay in *Journal of Contemporary African Studies*, and the numerous publications of Victor LeVine. The recent Joseph Takoukang and Milton Krieger, *African State and Society in the 1990s,* is an excellent study of the politics of the late 1980s and 1990s. The political crisis of these decades, democratization, and the move to a multiparty state are well covered. Collections of the speeches and thoughts of presidents Ahmadou Ahidjo and Paul Biya are available; the reports of Cameroon National Union (CNU) and Cameroon People's Democratic Movement (CPDM) congresses are useful sources on official policy. Mongo Beti, *Main basse sur le Cameroun*, is a stinging attack on the Ahidjo administration. Also see the UPC view in N. Woungly-Massaga, *Ou va le Kamerun*? Jacques Benjamin, *Les camerounais occidentaux*, analyzes the position of West Cameroon in the Federal Republic.

Peter Geschiere, *Village Communities and the State*, presents a rare—and thorough—analysis of local government–central government relationships. The works by Miriam Goheen are a valuable contribution to our understanding of rural developments and the role of women in Cameroon rural society. Other valuable studies of the political system include the publications of Willard Johnson, Ndiva Kofele-Kale, and Victor Kamga for the earlier years. The work of Nicolas van de Walle is especially significant for the 1990s. Foreign relations are analyzed in essays by Mark DeLancey, Ndiva Kofele-Kale, and the volume by Dieudonné Oyono, *Avec ou sans la France? La politique africaine du Cameroun depuis 1960*.

For an introduction to the geography of Cameroon, Aaron S. Neba, *Modern Geography of the Republic of Cameroon,* is elementary but useful. G. Laclavere (ed.), *Atlas of the United Republic of Cameroon*, although a bit old, is adequate. Much more detail is available in the two volumes of Pierre Billard, *Cameroun fédéral*; unfortunately, this work is somewhat dated. The most current material appears in the journal *Revue de Géographie du Cameroun*, published in Yaoundé. This, like most items published in Cameroon, is difficult to find in foreign universities.

There is no up-to-date survey of the Cameroon economy. Chapters in general books on Cameroon, as in Mark W. DeLancey's 1989 publication, provide some general coverage, but in-depth analysis of the economy is available only in articles concerned with specific aspects of the economic system. Agriculture has received more attention than any other sector. See especially the essays by Virginia DeLancey. Perhaps the best brief survey is provided by the World Bank, *Republic of Cameroon, the Challenge*. Also see Nantang Jua, *Economic Mismanagement in a Neo-colonial State,* for a very critical analysis of the Cameroon economic system. Also useful is Ekema Manga, *The African Economic Dilemma*.

Although comprehensive studies of the arts in Cameroun are uncommon, several significant publications are available on selected aspects of the arts. The volume by Christian Seignobos, *Montagnes et hautes terres du nord Cameroun*, and the older J. P. Beguin, *L'habitat au Cameroun*, analyze architecture. Also see the special edition of *Paideuma* (vol. 31) devoted to

Grassfields palaces. Jocelyne Etienne-Nugue and Harri Peccinotti, *Crafts and the Arts of Living in Cameroon*; Venice and Alastair Lamb, *Au Cameroun: Weaving*; and Englebert Mveng, *L'art et l'artisanat africains*, provide analysis and excellent photographs of arts and crafts. Francis Bebey, *African Music*, relies heavily on Cameroon examples. Cameroon music gets good treatment in Sean Barlow and Banning Eyre, *Afropop!*

The best reference to African literature is Hans Zell et al., *A New Readers Guide to African Literature*, but also see the bibliographic essay on Cameroon by Richard Bjornson. Bjornson's *The African Quest for Identity and Freedom* is a very important study, worth reading by political scientists and historians as well as students of literature. The novels by Bebey, Beti, Nanga, and Oyono are the most famous of Cameroon fiction. For a listing of older studies of folklore, refer to Mark W. and Virginia DeLancey's general bibliography.

Cameroun contains numerous and quite varied ethnic groups. No single source can provide description or analysis of these many societies. Many groups have not appeared in published works, and those that have been frequently reported on are not necessarily the largest or most significant politically, economically, or in other respects. In the available literature there are several excellent studies by both Cameroonian and foreign scholars. These are organized by geographic region in the bibliography, but this does not signify that the groups described in any section are necessarily similar or "related" to each other. An older work of outstanding value is *Women in Grassfields* by Phyllis Kaberry, which analyzes the position of women in the Bamenda region. Sultan Njoya, *Histoire et coutumes des Bamum*, is one of the earliest studies of Cameroon society written by a Cameroonian. Other more recent works in English include the several items by Paul Nkwi (e.g., *Traditional Government and Social Change*, but also see his works listed under "History"). Other anglophone scholars include Bongfen Chem-Langhee, Paul N. Mzeka, and Bejing Soh. The publications of S. N. Ejedepong-Koge on the Bakossi are useful but difficult to find. Francophone Cameroonian anthropologists include Enoch K. Kwayeb and Manga Bekombo. Also see the publications of Eldridge Mohammadou under "History."

Studies of religion in Cameroon relate mainly to Christianity. Much of this is biographical or autobiographical, written by foreign missionaries. The several publications of Jean Kenyon Mackenzie provide much information on the peoples of southeastern Cameroon at about 1900. Louis Ngongo's *Histoire des forces religieuses au Cameroun* presents detailed analysis of the Christian missions and churches. Briefer studies of particular missions include Paul Nkwi, *The Catholic Church in Kom*, Lloyd Kwast, *The Disci-*

plining of West Cameroon: A Study of Baptist Growth, and Nyansako-ni-Nku (ed.), *Journey in Faith.* Jean-Marc Ela, *My Faith as an African,* provides a Cameroon perspective on the meaning of the Catholic faith.

Analysis of Cameroon religions is found in many of the anthropological works, but for an overall view and philosophical analysis, refer to J. C. Bahoken, *Clairières metaphysique Africaines*. Studies limited to particular ethnic groups include Philippe Laburthe-Toba, *Initiations et sociétés secrètes au Cameroun*; Philip A. Noss, *Grafting Old Rootstock;* and H. Balz, *Where the Faith Has to Live*. Nwel P. Titi, *Thong Likeng*, examines the Nyambe-Bantu religion, an example of a Cameroon syncretic movement, and its founder.

GENERAL

Bibliographies and Dictionaries

Bridgman, Jon, and David Clarke. *German Africa: A Select Annotated Bibliography.* Stanford, Calif.: Hoover Institute, Stanford University, 1965.

Carlson, Andrew R. *German Foreign Policy, 1890–1914, and Colonial Policy to 1914: A Handbook and Annotated Bibliography*. Metuchen, N.J.: Scarecrow, 1970.

DeLancey, Mark W, et al. *African International Relations: An Annotated Bibliography.* 2d ed. Boulder, Colo.: Westview, 1997.

DeLancey, Mark W., and Virginia H. DeLancey. *A Bibliography of Cameroon*. New York: Africana, 1974.

DeLancey, Mark W., and Peter J. Schraeder. *Cameroon*. World Bibliographical Series, vol. 63. Oxford: Clio, 1986.

Dippold, Max F. *Une Bibliographie de Cameroun: Les Ecrits en langue allemande* [A Bibliography of Cameroon: Works in German]. Yaoundé: CLE, 1971.

L'Encyclopédie de la République Unie du Cameroun [Encyclopedia of the United Republic of Cameroon]. Abidjan: Nouvelles Editions Africaines, 1981. 4 vols. Vol. 1. "The Physical Context and the People." Vol. 2. "History and the State." Vol. 3. "The Economy." Vol. 4. "The Life of the Nation."

Imbert, Jean. *Le Cameroun* [Cameroon]. Paris: Presses Universitaires de France, 1982.

Know Your Country: Know Cameroon. Paris: Afrique Biblio Club, 1979.

LeVine, Victor T., and Roger P. Nye. *Historical Dictionary of Cameroon*. Metuchen, N.J.: Scarecrow, 1974.

Mcllwaine, John. *Writings on African Archives*. London: Zell for SCOLMA, 1996.

Scheven, Yvette. *Bibliographies for African Studies 1987–1993.* London: Zell, 1994.

Schrader, T. H. *Man, Environment and Development: A Bibliography of the Extreme North of Cameroon.* Leiden, Netherlands: Institute for Cultural and Social Studies, 1987.

Westfall, Gloria D. *French Colonial Africa: A Guide to Official Sources.* London: Zell, 1992.

Guidebooks, Travel, and Description

L'Année politique et économique africaine [The African Political and Economic Year]. Dakar: Société Africaine d'Edition, annual.

Balfour, Patrick. *Lords of the Equator: An African Journey*. London: Hutchinson, 1939.

Burthe d'Annelet, J. L. C. de. *Du Cameroun à Alger* [From Cameroon to Algiers], 2 vols. Paris: Roger, 1932.

Calvert, Albert F. *The Cameroons*. London: T. Werner Laurie, 1917.

Camus, Alain. *Au Cameroun* [To Cameroon]. Paris: Hachette, 1981.

Cottes, Anthony. *La Mission Cottes au sud Cameroun, 1905–1908* [The Cotte Mission in Southern Cameroon, 1905–1908]. Paris: Leroux, 1911.

Darras, Jacques. "Le voyage en Afrique [African Journey]." *Esprit* 128, no. 7 (1987): 1–12.

Dominik, Hans. *Vom Atlantik zum Tschadsee* [From the Atlantic to Lake Chad]. Berlin: Mittler, 1908.

Egerton, F. Clement C. *African Majesty: A Record of Refuge at the Court of the King of Bangangte in the French Cameroons*. New York: Scribner's, 1939.

Escherich, Georg. *Quer durch den Urwald von Kamerun* [All across the Jungle of Cameroon]. Berlin: Stilke, 1923.

Finlay, Hugh, et al. *Africa on a Shoestring*. Hawthorn, Australia: Lonely Planet, 1998.

Friedrich, Adolf, ed. *From the Congo to the Niger and the Nile*, 2 vols. London: Duckworth, 1913.

Hudgens, Jim, and Richard Trillo. *West Africa: The Rough Guide*. London: Rough Guides, 1995.

International Women's Club of Yaoundé. *Travel Cameroon*. Bamenda, Cameroon: Gospel, 1994.

Kima, Ayuk A., and Daniel Lyonga Matute. *Introducing Limbe: Environment and Tourism*. Limbe, Cameroon: Business Promotion Consultants, 1990.

Langheld, Wilhelm. *Zwanzig Jahre in deutschen Kolonien* [Twenty Years in German Colonies]. Berlin: Weicher, 1909.

Legum, Colin, ed. *Africa Contemporary Record: Annual Survey and Documents*. London: Collings, annual.

Lyee de Belleau, M. de. *Du Cameroun au Hoggar* [From Cameroon to Hoggar]. Paris: Alsatia, 1945.

Maistre, Camille. *A Travers l'Afrique centrale* [Across Central Africa]. Paris: Hachette, 1895.

Migeod, Frederick William Hugh. *Through British Cameroons*. London: Heath Cranton, 1925.

Morgen, Curt von. *A Travers le Cameroun de sud au nord: Voyages et explorations dans l'arrière-pays de 1889 à 1891* [Across Cameroon from South to North: Voyages and Explorations in the Backcountry from 1889–1891]. Yaoundé: Université Fedérale du Cameroun, 1972.

Passarge, Siegfried. *Adamaua* [Adamawa]. Berlin: Reimer, 1895.

Riebe, Otto. *Drei Jahre unter die deutscher Flagge im Hinterland von Kamerun* [Three Years under the German Flag in the Hinterland of Cameroon]. Berlin: Hayn, 1987.

Thorbecke, Marie P. *Auf der Savanne* [In the Savanna]. Berlin: Mittler, 1914.

United Kingdom. Naval Intelligence Division. *French Equatorial Africa and Cameroons*. London: His Majesty's Stationery Office, 1942.

Zimmermann, K., et al. *Die Grenzgebiete Kameruns im Süden und Osten* [The Cameroon Border Regions of the South and East]. 2 vols. Berlin: n.p., 1914.

Zoller, Hugo. *Forschungsreisen in der deutschen Kolonie Kamerun* [Research Trip in the German Cameroon Colony]. 3 vols. Berlin: Spemann, 1885.

HISTORY

General

Austen, Ralph A. "The Metamorphoses of Middlemen: The Duala, Europeans and the Cameroon Hinterland, ca. 1800–ca. 1960." *International Journal of African Historical Studies* 16, no. 1 (1983): 1–24.

Birmingham, David, and Phyllis M. Martin, eds. *History of Central Africa*. London: Longman, 1983.

DeLancey, Mark W., and Mark D. DeLancey. *Cameroon*. Oxford: ABC-CLIO, 1999.

DeLancey, Mark W., and H. Mbella Mokeba. *Historical Dictionary of the Republic of Cameroon*. Metuchen, N.J.: Scarecrow, 1990.

Epale, Simon-Joseph. *Plantations and Development in Western Cameroon 1885–1975: A Study in Agrarian Capitalism*. New York: Vantage, 1985.

Fanso, Verkijika G. "Traditional and Colonial African Boundaries: Concepts and Functions in Inter-Group Relations." *Presence Africaine* 137–138 (1986): 58–75.

Fowler, Ian, and David Zeitlyn, eds. *African Crossroads: Intersections between History and Ethnography in Cameroon*. Oxford: Berghahn, 1996.

——. eds. *Perspectives on the State: From Political History to Ethnography in Cameroon: Essays for Sally Chilver.* Stuttgart: Steiner, 1995.

Gardi, R. *Momente des Alltags: Fotodokumente aus Nordkamerun, 1950–1985 (Tschadsee, Mandara, Alantika)/Scenes de la vie quotidienne: Photographiques sur le nord du Cameroun, 1950–1985 (Lac Tchad, Mandara, Alantika)* [Scenes from Daily Life: Photographic Documents in the North of Cameroon, 1950–1985 (Lake Chad, Mandara, Alantika)]. Basel, Switzerland: Museum für Völkerkunde und Schweizerische Museum für Völkskunde, 1995.

Geary, Christraud M. "Impressions of the African Past: Interpreting Ethnographic Photographs from Cameroon." *Visual Anthropology* 3, nos. 2/3 (1990): 289–315.

Geschiere, Peter, and Piet Konings, eds. *Conference on the Political Economy of Cameroon—Historical Perspectives, Leiden, June 1988.* Leiden, Netherlands: African Studies Centre, 1989.

Gouellain, René. *Douala: Ville et histoire* [Douala: City and History]. Paris: Institut d'Ethnologie, Museé de l'Homme, 1975.

Hengue, Paul. "Foumban, ou le destin d'une ville ancienne [Foumban, or the Destiny of an Old City]." *Presénce Africaine* 148 (1988): 91–98.

Hepper, F. "Centenary of Limbe Botanic Gardens, Cameroon 1892–1992." *Nigerian Field* 60, nos. 1/2 (1995): 34–41.

Hurault, J. "History of the Mambila Chiefdom of Mbor (Sonkolong)." *Journal of the Anthropological Society of Oxford* 26, no. 1 (1995): 87–98.

Lockhart, V. *A Socio-historical Study of Social Change among the Bangwa of Cameroon*. Edinburgh: Centre of African Studies, Edinburgh University, 1994.

Mainet, Guy. *Douala: Croissance et servitudes* [Douala: Growth and Servitude]. Paris: Harmattan, 1985.

Mbaugbaw, Tambi Eyongetah, Robert Brain, and Robin Palmer. *A History of the Cameroon*. Harlow, Essex: Longman, 1987.

Mveng, Engelbert. *Histoire du Cameroun* [History of Cameroon]. Paris: Présence Africaine, 1963.

——. *L'Eglise Catholique au Cameroun, 100 ans d'évangélisation, Album du Centenarie 1890–1990* [The Catholic Church in Cameroon: 100 Years of Evangelism, Album of the Centenary, 1890–1990]. Yaoundé: Conférence Episcopale Nationale du Cameroun, 1990.

Ngoh, Victor J. *Cameroon 1884–1985*. Yaoundé: Navi, 1988.

Njeuma, Martin Z. "Notes on the Sources of Cameroon History from Prehistoric to Colonial Times." *Annales de la faculté des lettres et sciences humaines, Université de Yaoundé* 11 (1983): 121–40.

Njoya, Sultan. *Histoire et coutumes des Bamum* [History and Customs of the Bamoum]. Yaoundé: Institut Français d'Afrique Noire, Centre du Cameroun, 1952.

O'Neil, Robert. *Mission to the British Cameroons*. London: Mission Book Service, 1991.

Ouden, Jan H. B. den. "In Search of Personal Mobility: Changing Interpersonal Relations in Two Bamiléké Chiefdoms, Cameroon." *Africa, Journal of the International African Institute* 57, no. 1 (1987): 3–27.

Roitman, Janet. "La Garison-entrepôt [The Garrison Depot]." *Autrepart* 6 (1998): 39–51.

Soulillou, Jacques. *Douala: Un Siècle en images* [Douala: A Century in Pictures]. Paris: Author, 1982.

Stoppiello, A. A. "Strumenti e prime forme de popolamento in Africa centrale al Museo di Duala (Camerun)." *Africa* (Rome) 49, no. 1 (1994): 96–107.

Precolonial

Abubakar, Salad. *The Lamibe of Fombina: A Political History of Adamawa, 1809–1901*. Zaria: Ahmadu Bello University Press, 1977.

Abwa, Daniel. "The Banen and Slavery." *Paideuma* 41 (1995): 107–25.

Ardener, Edwin. *Kingdom on Mount Cameroon: Studies in the History of the Cameroon Coast, 1500–1970.* Providence, R.I.: Berghahn, 1996.

Austen, Ralph A. "Tradition, Invention and History: The Case of the Ngondo (Cameroon)." *Cahiers d'études africaines* 32, no. 126 (1992): 285–309.

——. "Slavery and the Slave Trade on the Atlantic Coast: The Duala of the Littoral." *Paideuma* 41 (1995): 127–52.

Bah, Thierno Mouctar. "Les armées Peul de l'Adamawa au 19e siècle [The Fulani Armies of Adamawa in the Nineteenth Century]." In *Pastoralists of the West African Savanna*, ed. Mahdi Adamu and A. Kirk-Greene. London: International African Institute, 1986.

Bassoro, Ahmadou, and Eldridge Mohammadou. *Histoire de Garoua: Cité Peule de XIX siècle* [History of Garoua: Fulani City of the Nineteenth Century]. Garoua: ONAREST, 1977.

Blench, Roger M. "Linguistic Evidence for Cultivated Plants in the Bantu Borderland." *Azania* 29/30(1994/1995): 83–102.

Bouchaud, Joseph. *La Côte du Cameroun dans l'histoire et la cartographie, des origines à l'annexation allemande* [The Coast of Cameroon in History and Cartography, from Origin to German Annexation]. Paris: IFAN, 1952.

Boutrais, Jean. "L'Expansion des éléveurs peuls dans les savanes humides du Cameroun [The Expansion of Fulani Herders into the Humid Savannahs of Cameroon]." In *Pastoralists of the West African Savanna*, ed. Mahdi Adamu and A. H. M. Kirk-Greene. London: International African Institute, 1986, pp. 145–60.

Chem-Langhëë, Bongfen. "Slavery and Slave Marketing in Nso in the Nineteenth Century." *Paideuma* 41 (1995): 177–90.

Chilver, S. "Nineteenth Century Trade in the Bamenda Grassfields, Southern Cameroons." *Afrika und Übersee* 45, no. 4 (1962): 233–58.

——. *Traditional Bamenda: The Precolonial History and Ethnography of the Bamenda Grassfields*. Buea: Ministry of Primary Education and Social Welfare and West Cameroon Antiquities Commission, 1967.

——. "Chronology of the Bamenda Grasslands." *Journal of African History* 11, no. 2 (1970): 249–57.

Dike, K. Onwuka. *Trade and Politics in the Niger Delta, 1830–1956.* Oxford: Clarendon, 1956.

Dillon, Richard G. *Ranking and Resistance: A Precolonial Cameroonian Polity in Regional Perspective*. Stanford, Calif.: Stanford University Press, 1990.

Engard, Ronald K. "Myth and Political Economy in Bafut (Cameroon): The Structural History of an African Kingdom." *Paideuma* 34 (1988): 49–89.

Geschiere, Peter. "Slavery and Kinship among the Maka (Cameroon, Eastern Province)." *Paideuma* 41 (1995): 207–25.

Hurault, Jean. "History of the Mambila Chiefdom of Mbor (Sonkolong)." *Journal of the Anthropological Society of Oxford* 26, no. 1 (1996).

Kirk-Greene, A. H. M. *Adamawa, Past and Present: An Historical Approach to the Development of a Northern Cameroons Province*. London: Oxford University Press for the International African Institute, 1958.

Lyons, D. "The Politics of House Shape: Round vs. Rectilinear Domestic Structures in Dela Compounds, Northern Cameroon." *Antiquity* 70, no. 268 (1996): 351–67.

Marliac, Alain. "Connaissances et savoires pour l'histoire: Réflexions sur le cas du Nord-Cameroun [Knowledge and Learning for History: Reflections on the Case of North Cameroon." *Africa* 50, no. 3 (1995): 325–41.

Mohammadou, Eldridge. "Approche historique au probleme du peuplement des monts du Mandara [Historical Approach to the Problem of the People of the Mandara Mountains]." *Sudan Sahel Studies* (1984): 1–121.

———. "Envahisseur du Nord et Grassfields Camerounais aux XVIIIe siècle: Le Cas du Bamum [Invader from the North and the Cameroonian Grassfields in the Eighteenth Century: The Case of Bamoum]." *Sudan Sahel Studies* 2 (1986): 237–73.

———. *Fulbe Hooseere: Les Royaumes Foulbe du plateau de L'Adamaoua au XIX siècle: Tibati, Tignère, Banyo, Ngaoundéré* [Fulani Hooseere: Fulani Kingdoms of the Adamawa Plateau in the 19th Century: Tibati, Tignere, Banyo, Ngaoundere]. Tokyo: Institute for the Study of Languages and Cultures of Asia and Africa, 1978.

———. ed. *L'Histoire des Peuls Ferobe du Diamare, Maroua et Pette* [History of the Ferobe Fulani of Diamare, Maroua, and Pette]. Tokyo: Institute for the Study of Languages and Cultures of Asia and Africa, 1976.

———. *L'Histoire de Tibati: Chefferie Foulbe du Cameroun* [The History of Tibati: Fulani Chiefdom of Cameroon]. Yaoundé: Abbia, 1965.

———. Peuples et royaumes du Fombina [Peoples and Kingdoms of Fombina]. Tokyo: Institute for the Study of Languages and Cultures of Asia and Africa, 1983.

Mohammadou, Eldridge, and Alhaji Hamadjoda Abdoullaye. *Ray ou Rey Bouba: Traditions historiques des Foulbé de l'Adamawa* [Ray or Rey Bouba: Historical Traditions of the Fulani of Adamawa]. Garoua: Musée Dynamique du Nord-Cameroun, ONAREST, and Paris: Editions du Centre National de la Recherche Scientifique, 1979.

Ngoh, Victor Julius. *Cameroon 1884–1985: A Hundred Years of History*. Yaoundé: Navi, 1987.

Njeuma, Martin Z. "Adamawa and Mahdism: The Career of Hayatu Ibn Sa'id in Adamawa, 1878–1898." *Journal of African History* 12, no. 1 (1971): 61–77.

———. *Fulani Hegemony in Yola (Old Adamawa), 1809–1902*. Yaoundé: Author, 1978.

———. ed. *Introduction to the History of Cameroon in the Nineteenth and Twentieth Centuries*. London: Macmillan, 1989.

Njoya, Aboubakar Njiasse. "Slavery in the Bamum Kingdom in the 19th and 20th Centuries." *Paideuma* 41 (1995): 227–37.

Nkwi, Paul Nchoji. "Slavery and Slave Trade in the Kom Country." *Paideuma* 41 (1995): 239–49.

———. *Traditional Diplomacy: A Study of Inter-Chiefdom Relations in the Western Grassfields, North West Province of Cameroon*. Yaoundé: Department of Sociology, University of Yaoundé, 1987.

Nyamndi, Ndifontah B., and Jean-Pierre Warnier. *Elements for a History of the Western Grassfields.* Yaoundé: University of Yaoundé, 1982.

Schultze, A. *The Sultanate of Bornu.* 1910. Reprint, London: Cass, 1968.

Shimada, Yoshihito. "Formation de la civilisation 'complexe' islam et vêtements en Afrique sub-saharienne: Etude de cas de l'Adamawa [Formation of the 'Complex' Islamic Civilization and Clothing in Sub-Saharan Africa: Study of the Case of Adamawa]." *Senri Ethnological Studies* 31 (1992): 373–422.

Tardits, Claude. "Le royaume Bamum: Un Etat africain traditionnel qui a traversé toute l'histoire [The Bamoum Kingdom: A Traditional African State Which Has Crossed All History]." *Mondes et cultures* 52, nos. 2/4 (1992): 671–94.

VerEecke, Catherine. "The Slave Experience in Adamawa: Past and Present Perspectives from Yola (Nigeria)." *Cahiers d'études africaines* 34, nos. 133/135 (1994): 23–53.

Victoria Centenary Committee. *Victoria, Southern Cameroons, 1858–1958.* Victoria: Basel Mission Book Depot, 1958.

Vincent, Jeanne-Françoise. "Données nouvelles sur la fondation et le peuplement de la chefferie de Marva (Nord-Cameroun) [New Facts on the Foundation and the Peopling of the Chiefdom of Marva (North Cameroon]." *Senri Ethnological Studies* 31 (1992): 481–501.

Warnier, Jean-Pierre. "Histoire du peuplement et genèse des paysages dans l'ouest Camerounais [History of the Population and Genesis of the Countrysides in West Cameroon]." *Journal of African History* 25, no. 4 (1984): 395–410.

——. *Echanges, développement et hiérarchies dans le Bamenda pré-colonial (Cameroun)* [Trade, Progress and Hierarchies in Precolonial Bamenda]. Wiesbaden: Sleinr, 1985.

——. "Traite sans raids au Cameroun [Trade without Raids in Cameroon]." *Cahiers d'études africaines* 29, no. 113 (1989): 5–32.

Colonial

General

Aymerich, J. G. *La Conquête du Cameroun* [The Conquest of Cameroon]. Paris: Payot, 1933.

Beer, George Louis. *African Questions at the Paris Peace Conference.* New York: Macmillan, 1923; London: Dawsons of Pall Mall, 1968.

Chiabi, Emmanuel. *The Making of Modern Cameroon: A History of Substate Nationalism and Disparate Union, 1914–1961.* Lanham, Md.: University Press of America, 1997.

DeLancey, Mark W. "Plantation and Migration in the Mt. Cameroon Region." In *Kamerun,* ed. Hans F. Illy. Mainz: Hase & Koehler, 1974.

——. "Health and Disease on the Plantations of Cameroon, 1884–1939." In *Disease in African History,* ed. Gerald W. Hartwig and K. David Patterson. Durham, N.C.: Duke University Press, 1978.

Diduk, Susan. "European Alcohol, History, and the State in Cameroon." *African Studies Review* 36, no. 1 (1993): 1–42.

Elango, Lovett Z. "The Anglo-French 'Condominium' in Cameroon, 1914–1916: The Myth and the Reality. *International Journal of African Historical Studies* 18, no. 4 (1985): 657–73.

Geschiere, Peter. "Chiefs and Colonial Rule in Cameroon: Inventing Chieftaincy, French and British Style." *Africa, Journal of the International African Institute* 63, no. 2 (1993): 151–75.

Houtkamp, John A. *Tropical Africa's Emergence as a Banana Supplier in the Inter-War Period*. Aldershot, England: Avebury for the African Studies Centre, Leiden, 1996.

Jaja, S. O., E. O. Erim, and B. W. Andah. *History and Culture of the Upper Cross River*. Enugu: Harris, 1990.

Konde, Emmanuel. *The Bassa of Cameroon: An Indigenous Africa Democracy Confronts European Colonialism*. Douala: MAPE, 1997.

Laburthe-Tolra, Philippe. "'Christianisme et ouverture au monde': Le Cas du Cameroun 1845–1915 [Christianity and Opening to the World: The Case of Cameroon 1945–1915]." *Revue française d'histoire d'outre-mer* 75, no. 279 (1988): 207–21.

———. "Inventions missionnaires et perception africaine: Quelques données Camerounaises [Missionary Inventions and African Perception: Some Cameroonian Facts]." *Civilisations* 41, nos. 1/2 (1993): 239–55.

LeVine, Victor T. *The Cameroons from Mandate to Independence*. Berkeley: University of California Press, 1964.

Logan, Rayford W. *The African Mandates in World Politics.* Washington, D.C.: Public Affairs Press, 1948.

Mbembe, Achille. "Domaines de la nuit et autorité onirique dans les maquis du Sud-Cameroun (1955–1958) [Domains of the night and Dream-like Authority in the Maquis of South Cameroon." *Journal of African History* 32, no. 1 (1991): 89–121.

Ngoh, Victor J. "Anglo-French Rivalry over the Misselele Plantations, 1916–1920: A Case Study in the Economic Motives for the Partition of Africa." *Journal of Third World Studies* 12, no. 2 (1995): 273–99.

Niba, Mathias L. "Bafut under Colonial Administration 1900–1949." *Paideuma* 41 (1995): 63–72.

Nijie, Peter Kalle. "Self-portrait of a Cameroonian: Maxwell Gabana Fohtung." *Paideuma* 38 (1992): 219–48.

Njeuma, Martin Z. "Reunification and Political Opportunism in the Making of Cameroon's Independence." *Paideuma* 41 (1995): 27–37.

Nkwi, Paul Nchoji. *The German Presence in the Western Grassfields 1891–1913: A German Colonial Account*. Leiden, Netherlands: African Studies Centre, 1989.

Takougang, Joseph. "Chief Johannes Manga Williams and the Making of a 'Native' Colonial Autocrat among the Bakweri of the Southern Cameroons." *Transafrican Journal of History* 23 (1994): 9–31.

Tardits, Claude. "Le Roi N'joya: L'Image allemande et l'image française d'un souverain africain [King Njoya: The German Image and the French Image of an African Sovereign]." *Paideuma* 36 (1990): 303–17.

German Rule

Austen, Ralph A. "Duala versus German in Cameroon: Economic Dimensions of a Political Conflict," *Revue française d'outre-mer* 64, no. 237 (1977): 477–97.

Bouba, A. "'Lauter breite Negergesichter': Die Darstellung der ausseren Erscheinung einiger Ethnien aus Deutsch-Nordkamerun in der Vorkolonial- und Kolonialzeit [Loud, Bright History of the Black Man: The Account of the External Appearance of an Ethnicity in German North Cameroon in the Pre-Colonial and Colonial Eras]." *Paideuma* 42 (1996): 63–84.

Dah, Jonas N. *Missionary Motivations and Methods: A Critical Examination of the Basel Mission in Cameroon, 1886–1914.* Basel: University of Basel, 1983.

France. *La conquête du Cameroun et du Togo* [The Conquest of Cameroon and Togo]. Paris: Imprimerie Nationale, 1931.

Gann, L. H., and Peter Duignan. *The Rulers of German Africa, 1884–1914.* Stanford, Calif.: Stanford University Press, 1977.

Halldén, Erik. *The Culture Policy of the Basel Mission in the Cameroons, 1886–1905*. Lund, Sweden: University of Uppsala, 1968.

Hausen, Karin. *Deutsche Kolonialherrschaft in Afrika: Wirtschaftsinteresse und Kolonialverwaltung in Kamerun vor 1914* [German Colonial Rule in Africa: Business Interests and Colonial Management in Cameroon before 1914]. Freiburg: Atlantis, 1970.

Louis, William Roger. *Great Britain and Germany's Lost Colonies, 1914–1919.* Oxford: Clarendon, 1967.

Mohammoudou, Eldridge. "Le Soulèvement mahdiste de Goni Waday dans la Haute-Bénoué (Juillet 1907) [The Mahdi Uprising of Goni Waday in the High Benue (July 1907)]." *Senri Ethnological Studies* 31 (1992): 423–64.

Moberly, F. J. *Military Operations: Togoland and the Cameroons, 1914–1916.* London: His Majesty's Stationery Office, 1931.

Njeuma, Martin Z. "The Usmanuya System, Radicalism and the Establishment of German Colonial Rule in Northern Cameroon, 1890–1907." *Paideuma* 40 (1994): 111–28.

Rudin, Harry R. *Germans in the Cameroons, 1884–1914: A Case Study in Modern Imperialism*. New Haven, Conn.: Yale University Press, 1938.

Stoecker, Helmuth. *German Imperialism in Africa*. Trans. B. Zollner. London: Hurst, 1986.

French Rule

Abwa, D. *André-Marie Mbida, Premier ministre camerounais (1917–1980)* [André-Marie Mbida, Cameroonian Prime Minister (1917–1980)]. Paris: Harmattan, 1993.

Amaazee, Victor Bong. "The Role of the French Cameroonians in the Unification of Cameroon, 1916–1961." *Transafrican Journal of History* 23 (1994): 195–234.

Beull, Raymond Leslie. *The Native Problem in Africa*. Cambridge, Mass.: Bureau of International Research, Harvard University and Radcliffe College, 1928; London: Cass, 1965.

Boutrais, J., et al. *Nord du Cameroun: Des Hommes, une region* [North of Cameroon: Some Men, One Region]. Paris: ORSTOM, 1984.

Chauleur, Pierre. *L'Oeuvre de la France au Cameroun* [The Work of France in Cameroon]. Yaoundé: Imprimerie du Gouvernement, 1936.

Chazelas, Victor. *Territoires africains sous mandat de la France: Cameroun et Togo* [African Territories under French Mandate: Cameroon and Togo]. Paris: Société d'Editions, 1931.

Cohen, William B. *Rulers of Empire: The French Colonial Service in Africa.* Stanford, Calif.: Hoover Institution Press, Stanford University, 1971.

Costedoat, René. *L'Effort français au Cameroun: Le Mandat français et la réorganisation des territoires du Cameroun*. [The French Effort in Cameroon: The French Mandate and the Reorganization of the Territories of Cameroon]. Besançon, France: Imprimerie Jacques et Demontrond, 1930.

Debusmann, Robert. "Santé et colonisation: Epidémiologie et démographie en AEF et au Cameroun [Health and Colonization: Epidemiology and Demography in AEF and in Cameroon]." In *Echanges franco-allemands sur l'Afrique: Lettres et sciences humaines*, ed. James Reisez and Hélène d'Almeida-Topor. Bayreuth, Germany: Bayreuth University, 1994.

Delavignette, Robert. *Freedom and Authority in French West Africa*. London: Cass, 1968.

Eyinga, Abel. *Démocratie de Yaoundé T 1: Syndicalisme d'abord, 1944–1946.* [Democracy of Yaoundé T 1: Unionism First, 1944–1946]. Paris: Harmattan, 1985.

——. *L'UPC: Une Révolution manquée?* [The UPC: A Lost Revolution?] Paris: Chada, 1991.

France. *Rapport annuel du gouvernement français aux nations unies sur l'administration du Cameroun placé sous la tutelle de la France* [Annual Report of the French Government to the United Nations on the Administration of Cameroon Placed under the Tutelage of France]. Paris: Imprimerie Nationale, annual.

Gardinier, David E. *Cameroon: United Nations Challenge to French Policy*. London: Oxford University Press, 1963.

Geschiere, Peter. "Working Groups or Wage Labour? Cash-Crops, Reciprocity and Money among the Maka of Southeastern Cameroon." *Development and Change* 26, no. 3 (1995): 503–23.

Guyer, Jane I. "Feeding Yaoundé, Capital of Cameroon." In *Feeding African Cities: Studies in Regional Social History,* ed. Jane I. Guyer. Manchester, England: Manchester University Press, 1987.

Joseph, Richard A. *Radical Nationalism in Cameroun: Social Origins of the U.P.C. Rebellion*. Oxford: Oxford University Press, 1977.

Lapeysonnie. *Moi, Jamot: Le vainqueur de la Maladie du Sommeil* [I, Jamot. The Conqueror of Sleeping Sickness]. Plaisir, France: INAM, 1987.

Leon, Kaptue. "De la clandestinité à la légalité: Protosyndicats et syndicalisme institutionnel au Cameroun de 1919 à 1944 [From Clandestine to Legality: Proto-Unions and Institutional Unions in Cameroon from 1919 to 1944]." *Afrika Zamani*, n.s., no. 3 (1995): 27–53.

Mbapndah, Ndobegang M. "French Colonial Agricultural Policy, African Chiefs, and Coffee Growing in the Cameroon Grassfields, 1920–1960." *International Journal of African Historical Studies* 27, no. 1 (1994): 41–58.

Mbembe, J. Achille. *Ruben Um Nyobe: Le Problème national kamerunais* [Ruben Um Nyobe: The Kamerun National Problem]. Paris: Harmattan, 1984.

——. *La Naissance du maquis dans le Sud-Cameroun, 1920–1960: Histoire des usages de la raison en colonie* [The Birth of the Maquis in South Cameroon, 1920–1960: History of the Use of Reason in the Colony]. Paris: Karthala, 1996.

Moumé-Etia, Léopold. *Cameroun: Les Années ardentes aux origines de la vie syndicale et politique* [Cameroon: The Fervent Years of the Origins of Union and Political Life]. Paris: Japress, 1991.

Ngongo, Louis. *Histoire des forces religieuses au Cameroun: De la première guerre mondiale à l'indépendance (1916–1955)* [History of Religious Forces in Cameroon: From the First World War to Independence (1916–1955)]. Paris: Karthala, 1982.

Oyono, D. *Colonie ou mandat international? La politique française au Cameroun de 1919 à 1946* [Colony or International Mandate? French Politics in Cameroon from 1919 to 1946]. Paris: Harmattan, 1992.

Shimada, Yoshihito. "Dynamique politique des états traditionnels sous l'indirect rule: Du pouvoir à l'autorité; étude de cas du Lamidat de Rey-Bouba [Political Dynamic of Traditional States under Indirect Rule: From Power to Authority: A Study of the Case of the Lamido of Rey-Bouba]." *Senri Ethnological Studies* 15 (1984): 289–359.

Takougang, J. "The Union des Populations du Cameroun and its Southern Cameroons Connection." *Revue française d'histoire d'outre-mer* 83, no. 310 (1996): 7–24.

Tientcheu, Abraham Ngueukam. "Ruben Um Nyobé: Le Héros national camerounais [Ruben Um Nyobe: The Cameroonian National Hero]." *Afrique 2000* 5 (1991): 75–87.

Wilbois, J. *Le Cameroun: Les Indignes, les colons, les missions, l'administration française* [Cameroon: The Natives, the Colonials, the Missions, the French Administration]. Paris: Payot, 1934.

British Rule

Amaazee, Victor Bong. "The 'Igbo Scare' in the British Cameroons, c. 1945–61." *Journal of African History* 31, no. 2 (1990): 281–93.

——. "The British versus Pro-Germanism in the British Southern Cameroons 1916–1922." *Transafrican Journal of History* 22 (1993): 5–73.

Booth, Bernard F. *The Mill Hill Fathers in the West Cameroon: Education, Health and Development, 1884–1970.* Bethesda, Md.: International Scholars Publications, 1996.

Chiabi, E. Mucho. "The Nigerian-Cameroonian Connection." *Journal of African Studies* 13, no. 2 (1986): 59–68.

Chilver, Elizabeth. "Native Administration in the West Central Cameroons 1902–1954." In *Essays in Imperial Government*, ed. Kenneth Robinson and Frederick Madden. Oxford: Blackwell, 1963.

Ebune, Joseph B. *The Growth of Political Parties in Southern Cameroon 1916–1960*. Yaoundé: CEPER, 1992.

Epale, Simon Joseph. *Plantations and Development in Western Cameroon, 1885–1975: A Study in Agrarian Capitalism*. New York: Vantage, 1985.

Gaillard, P. *Ahmadou Ahidjo: Patriote et despote, bâtisseur de l'état camerounais* [Ahmadou Ahidjo: Patriot and Despot, Builder of the Cameroon State]. Paris: JA Livres, 1994.

Goodridge, Richard A. "The Issue of Slavery in the Establishment of British Rule in the Northern Cameroun to 1927." *African Economic History* 22 (1994): 19–36.

———. "'In the Most Effective Manner?': Britain and the Disposal of the Cameroons Plantations, 1914–1924." *International Journal of African Historical Studies* 29, no. 2 (1996): 251–77.

Jua, Nantang. "Indirect Rule in Colonial and Post-Colonial Cameroon." *Paideuma* 41 (1995): 39–47.

Kale, P. M. *Political Evolution in the Cameroons.* Buea: Author, 1967.

Marc, Alexandre. *La politique économique de l'état britannique dans la région du Sud-Cameroun, 1920–1960* [The Economic Policy of the British State in the Southern Cameroon Region, 1920–1960]. Paris: Université de Paris, Institut d' Etudes Politiques, 1985.

Ngoh, Victor Julius. *Constitutional Developments in Southern Cameroons 1946–1961.* Yaoundé: CEPER, 1990.

Njeuma, Martin Z., and Nicodemus F. Awason. "The Fulani and the Political Economy of the Bamenda Grasslands, 1940–1960." *Paideuma* 36 (1990): 217–333.

O'Neill, R. J. "Authority, Witchcraft and Change in Old Moghamo (Cameroon): Suppression of the Sasswood Ordeal 1924–1925 and Its Consequences." *Anthropos* 86, nos. 1–3 (1991): 34–52.

Smith, Bryan Sharwood. *Recollections of British Administration in the Cameroons and Northern Nigeria 1921–1957: But Always as Friends."* Durham, N.C.: Duke University Press, 1969.

Takougang, Joseph. "The 'Union des Populations du Cameroun' and Its Southern Cameroons Connection." *Revue française d'histoire d'outre-mer* 83, no. 310 (1996): 7–24.

United Kingdom, Colonial Office. *Cameroons under United Kingdom Administration: Report for the Year*. London: H.M.S.O. Author, annual 1916–1960. (Annual, title varies.)

Yearwood, Peter J. "'In a Casual Way with a Blue Pencil': British Policy and the Partition of Kamerun, 1914–1919." *Canadian Journal of African Studies* 27, no. 2 (1993): 218–44.

Postindependence

Amin, Julius A. *The Peace Corps in Cameroon*. Kent, Ohio: Kent State University Press, 1992.

Chem-Langhëë, Bongfen. "The Road to the Unitary State of Cameroon 1959–1972." *Paideuma* 41 (1995): 17–25.

Guyer, Jane I. *Family and Farm in Southern Cameroon.* Boston: Boston University, African Studies Center, 1984.

Konings, Piet. "Chieftaincy, Labour Control and Capitalist Development in Cameroon." *Journal of Legal Pluralism and Unofficial Law* 37/38 (1996): 329–46.

Kuoh, Christian-Tobie. *Mon témoignage: Le Cameroun de l'indépendance (1958–1970)* [My Testimony: Cameroon from Independence (1958–1970)]. Paris: Karthala, 1990.

Zang-Atangana, Joseph-Marie. *Les forces politiques au Cameroun réunifié* [Political Forces in Reunified Cameroon]. 3 vols. Paris: L'Harmattan, 1989.

POLITICS

Domestic

Abada, Marcelin Nguele. "Ruptures et continuités constitutionnelles en République du Cameroun: Réflexions à propos de la réforme constitutionnelle du 18 janvier [Ruptures and Constitutional Continuities in the Republic of Cameroon: Reflections with Respect to the Constitutional Reform of January 18, 1996]." *Revue juridique et politique* 50, no. 3 (1996): 272–93.

Ahidjo, Ahmadou. *Contribution to National Construction*. Paris: Présence Africaine, 1964.

All Anglophone Conference. *The Buea Declaration*. Limbe, Cameroon: Nooremaac, 1993.

Azarya, Victor. *Aristocrats Facing Change: The Fulbe in Guinea, Nigeria, and Cameroon*. Chicago: University of Chicago Press, 1978.

Azevedo, Mario J. "Ethnicity and Democratization: Cameroon and Gabon." In *Ethnic Conflict and Democratization in Africa*, ed. Harvey Glickman. Atlanta: African Studies Association Press, 1995.

Banock, M. *Le Processus de démocratisation en Afrique: Le Cas camerounais* [The Process of Democratization in Africa: The Cameroonian Case]. Paris: Harmattan, 1992.

Bayart, Jean-François. "Cameroon." In *Contemporary West African States*, ed. D. B. C. O'Brien et al. Cambridge: Cambridge University Press, 1989.

———. *L'Etat au Cameroun* [The State in Cameroon]. Paris: Presses de la Foundation Nationale des Sciences Politiques, 1979.

Benjamin, Jacques. *Les Camerounais occidentaux: La Minorité dans un état bicommunautaire* [West Cameroonians: A Minority in a Bicameral State]. Montreal: Presses de l'Université de Montréal, 1972.

Béti, Mongo. *Lettre ouverte aux Camerounais: Ou la deuxième mort de Ruben Um Nyobé* [An Open Letter to Cameroonians: Or the Second Death of Ruben Um Nyobe]. Paris: Editions des Peuples Noirs, 1986.

——. *Main basse sur le Cameroun: autopsie d'une décolonisation* [Looting in Cameroon: The Autopsy of Decolonization]. Montreal: Editions Québécoises, 1974; Paris: Maspero, 1977.

Bigombe Logo, Patrice, and Hélène-Laure Menthong. "Crise de légitimité et évidence de la continuité politique [Crisis of Legitimacy and Evidence of Political Continuity]." *Politique africaine* 62 (1996): 15–23.

Biya, Paul. *Communal Liberalism*. London: Macmillan, 1987.

Bopda, Athanase. "Genèse, mutation et problèmes de la chefferie 'traditionelle' à Yaoundé (Cameroun) [Genesis, Change and Problems of the 'Traditional' Chiefdom in Yaoundé (Cameroon)]." In *Pouvoirs et cités d'Afrique noire: Décentralisations en questions*, ed. Sylvy Jaglin and Alain Dubresson. Paris: Karthala, 1993.

Burnham, Philip. "L'Ethnie, la religion et l'état: Le Rôle des Peuls dans la vie politique et sociale du Nord-Cameroun [Ethnicity, Religion and the State: The Role of Fulani in the Political and Social Life of North Cameroon]." *Journal des africanistes* 61, fasc. 1 (1991): 73–102.

——. *The Politics of Cultural Difference in Northern Cameroon*. Edinburgh: Edinburgh University Press, 1996.

Cameroon National Union. *The Political Philosophy of Ahmadou Ahidjo.* Monte Carlo: Bory, 1968.

Le Cameroun éclaté? Une anthologie commentée des revendications ethniques [Splintered Cameroon: An Annotated Anthology of Ethnic Claims]. Yaoundé: Editions C3, 1992.

"Le Cameroun ou les occasions perdues [Cameroon or Lost Opportunities]." *Géopolitique africaine* (nouv. sér.) 12, no. 1 (1989): 127–45.

Champaud, J. "Cameroun: Au bord de l'affrontement [Cameroon: At the Brink of Confrontation]." *Politique africaine* 44 (1991): 115–20.

Collectif "Changer le Cameroun." *Changer le Cameroun: Pourquoi pas?* [To Change Cameroon: Why Not?]. Yaoundé: Sopecam, 1990.

——. *Le 11 Octobre 1992: Autopsie d'une élection présidentielle controversée* [October 11, 1992: Autopsy of a Controversial Presidential Election]. Yaoundé: Editions C3, 1993.

Courade, G. "Les Planteurs camerounais: Ont-ils été réévalués? [The Cameroon Planters: Have They Been Reevaluated?]" *Politique africaine* 54 (1994): 74–87.

Davis, Lucy. "Opening Political Space in Cameroon: The Ambiguous Response of the Mbororo." *Review of African Political Economy* 22, no. 64 (1995): 213–28.

Delancey, Mark W. "Ahmadou Ahidjo." In *Political Leaders of Contemporary Africa*. ed. Harvey Glickman. Westport, Conn.: Greenwood, 1992.

——. "The Construction of the Cameroon Political System: The Ahidjo Years, 1958-1982." *Journal of Contemporary African Studies* 6 (1987): 3–24.

——. "United Republic of Cameroon." In *World Encyclopedia of Political Systems and Parties*. Vol. 1., ed. G. Delury. New York: Facts on File, 1983.

Delavignette, Robert. *Freedom and Authority in French West Africa.* London: Cass, 1968.

Derrick, Jonathan. "Cameroon: One Party, Many Parties and the State." *Africa Insight* 22, no. 3 (1992): 165–77.

Dinka, Gorji. "Pour un nouveau contrat social [For a New Social Contract]." *Peuples noirs-peuples africaines* 9, no. 50 (1986): 50–65.

Donfack, Lekene. "Le renouveau de la question fédérale au Cameroun [The Renewal of the Federal Question in Cameroon]."*Penant* 108, no. 826 (1998): 30–61.

Eloundou-Enyegue, P. M. *Solidarité dans la crise ou crise de solidarités familiales au Cameroun* [Solidarity in the Crisis or Crisis of Family Solidarity in Cameroon]. Paris: CEPED, 1992.

Emagna, Maximin. "Les Intellectuels camerounais sous le regime Ahidjo [Cameroonian Intellectuals under the Ahidjo Regime]." *Afrika Focus* 12, no. 1/3 (1996): 51–83.

Englebert, Pierre. "Cameroon: Background to a Crisis." *CSIS Africa Notes* 130 (November 1991): 1–8.

Epale, Simon Joseph. *The Economic and Social Council of the Republic of Cameroon: Antecedents, Precedents, Evolution.* Yaoundé: SOPECAM, 1991.

Eyinga, Abel. *Cameroun 1960–1989, la fin des élections: Un Cas d'évolution régressive de la démocratie* [Cameroon 1960–1989, The End of the Elections: A Case of Regressive Evolution of Democracy]. Paris: Harmattan, 1990.

Eyoh, Dickson. "Conflicting Narratives of Anglophone Protest and the Politics of Identity in Cameroon." *Journal of Contemporary African Studies* 16, no. 2 (1998): 249–76.

——. "Through the Prism of a Local Tragedy: Political Liberation, Regionalism and Elite Struggles for Power in Cameroon." *Africa, Journal of the International African Institute* 68, no. 3 (1998) 338–59.

Finken, M. *Communes et gestion municipale au Cameroun* [Communities and Municipal Management in Cameroon]. Yaoundé: Presses du Groupe Saint-François, 1996.

Fogui, Jean-Pierre. *L'Intégration politique au Cameroun: Une Analyse centre-périphérie* [Political Integration in Cameroon: A Center-Periphery Analysis]. Paris: Libraire Générale de Droit et de Jurisprudence, 1990.

——. *Plaidoyer pour l'unité* [Plea for the Defense of Unity]. Yaoundé: Editions de la Renaissance, 1994.

Fonchingong, Tangie Nsoh. "Multipartyism and Democratization in Cameroon." *Journal of Third World Studies* 15, no. 2 (Fall 1998): 119–36.

Fonge, Fuabeh Paul. *Modernization without Development in Africa: Patterns of Change and Continuity in Post-Independence Cameroonian Public Service*. Trenton, N.J.: Africa World Press, 1997.

Fonyuy Fisiy, Cyprian. "Chieftaincy in the Modern State: An Institution at the Crossroads of Democratic Change." *Paideuma* 41 (1995): 49–62.

Fonyuy Fisiy, Cyprian, and Peter Geschiere. "Judges and Witches, Or How Is the State to Deal with Witchcraft?: Examples from Southeast Cameroon." *Cahiers d'études africaines* 30, no. 118 (1990): 135–56.

Fotsing, Jean-Baptiste. "Le pouvoir fiscal local en Afrique: La Résistance du système traditionnel au système moderne: Cas de l'Ouest-Cameroun [Local Fiscal Power in Africa: Resistance of the Traditional System to the Modern System: The Case of West Cameroon]." *Penant* 100, no. 802 (1990): 73–116.

Frenay, Patrick. "Le Cameroun anglophone dans le procéssus d'intégration nationale: Les Conséquences de la marginalisation d'une région sur le développement des villes [Anglophone Cameroon in the Process of National Integration: The Consequences of Marginalization of a Region on the Development of Towns]." *Cahier d'outre-mer* 40, no. 159 (1987): 217–36.

Gaillard, P. "Pluralisme et régionalisme dans la politique camerounaise [Pluralism and Regionalism in Cameroonian Politics]." *Afrique 2000* 11 (1992): 97–109.

Geschiere, Peter. "Sorcellerie et politique: Les Pièges du rapport élite-village [Sorcery and Politics: The Snares of Elite-Village Communication." *Politique africaine* 63 (1996): 82–96.

——. *Village Communities and the State: Changing Relations among the Maka of Southeastern Cameroon since the Colonial Conquest.* Trans. James J. Ravell. London: Kegan Paul 1982.

Geschiere, Peter, and Cyprian Fonyug Fisiy. *Sorcellerie et politique en Afrique: La Viande des autres* [Sorcery and Politics in Africa: The Meat of Others]. Paris: Karthala, 1995.

Gros, J. G. "The Hard Lessons of Cameroon." *Journal of Democracy* 6, no. 3 (1995): 22–127.

Higgens, K. *The Politics of Sorcery in Southern Cameroon Contemporary Ambiguities.* Dallas, Tex.: International Museum of Cultures, 1992.

Hond, Jean Tobie. "Étude de science administrative de la mutation des services publics en Afrique subsaharienne francophone: L'Expérience du Cameroun [Study of the Administrative Science of Change in Public Services in Francophone Sub-Saharan Africa: The Experience of Cameroon]." *Cahiers africains d'administration publique* 45 (1995): 71–184.

Johnson, Willard R. *The Cameroon Federation: Political Integration in a Fragmentary Society*. Princeton, N.J.: Princeton University Press, 1970.

Joseph, Richard, ed. *Gaullist Africa: Cameroon under Ahmadou Ahidjo.* Enugu, Nigeria: Fourth Dimension, 1978.

Jua, N. "Cameroon: Jump-starting an Economic Crisis." *Africa Insight* 21, no. 3 (1991): 162–71.

Kamto, Maurice. "La participation des étrangers à l'Administration publique camerounais (L'Idée d'un tiers-droit de la Fonction publique) [The Participation of Foreigners in the Cameroonian Public Administration (The Idea of a Third Right of Public Service)]." *Penant* 99, no. 801 (1989): 403–32.

——. "Quelques réflexions sur la transition vers le pluralisme politique au Cameroun [Some Reflections on the Transition toward Political Pluralism in Cameroon]." In *L'Afrique en transition,* ed. G. Conac. Paris: Economica, 1993.

Konings, Piet. "L'Etat, l'agro-industrie et la paysannerie au Cameroun [The State, Agro-Industry and the Peasantry in Cameroon]." *Politique africaine* 22 (1986): 120–37.

———. "Privatization of Agro-Industrial Parastatals and Anglophone Opposition in Cameroon." *Journal of Commonwealth and Comparative Politics* 34, no. 3 (1996): 199–217.

———. "The Anglophone Problem in Cameroon." *Journal of Modern African Studies* 35, no. 2 (1997): 207–29.

———. "Unilever, Contract Farmers and Co-operatives in Cameroon: Crisis and Response." *Journal of Peasant Studies* 26 (1999): 112–38.

Krieger, Milton. "Cameroon's Democratic Crossroads, 1990–94." *Journal of Modern African Studies* 32, no. 4 (1994): 605–28.

Kuoh, C. T. *Le Cameroun de l'après-Ahidjo* [Cameroon after Ahidjo]. Paris: Karthala, 1992.

———. *Une fresque du régime Ahidjo* [A Fresco of the Ahidjo Regime]. Paris: Karthala, 1991.

LeVine, Victor T. *The Cameroon Federal Republic*. Ithaca, N.Y.: Cornell University Press, 1971.

Lyonga, N., ed. *Socrates in Cameroon: The Life and Works of Bernard Nsokika Fonlon.* Yaoundé: University of Yaoundé, 1989.

Mama, T., et al. *Crise économique et politique de dérèglementation au Cameroun* [Economic and Political Crisis of Deregulation in Cameroon]. Paris: Harmattan, 1996.

Mané, Ibrahima, et al. "Violences ethniques [Ethnic Violence]." *Démocraties africaines* 4, no. 12 (1997): 21–48.

Mawhood, Philip. "Applying the French Model in Cameroon." In *Local Government in the Third World*, ed. P. Mawhood. Pretoria: Africa Institute, 1993.

Mbembe, J.-A. "Pouvoir des morts et langue des vivants: Les Errances de la mémoire nationaliste au Cameroun [Power of the Dead and Language of the Living: The Wanderings of the National Memory in Cameroon]." *Politique africaine* 22 (1986): 3–37.

———. "Power and Obscenity in the Post-Colonial Period: The Case of Cameroon." In *Rethinking Third World Politics,* ed. J. Manor. Harlow: Longman, 1991.

———. "Provisional Notes on the Postcolony." *Africa* 62, no. 1 (1992): 3–37.

———. "Le spectre et l'état: Des dimensions politiques de l'imaginaire historique dans le Cameroun postcolonial [The Ghost and the State: Some Political Dimensions of the Historical Imagination in Post-Colonial Cameroon]." *Revue de la Bibliothèque Nationale* 34 (1989): 2–13.

Mbondjo, P. M. "Le Retour au multipartisme au Cameroun [The Return to Multipartyism in Cameroon]." In *L'Afrique en transition*, ed. G. Conac. Paris: Economica, 1993.

Mbuyinga, E. *Tribalisme et problème national en Afrique: Le Cas du Cameroun* [Tribalism and the National Problem in Africa: The Case of Cameroon]. Paris: Harmattan, 1989.

Menthong, Hélène-Laure. "La question locale dans le débat constitutionnel au Cameroun: Chassé-Croisé entre unité et pluralisme [The Local Question in the

Constitutional Debate in Cameroon: The Dance between Unity and Pluralism].” *Africa Development* 23, no. 1 (1998): 5–40.

———. “Vote et communautarisme au Cameroun: ‘Un vote de coeurs, de sang et de raison’ [Vote and Communitarianism in Cameroon: ‘A Vote of the Heart, of Blood and of Reason’].” *Politique africaine* 69 (1998): 40–52.

Miaffo, D., ed. *Chefferie traditionelle et démocratie: Réflexion sur le destin du chef en régime pluraliste* [Traditional Chiefdom and Democracy: Reflection on the Destiny of the Chief in a Pluralist Regime]. Yaoundé: LAAKAM, 1993.

Momo, B. “L’Evaluation des emplois et des performances dans la fonction publique camerounaise [The Evaluation of Employees and of Performances in the Cameroonian Public Service].” *Cahiers africains d’administration publique* 42 (1994): 93–108.

Monga, Celestin. *The Anthropology of Anger: Civil Society and Democracy in Africa.* Boulder, Colo.: Rienner, 1996.

Monono, C. E. *The Throne and the Torch: The Political Philosophy of Bernard Fonlon*. Yaoundé: Sopecam, 1991.

Mouiche, Ibrahim. “Ethnicité et pouvoir au Nord-Cameroun [Ethnicity and Power in North Cameroon].” *Verfassung und Recht in Ubersee* 30, no. 2 (1997): 182–216.

Moukoko-Priso. *Cameroun/Kamerun: La Transition dans l’impasse* [Cameroon: The Transition in the Impasse]. Paris: Harmattan, 1994.

Mukong, Albert, ed. *The Case for the Southern Cameroons.* n.p.: Camfeco, 1990.

———. *Prisoner without a Crime.* Paris: Nubia, 1990.

———. *Stewardship in the Cameroon Struggle.* Bamenda, Cameroon: Author, 1992.

Muna, Bernard A. *Cameroon and the Challenges of the 21st Century.* Yaoundé: Tama, 1993.

National Democratic Institute for International Affairs. *An Assessment of the October 11, 1992 Election in Cameroon.* Washington, D.C.: Author, 1993.

Ndi Mbarga, V. *Ruptures et continuités au Cameroun* [Ruptures and Continuities in Cameroon]. Paris: Harmattan, 1993.

Ndue, P. N. *Decentralisation and Local Government in Cameroon*. Yaoundé: DIHACO, 1994.

Ngniman, Zacharie. *Cameroun: La Démocratie emballée* [Cameroon: The Arrested Democracy]. Yaoundé: CLE, 1993.

Ngwane, G. *Fragments of Unity (To Every Son and Daughter of the South West).* Limbe: Nooremac, 1992.

Nkainfon Pefura, Samuel. *Le dossier de la fonction preféctorale au Cameroun* [The Record of the Prefectorial Service in Cameroon]. Yaoundé: SOPECAM, 1990.

———. *Le Cameroun, du multipartisme au multipartisme* [Cameroon, From Multipartyism to Multipartyism]. Paris: Harmattan, 1996.

Nkwi, Paul Nchoji. “Cameroon Grassfield Chiefs and Modern Politics.” *Paideuma* 25 (1979): 99–115.

Nkwi, Paul Nchoji, and Francis B. Nyamnjoh, eds. *Regional Balance and National Integration in Cameroon: Lessons Learned and the Uncertain Future.* Leiden, Netherlands: African Studies Centre, 1997.

Nkwi, Paul Nchoji, and Bea Vidacs. "Football, Politics and Power in Cameroon." In *Entering the Field: New Perspectives on World Football*, ed. Gary Armstrong and Richard Giulianotti. New York: Berg, 1997.

O'Brien, D. B. C., et al, eds. *Contemporary West African States.* Cambridge: Cambridge University Press, 1989.

Ododa, Harry. "Voluntary Retirement of Presidents in Africa." *Journal of African Studies* 15, nos. 3/4 (1988): 94–100.

Okala, J. T. *La Décennie Biya au Cameroun: De la grace à la disgrace* [The Biya Decade in Cameroon: From Grace to Disgrace]. Paris: Harmattan, 1996.

Olinga, Alain Didier. "Cameroun: Vers un présidentialisme démocratique: Réflections sur la révision constitutionelle du 23 avril 1991 [Cameroon: Toward a Democratic Presidency: Reflections on the Constitutional Revision of April 23, 1991]." *Revue juridique et politique* 46, no. 4 (1992): 419–29.

Owona Nguini, M. E. "Cameroun: La Controverse Bikutsi–Makossa—musique, politique et affinités régionales (1990–1994) [Cameroon: The Bikutsi–Makossa Controversy—Music, Politics and Regional Affinities]." *Afrique politique* (1995) 267–76.

Pondi, Paul. *La police au Cameroun: Naissance et évolution* [The Police in Cameroon: Birth and Evolution]. Yaoundé: CLE, 1988.

Rowlands, Michael, and J.-P. Warnier. "Sorcery, Power and the Modern State in Cameroon." *Man* 23, no. 1 (1988): 118–32.

Schilder, Kees. "La démocratie aux champs: Les Présidentielles d'octobre 1992 au Nord-Cameroun [Democracy in the Fields: The Presidential Elections of October 1992 in North Cameroon]." *Politique africaine* 50 (1993): 115–92.

——. "État et islamisation au Nord-Cameroun (1960–1982) [State and Islamization in North Cameroon (1960–1982)]." *Politique africaine* 41 (1991): 144–48.

——. "Local Rulers in Northern Cameroun: The Interplay of Politics and Conversion." *Afrika focus* 9, nos. 1/2 (1993): 43–72.

Séraphin, Gilles. "L'Interprétation du crash du 'Nyong' comme révélateur des tensions politiques et de l'imaginaire [The Interpretation of the Crash of 'Nyong' as Revealing Political and Imaginary Tensions]." *Politique africaine* 66 (1997): 121–26.

Shanda, Tonme. *Crise du SDF et problème bamiléké: Les Clarifications* [Crisis of the SDF and the Bamiléke Problem: Clarifications]. Yaoundé: Montagnes, 1995.

Sindjoun, Luc. "Caméroun: Le Système politique face aux enjeux de la transition démocratique [Cameroon: The Political System Facing the Stakes of Democratic Transition]." *L'Afrique politique* (1994): 143–65.

——. "La Cour suprême, la compétition électorale et la continuité politique au Cameroun: La Construction de la démocratisation passive [The Supreme Court: The Electoral Competition and Political Continuity in Cameroon: The Construction of Passive Democratization." *Africa Development* 19, no. 2 (1994): 21–69.

——. "Mobilisation politique du pluralisme culturel et crise de l'État-nation au Cameroun [Political Mobilization of Cultural Pluralism and the Crisis of the Nation-State in Cameroon." In *Etat, démocratie, sociétés et culture en Afrique:*

Actes du colloque. Les dimensions sociales et culturelles de la démocratie en Afrique. Dakar: Démocraties Africaines, 1996.

———. *Le Président de la République au Cameroun (1982–1996): Les Acteurs et leur rôle dans le jeu politique* [The President of the Republic of Cameroon (1982–1996): The Actors and Their Role in the Political Game]. Bordeaux: Centre d'Etude d'Afrique Noire, 1996.

———. *Le président de la république à l'épreuve du changement politique au Cameroun: De l'alternance néo-patrimoniale à la transition démocratique* [The President of the Republic in the Test of Political Change in Cameroon: From Neo-patrimonial Alternation to Democratic Transition]. Talence, France: Université de Bordeaux, CEAN, 1996.

Sipa, J. B. *Outrage à la République. Tome I: Une transition manquée* [Insult to the Republic. Vol. I: A Failed Transition]. Douala: SEPEC, 1992.

Sonné, Wang. "Cameroun: Pourquoi les noms des grandes figures historiques des années 1950 sont-ils tabous dans la bouche du président Paul Biya? [Cameroon: Why Are the Names of the Great Historical Figures of the 1950s Taboos in the Mouth of President Paul Biya?]" *Africa Development* 22, no. 2 (1997): 131–49.

Tabetsing, C. *Cameroun: Sursaut ou suicide?* [Cameroon: Start or Suicide?] N.p.: Arthaud, 1991.

Takougang, Joseph. "Cameroon at the Democratic Crossroads: The Struggle for Power and Authority in an African State." *Asian and African Studies* 27, no. 3 (1993): 241–62.

———. "The Demise of Biya's New Deal in Cameroon." *Africa Insight* 23, no. 2 (1993): 91–101.

Takougang, Joseph, and Milton Krieger. *African State and Society in the 1990s: Cameroon's Political Crossroads*. Boulder, Colo.: Westview, 1998.

Tappa, Louise. "The Isolation of the State and the Church in Africa." In *Civil Society, the State and African Development in the 1990s.* Nairobi: All Africa Council of Churches, 1993.

Tchuente, Barthelemy Kom. *Développement communal et gestion urbaine au Cameroun: Les Enjeux de la gestion municipale dans un système décentralisé* [Communal Development and Urban Management in Cameroon: The Stakes of Municipal Management in a Decentralized System]. Yaoundé: CLE, 1996.

Tedga, P. J. M. *Entreprise publiques, état et crise au Cameroun: faillite d'un système* [Public Enterprises, State and Crisis in Cameroon: Bankruptcy of a System]. Paris: Harmattan, 1990.

Tolen, Aaron. *The Electoral Process in Cameroon.* Yaoundé: FEMEC, 1997.

Torimiro, F. B. "Personal Rule and the Search for Political Pluralism in Cameroon." In *Civilian Rule in the Developing World*, ed. C. P. Danapoulos. Boulder, Colo.: Westview, 1992.

Toulabor, Comi M. "Déclaration de Buea [The Buea Declaration]." *Politique africaine* 51 (1993): 139–51.

Walle, Nicolas van de. "Neopatrimonialism and Democracy in Africa, with an Illustration from Cameroon." In *Economic Change and Political Liberalization in Sub-Saharan Africa.* Baltimore, Md.: Johns Hopkins University Press, 1994.

———. "The Politics of Nonreform in Cameroon." In *Hemmed In,* ed. B. Grosh and R. S. Mukandala. New York: Columbia University Press, 1994.

———. "The Politics of Public Enterprise Reform in Cameroon." In *State-Owned Enterprise, in Africa,* ed. B. Grosh and R. Mukandala. Boulder, Colo.: Westview, 1994.

———. "Rice Politics in Cameroon: State Commitment, Capability, and Urban Bias." *Journal of Modern African Studies* 27, no. 4 (1989): 579–99.

Welch, Claude E. *Dream of Unity: Pan-Africanism and Political Unification in West Africa*. Ithaca, N.Y.: Cornell University Press, 1966.

Willame, Jean-Claude. "Cameroun: Les Avatars d'un liberalisme planifié [Cameroon: The Avatars of a Planned Liberalism]." *Politique Africaine* 18 (1985): 44–70.

Wonyu, Emmanuel. "Regards sur le Cameroun de Paul Biya [A Look at the Cameroon of Paul Biya]." *Afrique 2000* 14 (1993): 133–37.

Woungly-Massaga, Ngouo. *O va le Kamerun?* [Where Is Kamerun Going?] Paris: Harmattan, 1984.

Foreign Relations

Ahidjo, Ahmadou. *In Defense of Peace, Justice and Solidarity in International Society*. Yaoundé: n.p., [1970].

Ate, Bassey E, and Bola A. Akinterinwa, eds. *Nigeria and Its Immediate Neighbours: Constraints and Prospects of Sub-Regional Security in the 1990s.* Lagos: Nigerian Institute of International Affairs in cooperation with Pumark Nigeria, 1992.

Barkindo, Bawaro, M. "The Mandara Astride the Nigeria-Cameroon Boundary." In *Partitioned Africans*, ed. A. I. Asiwaju. Lagos: University of Lagos Press, 1985, pp. 29–49.

Bekong, Njinkeng Julius. "International Dispute Settlement: Land and Maritime Boundary between Cameroon and Nigeria—Origin of the Dispute and Provisional Measures." *African Journal of International and Comparative Law* 9, no. 2 (1997): 287–310.

Brownlie, Ian. *African Boundaries: A Legal and Diplomatic Encyclopedia*. London: Hurst; Berkeley: University of California Press, 1979.

DeLancey, Mark W. "Cameroon's Foreign Relations." In *The Political Economy of Cameroon*, ed. William Zartman and Michael G. Schatzberg. Baltimore, Md.: Johns Hopkins University Press, 1985.

Dibengue, A., and W. Böttcher, eds. *Zur Vormachtstellung Frankreichs im frankophone Afrika: Die Beziehungen Kameruns zu Frankreich und der Bundesrepublik Deutschland von 1960 bis Anfang der achtziger Jahre im Vergleich* [The French

Supremacy in Francophone Africa: The Relations of Cameroon to France and Germany from the Beginning of 1960 Compared to the 1980s]. Aachen: Alano, 1994.
Hertslet, Edward. *The Map of Africa by Treaty.* 3rd ed., 3 vols. London: His Majesty's Stationery Office, 1909.
Jua, Nantang. "UDEAC: Dream, Reality or the Making of Subimperial States." *Afrika Spectrum* 21, no. 2 (1986): 211–23.
Kombi, Narcisse Mouelle. *La politique étrangère du Cameroun* [Foreign Policy of Cameroon]. Paris: Harmattan, 1996.
Mabe, J. E. *Deutsche Entwicklungspolitik in Kamerun* [German Development Policy in Kamerun]. Frankfurt: Lang, 1993.
Mbaku, John M., and David R. Kamerschen. "Integration and Economic Development in Sub-Saharan Africa: The Case of UDEAC." *Journal of Contemporary African Studies* 7, nos. 1/2 (1998): 3–21.
Mbome, François Xavier. "Les Relations entre le Cameroun et le Nigéria: L'Affaire Bakassi [Relations between Cameroon and Nigeria: The Bakassi Affair]." *Afrique 2000* 25 (1996): 45–60.
Ngniman, Z. *Nigeria-Cameroun: La Guerre permanente* [Nigeria-Cameroon: The Permanent War]. Yaoundé: CLE, 1996.
Njoya, Adamou Ndam. *Le Cameroun dans les relations internationales* [Cameroon in International Relations]. Paris: Pichon et Durand-Auzias, 1976.
Owolabi, Ajamu Olayiwola. "Nigeria and Cameroon: Boundary Disputes and the Problem of Border Security." *African Notes* 15, nos. 1/2 (1991): 39–47.
Oyono, Dieudonné. *Avec ou sans la France? La politique Africaine du Cameroun depuis 1960* [With or without France? African Policy of Cameroon since 1960]. Paris: Harmattan, 1990.
Pondi, Jean-Emmanuel. *Relations internationales africaines* [African International Relations]. Berlin: Lang, 1993.
Sall, Alioune. "Actualité des conflits frontaliers en Afrique [Present Interests of Frontier Conflicts in Africa]." *African Journal of International and Comparative Law* 9, no. 1 (1997): 183–94.
Sindjoun, L. "L'Action internationale de l'Assemblée Nationale du Cameroun: Eléments d'analyse politique [International Action of the National Assembly of Cameroon: Elements of Political Analysis]." *Etudes internationales* 24, no. 4 (1993): 813–44.
Weiss, Thomas Lothar. "Migrations et conflits frontaliers: Une relation Nigeria-Cameroun contrariée [Migration and Border Conflicts: A Thwarted Nigerian-Cameroon Relation]." *Afrique contemporaine*, no. 180 (1996): 39–51.

Law

Abada, Marcelin Nguele. "De l'empêchement du président de la République au Cameroun [On the Impeachment of the President of the Republic of Cameroon]." *African Journal of International and Comparative Law* 7, no. 2 (1995): 380–99.

Abada, Marcelin Nguele. "Etat et droit et libertés fondamentales au Cameroun [State and Law and Fundamental Freedoms in Cameroon]." *Revue juridique et politique* 49, no. 3 (1995): 285–303.

Africa Watch. "Cameroon." In *Academic Freedom and Human Rights Abuses in Africa.* New York: Africa Watch, 1991.

——. *Cameroon: Attacks against Independent Press.* Washington, D.C.: Africa Watch, 1991.

Amnesty International. *Cameroon: Blatant Disregard for Human Rights.* New York: Amnesty International, 1997.

Anyangwe, Carlson. "Land Tenure and Interest in Land in Cameroonian Indigenous Law." *Revue camerounaise de droit* 27 (1984): 29–41.

——. "'Prima facie' Presumption of Guilt in the Cameroonian Criminal Process." *First Annual Conference, African Society of International and Comparative Law* 1 (1989): 132–47.

Article 19. *Cameroon: The Press in Trouble.* London: Author, 1993.

——. *Northern Cameroon: Attacks on Freedom of Expression by Governmental and Traditional Authorities.* London: Author, 1995.

Bringer, Peter. "The Abiding Influence of English and French Criminal Law in One African Country." *Journal of African Law* 25, no. 1 (1981): 1–13.

Churchill, E. M. "The Right to Inform and the 1990 Press Law in Cameroon." *Africa Media Review* 6, no. 3 (1992): 19–29.

Debusmann, Robert, and Stefan Arnold, eds. *Land Law and Land Ownership in Africa: Case Studies from Colonial and Contemporary Cameroon and Tanzania.* Bayreuth, Germany: Bayreuth African Studies Breitinger, 1996.

Dipanda Mouelle, Alexis. "Les techniques de codification au Cameroun [The Techniques of Codification in Cameroon]." *Revue juridique et politique* 40, no. 3/4 (1996): 297–306.

Documentation législative africaine. Paris: Centre de Recherche, d'Etude et de Documentation sur les Institutions et les Législations Africaines, annual.

Eckert, Andreas. "'What Makes My Land My Land?': Bodenrecht, Entwicklung und Landkonflikte in Kamerun [Land Rights, Development and Land Conflict in Cameroon]." *Afrika Spectrum* 29, H. 3 (1994): 285–302.

Enonchong, H. Nelson A. *Cameroon Constitutional Law: Federalism in a Mixed Common Law and Civil Law System.* Yaoundé: Centre d'Edition et de Production de Manuels et d'Auxiliaires de l'Enseignement, 1967.

——. "Public Policy and 'Ordre Public': The Exclusion of Customary Law in Cameroon." *African Journal of International and Comparative Law* 5, no. 3 (1993): 503–24.

Fombad, Charles Manga. "Freedom of Expression in the Cameroonian Democratic Transition. *Journal of Modern African Studies* 33, no. 2 (1995): 211–26.

——. "Judicial Power in Cameroon's Amended Constitution of 18 January 1996." *Lesotho Law Journal* 9, no. 2 (1996): 1–11.

——. "The Scope for Uniform National Laws in Cameroon." *Journal of Modern African Studies* 29, no. 3 (1991): 443–56.

Fonyuy Fisiy, Cyprian. "Colonial and Religious Influences on Customary Law: The Cameroonian Experiences." *Africa (Rome)* 43, no. 2 (1988): 262–75.

———. *Palm Tree Justice in the Bertoua Court of Appeal: The Witchcraft Cases.* Leiden, Netherlands: African Studies Centre, 1990.

———. *Power and Privilege in the Administration of Law: Land Law Reforms and Social Differentiation in Cameroon.* Leiden, Netherlands: African Studies Centre, 1992.

Geschiere, Peter. "Domesticating Personal Violence: Witchcraft, Courts and Confessions in Cameroon." *Africa, the Journal of the International African Institute* 64, no. 3 (1994): 323–41.

Goheen, Mitzi. "Land Accumulation and Local Control: The Manipulation of Symbols and Power in Nso, Cameroon." *Land and Society in Contemporary Africa.* ed. R. E. Downs and S. P. Reyna. Hanover: University of New Hampshire Press, 1988.

———. "Chiefs, Sub-chiefs and Local Control: Negotiations over Land, Struggles over Meaning." *Africa, the Journal of the International African Institute* 62, no. 3 (1992): 389–412.

International Court of Justice. *Case concerning the Northern Cameroons: Cameroon v. United Kingdom*. The Hague: Author, 1963.

Johnson, D. H. N. "The Case concerning the Northern Cameroons." *International and Comparative Law Quarterly* 13, no. 4 (1964): 1143–92.

Kéré, G. K. "La polygamie et le devoir de fidélité en droit positif camerounais [Polygamy and the Oath of Fidelity in Cameroonian Positive Law]." *Penant* 106, no. 821 (1996): 129–36.

Kom, Ambroise. "Writing under a Monarchy: Intellectual Poverty in Cameroon." *Research in African Literatures* 22, no. 1 (1991): 83–92.

Mbarga, E. "La Reforme des articles 5 et 7 de la constitution de la République Unie du Cameroun [Reform of Articles 5 and 7 of the Constitution of the United Republic of Cameroon]." *Penant* 90, no. 769 (1980): 262–87.

Mbome, François. "Les Expériences de révisions constitutionnelle au Cameroun [The Experiences of Constitutional Revisions in Cameroon]." *Penant* 102, no. 808 (1992): 19–45.

Meek, C. K. *Land Tenure and Land Administration in Nigeria and the Cameroons*. London: Her Majesty's Stationery Office, 1957.

Mukong, A. "The Tale of a Lesson Learned Too Well—Cameroon Police Searches and Repression." *Index on Censorship* 20, no. 2 (1991): 24–27.

Nguiffo Tene, S. A. *La Nouvelle législation forestière au Cameroun* [New Forestry Legislation in Cameroon]. Yaoundé: DIHACO, 1994.

Ngwasiri, C. N. "The Effect of Legislation on Foreign Investment: The Case of Cameroon." *Journal of African Law* 33, no. 2 (1989): 192–204.

Nkolo, Pierrette. "L'Option matrimoniale au Cameroun [The Matrimonial Option in Cameroon]." *Penant* 97, no. 793 (1987): 87–116.

Nkot, Pierre Fabien. "Révision constitutionnelle du 18 janvier 1996 au Cameroun: Commentaire de quelques 'avis informes' [Constitutional Revision of January

18, 1996 in Cameroon: Commentary on Some 'Informal Opinions']." *Penant* 108, no. 286 (1998): 82–96.

Nlep, Roger Gabriel. "Censure, saisie et interdiction des écrits en droit camerounais [Censure, Seizure and Interdiction of Writing in Cameroonian Law]." *Penant* 106, no. 822 (1996): 324–39.

Olinga, Alain Didier. "Considérations sur les traités dans l'ordre juridique camerounais [Consideration on Treaties in the Cameroonian Juridical Order]." *African Journal of International and Comparative Law* 8, pt. 2 (1996): 283–308.

Penn, Godfred A. E., and Wawa A. Ngenge. "The Evolution of Cooperative Legislation in Cameroon." *Verfassung und Recht in Übersee* 26, no. 4 (1993): 372–98.

Schilder, Kees. *State Formation, Religion and Land Tenure in Cameroon: A Bibliographical Survey.* Leiden, Netherlands: African Studies Centre, 1988.

Zeitlyn, David. "Spiders in and out of Court, or 'the Long Legs of the Law': Styles of Spider Divination in Their Sociological Contexts." *Africa, Journal of the International African Institute* 63, no. 2 (1993): 219–40.

ECONOMY

General

Benjamin, N. "Adjustment and Income Distribution in an Agricultural Economy: A General Equilibrium Analysis of Cameroon." *World Development* 24, no. 6 (1996): 1003–14.

Bizeme, M. E., and J. P. Komon. "La crise économique continue [The Economic Crisis Continues]." *Africa Development* 21, nos. 2/3 (1996): 67–77.

Boutat, A. *Technologies et développement au Cameroun: Le Rendez-vous manqué* [Technologies and Development in Cameroon: The Missed Engagement]. Paris: Harmattan, 1991.

"Cameroon." In *Trends in Developing Economies.* Vol. 3. Washington, D.C.: World Bank, 1995.

Cameroon, Ministry of Economic Affairs and Planning. *The Fifth Five-Year Economic, Social and Cultural Development Plan 1981–1986*. Yaounde: Author, 1981.

Cameroon, Ministry of Planning and Territorial Development. *What You Should Know about the Third Plan*. Yaoundé: Author, 1971.

Derrick, Jonathan. "Cameroon: From Oil Boom to Recession." *Africa Recovery* 6, no. 2 (August 1992): 16–21.

Dijk, Meine Pieter van. "Successful and Unsuccessful Adjustment and Its Effects on Employment: The Cases of Cameroon and Zimbabwe." *African Development Perspectives Yearbook 1994/95.* Berlin: Lit, 1995.

Dubois, J. L. "L'Expérience du programme 'Dimensions sociales de l'ajustement': Apports méthodologiques et réflexions d'ensemble [The Experience of the 'Social Dimensions of Adjustment' Program: Methodological Properties and Reflections of the Group]." *Cahiers des sciences humaines* 32, no. 2 (1996): 379–404.

Eboua, S. *Le changement au Cameroun* [Change in Cameroon]. Paris: Harmattan, 1996.

Evalds, Victoria K. *National Union List of African Development Plans, Censuses and Statistical Abstracts.* Oxford: Zell, 1985.

Feumetio, E. B. *Cameroun: Radioscopie d'une économie dans le sillage de la faillite: Implications stratégiques* [Cameroon: X-ray of an Economy in the Wake of Bankruptcy: Strategic Implications]. Douala: F and GR, 1992.

Gankou, J. M. *La politique économique du Cameroun: son impact sur le croissance depuis 1960* [The Political Economy of Cameroon: Its Impact on Growth since 1960]. Neuchatel, Switzerland: Centre de Recherche sur le développement, 1991.

Geschiere, Peter, and Piet Konings, eds. *Itinéraires d'accumulation au Cameroun: Pathways to Accumulation in Cameroun.* Paris: Karthala, 1993.

Gilguy, Christine. ed. "Spécial Cameroun." *Marchés tropicaux et méditerranéens* 50, no. 2613 (1995): 2703–55.

Gilles, Bertrand. *Cameroun.* Paris: Moreux, 1998.

Hillebrand, E., et al. *Le Secteur informel au Cameroun: Importance et perspectives* [The Informal Sector in Cameroon: Importance and Prospects]. Yaoundé: Friedrich Ebert Foundation, 1991.

Jua, Nantang. *Economic Mismanagement in Neo-colonial States: A Case Study of Cameroon.* Leiden, Netherlands: African Studies Centre, 1990.

Ketchekmen, Benoît. "Problématique de la compétitivité de l'économie camerounaise [Problem of the Competitiveness of the Cameroonian Economy]." In *Etudes et statistiques/Banque des Etats de l'Afrique Centrale* 211 (1994): 247–62.

Mama, Touna, and Magloire Louis Bikomen. *Crise économique et politique de dérèglementation au Cameroun* [Economic and Political Crisis of Deregulation in Cameroon]. Paris: Harmattan, 1996.

Manga, Ekema J. *The African Economic Dilemma: The Case of Cameroon.* Lanham, Md.: University Press of America, 1998.

Manning, Patrick. "African Economic Growth and the Public Sector: Lessons from the Historical Statistics of Cameroon." *African Economic History* 19 (1990/91): 135–70.

Mbe Emane, Pierre. "Intégration économique et sociale en Afrique centrale: Aperçu générale et perspectives [Economic and Social Integration in Central Africa: Overview and Perspectives]." *Etudes et statistiques/Banque des Etats de l'Afrique Centrale* 215 (1995): 89–97.

Mouafo, Dieudonné. "Les Difficultés de l'intégration économique inter-régionale en Afrique noire: L'Exemple de la zone UDEAC [Difficulties of Inter-Régional Economic Integration in Black Africa: The Example of the UDEAC Zone]." *Les cahiers d'outre-mer* 44, no. 174 (1991): 167–85.

Ndongko, Wilfred A., and Franklin Vivekananda. *Economic Development of Cameroon.* Stockholm: Bethany, 1989.

Njinkeu, D. "Evaluation of the Incentive Structure: A Survey and Application to Cameroon." *World Development* 24, no. 3 (1996): 557–68.

Nkwi, Paul N. "Rethinking the Role of Elites in Rural Development: A Case Study from Cameroon." *Journal of Comtemporary African Studies* 15, no. 1 (1997): 67–86.

Oyowe, Augustin. "The Economy of Cameroon: Better Prospects—But a Long Way to Go." *The Courier* 158 (July–August 1996): 5–9.

Subramanian, Shankar. "Vulnerability to Price Shocks under Alternative Policies in Cameroon." In *Economic Reform and the Poor in Africa,* ed. David E. Sahn. Oxford: Clarendon, 1996.

Tafah Edokat, E. O. "Analysis of Public Sector Earnings Profiles and Implications for Human Capital Investment and Utilization: A Case Study of Cameroon." *Journal of Third World Studies* 11, no. 2 (1994): 386–406.

World Bank. *Republic of Cameroon, the Challenge: Harnessing Unrealized Potential, a Private Sector Assessment.* Washington, D.C.: World Bank, 1996.

Agriculture and Pastoralism

Amin, A. A. *The Effects of Exchange Rate Policy on Cameroon's Agricultural Competitiveness*. Nairobi, Kenya: African Economic Research Consortium, 1996.

Bederman, Sanford H. *The Cameroons Development Corporation: Partner in National Growth*. Bota, West Cameroon: Cameroons Development Corporation, 1968.

Bederman, Sanford H., and Mark W. DeLancey. "The Cameroon Development Corporation, 1947–1977: Cameroonization and Growth." In *An African Experiment in Nation-Building*, ed. Ndiva Kofele–Kale. Boulder, Colo.: Westview, 1980.

Benjamin, Nancy. "Adjustment and Income Distribution in an Agricultural Economy: A General Equilibrium Analysis of Cameroon." *World Development* 24, no. 6 (1996): 1003–13.

Bopda, A. "Le Secteur vivrier sud-camérounais face à la crise de l'économie cacaoyère [South Cameroonian Alimentary Sector Faces the Economic Crisis in Cocoa]." *Travaux-Institut de géographie de Reims* 83/84 (1993): 109–22.

Boutrais, Jean. "Les Foulbé de l'Adamaoua et l'élevage: De l'idéologie pastorale à la pluri-activité [The Fulani of Adamawa and Stock Rearing: From Pastoral Ideology to Mixed Farming]." *Cahiers d'études africaines* 34, no. 133–35 (1994): 175–96.

Bray, M. "The Problems That Arise in Relation to Local Communities and the State in Contemporary West Africa: The Case of the Bamiléké in Cameroun." *Bulletin of Francophone Africa*, no. 3 (1993): 26–36.

Clarence–Smith, William G. "Plantation versus Smallholder Production of Cocoa: The Legacy of the German Period in Cameroon." In *Itinéraires d'accumulation au Cameroun–Pathways to Accumulation in Cameroon,* ed. Peter Geschiere and Piet Konings. Paris: Karthala, 1993.

Claude, Dominique. "Production and Commercialisation of Rice in Cameroon: The SEMRY Project." In *Structural Adjustment in Africa.* ed. Bonnie K. Campbell and John Loxley. New York: St. Martin's, 1989.

Courade, Georges. "Des complexes qui coûtent cher: La Priorité agro-industrielle dans l'agriculture camerounaise [Expensive Complexes: The Agro-Industrial Priority in Cameroonian Agriculture]." *Politique africaine* 14 (1984): 75–91.

DeLancey, Mark W. "Cameroon National Food Policies and Organizations: The Green Revolution and Structural Proliferation." *Journal of African Studies* 7, no. 2 (Summer 1980): 109–22.

———. "Women's Cooperatives in Cameroon." *African Studies Review* 30, no. 1 (March 1987): 1–18.

DeLancey, Virginia. "Agricultural Productivity in Cameroon." In *The Political Economy of Cameroon*, ed. I. William Zartman and Michael G. Schatzberg. Baltimore, Md.: Johns Hopkins University Press, 1985.

———. "Cameroon Agricultural Policy: The Struggle to Remain Food Self–Sufficient." In *Dependency Theory and the Return to High Politics*, ed. M. A. Tetreault and R. Able. Westport, Conn.: Greenwood, 1986.

———. "The Impact of the Credit Union Movement on Production and Accumulation in the Agricultural Sector of Cameroon." *Conference on the Political Economy of Cameroon, Historical Perspectives.* Leiden, Netherlands: African Studies Centre, 1989.

Douffisa, A. *L'Elevage bovin dans le Mbéré (Adamaoua camerounais)* [Cattle Breeding in Mbere (Cameroonian Adamawa)]. Paris: Orstom, 1993.

Dumont, R., et al. *Les Ignames au Cameroun* [Yams in Cameroon]. Montpellier: CIRAD, 1994.

Fisiy, Cyprian Fonyuy. "The Death of a Myth System: Land Colonization on the Slopes of Mount Oku, Cameroon." *Land Tenure and Sustainable Land Use,* ed. Reint J. Baxema. Amsterdam: Royal Tropical Institute, Agricultural Development Section, 1994.

Gros, Jean–Germain. "Of Cattle, Farmers, Veterinarians and the World Bank: The Political Economy of Veterinary Services Privatization in Cameroon." *Public Administration and Development* 14, no. 1 (1994): 37–51.

Gubry, P., et al. *Le Retour au village: Une Solution à la crise économique au Cameroun* [Return to the Village: A Solution to the Economic Crisis in Cameroon]. Paris: Harmattan, 1996.

Gurgand, Marc, Glenn Pederson, and Jacob Yaron. *Outreach and Sustainability of Six Rural Institutions in Sub-Saharan Africa* Washington, D.C.: World Bank, 1994.

Guyer, Jane I. "From Seasonal Income to Daily Diet in a Partially Commercialized Rural Economy (Southern Cameroon)." In *Seasonal Variability in Third World Agriculture: The Consequences for Food Security,* ed. David E. Sahn. Baltimore, Md.: Johns Hopkins University Press, 1989.

Janin, P. "Tout change pour que tout reste pareil: Ruptures et continuités en économie de plantation Bamiléké et Béti (Cameroun) en période de crise [All Changes so That All Remains the Same: Ruptures and Economic Continuities in the Plantation Economy of Bamiléké and Béti in a Period of Crisis]." *Cahiers des sciences humaines* 32, no. 3 (1996): 577–96.

Jones, Christine. "The Mobilization of Women's Labor for Cash Crop Production." *American Journal of Agricultural Economics* 65, no. 5 (1983): 1049–54.

Kennes, Walter. "European Communities Assistance for Agricultural Development in Cameroon, Senegal and Tanzania, 1960–1987." In *Aid to African Agriculture.* Baltimore, Md.: Johns Hopkins University Press, 1992.

Konings, Piet. "Plantation Labour and Economic Crisis in Cameroon." *Development and Change* 26, no. 3 (1995): 525–49.

——. "Privatisation of Agro-Industrial Parastatals and Anglophone Opposition in Cameroon." *Journal of Commonwealth & Comparative Politics* 34, no. 3 (1996): 199–217.

Langham, Max R., and François Kamajou, eds. *Agricultural Policy Analysis in Sub-Saharan Africa.* Gainesville: University of Florida, Office of International Programs, 1992.

Mouafo, Dieudonné. "L'Hévéaculture au Cameroun [Rubber Production in Cameroon]." *Revue de géographie du Cameroun* 9, nos. 1/2 (1990): 16–30.

——. "La Production camerounaise de caoutchouc naturel: Evolution et perspectives de commercialisation [Cameroonian Production of Natural Rubber: Evolution and Perspectives of Commercialization]." *Canadian Journal of African Studies* 26 no. 1 (1992): 92–116.

Nebasina, Ngwa. "Village Food Co-operatives as Institutions of Rural Uplift." *Revue de géographie du Cameroun* 9, nos. 1/2 (1990): 48–59.

Ngwa, N. E. "Land Use Dynamics and Restructuring on Some Sectors of the Grassfields Plateau, Cameroon." *GeoJournal* 20, no. 3 (1990): 203–08.

Njiti, C. F., and D. M. Sharpe. "A Goal–Programing Approach to the Management of Competition and Conflict among Land Uses in the Tropics: The Cameroon Example." *Ambio* 23, no. 2 (1994): 112–19.

Nyemba, Jean Ambela. "Développement rural au Cameroun: Et si les paysans le conçevaient autrement? [Rural Development in Cameroon: And If the Peasants Thought Otherwise?]." *African Development* 17, no. 4 (1992): 29–45.

——. "The Social Significance of Cooperatives and Farmers' Involvement in the Littoral Province of Cameroon: An Empirical Analysis Using Multiple Regression Equations." *Discovery and Innovation* 7, no. 3 (1995): 221–28.

Phelinas, Pascale. "Le Riz: Politique des prix et relance de la production (Cameroun, Côte d'Ivoire, Madagascar et Senegal) [Rice: Politics of Price and the Relaunching of Production (Cameroon, Ivory Coast, Madagascar and Senegal]." *Politique africaine* 37 (1990): 71–75.

Tambi, Emmanuel N., and Michael B. Vabi. "Household Consumption Patterns of Dairy Products in Bamenda Urban Town." *Journal of International Food & Agribusiness Marketing* 7, no. 2 (1995): 65–78.

Thillard, Robert. *L'Agriculture et l'élevage au Cameroun* [Agriculture and Cattle Breeding in Cameroon]. Paris: LaRose, 1920.

Wells, F. A., and W. A. Warmington. *Studies in Industrialization: Nigeria and the Cameroons.* London: Oxford University Press, 1962.

Wong, Jennifer. "Two Cooperative Unions in Africa: Views from the Inside." *Aproma* 34 (1993): 8–14.

Zuiderwijk, Adri. *Farming Gently—Farming Fast; Migration, Incorporation and Agricultural Change in the Mandara Mountains of Northern Cameroon.* Leiden, Netherlands: Programme of Environment & Development, Centre of Environmental Science, 1988.

Finance, Credit, and Banking

Bekolo Ebem, B. "Dynamique nouvelle de financement et sortie de crise au Cameroun [New Dynamics of Finance and Escaping the Crisis in Cameroon]." *Mondes en développement* 20, no. 77/78 (1992): 101–18.

Ben Barka, Mahamad Amine. "Les problèmes de déséquilibre de la balance des paiements en Afrique centrale [The Problems of Disequilibrium of the Balance of Payments in Central Africa]." *Etudes et statistiques/Banque des Etats l'Afrique Centrale* 218 (1995): 168–200.

Biao, Barthélémy. "Expérience de coopération économique et monétaire en zone UDEAC-BEAC et théorie des zones monétaires optimales [Experience of Economic and Monetary Cooperation in the UDEAC-CEMAC Zone and Theory of Optimal Monetary Zones]." *Etudes et statistiques/Banque des Etats de l'Afrique Centrale* 235 (1997): 127–41.

Blandford, D., et al. "Oil Boom or Bust: The Harsh Realities of Adjustment in Cameroon." In *Adjusting to Policy Failure in African Economies*, ed. D. E. Sahn. Ithaca, N.Y.: Cornell University Press, 1994.

Cogneau, D., et al. "La Dévaluation du franc CFA au Cameroun: Bilan et perspectives [The Devaluation of the CFA Franc in Cameroon: Balance and Prospects]." *Economies et sociétés* 30, no. 1 (1996): 169–203.

DeLancey, Mark W. "Credit for the Common Man in Cameroon," *Journal of Modern African Studies* 15, no. 2 (1977): 316–22.

———. "Institutions for the Accumulation and Redistribution of Savings amongst Migrants." *Journal of Developing Areas* 12, no. 2 (January 1978): 209–24.

———. "The U.S. Peace Corps Program for Credit Union and Cooperative Development in Cameroon, 1969–1976." *Studies in Comparative International Development* 17, nos. 3–4 (Fall–Winter 1982): 92–123.

Gako, Samuel. "Environment juridique et développement d'un marché financier en Afrique centrale: Quelques enjeux à prendre en compte [Legal Environment and Development of a Financial Market in Central Africa: Some Stakes to Take into Account]." *Etudes et statistiques/Banque des Etats de l'Afrique Centrale* 23 (1997): 87–111.

Henry, Alain, Guy-Honoré Tchente, and Philippe Guillerme-Dieumegard. *Tontines et banques au Cameroun: Les Principes de la société des amis* [Tontines and Banks in Cameroon: The Principles of the Society of Friends]. Paris: Karthala, 1991.

Herrera, Javier. "Sur l'inconvertibilité du Franc CFA au Cameroun [On the Unconvertibility of the CFA Franc in Cameroon]." *Politique africaine* 54 (1994): 47–65.

Lubin, Doe. "Managing Cameroon's Banking Sector: In and Out of Crisis: The Role of the Government." *African Development Review* 7, no. 1 (1995): 103–66.

Masini, M., et al. *Rural Finance Profiles in African Countries.* Vol. 2. Milan: Finafrica-Cariplo, 1989.

M'bet, Allechi. *European Economic Integration and the Franc Zone: The Future of the CFA Franc after 1996.* Nairobi: African Economic Research Consortium, 1993.

Nana-Fabu, Rosemary. "Mobilizing Savings in Cameroon." In *Saving for Economic Recovery in Africa,* ed. J. H. Frimpong-Ansah and Barbara Ingham. London: Currey; Portsmouth, N.H.: Heinemann for the African Centre for Economic Policy Research, 1992.

Ndongko, Wilfred A. "Cameroon." In *Impact of Structural Adjustment on the Population of Africa*, ed. A. Adepoju. London: Currey, 1993.

——. "The Experience of Cameroon." In *Instruments of Economic Policy in Africa,* ed. African Centre for Monetary Studies. London: Currey; Portsmouth, N.H.: Heinemann, 1992.

Ojo, Oladeji O. "The CFA Franc Devaluation and the Future of Monetary Cooperation in Africa." In *Africa and Europe,* ed. O. O. Ojo London: Zed, 1996.

Peltzer, R. "Der Fall Kamerun: Erste Auswirkungen und Perspektiven der FCFA-Abwertung [The Case of Cameroon: The First Effects and Prospects of the Devaluation of the CFA Franc]." *Afrika Spectrum* 29, no. 2 (1994): 207–15.

"Un rapport de la banque mondiale: Ou les comptes fantastiques d'Ahmadou Ahidjo, Paul Biya et quelques autres qu'il ne faut pas oublier [A World Bank Report: Or the Fantastic Accounts of Ahmadou Ahidjo, Paul Biya and a Few Others Who Should Not Be Forgotten]" *Peuples noirs—peuples africains* 10, no. 55/58 (1987): 340–528.

Tabbed, James. "Firm–level Responses to the CFA Devaluation in Cameroon." *Journal of African Economics* 6, no. 1 (1997): 3–34.

Talom, Pierre. "Réforme des instruments de régulation de la liquidité bancaire dans les Etats de la zone CEMAC [Reform of Regulation Instruments for Banking Liquidity in the States of the CEMAC Zone]." *Études et statistiques/Banque des États de l'Afrique Centrale* 239 (1997): 277–302.

Tamba, I., and L. T. Djine. "De la crise à la reforme des institutions bancaires africaines: Le Cas du Cameroun [From the Crisis to the Reform of African Banking Institutions: The Case of Cameroon]." *Revue tiers–monde* 36, no. 144 (1995): 813–36.

Foreign Aid, Trade, and Investment

Agbor-Tabi, Peter. *U.S. Bilateral Assistance in Africa: The Case of Cameroon*. Lanham, Md.: University Press of America, 1984.

Andely, Rigobert Roger. "Financement des investissements en zone BEAC: Blocages actuels et stratégie de relance par le marché financier [Financing Investments in the CEMAC Zone: Current Blocks and Strategy for Relaunching by the Financial Market]." *Etudes et statistiques/Banque des Etats de l'Afrique Centrale* 236 (1997): 154–87.

Bennafla, Karine. "Mbaiboum: Un Marché au carrefour de frontières multiples [Mbaiboum: A Market at the Crossroads of Many Borders]." *Autrepart* 6 (1998): 53–72.

Biakan, Jacques. "L'Idée de rationalisation des relations entre L'Etat et les entreprises publiques au Cameroun: L'Approche des contrats de performance [The Idea of Rationalizing Relations between the State and Public Enterprises in Cameroon: The Coming of Performance Contracts]." *Revue juridique et politique* 51, no. 1 (1997): 103–10.

Devarajan, S., and D. Rodrik. "Pro–competition Effects of Trade Reform: Results from a CGE Model of Cameroon." *European Economic Review* 35, no. 5 (1991): 1157–84.

Fielding, David. "Investment in Cameroon 1978–88." *Journal of African Economies* 4, no. 1 (1995): 29–51.

Fodouop, Kengné. "La Contrebande entre le Cameroun et le Nigéria [Smuggling between Cameroon and Nigeria]." *Cahiers d'outre-mer* 41, no. 161 (1988): 5–25.

Massuyeau, Benoit. "La formation des prix dans le commerce trans-frontalier: Les Produits manufacturés nigérians sur les marchés nord-camerounais [Price Formation in Transborder Commerce: Nigerian Manufactured Products in the Markets of North Cameroon]." *Autrepart* 6 (1998): 163–80.

Mbaku, J. M. "Foreign Aid and Economic Growth in Cameroon." *Applied Economics* 25, no. 10 (1993): 1309–14.

Njinkeu, Dominique. "Evaluation of the Incentive Structure: A Survey and Application to Cameroon." *World Development* 24, no. 3 (1996): 557–68.

United Nations Organization for Economic Cooperation and Development. *Geographical Distribution of Financial Flows to Developing Countries.* Paris: Author, annual.

Walle, Nicolas van de. "The Politics of Public Enterprise Reform in Cameroon." In *State-Owned Enterprises in Africa*, ed. Barbara B. Gosh and Rwekaza S. Mukandala. Boulder, Colo.: Reinner, 1994.

Yenshu, Emmanuel. "The Evolution of Official Attitudes towards Grassroots Initiatives in Cameroon." *Community Development Journal* 33, no. 1 (1998): 41–48.

Mining, Industry, Commerce, and Communication

Benjamin, Nancy. "Investment, the Real Exchange Rate, and Dutch Disease: A Two-Period General Equilibrium Model for Cameroon." *Journal of Policy Modeling* 12, no. 1 (1990): 77–92.

Benjamin, N. C., et al. "The 'Dutch' Disease in a Developing Country: Oil Reserves in Cameroon." *Journal of Development Economics* 30, no. 1 (1989): 71–92.

Benjamin, Nancy, and Shantayanan Devarajan. *Oil Revenues and Economic Policy in Cameroon: Results from a Computable General Equilibrium Model.* Washington D.C.: World Bank, 1985.

Boisvert, J., and E. Kamdem. "La formation permanente en gestion au Cameroun [The Continuing Education of Management in Cameroon]." *Afrique 2000* 10 (1992): 67–85.

Boyer, N. A., and C. G. Davis. "Exploitation and Inefficiency in Cameroon Food Marketing Systems—Myth or Reality? Some Evidence from the West Province." *Review of Black Political Economy* 18, no. 4 (1990): 69–97.

Cook, A. "Quelques réflexions sur le tourisme au Cameroun [Some Reflections on Tourism in Cameroon]." *Bulletin of Francophone Africa* 3 (1993): 37–55.

Courcelle, M., et al. *Le Secteur privé au Cameroun* [The Private Sector in Cameroon]. Paris: OECD, 1990.

Clarke, John I. "The Transcameroonian." *Geographical Magazine* 40, no. 15 (July 1968): 1268–77.

Eding, B. "Les Dix ans de raffinage et l'approvisionnement du Cameroun [Ten Years of Refining and the Supplying of Cameroon]." In *Ajustements structurels et gestion du secteur énergétique en Afrique*, ed. A. La Pointe and G. Zaccour. Paris: Technip, 1993.

Ejangue, T. K., and E. Noubissie Ngankam. *Les Privatisations au Cameroun: Bilan et perspectives* [Privatizations in Cameroon: Balance Sheet and Prospects]. Yaoundé: Friedrich Ebert Foundation, 1995.

Essombe Edimo, J.-R. "Désengagement de l'Etat et réhabilitation des entreprises parapubliques au Cameroun [Disengagement of the State and Rehabilitation of Parastatal Enterprises in Cameroon]." *Mondes en développement* 19, nos. 75/76 (1991): 67–73.

Fodouop, Kengne. "Les Transports 'clandestins' autour de Yaoundé ['Clandestine' Transport around Yaoundé]." *Cahiers d'outre-mer* 38, no. 150 (1985): 175–95.

———. *Le Secteur informel porteur de technologies de la ville de Yaoundé: Bilan d'un enquête* [The Informal Sector, Carrier of Yaoundé's Technology: The Balance-Sheet of an Inquiry]." Yaoundé: Imprimerie St. Paul, 1992.

———. "Le Secteur informel dans le contexte des ajustments au Cameroun: L'Exemple de la 'vente à la sauvette' [The Informal Sector in the Context of Adjustments in Cameroon: The Example of 'Unauthorized Sales']." *Labour, Capital and Society* 26, no. 1 (1993): 42–61.

Fombad, C. M. "Adjusting Working Conditions to the Economic Crisis: The Cameroonian Experience." *Labor Law Journal* 47, no. 4 (1996): 454–64.

Hesp, Paul. "Industrial Development and Industrial Policy-making in Cameroon." In *Conference on the Political Economy of Cameroon.* Leiden, Netherlands: African Studies Centre, 1989.

Herera, Javier. "Du 'fédéral' et des 'Koweitiens': La Fraude de l'essence nigériane au Cameroun [Of 'Federal' and Kuwaitians: Nigerian Gasoline Fraud in Cameroon]." *Autrepart* 6 (1998): 181–202.

Hsaini, Abderraouf. "Cameroun." In *L'Energie en Afrique: Situation énergétique de 34 pays* [Energy in Africa: The Energy Situation in 34 Countries]. Dakar: Enda, 1995.

Iyebi-Mandjek, Olivier. "Distribution et commerce de l'eau potable à Maroua (Cameroun) [Distribution and Sale of Potable Water in Maroua (Cameroon)]." *Cahiers d'outre-mer* 47, no. 187 (1994): 305–27.

Kamdem, M. S. "Basket-making, a Rural Micro-enterprise in Africa (North Cameroun)." *Frankfurter Wirtschaft und Sozialgeographische Schriften* 63 (1993): 63–94.

Karmiloff, Igor. "Cameroon." In *Manufacturing in Africa*, ed. R. C. Riddell. London: Currey, 1990.

Minlend, Aurore Sara Mbock. "L'Equipement hydroelectrique du Cameroun [Hydroelectric Equipment of Cameroon]." *Revue de géographie du Cameroun* 9, nos. 1/2 (1990): 68–80.

Mouafo, Dieudonné. "Les Zones industrielles MAGZI de Douala (Cameroun) [The MAGZI Industrial Zones of Douala (Cameroon)]." *Revue de géographie du Cameroun* 10, no. 1 (1991): 53–63.

Oumarou, A. "La Privatisation au Cameroun [Privatization in Cameroon]." *Cahiers africains d'administration publique* 47 (1996): 83–88.

Pettang, Chrispin, Paul Vermande, and Monique Zimmerman. "L'Impact du secteur informel dans la production de l'habitat au Cameroun [The Impact of the Informal Sector in the Production of Housing in Cameroon]." *Cahiers des sciences humaines* 31, no. 4 (1995): 883–903.

Richard, C., and P. Huster. "Energie: Les Choix du Cameroun [Energy: Cameroon's Choices]." *Jeune Afrique* 1572 (1991): 61–80.

Roubaud, F. "Le Marché du travail à Yaoundé, 1983–1993: La Décennie perdue [The Labor Market in Yaoundé, 1983–1993: The Lost Decade]." *Revue tiers monde* 35, no. 140 (1994): 751–78.

Thomas, Mark, and Luc Vallée. "Labour Market Segmentation in Cameroonian Manufacturing." *Journal of Development Studies* 32, no. 6 (1995/1996): 876–98.

Warnier, Jean-Pierre. *L'Esprit d'entreprise au Cameroun* [The Spirit of Enterprise in Cameroon]. Paris: Karthala, 1993.

SOCIETY

Anthropology

General

Bahoken, J. C., and Engelbert Atangana. *Cultural Policy in the United Republic of Cameroon.* Paris: UNESCO Press, 1976.

Brain, Robert. *Art and Society in Africa*. London: Longman, 1980.

Cameroon Ministry of Information and Culture. *The Cultural Identity of Cameroon*. Yaoundé: MINFOC, 1985.

Collectif Changer le Cameroun. *Ethnies et développement national: actes du colloque de Yaoundé 1993* [Ethnicity and National Development: Documents from the Yaoundé Colloquium 1993]. Yaoundé: CRAC; Editions C3, 1994.

Fisiy, Cyprian Fonyuy, and Peter Geschiere. "Witchcraft, Violence and Identity: Different Trajectories in Postcolonial Cameroon." In *Postcolonial Identities in Africa,* ed. Richard Werbner and Terence Ranger. London: Zed, 1996.

Fotso, E. F. *Faut-il brûler les chefferies traditionelles?* [Is It Necessary to Do Away with the Traditional Chiefs?]. Yaoundé: CRAC, 1991.

Fowler, Ian, and David Zeitlyn, eds. *African Crossroads: Intersection between History and Anthropology in Cameroon.* Providence, R.I.: Berghahn, 1996.

Geschiere, Peter. "Chiefs and the Problem of Witchcraft: Varying Patterns in South and West Cameroon." *Journal of Legal Pluralism and Unofficial Law* 37/38 (1996): 307–27.

Guyer, Jane I. "Wealth in People as Wealth in Knowledge: Accumulation and Composition in Equatorial Africa." *Journal of African History* 36, no. 1 (1995): 91–120.

Heritier-Augé, F., and E. Copet-Rougier, eds. *Les Complexités de l'alliance* [The Complexities of the Alliance]. Paris: Archives Contemporaines, 1990.

Idowu, K. E. *Auntie Kate's Cookery Book*. London: Macmillan Education, 1982.

Bamiléké and Related

Albert, A. *In French Cameroons, Bandjoon*. Ottawa: Éditions de l'Arbre, 1943.

Brain, Robert. *Bangwa Kinship and Marriage.* Cambridge: Cambridge University Press, 1972.

——. "Friends and Twins in Bangwa." In *Man in Africa*, ed. Mary Douglas and Phyllis M. Kaberry. Garden City, N.Y.: Anchor, 1971.

Brain, Robert, and Adam Pollock. *Bangwa Funerary Sculpture*. London: Duckworth, 1971.

Geary, Christaud. *Images from Bamum: German Colonial Photography at the Court of King Njoya, Cameroon, West Africa 1902–1915.* Washington, D.C.: Smithsonian Institution Press, 1988.

Geschiere, Peter. "Slavery and Kinship in the Old Political Economy of the Maka (Cameroon, Eastern Province)." *Paideuma* 41 (1995): 207–26.

Lecoq, Raymond. *Les Bamiléké: Une Civilisation africaine* [The Bamiléké: An African Civilization]. Paris: Présence Africaine, 1953.

McCullock, Merran, Margaret Littlewood, and I. Dugast. *Peoples of the Central Cameroons.* London: International African Institute, 1954.

Njoya, Sultan. *Histoire et coutumes des Bamum* [History and Customs of the Bamoum]. Yaoundé: Institut Français d'Afrique Noire, Centre du Cameroun, 1952.

Ouden, Jan H. B. den. "In Search of Personal Mobility: Changing Interpersonal Relations in Two Bamiléké Chiefdoms, Cameroon." *Africa, Journal of the International African Institute* 57, no. 1 (1987): 3–27.

Pradelles de Latour, Charles-Henri. "The Initiation of the Dugi among the Pere." *Journal of the Anthropological Society of Oxford* 26, no. 1 (1995): 81–86.

———. "Marriage Payments, Debt and Fatherhood among the Bangoua: A Lacanian Analysis of a Kinship System." *Africa, Journal of the International African Institute* 64, no. 1 (1994): 21–33.

———. "Witchcraft and the Avoidance of Physical Violence in Cameroon." *Journal of the Royal Anthropological Institute* 1, no. 3 (1995): 599–610.

Rohde, E. *Chefferie Bamueke Tradition, Herrschaft und Kolonialsystem* [Bamueke Traditional Chiefdom, Power and the Colonial System]. Münster: Lit, 1990.

Sofotso, G. T. *Bandjoun: Un Peuple, une civilisation* [Bandjoun: A People, A Civilization]. Yaoundé: CRAC, 1995.

Tardits, Claude. *Le royaume Bamoum* [The Kingdom of the Bamoum]. Paris: Colin, 1980.

Tessmann, Gunter. *Die Bafia und die Kultur der mittelkamerun Bantu* [The Bafia and the Culture of Central Cameroon Bantu]. Stuttgart: Strecker & Schroder, 1934.

Wazaki, Haruka. "The Political Structure of the Bamum Kingdom in Cameroon and the Urban–Rural Relationship." *Senri Ethnological Studies* 31 (1992): 303–71.

Central South

Alexandre, Pierre, and Jacques Binet. *Le Groupe dit Pahouin (Fang–Boulou–Beti)* [The Pahouin Speaking Group [Fang–Boulou–Beti]. Paris: Presses Universitaires de France, 1958.

Burnham, Philip. *Opportunity and Constraint in a Savanna Society: The Gbaya of Meiganga, Cameroon*. London: Academic Press, 1980.

Copet-Rougier, Elisabeth. "Du clan la chefferie dans l'est du Cameroon [From Clan to Chiefdom in the East of Cameroon]." *Africa* 57, no. 2 (1987): 345–65.

Dimi, Charles-Robert. *Sagesse Boulou et philosophie* [Bulu Wisdom and Philosophy]. Paris: Silex, 1982.

Dugast, Idelette. *Monographie de la tribu des Ndiki (Banen du Cameroun)* [Monograph on the Tribe of the Ndoko (Banen of Cameroon)]. Paris: Institut d'Ethnologie, 1959.

Guyer, Jane I. "The Value of Beti Bridewealth." In *Money Matters: Instability, Values and Social Payments in the History of West African Communities,* ed. Jane Guyer. Portsmouth, N.H.: Heinemann, 1995.

Hilberth, John. *Les Gbaya* [The Gbaya]. Uppsala: Studia Ethnographica Upsaliensia, 1962.

Hilberth, Ellen, and John Hilberth. *Contribution à l'ethnographie des Gbaya* [Contribution to the Ethnography of the Gbaya]. Uppsala: Institut for Allmann och Jamforande Etnografi, 1968.

Trilles, H. *L'Ame des Pygmées d'Afrique* [The Spirit of the African Pygmies]. Paris: Cerf, 1945.

Coastal and Southern

Ardener, Edwin. *Coastal Bantu of the Cameroons*. London: International African Institute, 1956.

Bahuchet, S. *La Rencontre des agriculteurs: Les Pygmées parmi les peuples d'Afrique centrales* [The Meeting of the Farmers: Pygmies among the Peoples of Central Africa]. Paris: Peeters, for SELAF, 1993.

Bekombo, Manga. "Conception et exercice de la justice dans les sociétés de la côte du Cameroun [Conception and Exercise of Justice in the Societies of the Coast of Cameroon]." *Droit et cultures* 29 (1995): 141–57.

D'Epie, Charles Alobwede. "Naming and Names in Bakossi: A Study in Signs and Symbols." *Bulletin of the International Committee on Urgent Anthropological and Ethnological Research* 36 (1994): 173–84.

Dugast, Idelette. *Inventaire ethnique du Sud Cameroun* [Ethnic Inventory of South Cameroon]. Yaoundé: Institut Français d'Afrique Noire, 1949.

Ejedepang-Koge, S. N. *Tradition and Change in Peasant Activities: A Study of the Indigenous People's Search for Cash in the South-West Province of Cameroon.* Yaoundé: Author, 1975.

Imoagene, Oshomha. *Peoples of the Cross River Valley and the Eastern Delta*. Ibadan, Nigeria: New-Era, 1990.

Joiris, Daou V. "Baka Pygmy Hunting Rituals in Southern Cameroon." *Civilisations* 41, nos. 1/2 (1993): 51–81.

——. "A Comparative Approach to Hunting Rituals among the Baka Pygmies (Southeastern Cameroon)." In *Cultural Diversity among Twentieth-Century Foragers: An African Perspective*, ed. Susan Kent. Cambridge: Cambridge University Press, 1996.

——. "Elements of Techno-Economic Changes among the Sedentarised Bagyeli Pygmies." *African Studies Monographs* 15, no. 2 (1994): 83–95.

Mansfeld, Alfred. *Urwald Dokumente: Vier Jahre unter den Crossflussnegern Kameruns* [Documents of the Jungle: Four Years with Cross River Natives]. Berlin: Reimer, 1908.

Matute, Dan Lyonga. *Facing Mount Fako: An Ethnographic Study of the Bakweri of Cameroon.* Milwaukee, Wisc.: Omni, 1990.

Ndonko, Flavien Tiokou. "Ethnicité, nourriture et politique: L'Exemple des Yasa de la côte sud du Cameroun [Ethnicity, Nutrition and Politics: The Example of the Yasa of the South Coast of Cameroon]." *Afrika Focus* 9, nos. 1/2 (1993): 105–23.

Ruel, Malcolm. *Leopards and Leaders.* London: Tavistock, 1969.

North

Adala, H., and J. Boutrais, eds. *Peuples et cultures de l'Adamaoua, Cameroun* [Peoples and Cultures of the Adamawa, Cameroon]. Paris: Orstom, 1993.

Beek, W. E. A. van. "The Dirty Smith: Smell as a Social Frontier among the Kapsiki/Higi of North Cameroon and North-eastern Nigeria." *Africa. Journal of the International African Institute* 62, no. 1 (1992): 38–58.

Burnham, Philip. *The Politics of Cultural Difference in Northern Cameroon.* Washington, D.C.: Smithsonian Institution Press, 1996.

——. "Raiders and Traders in Adamawa: Slavery as a Regional System." *Paideuma* 41 (1995): 153–76.

Dognin, Rene. "L'Arbre peul [The Fulani Tree]." *Cahiers des sciences humaines* 26, no. 4 (1990): 505–29.

Dumas-Champion, Françoise. "Régicide et initiation: Limitation des règnes et le cycle initiatique dans les monts Mandara (Cameroun et Nigéria) [Regicide and Initiation: Limitation of Reigns and the Initiation Cycle in the Mandara Mountains (Cameroon and Nigeria)]." *Journal des africanistes* 65, no. 1 (1995): 5–34.

Frantz, Charles. "Fulani Continuity and Change under Five Flags." In *Pastoralists of the West African Savanna*, ed. Mahdi Adamu and A. H. M. Kirk-Greene. London: International African Institute, 1986.

Garine, Igor de. *Les Massa du Cameroun: Vie économique et sociale* [The Massa of Cameroon: Economic and Social Life]. Paris: Presses Universitaires de France, 1964.

Hallaire, Antoinette. *Paysans montagnards du nord-Cameroun: Les Monts Mandara* [Mountain Peasants of North Cameroon: The Mandara Mountains]. Paris: ORSTOM, 1991.

Hino, Shun'ya. "Fulbé People in African Urban Society: A Comparative Study of Cameroon and the Sudan." *Senri Ethnological Studies* 35 (1993): 61–85.

Hurault, Jean. "Les Noms attribués aux non-libres dans le lamidat de Banyo [Names Attributed to the Non-Free in the Lamidat of Banyo]." *Journal des africanistes* 64, no. 1 (1994): 91–107.

Izard, Michel. *Gens du pouvior; gens de la terre: Les Institutions politiques de l'ancien royaume du Yatenga* [People of Power; People of the Land: The Political Institutions of the Ancient Kingdom of the Yatenga]. Cambridge: Cambridge University Press, 1985.

Jouaux, Catherine. "Gudur: Chefferie ou royaume? [Gudur: Chiefdom or Kingdom]" *Cahiers d'études africaines* 114, vol. 29 (1989): 259– 88.

Kosack, G. "Aus der Zeit der Sklaverei (Nordkamerun): Alte Mafa erzählen [From the Time of Slavery (North Cameroon): Old Mafa Stories)]." *Paideuma* 38 (1992): 177–94.

Lavergne, George. *Une peuplade du haut Cameroun: Les Matakam* [A Clan of High Cameroon: The Matakam]. Paris: Servant-Crouzet, 1949.

Lebeuf, Annie M. D. *Les Principautés Kotoko: Essai sur le caractère sacré de l'autorité* [The Kotoko Principalities: Essay on the Sacred Character of Authority]. Paris: Editions du Centre National de la Recherche Scientifique, 1969.

Lebeuf, Jean-Paul. *L'Habitation des Fali: Montagnards du Cameroun septentrional* [The Habitation of the Fali: Mountain Dwellers of Northern Cameroon]. Paris: Hachette, 1961.

Lembezat, Bertrand. *Les populations païennes du Nord-Cameroun et de l'Adamaoua* [The Pagan Populations of North Cameroon and Adamawa]. Paris: Presses Universitaires de France, 1961.

Martin, Jean-Yves. *Le Matakam du Cameroun: Essai sur la dynamique d'une société préindustrielle* [The Matakam of Cameroon: Essay on the Dynamic of a Preindustrial Society]. Paris: ORSTOM, 1970.

Muller, J.-C. "Les Deux fois circoncis et les presque excisés: Le Cas des Dii de l'Adamaoua (nord Cameroun) [The Twice Circumcised and the Almost Excised: The Case of the Dii of Adamawa (North Cameroon)]." *Cahiers d'études africaines* 33, no. 132 (1993): 531–44.

Roitman, J. "Lost Innocence: The Production of Truth and Desire in Northern Cameroon." *Critique of Anthropology* 14, no. 3 (1994): 315–34.

Schilder, Kees. *Quest for Self Esteem: State, Islam, and Mundang Ethnicity in Northern Cameroon.* Leiden, Netherlands: African Studies Centre, 1994.

Vincent, Jeanne-Françoise. *Princes montagnards: Les Mofu-Diamané et le pouvoir politique (Cameroun du Nord)* [Mountain Princes: The Mofu-Diamané and Political Power (North Cameroon)]. Paris: Harmattan, 1991.

Northwest

Baeke, V. "Wuli Witchcraft." *Journal of the Anthropological Society of Oxford* 26, no. 1 (1995): 21–42.

Dillon, Richard G. "Ritual, Conflict, and Meaning in an African Society." *Ethos* 5, no. 2 (Summer 1977): 151–73.

Engard, Ronald. "Dance and Power in Bafut (Cameroon)." In *Creativity of Power: Cosmology and Action in African Societies.* Washington, D.C.: Smithsonian Institution Press, 1989.

Feldman-Sarelsberg, P. "Plundered Kitchens, Empty Wombs: Fear of Infertility in the Cameroonian Grassfields." *Social Science and Medicine* 39, no. 6 (1994): 463–74.

Fowler, I. "African Sacred Kings: Expectations and Performance in the Cameroun Grassfields." *Ethnology* 32, no. 3 (1993): 253–68.

Goheen, M. "Chiefs, Subchiefs and Local Control: Negotiations over Land, Struggles over Meaning." *Africa, Journal of the International African Institute* 62, no. 3 (1992): 389–412.

Gufler, H. "Social, Ritual and Religious Aspects of the Communal Hunt among the Yamba." *Baessler-Archiv* 43, no. 2 (1996): 197–228.

——. "Yamba Spider Divination." *Journal of the Anthropological Society of Oxford* 26, no. 1 (1995): 43–68.

Masquelier, Bertrand M. "Descent, Organisational Strategy, and Polity Formation in the Cameroon Highlands (Bamenda Grassfields)." *Anthropos* 88, nos. 3/4 (1993): 443–58.

Mbunwe-Samba, Patrick, Paul N. Mzeka, Mathias Niba, and Clare Wirwum. *Rites of Passage and Incorporation in the Western Grassfields of Cameroon: Birth,*

Naming, Childhood, Adolescence, the Incorporation of Royal Wives and Some Palace Rituals. Bamenda, Cameroon: Kaberry Research Centre, 1993.

Mumah, M. M. "Sacred Sites in the Bamenda Grassfields of Cameroun: A Study of Sacred Sites in the Nso' Fondom." In *Sacred Sites, Sacred Places*, ed. D. Charmichael et al. London: Routledge, 1994.

Nsamenang, B. A. "Perceptions of Parenting among the Nso of Cameroun." In *Father–Child Relations*, ed. B. S. Hewlett. New York: Aldine de Gruyter, 1992.

Probst, P. *Schrift, Staat und symbolisches Kapital bei den Wimbum: Ein ethnographischer Bericht aus dem Grasland von Kamerun* [Writing, State, and Symbolic Capital of the Wimbum: An Ethnographic Report from Cameroon]. Münster: Lit, 1992.

Probst, P., and B. Bühler. "Patterns of Control on Medicine, Politics, and Social Change among the Wimbum, Cameroon Grassfields." *Anthropos* 85, nos. 4/6 (1990): 447–54.

Ritzenthaler, Robert, and Pat Ritzenthaler. *Cameroons Village: An Ethnography of the Bafut.* Milwaukee, Wisc.: Milwaukee Public Museum, 1962.

Rowlands, Michael. "Accounting for Personal Success in Bamenda. *Concepts of the Body/Self in Africa*, ed. Joan Maw and John Pictor. Vienna: Afro-, 1992.

Rowlands, Michael. "Accumulation and the Cultural Politics of Identity in the Grassfields." In *Itinéraires d'accumulation au Cameroun: Pathways to Accumulation in Cameroon*, ed. Peter Geschiere and Piet Konings. Paris: Karthala; Leiden, Netherlands: African Studies Centre, 1993.

Shanklin, Eugenia. "Installation Rites in Kom Royal Court Compounds." *Paideuma* 36 (1990): 291–303.

Simo, J. A. M. "Structures of Control and Power and the Implications for Social Change in a Western Grassfields Chiefdom." *Paideuma* 41 (1995): 95–106.

Warnier, Jean-Pierre. "The King as a Container in the Cameroon Grassfields." *Paideuma* 39 (1993): 303–19.

——. "Slave-trading without Slave-raiding in Cameroon." *Paideuma* 41 (1995): 251–72.

Zeitlyn, D. "Professor Garfinkel Visits the Soothsayers: Ethnomethodology and Mambila Divination." *Man* 25, no. 4 (1990): 654–666.

——. "Spiders In and Out of Court, or, 'the Long Legs of the Law': Styles of Spider Divination in Their Sociological Context." *Africa* 63, no. 2 (1993): 219–40.

Education

Adick, D., ed. *Missions und Kolonialpedagogik* [Missions and Colonial Education]. Cologne: Böhlau, 1993.

Amin, J. A. "Continuity and Change in Cameroon's Education: The Case of Western Cameroon." *Journal of Asian and African Studies* 29, nos. 3/4 (1994): 248–59.

Betene, Pierre L., ed. *L'Enseignement catholique au Cameroun 1890–1990* [Catholic Teaching in Cameroon 1890–1990]. Yaoundé: Secretariat Permanent de l'Enseignement Catholique au Cameroun, 1992.

Boyle, Patrick M. "Parents, Private Schools, and the Politics of an Emerging Civil Society in Cameroon." *Journal of Modern African Studies* 34, no. 4 (1996): 609–22.

Courade, Christine, and Georges Courade. *Education in Anglophone Cameroon, 1915–1975.* Yaoundé: ONAREST, 1977.

Dupagne, Y. *Coopérant de l'éducation en Afrique ou l'expérience camerounaise d'un directeur de collège* [Working together for Education in Africa or the Cameroonian Experience of a College Director]. Paris: Harmattan, 1994.

Edokat, Tafah. "The Economics of Education: Evaluation of the Determinants of Primary School Performance in Cameroon." *Zimbabwe Journal of Educational Research* 2, no. 2 (1990): 93–110.

Fonlon, Bernard. "A Case for Early Bilingualism." *Abbia* (Yaoundé) 4 (December 1963): 56–94.

———. *The Genuine Intellectual.* Yaoundé: Buma Kor, 1978.

Maugenest, Denis. "L'Enseignement supérieur privé [Private Higher Education]." *Afrique contemporaine* 172 (1994): 174–85.

Mbala Owona, Rigobert. *Scolarisation et disparités socioéconomiques dans le Province de l'Est au Cameroun* [School Attendance and Socioeconomic Disparities in the East Province of Cameroon]. Yaoundé: CEPER, 1990.

Mfoulou, Jean. "Agricultural Education for Food Self–Sufficiency in Cameroon." In *Conference on the Political Economy of Cameroon, Historical Perspectives*, ed. Peter Geschiere and Piet Konings. Leiden, Netherlands: African Studies Centre, 1989.

Ndongko, Wilfred A. "Social Science Research and Policy-making in Africa: Status, Issues and Prospects." *Africa Development* 19, no. 1 (1994): 71–90.

Nju, Joseph L. *At What Price Higher Education in Africa? A Case Study of Higher Education Systems in Cameroon.* Ottawa: International Development Research Centre, 1992.

Nyamnjoh, F., ed. *The Cameroon G.C.E. Crisis: A Test of Anglophone Solidarity.* Limbe, Cameroon: Nooremac, 1996.

Paul, J.-J. "Technical Secondary Education in Togo and Cameroon: Research Note." *Economics of Education Review* 9, no. 4 (1990): 405–9.

Raaflaub, Fritz. *Die Schulen der Basler Mission in Kamerun: Ihre Geschichte und Gegenwartsaufgabe* [Schools of the Basel Mission in Cameroon: Their History and Present Task]. Basel: Basler Missionsbuchhandlung, 1948.

Saad, Hamman Tukur, and Isa Alkali Abba. "Islamic Scholarship across the Nigeria–Cameroon Border: The Case of Old Adamawa Emirate." *Frankfurter Afrikanistische Blätter* 6 (1994): 23–52.

Sikounmo, H. *L'Ecole du sous-developpement: Gros plan sur l'enseignement secondaire en Afrique* [The School of Underdevelopment: An Overview of Secondary Teaching in Africa]. Paris: Harmattan, 1992.

——. *Jeunesse et education en Afrique noire* [Youth and Education in Black Africa]. Paris: Harmattan, 1995.

Syndicat National des Enseignants du Supérieur. *La Dérive de l'université au Cameroun/The University in Cameroon: An Institution in Disarray*. Yaoundé: SYNES, 1992.

Tafah Edokat, E. O. "An Economic Analysis of the Determinants of Primary School Expenditures in Cameroon." *Journal of Third World Studies* 11, no. 1 (1994): 75–89.

Religion

Alembong, Nol. "Divine Images in Nweh Narratives, South West Province of Cameroon." *Bulletin of the International Committee on Urgent Anthropological and Ethnological Research* 36 (1994): 151–60.

Alexandre, Pierre. "Cameroun." In *Islam in Africa*, ed. James Kritzeck and William H. Lewis. New York: von Nostrand-Reinhold, 1969.

Bahoken, Jean Calvin. *Clairières métaphysiques africaines: Essai sur la philosophie et la religion chez les Bantu du Sud-Cameroun* [Metaphysical African Clearings: Essays on Philosophy and Religion among the Bantu of South Cameroon]. Paris: Présence africaine, 1967.

Beek, W. E. A. van. "The Innocent Sorcerer: Coping with Evil in Two African Societies (Kapsiki and Dogon)." In *Religion in Africa: Experience and Expression*, ed. T. D. Blakely et al. London: Currey, 1994.

Braukamper, Ulrich. *Der Einfluss des Islam auf die Geschichte und Kulturentwicklung Adamauas* [The Influence of Islam on the History and Cultural Evolution of Adamawa]. Weisbaden: Steiner, 1970.

Brutsch, Jean-René. "Origine et développement d'une église indépendante africaine: L'Eglise Baptiste camerounaise [Origin and Development of an Independent African Church: The Cameroonian Baptist Church]." *Monde non Chrétien* 12 (October–December 1949): 408–24.

Christensen, T. G. *An African Tree of Life*. Maryknoll, N.Y.: Orbis, 1990.

Criaud, Jean. *Ils ont planté l'église au Cameroun: Les Pallottins,1890–1915* [They Planted the Church in Cameroon: The Pallottins, 1890–1915]. Yaoundé: IMA, 1989.

Curley, Richard T. "Private Dreams and Public Knowledge in a Cameroonian Independent Church." In *Dreaming, Religion and Society in Africa*, ed. M. C. Jedrej and Rosalind Shaw. Leiden, Netherlands: Brill, 1992.

Dentan, Anne. "Lotin a Same et la Native Baptist Church: chronique de la première église au Cameroun [Lotin a Same and the Native Baptist Church: Chronicle of the First Church in Cameroon]." *Genève-Afrique* 28, no. 1 (1990): 36–64.

Ela, Jean-Marc. *My Faith as an African*. London: Chapman, 1989; Maryknoll, N.Y.: Orbis, 1988.

——. *African Cry*. Maryknoll, N.Y.: Orbis, n.d.

Engonga Bikoro, Blandine. "Cosmologie Bantu: Origine de la vie, du monde et de Dieu chez les Fang [Bantu Cosmology: Origin of Life, of the World and of God among the Fang]." *Muntu* 6 (1987): 105–19.

Fardon, Richard. *Between God, the Dead and the Wild: Chamba Interpretations of Religion and Ritual.* Washington, D.C.: Smithsonian Institution Press, 1990.

Fouda, Basile J. "Philosophical Dialogue and the Problem of Evil amongst the Beti (Southern Cameroon)." *Journal of African Religion and Philosophy* 1, no. 2 (1990): 43–52.

Gausset, Quentin. "Contribution à l'étude du pouvoir sacré chez les Wawa (Adamawa, Cameroun) [Contribution to the Study of Sacred Power among the Wawa (Adamawa, Cameroon)]." *Journal des africanistes* 65, no. 2 (1995): 179–200.

Innes, Alexander. *The Cameroons and the Baptist Mission in Four Parts.* Birkenhead, England: Author, 1895.

Kofon, N. Engelbert. *Polygyny in Pre-Christian Bafut and New Moral Theological Perspectives*. Frankfurt am Main: Lang, 1992.

Mbunwe-Samba, P. *Witchcraft, Magic and Divination: A Personal Testimony*. Bamenda: Catholic Education Secretariat, 1996.

Mbuy, Tatah H. *African Traditional Religion as Anonymous Christianity: The Case of the Tikars of the Bamenda Grassfields*. Bamenda: Unique Printers, 1994.

———. ed. *Shepherd on the Bamenda Highlands: The Pastoral Views of Paul Verdezekov, Archbishop of Bamenda*. N.p.: Jubilee Publication Committee, 1995.

Mve-Ondo, Bonaventure. "Pour une lecture philosophique des textes traditionnels africains [For a Philosophical Lecture of Traditional African Texts]." *Studia Africana* 6 (1995): 97– 104.

Nkoe, B. *De la procuration à la conviction: Cent ans d'évangelisation du Cameroun* [From the Proxy to the Conviction: 100 Years of Evangelization of Cameroon]. Yaoundé: Sopecam, 1991.

Okafor, Gabriel Maduka. *Christians and Muslims in Cameroon*. Wurzburg, Germany: Echter, 1994.

O'Neil, Robert J. *Mission to the British Cameroons*. London: Mission Book Service, 1991.

Rosny, Eric de. *Healers in the Night*. Maryknoll, N.Y.: Orbis, 1985.

Saker, E. M. *Alfred Saker: The Pioneer of the Cameroons.* London: The Religious Tract Society, 1908.

Santen, J. C. M. van. *They Leave Their Jars Behind: The Conversion of Mafa Women to Islam.* Leiden: Centrum Vrouwen en Autonomie, 1993.

Slageren, Jaap Van. *Histoire de l'église en Afrique (Cameroun)* [History of the Church in Africa (Cameroon)]. Yaoundé: CLE, 1969.

Titi, Nwel P. *Thong Likeng: Fondateur de la religion Nyambe-Bantu* [Thong Likeng: Founder of the Nyambe-Bantu Religion]. Paris: Harmattan, 1986.

Wan-Tatah, Fon Victor. *Emancipation in African Theology: An Inquiry on the Relevance of Latin American Liberation Theology to Africa*. New York: Lang, 1989.

Weber, Charles W. *International Influences and Baptist Mission in West Cameroon: German–African Missionary Endeavor under International Mandate and British Colonialism*. Leiden, Netherlands: Brill, 1993.

Westermann, Diedrich. *Die Verbreitung des Islams in Togo und Kamerun* [The Spread of Islam in Togo and Cameroon]. Berlin: Reimer, 1914.

Zeitlyn, David. *Sua in Somié: Aspects of Mambila Traditional Religion.* St. Augustin: Academia, 1994.

Sociology

Abega, Prosper. "Prêtre à la Briqueterie [A Priest in Briqueterie]." *Politique africaine* 35 (1989): 39–49.

Achu Gwan, Emmanuel. "Labour Migration in Cameroon Republic." *Revue de géographie du Cameroun* 10, no. 1 (1991): 9–19.

Amin, Aloysius Ajab. "The Socio-economic Impact of Child Labour in Cameroon." *Labour, Capital and Society* 27, no. 2 (1994): 235–48.

Ardener, Edwin, Shirley Ardener, and W. A. Warmington. *Plantation and Village in the Cameroons.* London: Oxford University Press for the Nigerian Institute of Social and Economic Research, 1960.

Awambeng, Christopher M. *Evolution and Growth of Urban Centres in the North-West Province (Cameroon).* Bern: Lang, 1991.

Ba, C. O. "Un Exemple d'essoufflement de l'immigration sénégalaise: Les Sénégalais au Cameroun [An Example of the Dwindling of Senegalese Immigration: The Senegalese in Cameroon]." *Mondes en développement* 23, no. 91 (1995): 31–44.

Bekombo, Manga. "Viellissement, culture et société en Afrique [Ageing, Culture and Society in Africa]." *Viellir en Afrique,* ed. Claudine Attias-Donfut and Léopold Rosenmayr. Paris: Presses Universitaires de France, 1994.

Bissek, P. *Habitat et démocratisation au Caméroun* [Housing and Democratization in Cameroon]. Paris: Karthala, 1994.

Breton, Roland, and Michel Dieu. "More Than 230 Languages in Cameroon." *Courier* 80 (July–August 1980): 92–95.

Courade, Georges, ed. *Le Village camerounais à l'heure de l'ajustement* [The Cameroonian Village at the Time of Adjustment]. Paris: Karthala, 1994.

DeLancey, Mark W. "Plantation and Migration in the Mt. Cameroon Region." In *Kamerun*, ed. Hans F. Illy. Mainz, Germany: Hase & Koehler, 1974.

Ejedepang-Koge, S. N. *Change in Cameroun*. Yaoundé: Author, 1985.

Fisiy, C., and Peter Geschiere. "Witchcraft, Violence and Identity: Different Trajectories in Postcolonial Cameroon." In *Postcolonial Identities*, ed. R. Werbner and T. Ranger. London: Zed, 1996.

Fodouop, R. *Les Petits métiers de rue et l'emploi: Le Cas de Yaoundé* [Small Trades of the Street and Employment: The Case of Yaoundé]. Yaoundé: SOPECAM, 1991.

Frenay, Patrick. "Le Cameroun anglophone dans le procéssus d'integration nationale: Les Consequences de la marginalisation d'une region sur le développement des villes [Anglophone Cameroon in the Process of National Integration: The Consequences of Regional Marginalization on the Development of Towns].” *Cahiers d'outre-mer* 40, no. 159 (1987): 217–36.

———. “Du quelques faits nouveaux de la dynamique urbaine de Cameroun [Some New Facts on the Urban Dynamics of Cameroon].” In *La Recherche en sciences humaines au Cameroun: D'Etude Bruxelles, 20 juin 1989*, ed. P. Salmon and J.-J. Symoens. Brussels: Académie Royale des Sciences d'Outre-Mer, 1991.

Garine, Igor de. “Facteurs socio-culturels et saisonnalité dans l'alimentation: L'Exemple de deux populations du Tchad et du Cameroun (Massa-Moussey) [Socio-Cultural Factors and Seasonality of Food: The Example of Two Populations of Chad and Cameroon].” In *Les Changements des habitudes et des politiques alimentaires en Afrique: Aspects des sciences humaines, naturelles et sociales*, ed. Igor de Garine. Paris: Publisud, 1991.

Geschiere, Peter. “The Modernity of Witchcraft: Examples from Cameroon.” *Leidschrift* 10, no. 2 (1994): 69–87.

Iyebi-Mandjek, Olivier. “Les Migrations saisonnières chez les Mafas, montagnards du Nord-Cameroun: Une Solution au surpeuplement et un frein à l'émigration définitive [Seasonal Migrations among the Mafa, Mountain Folk of North Cameroon: A Solution to Overpopulation and a Brake on Permanent Migration].” *Cahiers des sciences humaines* 29, nos. 2/3 (1993): 419–41.

Konings, P. *Labour Control and Labour Resistance in the Agro-Industrial Plantations of Cameroon: The Case of the Cameroon Development Corporation*. London: Kegan Paul International, 1991.

———. *Labour Resistance in Cameroon: Managerial Strategies and Labour Resistance in the Agro-Industrial Plantations of the CDC 1947–1987*. London: Currey, 1993.

Mainet, Guy. “Pauvreté relative et dynamique populaire dans l'agglomération doualaise [Relative Poverty and Popular Dynamics in a Douala Suburb].” In *Pauvreté et développement dans les pays tropicaux*, ed. T. Singaravelou. Bordeaux: Centre d'Etudes de Géographie Tropicale, Université de Bordeaux, 1989.

Njoh, A. J. “Building and Urban Land Use Controls in Developing Countries: A Critical Appraisal of the Kumba (Cameroon) Zoning Ordinance.” *Third World Planning Review* 17, no. 3 (1995): 337–56.

———. “Institutional Impediments to Private Residential Development in Cameroon.” *Third World Planning Review* 14, no. 1 (1991): 21–37.

Ouden, J. H. B. Den. “In Search of Personal Mobility: Changing Interpersonal Relations in Two Bamiléké Chiefdoms.” *Africa* 57, no. 1 (1987): 3–27.

Timnou, J. P. *Migration, Urbanisation et développment au Cameroun* [Migration, Urbanization and Development in Cameroon]. Paris: IFORD/CEPED, 1993.

Tsala Tsala, Jacques Philippe. “La Dot endettée ou la question du père: Problématique psychologique de la dot au Cameroun [The Dowry Debt or the Question of the Father: Psychological Problem of the Dowry in Cameroon].” *Cahiers de sociologie économique et culturelle* 14 (1990): 85–96.

——. "Souffrance familiale et famille en souffrance: La Famille Camerounaise entre le village et la ville [Family Suffering and Families on Sufferance: The Cameroon Family between the Village and the City]." *Cahiers de sociologie économique et culturelle* 18 (1992): 99–113.

United Nations Development Program. *Rapport sur le développement humain au Cameroun—1993* [Report on Human Development in Cameroon—1993]. Yaoundé: Author, 1993.

UNESCO. "Succor for Youth: The Hostel of Hope, Cameroon." In *Working with Street Children.* Paris: Author, 1995.

"La vie urbaine et municipale Douala [Urban Life and Douala City]." *Marchés tropicaux et méditerranéens* 45, no. 2267 (1989): 1061–90.

Wautelet, J. M. "Disparités régionales et differenciation des paysanneries au Cameroun [Regional Disparities and Differentiation of the Peasantries in Cameroon]." *Revue tiers-monde* 36, no. 141 (1995): 87–101.

Zoa, A. S. *Les Ordures à Yaoundé: Urbanisation, environment et politique au Cameroun* [The Garbage in Yaoundé: Urbanization, Environment and Politics in Cameroon]. Paris: Harmattan, 1996.

Women

Abega, Cécile Sévérin. "La Bru tueuse [The Killer Daughter-in-Law]." *Journal des Africanistes* 62, no. 1 (1992): 95–106.

——. "Le Refus de l'acte de mariage chez les femmes Mafa [The Refusal of Marriage among Mafa Women]." *African Anthropology* 1, no. 1/2 (1994): 94–102.

Adler, A. "La Fillette amoureuse des masques: Le Statut de la femme chez les Moudang [The Little Girl in Love with Masks: The Status of Women among the Moudang]." *Journal des Africanistes* 59, no. 1–2 (1989): 63–97.

Ardener, Edwin. *Divorce and Fertility: An African Study*. London: Oxford University Press, 1962.

Ardener, Shirley, ed. *Persons and Powers of Women in Diverse Cultures.* Oxford: Berg, 1992.

Barbier, Jean-Claude, ed. *Femmes du Cameroun: Mères pacifiques, femmes rebelles* [Women of Cameroon: Peaceful Mothers, Rebel Wives]. Paris: Karthala, 1985.

Beat-Songue, Paulette. "Prostitution, à 'petit–métier' during Economic Crisis: A Road to Women's Liberation?: The Case of Cameroon." In *Courtyards, Markets, City Streets: Urban Women in Africa*, ed. Kathleen Staudt. Boulder, Colo.: Westview, 1996.

Berg, Adri van den. "Les Femmes et les terres: Mariage malheureux ou alliance stratégique? [Women and Land: Unfortunate Marriage or Strategic Alliance?]." In *Phénomènes informels et dynamiques culturelles en Afrique*, ed. G. De Villers. Brussels: Institut Africain, CEDAF, 1996.

——. "Land and Marriage: Women's Strategies in the Extreme North of Cameroon." *Focaal* 22/23 (1994): 65–81.

Bowie, Fiona. "The Elusive Christian Family: Missionary Attempts to Define Women's Roles. Case Studies from the Cameroon." In *Women and Mission: Past and Present: Anthropological and Historical Perspectives*, ed. Fiona Bowie, D. Kirkwood, and S. Ardener. Oxford: Berg, 1993.

Copet-Rougier, Elisabeth. "'L'Antilope accouche toujours de l'éléphant'(devinette Mkako): Etude de la transformation du mariage chez les Mkako du Cameroun [The Antelope Always Gives Birth to the Elephant (Mkako Riddle): Study on the Transformation of Marriage in the Mkako of Cameroon]." In *Transformations of African Marriage*, ed. David Parkin and David Nyamwaya. Manchester, England: Manchester University Press, 1987.

DeLancey, Mark W. "Women's Cooperatives in Cameroon: The Cooperative Experiences of the Northwest and Southwest Provinces." *African Studies Review* 30, no. 1 (1987): 1–18.

DeLancey, Virginia. "Wage Earner and Mother: Compatibility of Roles on a Cameroon Plantation." In *Women, Education and Modernization of the Family*, ed. Helen Ware. Canberra: Australian National University, 1981.

Diduk, Susan. "Women's Agricultural Production and Political Action in the Cameroon Grassfields." *Africa, Journal of the International African Institute* 59, no. 3 (1989): 338–55.

Dong'Aroga, Joseph. "La Place de la femme dans la société camerounaise traditionnelle d'après la littérature orale [The Place of the Woman in Traditional Cameroonian Society according to Oral Literature]." *Bulletin of the International Committee on Urgent Anthropological and Ethnological Research* 37/38 (1995/96): 171–83.

Feldman-Savelsberg, P. "Cooking Inside: Kinship and Gender in Bangangté Idioms of Marriage and Procreation." *American Ethnologist* 22, no. 3 (1995): 483–501.

Freudenberger, K. S. "New Technology for Rural Women: Paradoxes of Sustainability." *Development in Practice* 4, no. 1 (1994): 13–22.

Goheen, Miriam. "The Ideology and Political Economy of Gender: Women and Land in Nso', Cameroon." In *Structural Adjustment and African Women Farmers*, ed. C. H. Gladwin. Gainesville: University of Florida Press, 1991.

———. "Land and the Household Economy: Women Farmers of the Grassfields Today." In *Agriculture, Women, and Land: The African Experience*, ed. Jean Davison. Boulder, Colo.: Westview, 1988.

———. *Men Own the Fields, Women Own the Crops: Gender and Power in the Cameroon Grassfields.* Madison: University of Wisconsin Press, 1996.

Holtedahl, Lisbet. "Education, Economics and the 'Good Life': Women in Ngaoundéré, Northern Cameroon." In *Itinéraires d'accumulation au Cameroun–Pathways to Accumulation in Cameroon*, ed. Peter Geschiere and Piet Konings. Paris: Karthala, 1993.

Houseman, Michael. "Social Structure Is Where the Hearth Is: A 'Women's Place' in Beti Society." *Africa, Journal of the International African Institute* 58, no. 1 (1988): 51–69.

Kaberry, Phyllis M. *Women of the Grassfields: A Study of the Economic Position of Women in Bamenda, British Cameroons*. London: Her Majesty's Stationery Office, 1952.

Kondé, E. *The Use of Women for the Empowerment of Men in African Nationalist Politics: The 1958 "Anlu" in Cameroon.* Boston: African Studies Center, Boston University, 1990.

Konings, Piet. *Gender and Class in the Tea Estates of Cameroon.* Leiden, Netherlands: African Studies Centre, 1995.

Kosack, G. "Denn die Erde gehört dem Mann: Frauen in Kamerun [Because the Earth Belongs to Man: Women in Cameroon]." *Marxistische Blätter* 4 (1996): 68–75.

Krieger, Judith. "Rural Women, Urban Food." *African Rural and Urban Studies* 2, no. 1 (1995): 89–109.

Lewis, B. "Farming Women, Public Policy and the Women's Ministry: A Case Study from Cameroon." In *Women, International Development, and Politics*, ed. Kathleen Staudt. Philadelphia: Temple University Press, 1990.

Mope Simo, J. A. "Ideology and Differentiation in the Ndop Plains: Rural Women's Strategies for Economic Independence." In *Conference on the Political Economy of Cameroon*, ed. Peter Geschiere and Piet Konings. Leiden, Netherlands: African Studies Centre, 1989.

Mope Simo, J. A. "Royal Wives in the Ndop Plain." *Canadian Journal of African Studies* 25, no. 3 (1991): 418–31.

Ngwa, N. E. "The Role of Women in Environmental Management: An Overview of the Rural Cameroonian Situation." *Geojournal* 35, no. 4 (1995): 515–20.

Ngwafar, E. "Cameroon Property Rights for Women—A Bold Step in the Wrong Direction." *Journal of Family Law* 29, no. 2 (1991): 297–303.

Nkwi, Paul N. "The Changing Role of Women and Their Contributions to the Domestic Economy in Cameroon." In *Transformations of African Marriages*, ed. D. Parkin and D. Nyamwaya. Manchester: Manchester University Press for the International African Institute, 1987.

Ombolo, J. P. *Sexe et société en Afrique noire: L'Anthropologie sexuelle Beti. Essai analytique, critique et comparatif* [Sex and Society in Black Africa: The Sexual Anthropology of the Beti. An Analytical, Critical and Comparative Essay]. Paris: Harmattan, 1991.

Shanklin, Eugenia. "Anlu Remembered: The Kom Women's Rebellion of 1958–61." *Dialectical Anthropology* 15 (1990): 159–81.

Smith, Suzanna, and Barbara Taylor. "Curriculum Planning for Women and Agricultural Households: The Case of Cameroon." In *Structural Adjustment and African Women Farmers*. Gainesville: University of Florida Press, 1991.

Tsala Tsala, Jacques-Philippe. "Grossesse et interdits chez la femme beti du Sud Cameroun [Pregnancy and Taboos among the Beti Women of South Cameroon]." *Cahiers de sociologie économique et culturelle* 25 (1996): 85–94.

Westermann, V. *Women's Disturbances: Der Anlu-Aufstand bei den Kom 1958–1960* [Women's Disturbances: The Anlu Uprising among the Kom 1958–1960]. Münster: Lit, 1990.

Woodhouse, H., and T. M. Ndongko. "Women and Science Education in Cameroon: Some Critical Reflections." *Interchange* 241/2 (1993): 131–58.

Yana, Simon David. "Statuts et rôles féminins au Cameroun: Réalités d'hier, images d'aujourd'hui [Status and Feminine Roles in Cameroon: Realities of Yesterday, Images of Today]." *Politique africaine* 65 (1997): 35–47.

CULTURE

Archaeology and Prehistory

Annaud, Mathilde. "Des animaux à carapace molle: Organisation spatiale des relations sociales dans la société Tikar du territoire de Cindji, Cameroun central [Soft-Shelled Animals: Spatial Organization of Social Relations in Tikar Society in the Cindji Territory, Central Cameroon]." *Préhistoire anthropologie méditerranéenne* 6 (1997): 155–84.

Buisson, E. M. "Matériaux pour servir à la prehistoire du Cameroun [Materials for Use in the Prehistory of Cameroon]." *Bulletin de la Société Préhistorique Française* 30 (1933): 335–48.

David, Nicholas C. "Between Bloomery and Blast Furnace: Mafa Iron-smelting Technology in North Cameroon." *African Archaeological Review* 7 (1989): 183–208.

De Maret, P. "La Recherche archéologique au Cameroun [Archaeological Research in Cameroon]." In *La Recherche en sciences humaines au Cameroun: Journée d'étude Bruxelles, 20 juin 1989*, ed. P. Salmon and J.-J. Symoens. Brussels: Académie Royale des Sciences d'Outre-Mer, 1991.

Essomba, Joseph-Marie. *L'Archéologie au Cameroun: Actes du premier Colloque international de Yaoundé* [Archaeology in Cameroon: Proceedings of the First International Colloquium of Yaoundé]. Paris: Karthala, 1988.

——. *Bibliographie critique de l'archéologie camerounaise* [Critical Bibliography of Cameroon Archaeology]. Yaoundé: University of Yaoundé, 1986.

——. *Civilisation de fer en sociétés en Afrique centrale* [Iron Civilization in Central African Societies]. Paris: Harmattan, 1992.

——. "Dix ans de recherches archéologiques au Cameroun méridional (1979–1989) [Ten Years of Archaeological Research in Southern Cameroon (1979–1989)]." *Nsi* 6 (1989): 33–57.

Fowler, I. "The Oku Iron Industry in Its Regional Setting: A Descriptive Account." *Basler-Archiv* 43, no. 1 (1995): 89–126.

Griaule, Marcel. *Les Sao légendaires* [The Legendary Sao]. Paris: Gallimard, 1943.

Holl, Augustin. "The Cemetery of Houlouf in Northern Cameroon (AD 1500–1600): Fragments of a Past Social System." *African Archaeological Review* 12 (1994): 133–70.

MacEachern, Scott. "Selling the Iron for Their Shackles: Wandala-Montagnard Interactions in Northern Cameroon." *Journal of African History* 34, no. 2 (1993): 247–70.

Marliac, Alain. *De la préhistoire à l'histoire au Cameroun septentrional* [From Prehistory to History in Northern Cameroon]. Paris: ORSTOM, 1991.

Marliac, Alain, and O. Langlois. "Les Civilisations de l'age du fer au Diamare (Cameroun septentrional): Des Cultures aux ethnies [Civilizations of the Iron Age in Diamaré (Northern Cameroon): From Cultures to Ethnic Groups]." *Anthropologie* 100, no. 2/3 (1996): 420–56.

Pwiti, Gilbert, and Robert Soper, eds. *Aspects of African Archaeology*. Harare: University of Zimbabwe Publications, 1996.

Vogel, Joseph O., ed. *Encyclopedia of Precolonial Africa: Archaeology, History, Languages, Cultures, and Environments.* Walnut Creek, Calif.: Alta Mira, 1997.

Warnier, Jean-Pierre. "Métallurgie du groupe Chap des Grassfields Camerounais [Metallurgy of the Chap Group from the Cameroonian Grasslands]." *Muntu* 8 (1988): 9–25.

Architecture

Aradeon, Susan B. "Mofou Architecture." *African Arts* 14, no. 1 (November 1980): 58–60, 88.

Beguin, J. P., et al. *L'Habitat au Cameroun* [The Habitat in Cameroon]. Paris: ORSTOM and Union Française, 1952.

Gebauer, Paul. "Architecture of Cameroon." *African Arts* 5, no. 1 (1971): 40–49.

Ghomsi, Emmanuel. "Organisation et fonctions des résidences royales dans les Grassfields du Cameroun [Organization and Functions of the Royal Residences in the Grassfields of Cameroon]." *Paideuma* 31 (1985): 49–63.

Labouret, Henri. "L'Ancien palais royal de Foumban [The Old Foumban Royal Palace]." *Togo-Cameroun* (April–July 1935): 121–26.

Lauber, Wolfgang. *Deutsche architektur in Kamerun 1884–1914: Deutsche architekten und Kameruner wissenschaftler dokumentieren die bauten der deutschen epoche in Kamerun/Afrika* [German Architecture in Cameroon 1884–1914: German Architects and Cameroon Scientists Document the Building of the German Epoch in Cameroon/Africa]. Stuttgart: Kramer, 1988.

———. *Palaste und gehofte im Grasland von Kamerun: Traditionelle holzarchitektur eines westafrikanischen Landes* [Palaces and Farmstands in Cameroon: Traditional Wooden Architecture of a West African Land]. Stuttgart: Kramer, 1990.

Lebeuf, Jean-Paul. "Maisons Peules du Cameroon [Fulani Houses of Cameroon]." *Itinerances . . . en pays Peul et ailleurs,* vol. 2. Paris: Société des Africanistes, 1981.

Lyons, Diane. "The Politics of House Shape: Round vs. Rectilinear Domestic Structures in Déla Compounds, Northern Cameroon." *Antiquity* 70, no. 268 (June 1996): 351–67.

Robert, Marc. *La Restauration du palais des Sultans de Bamoum à Foumban* [The Restoration of the Palace of the Sultans of Bamoum in Foumban]. Paris: UNESCO, 1980.

Rowlands, Michael. "Notes on the Material Symbolism of Grassfields Palaces." *Paideuma* 31 (1985): 203–13.

Seignobos, Christian. *Montagnes et hautes terres du Nord Cameroun* [Mountains and High Lands of North Cameroon]. Roquevaire, France: Parenthèses, 1982.

Arts, Artisanry, and Music

Baeke, Viviane. "Water Spirits and Witchcraft: Rituals, Myths and Objects (Mfumte-Wuli, Western Cameroon)." In *Objects: Signs of Africa*, ed. Luc de Heusch. Tervuren, Belgium: Musée Royal de l'Afrique Centrale, 1995.

Barley, N. "The Linguistic Image in the Interpretation of African Objects." *African Languages and Cultures* 1, no. 2 (1988): 93–105.

Barlow, Sean, and Banning Eyre. *Afropop! An Illustrated Guide to Contemporary African Music*. Edison, N.J.: Chartwell, 1995.

Bascom, William R., Paul Gebauer, and Robert F. Ritzenthaler. *Handbook of West African Art.* Milwaukee, Wisc.: Public Museum, 1953.

Bebey, Francis. *African Music: A People's Art*. Westport, Conn.: Hill, 1975.

Beek, Walter E. A. van. "Iron, Brass and Burial: The Kapsiki Blacksmith and His Many Crafts." In *Forge et forgerons: Actes du IV colloque mega-Tchad CNRS/ORSTOM, Paris du 14 au 16 Sept. 1988.* Vol. 1, ed. Yves Moñino. Paris: ORSTOM, 1991.

Bender, Wolfgang. "Soul Makossa and African Chanson: Cameroun." In *Sweet Mother: Modern African Music*. Chicago: University of Chicago Press, 1991.

Beumers, Erna, and Hans-Joachim Koloss. *Kings of Africa: Art and Authority in Central Africa: Collection Museum für Völkerkunde, Berlin.* Utrecht, Netherlands: Foundation Kings of Africa, 1992.

Blier, Suzanne P. *Africa's Cross River: Art of the Nigerian–Cameroon Border.* New York: L. Kahan Gallery, 1980.

Campbell, Kenneth F. "L'Agwe, masque spécifiquement Widekum [L'Agwe, a Specifically Widekum Mask." *Arts d'Afrique Noire* 67 (Autumn 1988): 17–27.

Caraway, Caren. *African Designs of Nigeria and the Cameroons.* Owins Hills, Md.: Stemmer House, 1984.

Dibango, Manu. *Three Kilos of Coffee: An Autobiography.* Chicago: University of Chicago Press, 1994.

Edelman, Nancy W. *Guide de l'art Camerounais du Musée Monastère Benedictin Monte Febe, Yaoundé: Une Visite guidée en compagnie du père Omer Bauer* [Guide to the Cameroonian Art of the Mount Febe Monastery Museum: A Guided Visit in the Company of Father Omer Bauer]. Yaoundé: Mount Febe Benedictine Monastery Museum, 1989.

Elouga, M. "Semiologie des motifs décoratifs de la céramique actuelle d'un groupe Bantu du sud-Cameroun: Les Beti de la Lekie [Semiology of the Decorative Motifs of the Existing Ceramics of a Bantu Group of South-Cameroon: The Beti of the Lekie]." *Nsi* 10/11 (1992): 7–24.

Eno Belinga, S. M. *Ballades et chansons africaines* [African Ballads and Songs]. Yaoundé: CEPER, 1982.

Erlman, Veit. "Model, Variation and Performance: Praise Song of the Fulani." *Yearbook for Traditional Music* 17 (1985): 88–112.

Essomba, Joseph-Marie. L'Art traditionnel au Cameroun: Statues et masques [Traditional Art in Cameroon: Statues and Masks]. Suresnes, France: Dupuch, 1982.

Etienne-Nugue, Jocelyne, and Harri Peccinotti. *Crafts and the Arts of Living in Cameroon.* Baton Rouge: Louisiana State University Press, 1982.

Fagg, William Butler. *African Majesty from Grassland and Forest*. Toronto: Art Gallery of Ontario, 1981.

Geary, Christraud M. "Art and Political Process in the Kingdoms of Bali-Nyonga and Bamum (Cameroon Grassfields)." *Canadian Journal of African Studies* 22, no. 1 (1988): 11–41.

———. "Art, Politics, and the Transformation of Meaning: Bamum Art in the Twentieth Century." In *African Material Culture*, ed. Mary Jo Arnoldi, Christraud M. Geary, and Kris L. Hardin. Bloomington: Indiana University Press, 1996.

———. "Basketry in the Aghem-Fungom Area of the Cameroon Grassfields." *African Arts* 20, no. 3 (May 1987): 42–53, 89–90.

———. *Images from Bamum: German Colonial Photography at the Court of King Njoya, Cameroon, West Africa, 1902–1915.* Washington, D.C.: Smithsonian Institution Press, 1988.

———. "Messages and Meaning of African Court Arts: Warrior Figures from the Bamum Kingdom." *Art Journal* 47, no. 2 (Summer 1988): 103–13.

———. *Patterns from Without, Meaning from Within: European-style Military Dress and German Colonial Politics in the Bamum Kingdom (Cameroon).* Boston: Boston University: African Studies Centre, 1989.

———. *The Voyage of King Njoya's Gift: A Beaded Sculpture from the Bamum Kingdom, Cameroon, in the National Museum of African Art, Smithsonian Institution, Washington, DC.* Washington, D.C.: Smithsonian Institution, National Museum of African Art, 1994.

Graham, Ronnie. "Cameroon." In *The Da Capo Guide to Contemporary African Music.* New York: Da Capo; London: Zwan 1988.

———. "Cameroon." In *The World of African Music: Stern's Guide to Contemporary African Music, Vol. 2.* London: Pluto, 1992.

Haafkens, J. *Chants Musulmans en Peul: Textes de l'héritage de la communauté Musulmane de Maroua, Cameroun* [Muslim Songs in Fulani: Texts of the Heritage of the Muslim Community of Maroua, Cameroon]. Leiden: Brill, 1983.

Harter, Pierre. "Arts anciens du Cameroun [Ancient Arts of Cameroon]." *Arts d'Afrique Noire* 40 suppl. (1986): 374.

———. "The Beads of Cameroon." *Beads: Journal of the Society of Bead Researchers* 4 (1992): 5–20.

———. "Royal Commemorative Figures in the Cameroon Grasslands: Ateu Atsa, a Bangwa Artist." *African Arts* 23, no. 4 (October 1990): 70–77, 96.

Herbert, Eugenia. "Lost-wax Casting in the Cameroon Grassfields." In *West African Economic and Social History: Studies in Memory of Marion Johnson*, ed. David Henige and T. C. McCaskie. Madison: University of Wisconsin Press, 1990.

Jarocki, Barbara. *Cameroon: Art and Life Interwoven*. Chicago: May Weber Museum of Cultural Arts in cooperation with L. Kahan Gallery, New York City, 1988.

Kayo, Patrice. *Chansons populaires Bamiléké suivies de déchirements* [Popular Bamiléké Songs of Sadness Following Heartbreak]. Paris: Silex, 1983.

Lamb, Venice, and Alastair Lamb. *Au Cameroun: Weaving-tissage* [In Cameroon: Fabric Weaving]. Douala: Elf Serepca Cameroun, 1981.

Massa, Gabriel. *Masques animaux d'Afrique de l'ouest* {Animal Masks of West Africa]. Paris: Sepia, 1985.

Mveng, Engelbert. *L'Art et l'artisanats africain* [African Art and Crafts]. Yaoundé: CLE, 1980.

Ndiaye, Francine. *Emblèmes du pouvoir: Collection Mourtala Diop, Nigeria–Cameroun* [Emblems of Power: Mourtala Diop Collection, Nigeria–Cameroon]. Paris: Sépia, 1994.

Neeley, Paul. "Drummed Transactions: Calling the Church in Cameroon."*Anthropological Linguistics* 38, no. 4 (Winter 1996): 683–717.

Nicklin, Keith. "Cross River Studies." *African Arts* 18, no. 1 (November 1984): 24–27, 96.

Nicklin, Keith, and Jill Salmons. "Cross River Art Styles." *African Arts* 18, no. 1 (November 1984): 28–43, 93–94.

Njoya, Aboubakar Njiassé. "Chants dynastiques et chants populaires Bamum: Sources d'informations historiques [Bamum Dynastic and Popular Songs: Sources of Historical Information." In *Sources orales de l'histoire de l'Afrique*, ed. Claude-Hélène Perrot et al. Paris: Centre National de la Recherche Scientifique, 1989.

———. "Le collier de bronze royal Bamoum: Mgba-Mgba. [The Bronze Necklace of the Royal Bamoum: Mgba-Mgba]." *Art Tribal* (1995): 13–22.

Notué, J.-P. *Batcham: Sculptures du Cameroun: Nouvelles perspectives anthropologiques* [Batcham: Sculptures of Cameroon: New Anthropological Perspectives]. Marseilles: Musée d'Arts Africains, Océaniens, Amérindiens, 1993.

Perrois, Louis. *Arts royaux du Cameroun* [Royal Arts of Cameroon]. Geneva, Switzerland: Musée Barbier–Mueller, 1994.

———. *Byeri Fang: Sculptures d'ancêtres en Afrique* [Byeri Fang: Sculptures of Ancestors in Africa]. Marseilles, France: Musée d'Arts Africains, Océaniens, Amérindiens, 1992.

———. *Legs Pierre Harter: Les Rois sculpteurs: Art et pouvoir dans le Grassland Camerounais* [The Bequest of Pierre Harter: The Sculpter Kings: Art and Power in the Cameroon Grasslands]. Paris: Musée National des Arts d'Afrique et d'Océanie, 1993.

———. "Sculptures du Nord-Ouest du Cameroun. [Sculptures from North-west Cameroon]." *Dossiers Histoire et Archéologie* 130 (September 1988): 62–79.

Perrois, Louis, and Jean-Paul Notué. "Contribution à l'étude des arts plastiques du Cameroun [Contribution to the Study of the Plastic Arts of Cameroon]." *Muntu: Revue scientifique et culturelle du CICIBA* 4–5 (1986): 165–222.

Schneider, Gilbert D. "Celebrating the Achievements of Nyangabo: The Funeral of a Kom Elder." *African Arts* 28, no. 2 (Spring 1995): 58– 63.

Shanklin, Eugenia. "The Odyssey of the Afo-a-Kom." *African Arts* 23, no. 4 (October 1990): 62–69, 95–96.

Tardits, Claude. "Cadeau royal Bamoum: Une Pipe [A Bamoum Royal Gift: A Pipe]." *Art Tribal* (1993): 47–62.

———. "The Kingdom of Bamum (Cameroon)." In *Kings of Africa: Art and Authority in Central Africa*, ed. Erna Beumers and Hans-Joachim Koloss. Maastricht, Netherlands: Foundation Kings of Africa, 1992.

Ute, Rochenthaler. *Die Kunst der Frauen: Zur Komplementarität von Nacktheit und Maskierung bei den Ejagham im Südwesten Kameruns* [The Art of Women: The Complementarity of Nakedness and Masking among the Ejagham in Southwest Cameroon]. Berlin: Wissenschaft und Bildung, 1993.

Webb, Virginia-Lee. "The Photographs of Paul Gebauer." *African Arts* 20, no. 2 (February 1987): 46–51.

Language

Agence de Coopération Culturelle et Technique. *Atlas Linguistique de L'Afrique Centrale: Atlas Linguistique du Cameroun: Inventaire Préliminaire* [Linguistic Atlas of Central Africa: Linguistic Atlas of Cameroon: Preliminary Survey]. Paris: Author, 1983.

Barreteau, Daniel *Bibliographie des langues camerounaises* [Bibliography of Cameroonian Languages]. Paris: ORSTOM, 1993.

Barreteau, Daniel, and Robert Hedinger, eds. *Descriptions de langues camerounaises* [Descriptions of Cameroonian Languages]. Paris: ORSTOM. 1989.

Bot ba Njock, Henri Marcel. "Le problème linguistique au Cameroun [The Linguistic Problem in Cameroon]." *Afrique et Asie* 73 (1963): 3–13.

Brann, C. M. B. "Language and Society in West Africa." *West African Journal of Modern Languages* 3 (1978): 194–219.

Breton, Roland, and Michel Dieu. "More Than 230 Languages in Cameroon." *Courier* 80(July–August 1980): 92–95.

Chia, Emmanuel. "Cameroon Home Languages." In *A Sociolinguistic Profile of Urban Centers in Cameroon*, ed. Edna L. Koenig, Emmanuel Chia, and John Povey. Los Angeles: Crossroads, 1983.

Cook, A. C. "Cameroun: L'Etonnant bilinguisme [Cameroon: Surprising Bilingualism]." *Bulletin of Francophone Africa* 1 (1992): 74–82.

Fonlon, Bernard. "The Language Problem in Cameroon." *Comparative Education* 5, no. 1 (1969): 25–49; *Abbia* 22 (1969): 5–40.

Gfeller, Elisabeth, ed. *Multilingual Cameroon: Reader in Cameroonian Languages*. Yaoundé: Société International de Linguistique, 1990.

Grimes, Barbara F. "Cameroon." In *Ethnologue: Languages of the World*, ed. B. F. Grimes. Dallas: Summer Institute of Languages, 1988.

Kishani, Bongasu Tanla. "Language Problems in Anglophone Cameroon: Present Writers and Future Readers." *Quest* 8, no. 2 (1994): 101– 29.

Koenig, Edna L., Emmanuel Chia and John Povey, eds. *A Sociolinguistic Profile of Urban Centers in Cameroon*. Los Angeles: Crossroads, 1983.

Krieger, Milton. *Languages in Cameroon, 1960–1990: Bilingual Policy, Multilingual Practice*. Boston: Boston University, African Studies Center, 1991.

Lacroix, Pierre-Francis. "Distribution géographique et sociale des parleurs Peul du Nord Cameroun [Geographic and Social Distribution of Fulani Speakers in North Cameroon]." *L'Homme* 2, no. 3 (1962): 75–101.

Ownens, Jonathan. "Arabic Dialects of Chad and Nigeria (and Partially Cameroun)." *Journal of Arabic Linguistics* 14 (1985): 45–61.

Pradelles de Latour, Marie-Lorraine. "Pidgin in Douala." *York Papers in Linguistics* 11 (1984): 265–69.

Renaud, Patrick. "La situation linguistique du Cameroun, 1. coup d'oeil sur les langues, 2. aspects sociolinguistiques [The Linguistic Situation of Cameroon, 1. The Languages at a Glance, 2. Sociolinguistic Aspects]." In *Inventaire des études linguistiques sur les pays d'Afrique noire d'expression française et sur Madagascar*, ed. D Barreteau. Paris: Conseil International de Langue Française, 1978.

Robinson, Clinton D. W. "Is Sauce for the Goose Sauce for the Gander? Some Comparative Reflections on Minority Language Planning in North and South." *Journal of Multilingual and Multicultural Development* 15, no. 2/3 (1994): 129–45.

——. "The Place of Local-language Literacy in Rural Development in Cameroon." *African Studies Review* 33, no. 2 (1990): 53–64.

Stumpf, Rudolf. "The Emergence of a Sacred Language: Sectorization of Languages among High School Students in Kumba, Cameroon." *Africana Journal* 16 (1994): 292–99.

Tadajeu, Maurice. "L'Intégration linguistique au Cameroun [Linguistic Integration in Cameroon]." *New Horizons* 2, no. 2 (1982): 99–127.

Tangwa, G. "Colonial Legacy and the Language Question in Cameroon: A Reply to Dissenting Voices." *Quest* 11, no. 1 (1995): 121–30.

——. "Colonial Legacy and the Language Situation in Cameroon." *Quest* 6, no. 2 (1992): 24–43.

Tardits, C. "L'Ecriture, la politique et le secret chez les Bamum [Writing, Politics and Secrecy among the Bamoum]." *Africa, Istituto Italo-Africano* 46, no. 2 (1991): 224–40.

Ze Amvela, Etienne. "The 'Franglais' Phenomenon." *Bulletin de l'AELIA* 6 (1983): 419–29.

Literature and Folklore

Almeida, Fernando d'. *L'Espace de la parole* [The Place of the Word]. Paris: Silex, 1984.

Arnold, Stephen. H. "Preface to a History of Cameroon Literature in English." *Research in African Literatures* 14 (1983): 498–515.

——. ed. *Critical Perspectives on Mongo Beti.* Boulder, Colo.: Rienner, 1998.

Asongwed, Tah. *Born to Rule: Autobiography of a Life President.* Silver Spring, Md.: Heritage, 1993.

Austen, Ralph, A. *The Elusive Epic: Performance, Text and History in the Oral Narrative of Jeki la Njambè Cameroon Coast.* Atlanta: African Studies Association Press, 1995.

Baumgardt, Ursula. "La Représentation de l'autre: L'Exemple du répertoire d'une conteuse peule de Garoua (Cameroun) [The Representation of the Other: An Example from the Repertoire of a Fulani Storyteller of Garoua (Cameroon)]." *Cahiers d'études africaines* 34, no. 133/135 (1994): 295–311.

Bebey, Francis. *Agatha Moudio's Son*. Trans. by Joyce A. Hutchinson. London: Heinemann Educational, 1971.

——. *King Albert.* Translated by Joyce A. Hutchinson. Westport, Conn.: Hill, 1981; Yaoundé: CLE, 1976.

Beti, Mongo. *L'Histoire du fou* [The Story of a Madman]. Paris: Julliard, 1994.

——. *King Lazarus*. New York: Collier, 1971. Originally published as *Le Roi miraculé* (Paris: Buchet-Chastel-Corréa, 1958).

——. *Lament for an African Fool*. Trans. by R. Bjornson. Washington, D.C.: Three Continents, 1985. Originally published as *La Ruine presque cocasse d'une polichinelle* (Paris: Peuples Noirs, 1979).

——. *Mission to Kala*. New York: Collier, 1971; Paris: Corréa-Buchet-Chastel, 1957; London: Muller, 1958.

——. *Perpetua and the Habit of Unhappiness.* Trans. John Reed and Clive Wake. London: Heinemann, 1978. Originally published as *Perpétue et l'habitude du malheur* (Paris: Buchet & Chastel, 1974).

——. *The Poor Christ of Bomba*. Trans. Gerald Moore. London: Heinemann Educational, 1971; Paris: Laffont, 1956.

——. *Remember Ruben*. Trans. Gerald Moore. London: Heinemann, 1980; Paris: Éditions 10/18, 1974.

Beyala, Calixthe. *Assèze, l'Africaine* [Assèze, the African]. Paris: Albin Michel, 1994.

——. *Tu t'appelleras Tanga* [You Will Call Yourself Tanga]. Paris: Stock, 1988.

Bjornson, Richard. *The African Quest for Freedom and Identity: Cameroonian Writing and the National Experience.* Bloomington: Indiana University Press, 1991.

——. "A Bibliography of Cameroonian Literature." *Research in African Literature* 17, no. 1 (1986): 85–126.

Breitinger, E. "Kamerun: Literaten kämpfen gegen die Zensur [Cameroon: Writers' Struggle against the Censor." *Internationales Afrikaforum* 28, no. 3 (1992): 255–65.

Brière, Eloïse. "Resistance à l'acculturation dans l'oeuvre de Mongo Beti [Resistance to Acculturation in the Work of Mongo Beti]." *Canadian Journal of African Studies* 15, no. 2 (1981): 181–99.

——. *Le roman camerounais et ses discours* [The Cameroonian Novel and Its Discourses]. Ivry, France: Nouvelles du Sud, 1993.

Cazenave, Odile. "Calixthe Beyala and the Politics of Sexuality: The Example of 'Assèze l'Africaine' (1994)." *Présence africaine* 154 (1996): 283–98.

Cornwell, JoAnne. "Neurosis and Creativity: Early Novels by Mongo Beti." *French Review* 60, no. 5 (1987): 644–52.

Dentan, Anne. "Théatre dans la ville de Douala [Theater in the City of Douala]." *Genève–Afrique* 26, no. 2 (1988): 109–16.

Dipoko, Mbella Sonne. *Because of Women*. London: Heinemann, 1970.

———. *A Few Nights and Days.* London: Heinemann Educational, 1970.

———. *The Overloaded Ark*. New York: Tower, 1953; London: Faber & Faber, 1963.

Durrell, Gerald M.. *The Bafut Beagles*. New York: Tower, 1954.

———. *The New Noah*. Harmondsworth, England: Penguin, 1966.

———. *A Zoo in My Luggage.* Harmondsworth, England: Penguin, 1964.

Eba, Nsanda. *The Good Foot*. Ibadan: Oxford University Press, 1977.

Ebot, Wilson Atem. "Language and Action in Kenjo Jumbam's Prose Narratives." *Research in African Literature* 29, no. 2 (1998): 43– 56.

Edebiri, U. "Giullaume Oyono-Mbia: A Bilingual Playwright." In *The Question of Language in African Literature Today*, ed. E. D. Jones et al. London: Currey, 1991.

Eguchi, Paul K. "The Europeans Are Not Good: A Fulbé 'Mbooku' Poem of Protest." *Senri Ethnological Studies* 31 (1992): 1–74.

———. "'Fulbé-ness' in Fulbé Oral Literature of Cameroon." *Senri Ethnological Studies* 35 (1993): 37–104.

———. "Let Us Insult Pella: A Fulbe *Mbooku* Poem." *Senri Ethnological Studies* 15 (1984): 197–246.

———. "Pastoralism in Fulbé Folktales." *Cahiers d'études africaines* 34, nos. 133/135 (1994): 461–71.

Ellerman, E. "The Passion of Perpetua: A Generic Approach to Beti's Perpetué." *Research in African Literature* 24, no. 3 (1993): 25–34.

Eno-Belinga, Samuel-Martin. "La littérature orale du mvet à travers les pays de l'Afrique Centrale: Cameroun, Gabon, Guinée Equatoriale [The Oral Literature of the Mvet across the Countries of Central Africa: Cameroon, Gabon, Equatorial Guinea]." In *La tradition orale: Source de la littérature contemporaine en Afrique.* Dakar: Nouvelles Éditions Africaines, 1984.

Essomba, J. R. *Les Lanceurs de foudre* [The Lightening Throwers]. Paris: Harmattan, 1995.

Fonge, Michael Fotoh. *A Collection of African Folklore.* Houston, Tex.: Lebock, 1995.

Harrow, Kenneth H. "Cameroonian Theater: The Dialectic of Modern and Traditional." *The French View* 55, no. 6 (May 1982): 846–54.

Hunwick, John O., Razaq Abu Bakre, Hamidu Bobboyi, Roman Loimier, Stefan Reichmuth, and Muhammad Sami Umar. *The Writings of Central Sudanic Africa.* Leiden, Netherlands: Brill, 1995.

Jacquey, Marie-Clotilde, and Ambroise Kom. "Littérature camerounaise: 1. L'Eclosion de la parole; 2. le livre dans tous ses états [Cameroonian Literature: 1. The Blooming of the Word; 2. The Book in All Its Forms]." *Notre Librairie* 99 (1989): 1–206; no. 100 (1991): 1–141.

Jumban, Kenjo. *The White Man of God*. London: Heinemann, 1980.

Karone, Yodi. *Nègre de paille* [The Straw Negro]. Paris: Silex, 1982.

Kayo, Patrice. *Les Sauterelles* [The Grasshoppers]. Yaoundé: CLE, 1986.

Kom, A. "Mongo Beti Returns to Cameroun." *Research in African Literature* 22, no. 4 (1991): 147–53.

Krieger, M. "Building the Republic through Letters: Abbia: Cameroon Cultural Review, 1963–1982, and Its Legacy." *Research in African Literatures* 27, no. 2 (1996): 155–77.

Lyonga, Nalova, Eckhard Breitinger, and Bole Butake, eds. *Anglophone Cameroon Writing.* Bayreuth, Germany: Bayreuth University, 1993.

Maimo, Sankie. *Adventuring with Jaja*. Yaoundé: Author, 1976.

Mbangwana, I. "Some Instances of Linguistic and Literary Resource in Certain Humorous Cameroonianisms." *Humor* 6, no. 2 (1993): 195–222.

Mbembe, Achille. "La 'chose' et ses doubles dans la caricature camerounaise [The 'Thing' and Its Duplicates in Cameroon Caricatures]." *Cahiers d'études africaines* 36, cahier 141/142 (1996): 143–70.

Mokoso, Ndeley. *Man Pass Man and Other Stories.* Burnt Mill, England: Longman, 1987.

Mortimer, Mildred, Fernando Lambert, and Debra Popkin. "Cameroonian Literature." In *African Literatures in the 20th Century: A Guide*, ed. Leonard S. Klein. New York: Ungar, 1986.

Nanga, Bernard. *Les chauves-souris* [The Bats]. Paris: Présence Africaine, 1980.

———. *La Trahision de Marianne* [The Treachery of Marianne]. Dakar: Nouvelles Éditions Africaines, 1984.

Nchami, Azanwi. *Footprints of Destiny.* Limbe, Cameroon: Alfresco, 1985.

Nkashama, Pius Ngandu. *Littératures et écritures en langues africaines* [Literature and Writing in African Languages]. Paris: Harmattan, 1992.

Nkoa Atenga, Camille. *Kameroona: Le Hors-la-Loi rebelle* [Kameroona: The Outlawed Rebel]. Yaoundé: CLE, 1995.

Nkwi, Paul N. "The Lake Nyos Gas Explosions: Different Perceptions of the Phenomenon." *Discovery and Innovation* 2, no. 2 (1990): 7– 19.

Nyamnjoh, Francis B. *Mind Searching.* Awka, Nigeria: Kucena Damian, 1991.

Ongoum, Louis-Marie. "Erotic Poetry of the Grasslands." *Research in African Literatures* 24, no. 2 (Summer 1993): 101–8.

Oyono, Ferdinand. *Houseboy.* Trans. John Reed. London: Heinemann Educational, 1966. Also published as *Boy!* NewYork: Collier, 1970.

———. *The Old Man and the Medal*. Trans. John Reed. London: Heinemann, 1969. Originally published as *Le Vieux nègre et la médaille* (Paris: Julliard, 1956).

———. *Road to Europe*. Trans. Richard Bjornson. Washington, D.C.: Three Continents Press, 1989.

Oyono-Mbia, Guillaume. *Jusqu'à nouvel avis* [Until Further Notice]. Yaoundé: CLE, 1978.

———. *Three Suitors: One Husband and until Further Notice*. London: Methuen, 1968. Originally published as *Trois prétendants: Un Mmari* (Yaoundé: CLE, 1964).

Penda, Patrice Ndedi. *Le Caméléon suivi de les épouses stériles* [The Camelion Followed by Sterile Spouses]. Yaoundé: CLE, 1981.

Pliga, Jean. *Kondo, le Requin* [Kondo, the Shark]. Yaoundé: CLE, 1981.

Riesz, Janos, ed. *Semper aliquid novi: Littérature comparée et littératures d'Afrique. Mélanges offers à Albert Gérard* [Semper aliquid novi: Comparative Literature and African Literatures. A Mixture Presented to Albert Gerard]. Tübingen: Narr, 1990.

Schuerkens, Ulrike. "Change in Habitat, Village, and City Form in the Literary Work of the Cameroonian Author Mongo Beti." In *External vs. Internal Representations in Traditional Environments*, ed. Nezar Alsayyad. Berkeley: University of California at Berkeley, Center for Environmental Design Research, 1992.

Shanklin, Eugenia. "Exploding Lakes and Maleficient Water in Grasslands Legends and Myth." *Journal of Volcanology and Geothermal Research* 39, nos. 2/3 (1989): 233–46.

——. "The Track of the Python: A West African Origin Story." In *Signifying Animals: Human Meaning in the Natural World*, ed. R. G. Willis. London: Unwin Hyman, 1990.

Taille, Geneviève de la, Kristine Werner, and Victor Tarkang. *Balafon: An Anthology of Cameroon Literature in English.* Burnt Mill, England: Longman, 1986.

Tala, Kashim I. "Ten Years of Cameroon Literature." *New Horizons* 2, no. 2 (1982): 4–26.

Têko-Agbo, Ambroise. "Werewere Liking et Calixthe Beyala: Le Discours féministe et la fiction [Werewere Liking and Calixthe Beyala: Feminist Discourse and Fiction]." *Cahiers d'études africaines* 37, no. 145 (1997): 39–58.

Tsala Tsala, Jacques-Philippe. "La Folie parlée ou la déficience intellectuelle à travers les proverbes Beti du sud Cameroun [Spoken Folly or Intellectual Deficiency through Beti Proverbs of South Cameroon]." *Cahiers de sociologie économique et culturelle* 29 (1998): 101–9.

Werewere, Liking. *Elle sera de jaspe et de corail* [She Will Be of Jasper and of Coral]. Paris: Harmattan, 1983.

Wright, Katheryn. "Werewere Liking: From Chaos to Cosmos." *World Literature Today* 69, no. 1 (Winter 1995): 56–62.

Wufela, André yaek'Olingo. "Indépendances Africaines et déscolarisation de la jeunesse: L'Ecole occidentale dans la littérature Africaine avant et après l'indépendance [African Independence and the Descholarization of Youth: The Western School in African Literature before and after Independence]." *Journal of African and Asian Studies* 44 (1992): 145–66.

Zimmer, Wolfgang. *Répertoire du théâtre camerounais* [Catalogue of Cameroonian Theater]. Paris: Harmattan, 1986.

Media and Publishing

Bayemi, J. P. *L'Effort camerounais, ou la tentation d'une presse libre* [L'Effort Camerounais, or the Temptation of a Free Press]. Paris: Harmattan, 1980.

Breitinger, Eckhard. "'Lamentations patriotiques': Writers, Censors and Politics in Cameroon." *African Affairs* 92, no. 369 (1993): 557–75.

Cameroon Tribune. Yaoundé: 1974–. (Daily.)

Fondation Friedrich Ebert. *La Justice des medias au Cameroun* [Justice for the Media in Cameroon]. Yaoundé: DIHACO, 1994.

Mehler, A. *Presse und politischer Aufbruch in Kamerun: Kommenterie Presseschau für das Jahr 1990* [The Separation of Politics and the Press in Cameroon: A Commentary from the View of the Press for the Year 1990]. Hamburg: Institut für Afrika-Kunde, 1991.

Le Messager. Douala: 1979–. (Biweekly.)

Newton, Diana C. "Autonomous Publishing in Cameroon." *African Book Publishing Record* 17, no. 2 (1991): 95–102.

Nga Ndongo, Valentin. *Les Médias au Cameroun: Mythes et délires d'une société en crise* [The Media in Cameroon: Myths and Delirium of a Society in Crisis]. Paris: Harmattan, 1993.

Ngwafor, E. N. *Ako-Aya: An Anthology*. London: Institute of Third World Art and Literature, 1989.

Ngwainmbi, Emmanuel K. *Communication Efficiency and Rural Development in Africa.* Lanham, Md.: University Press of America, 1995.

Nyamnjoh, Francis Beng. "Contrôle de l'information au Cameroun: Implication pour les recherches en communication [Control of Information in Cameroon: Implication for Research in Communication]." *Afrika Spectrum* 28, no. 1 (1993): 93–115.

———. *Mass Media and Democratisation in Africa.* Yaoundé: Friedrich Ebert Foundation, 1996.

Nyamnjoh, Francis Beng, Francis Wete, and Tangle Fonchin-Gong. "Media and Civil Society in Cameroon." *Africa Media Review* 10, no. 3 (1996): 37–66.

Shelby, Barry. "The Measure of Freedom." *Africa Report* 38, no. 3 (May/June 1993): 60–63.

Takougang, J. "The Press and the Democratization Process in Africa: The Case of the Republic of Cameroon." *Journal of Third World Studies* 12, no. 2 (1995): 326–49.

SCIENCE

Geography, Geology, and Meteorology

Battistini, Rene. "Le Littoral du mont Cameroun: Etude géomorphologique [The Coast of Mount Cameroon: Geomorphologic Study]." *Revue de géographie du Cameroun* 4, no. 1 (1983): 55–72.

Billard, Pierre. *Le Cameroun fédéral* [Federal Cameroon]. 2 vols. Lyon: Tixier, 1968.

Cabot, Jean. *Le Bassin du moyen Logone* [The Basin of the Middle Logone]. Paris: ORSTOM, 1965.

Chevrier, R.-M. "Lake Nyos: Phenomenology of the Explosive Event of December 30, 1986." *Journal of Volcanology and Geothermal Research* 42, no. 4 (1990): 387–90.

Clarke, John I. "The Transcameroonian." *The Geographical Magazine* 40, no. 15 (July 1968): 1268–77.

Courade, Georges. *Atlas régional ouest I* [Regional Atlas West I]. Yaoundé: ORSTOM, n.d.

Eno Belinga, S. M. *Géologie du Cameroun*. Yaoundé: University of Yaoundé, 1984.

Fodouop, François Kengne. "Le système de marchés du Sud–Cameroun à l'est de la plaine cotière [The System of Markets of South Cameroon to the East of the Coastal Plain]." *Revue de géographie du Cameroun* 5, no. 2 (1986): 124–38.

Freeth, S. J. "The Anecdotal Evidence, Did It Help or Hinder Investigation of the Lake Nyos Gas Disaster?" *Journal of Volcanology and Geothermal Research* 42, no. 4 (1990): 373–80.

———. "Lake Bambuluwe: Could It Be the Source for a Third Gas Disaster in Western Cameroon?" *Journal of Volcanology and Geothermal Research* 42, no. 4 (1990): 393–95.

Giggenbach, W. F. "Water and Gas Chemistry of Lake Nyos and Its Bearing on the Eruptive Process." *Journal of Volcanology and Geothermal Research* 42, no. 4 (1990): 337–62.

Guillaume, G. M. D. *Notes on the Cameroon Mountain*. Buea: Government Printer, 1966.

Hallaire, Antoinette. "Les montagnards du Nord du Cameroun et leur environnement [The Mountain People of North Cameroon and their Environment]." *Afrique contemporaine* 161 (1992): 144–55.

Laclavère, G., ed. *Atlas of the United Republic of Cameroon*. Paris: Éditions Jeune Afrique, 1980.

Morin, Serge. "Colonisation agraire, espaces pastoraux et dégradation des milieux dans les hautes terres de l'ouest Cameroun [Agrarian Colonization, Pastoral Spaces and Degradation of Environment in the Highlands of West Cameroon]." *Cahiers d'outre-mer* 47, no. 185 (1994): 79–104.

Morin, Serge, and Jean Pahi. "La catastrophe du Nyos [The Nyos Catastrophe]." *Revue de géographie du Cameroun* 6, no. 2 (1986): 81–105.

Morin, Serge, and Apollinaire Zogning. "L'Eruption du Monoun (pays de Bamiléké) du 16 août 1984 [The Eruption of Monoun (Bamiléké Country) of August 16, 1984]." *Revue de géographie du Cameroun* 6, no. 2 (1986): 107–19.

Mottet, Gerard, and Appolinaire Zogning. "Les Eruptions volcaniques récentes du Mont Cameroun [Recent Volcanic Eruptions of Mount Cameroon]." *Mondes et cultures* 45, no. 4 (1985): 805–16.

Neba, Aaron S. *Modern Geography of the Republic of Cameroon.* Camden, N.J.: NEBA Publishers, 1987.

Othman-Chande, M. "The Cameroon Volcanic Gas Disaster." *Disasters* 11, no. 2 (1987): 21–37.

Piboule, M., et al. "Radiometric Studies of Lake Nyos, Cameroon, Sediments: Evidence of Strong Mixing and Excess." *Journal of Volcanology and Geothermal Research* 42, no. 4 (1990): 363–72.

Reyment, Richard A. "On the Stratigraphy and Paleontology of the Cretaceous of Nigeria and the Cameroons." *Geologiska Foreningens I Stockholm Forhandlingar* 78 (1956): 17–96.

———. "The Stratigraphy of the Southern Cameroons." *Geologiska Foreningens I Stockholm Forhandlingar* 76 (1954): 661–83.

Rietsch, Britta J. "Périodisation des logiques de gestion des ressources naturelles et fondement d'une politique environnementale au Cameroun [Periodization of the Logic of Natural Resource Management and the Foundation of an Environmental Policy]." *Afrika Spectrum* 26, no. 3 (1991): 251–73.

Sabroux, J. C., et al. "Satellite Monitoring of the Vertical Temperature Profile of Lake Nyos, Cameroon." *Journal of Volcanology and Geothermal Research* 42, no. 4 (1990): 381–85.

Sano, Y., et al. "Helium and Carbon Fluxes in Lake Nyos, Cameroon: Constraint on Next Gas Burst." *Earth and Planetary Science Letters* 99, no. 4 (1990): 303–14.

Santoir, Christian, and Athanase Bopda. *Atlas régional Sud-Cameroun* [Regional Atlas of South Cameroon]. Paris: ORSTOM; Yaoundé: MINREST, 1995.

Seiny-Boukar, L., C. Floret, and R. Potanier. "Degradation of Savanna Soils and Reduction of Water for the Vegetation: The Case of Northern Cameroon Vertisols." *Canadian Journal of Soil Science* 72 (1992): 481–88.

Semmel, Arno. "Geomorphology as Part of Development Aid." *Applied Geography and Development* 23 (1984): 7–19.

Tazieff, H. "Mechanisms of the Nyos Carbon Dioxide Disaster and of So-called Phreatic Steam Eruptions." *Journal of Volcanology and Geothermal Research* 39, nos. 2/3 (1989): 21–32.

Tchawa, Paul. "La dégradation des sols dans le Bamiléké méridional, conditions naturelles et facteurs anthropiques [Deterioration of soils in Southern Bamiléké, Natural Conditions and Anthropic Factors]." *Cahiers d'outre-mer* 46, no. 181 (1993): 75–104.

Tchotsoua, Michel. "Dynamique informelle de l'espace urbain et érosion accélérée en milieu tropical humide: Le Cas de la ville de Yaoundé [Informal Dynamic of Urban Space and Accelerated Erosion in Humid Environment: The Case of Yaoundé]." *Cahiers d'outre-mer* 47, no. 185 (1994): 123–36.

Tebor, S. G. "Gas Emission and Hydrothermal Manifestation in the Lake Nyos Area: January 5, 1987, January 26, 1987, June 20, 1987." *Journal of Volcanology and Geothermal Research* 40, no. 4 (1990): 391–92.

Tsalafac, M. "Sécheresse, déforestation et érosion sur les montagnes de l'ouest du Cameroun [Drought, Deforestation and Erosion on the Mountains of West Cameroon]." *Cahiers d'outre-mer* 47, no. 185 (1994): 105–22.

Verheve, Didier. "Les Ressources minières des états d'Afrique centrale (CEEAC) [Mineral Resources of the Central African States (CEEAC)]." *Tiers-Monde* 27, no. 106 (1986): 457–65.

Health, Medicine, and Demography

Azevedo, M. J., G. S. Prater, and D. N. Lantum. "Culture, Biomedicine and Child Mortality in Cameroon." *Social Science and Medicine* 32, no. 12 (1991): 1341–51.

Baeke, Viviane. "L'Anthropologie dans les Grassfields: Systèmes de guerison traditionnels chez les Wuli-Mfumte [Anthropology in the Grassfields: Traditional Systems of Curing among the Wuli-Mfumte]." In *La Recherche en sciences humaines au Cameroun*, ed. P. Salmon and J.-J. Symoens. Brussels: Academie Royale des Sciences d'Outre-Mer, 1991.

Beat-Songue, P. *SIDA et prostitution aux Cameroun* [AIDS and Prostitution in Cameroon]. Paris: Harmattan, 1993.

Bella, N. "La Fecondité au Cameroun [Fertility in Cameroon]." *Population* 50, no. 1 (1995): 35–60.

Cameroon. Ministry of Economic Affairs and Planning, 1978. *Main Results of the April 1976 General Population and Housing Census*. Yaoundé: Ministry of Economic Affairs and Planning, Department of Statistics; Paris: Société d'Etudes pour le Développement Economique et Social, 1965.

Cameroon, National Department of the Second General Population and Housing Census. *Cameroon Demographic and Health Survey 1991.* Yaoundé: Author, 1992.

——. *Enquête démographique au Cameroun: Résultats définitifs pour la région nord* [Demographic Survey in Cameroon: Final Results for the North Region]. Paris: Sécretariat d'Etat aux Affaires Etrangères, 1964.

——. *Enquête démographique au Cameroun: Résultats définitifs pour la région sud-est* [Demographic Survey in Cameroon: Final Results for the South-East Region]. Paris: Secretariat d'Etat aux Affaires Etrangères, n.d.

——. *The Population of West Cameroon: Main Findings of the 1964 Demographic Sample Survey*. Paris: Société d'Etudes pour le Développment Economique et Social, 1965.

——. *Recensement général de la population et de l'habitat d'avril, 1976* [General Census of the Population and of Housing, April 1976]. 4 vols. Ministre de l' Economie et du Plan. Direction de la Statistique et de la Compatibilité Nationale. Yaoundé: Bureau Central du Recensement, 1978.

Cameroon, and U.S. Agency for International Development. *United Republic of Cameroon National Nutrition Survey.* Washington, D.C.: AID, 1978.

Cosmas, C., and B. Schmidt-Ehey. "Human Rights and Health in Developing Countries: Barriers to Community Participation in Public Health in the Cameroon." *Health and Human Rights* 1, no. 3 (1995): 244–54.

Debarge, J. *La Mission médicale au Cameroun* [Medical Mission in Cameroon]. Paris: Société des Missions Evangéliques, 1934.

Dhooge, J. *Churches and Medical Care: The Organization of Christian Medical Care in East Cameroon*. Louvain: Institute of Social Studies, Centre de Documentation sur l'Action des Eglises dans le Monde, 1969.

Dongmo, J. L. *L'Approvisionnement alimentaire de Yaoundé* [The Food Supply of Yaoundé]. Yaoundé: University of Yaoundé, 1990.

Eboko, Fred. "L'Etat camerounais et les cadets sociaux face à la pandémie du SIDA [The Cameroonian State and Youth Face the AIDS Pandemic]." *Politique africaine* 64 (1996): 135–45.

Einterz, Ellen M. "Family Planning and Tradition: A View from Northern Cameroon." *World Health Forum* 15, no. 4 (1994): 378–81.

Essomba, R. O., et al. "The Reorientation of Primary Health Care in Cameroon: Rationale, Obstacles and Constraints." *Health Policy and Planning* 8, no. 3 (1993): 232–39.

Geest, Sjaak van der. "The Articulation of Formal and Informal Medicine Distribution in South Cameroun." In *The Context of Medicines in Developing Countries*, ed. S. van der Geest and S. R. White. Amsterdam: Spinhuis, 1991.

———. "Health Care as Politics: Missed Chance in Rural Cameroon." *Cahiers du CEDAF* 2/4 (1986): 241–59.

Gracia, Mathieu. "Research Findings in Cameroon: Older Persons in Villages in the District of Dibombari." *Gerontologie Africaine* 3 (1985): 25–39.

Gubry, P., G. Negadi, and J. Tayo. "Le Recensement général de la population et de l'habitat au Cameroun de 1976 [The General Census of the Population and Housing in Cameroon of 1976]." *Revue science et technique* 1, no. 3 (1980/81): 29–37.

Hladik, C. M., et al., eds. *Tropical Forests, People and Food*. Paris: UNESCO, 1993.

Jamot, Eugene. "La Lutte contre la maladie du sommeil au Cameroun [The Struggle against Sleeping Sickness in Cameroon]." *Africa* 3 (1930): 161–77; *Annales de l'Institut Pasteur* 48 (1932): 481–539.

Kambou, Gerard, Shantayanan Devarajan, and Mead Over. "The Economic Impact of AIDS in an African Country: Simulations with a Computable General Equilibrium Model of Cameroon." *Journal of African Economics* 1, no. 1 (1992): 109–30.

Kamdoum, A. *Planification sanitaire et ajustement structurel au Cameroun* [Sanitary Planning and Structural Adjustment in Cameroon]. Paris: CEPED, 1994.

Koloss, Hans-Joachim. "Kefuh Myin: A Therapeutic Medicine in Oku (Cameroon Grassfields)." *Journal of the Anthropological Society of Oxford* 26, no. 1 (1996): 69–80.

Kuczynski, Robert R. *The Cameroons and Togoland: A Demographic Study*. London: Oxford University Press for the Royal Institute of International Affairs, 1939.

Lantum, D. N. *Traditional Medicine-Men of Cameroon: The Case of Bui Division*. Yaoundé: University Center for Health Sciences, 1985.

Lee, B. S., and L. G. Pol. "The Influnce of Rural-Urban Migration on Migrants' Fertility in Korea, Mexico and Cameroon." *Population Research and Policy Review* 12, no. 1 (1993): 3–26.

Litvak, J. I., and C. Bodart. "User Fees Plus Quality Equals Improved Access to Health Care: Results of a Field Experiment in Cameroon." *Social Science and Medicine* 37, no. 3 (1993): 369–83.

Martin, Gustave. *L'Existence au Cameroun* [Subsistence in Cameroon]. Paris: Larose, 1921.

Moutome-Ekambi, J. "De l'acceptabilitié social de la politique de population du Cameroun [Concerning the Social Acceptability of the Population Policy]." *African Anthropology* 1, nos. 1/2 (1994): 9–20.

Ngatchou, R. D., et al. "Les Inégalités géographiques de la mortalité au Cameroun [Geographic Inequalities of Mortality in Cameroon]." *Social Science and Medicine* 36, no. 10 (1993): 1285–90.

Nigeria. Regional Census Office. *Population Census of the Eastern Region of Nigeria. No. 2, Bamenda Province. No. 5, Cameroons Province.* Lagos: Government Statistician, 1953.

Nsamenang, A. B., and M. E. Lamb. "The Acquisition of Sociocognitive Competence by Nso' Children in the Bamenda Grassfields of Northwest Cameroon." *International Journal of Behavioural Development* 16, no. 3 (1993): 429–41.

Pool, Robert. *Dialogue and the Interpretation of Illness: Conversations in a Cameroon Village*. Oxford: Berg 1994.

———. "On the Creation and Dissolution of Ethnomedical Systems in the Medical Ethnography of Africa." *Africa, Journal of the International African Institute* 64, no. 1 (1994): 1–20.

Pradelles de Latour, C. *Ethnopsychanalyse en pays Bamiléké* [Ethnopsychoanalysis in Bamiléké Country]. Paris: EPEL, 1991.

Regnier-Desjarains, D. "Le Consommation alimentaire Garoua, permanances et changements [Nutritional Consumption in Garoua, Constants and Changes]." In *Alimentation: Techniques et innovations dans les regions tropicales*, ed. J. Muchnik. Paris: Harmattan, 1993.

Sauerborn, R., et al. "Recovery of Recurrent Health Service Costs through Provincial Health Funds in Cameroun." *Social Science and Medicine* 40, no. 12 (1995): 1731–39.

Schrieder, G. *The Role of Rural Finance for Food Security of the Poor in Cameroon.* Frankfurt: Lang, 1996.

Schrieder, G., and F. Heidhues. "L'Impact des marchés financiers ruraux sur la sécurité alimentaire des populations pauvres: Le Cas du Cameroun [The Impact of Rural Financial Markets on the Nutritional Security of Poor Populations: The Case of Cameroon]." *Economies et sociétés* 29, no. 3/4 (1995): 249–68.

Seignobos, Christian. "La Variole dans le Nord-Cameroun: Représentation de la maladie, soins et gestion sociale de l'épidémie [Smallpox in North Cameroon: Representation of Illness, Treatments and Management of the Epidemic]." *Cahiers des sciences humaines* 31, no. 1 (1995): 149–80.

United Nations. *Demographic Yearbook*. New York: Author, 1948 (annual).

United Nations Fund for Population Activities. *Demo 87.* Yaoundé: Author, n.d.

Flora and Fauna

Alpert, Peter. "Conserving Biodiversity in Cameroon." *Ambio* 22, no. 1 (February 1993): 44–49.

Aubreville, Andre. *Flore du Cameroun* [Flora of Cameroon]. Paris: Musée National d'Histoire Naturelle, 1965–68.

Banda, C. D. "The Future of Tropical Rain Forests: The Case of Cameroon." *D+C* 1 (1992): 24–26.

Duguma, B., and J. Tonye. "Screening of Multipurpose Tree and Shrub Species for Agroforestry in the Humid Lowlands of Cameroon." *Forest Ecology and Management* 64 (1994): 135–43.

Gartlan, S. *La Conservation des ecosystèmes forestiers du Cameroun* [The Conservation of Forest Ecosystems of Cameroon]. Gland, Belgium: IUCN, 1989.

Good, A. I. *The Birds of French Cameroon*. Yaoundé: Institut Français d'Afrique Noire, Centre du Cameroun, 1952 and 1953.

Lanz, Tobias J. "The Politics of Sustainable Development: A Case Study of the Korup Project in Cameroon." In *Dimensions of Contemporary African Development Strategies*, ed. F. W. Wambalaba, Dubuque, Iowa: Kendall Hunt, 1999.

Letouzey, R. *Flore du Cameroun.* Vol. 1, *Introduction phytogéogra-phique.* Paris: Musée Nationale d'Histoire Naturelle, 1963.

Maitland, T. D. "The Grassland Vegetation of the Cameroons Mountain." *Kew Bulletin* 9 (1932): 417–25.

Monod, T., ed. *Contribution à l'étude de la faune du Cameroun* [Contribution to the Study of the Fauna of Cameroon]. Paris: Société d'Editions Geographiques, Maritimes et Coloniales, 1927.

Morin, S. "L'Evolution actuelle des milieux naturels au Cameroun central et occidental [The Current Evolution of Natural Environments in Central and Western Cameroon]." *Travaux de l'Institut de Géographie de Reims* 45/46 (1981): 117–39.

Ngoufo, Roger. "Conservation de la nature et développement rural dans le cadre du projet Korup [Conservation of Nature and Rural Development in the Framework of the Korup Project]." *Revue de géographie du Cameroun* 10, no. 2 (1991): 99–115.

Njiforti, Hanson Langmia. "Preferences and Present Demand for Bushmeat in North Cameroon: Some Implications for Wildlife Conservation." *Environmental Conservation* 23, no. 2 (1996): 149–55.

Sharpe, Barrie. "First the Forest: Conservation, Community and Participation in South-West Cameroon." *Africa, Journal of the International African Institute* 68, no. 1 (1998): 25–45.

Stuart, S. N., ed. *Conservation of Cameroon Montane Forests*. Cambridge, England: International Council for Bird Preservation, 1986.

Tazo, Etienne. "Installations humaines et destructions d'une reserve de faune: L'Exemple de Santchou dans les hautes terres de l'Ouest-Cameroun [Human Settlements and the Destruction of an Animal Reserve: The Example of Santchou in the High Lands of West Cameroon." *Cameroon Geographical Review* 13, no. 1 (1997): 15–25.

Tchamba, M. N. "History and Present Status of the Human/Elephant Conflict in the Waza-Logone Region, Cameroon, West Africa." *Biological Conservation* 75, no. 1 (1996): 35–41.

Thiele, R., and M. Wiebelt. "National and International Policies for Tropical Rainforest Conservation: A Quantitative Analysis for Cameroon." *Environment and Resource Economics* 3, no. 6 (1993): 501–31.

———. "Policies to Reduce Tropical Deforestation and Degradation: A Computable General Equilibrium Analysis for Cameroon." *Quarterly Journal of International Agriculture* 33, no. 2 (1994): 162–78.

About the Authors

Mark W. DeLancey (B.A. Syracuse University; M.A. Indiana University; Ph.D. Indiana University) is a professor of political science in the Department of Government and International Studies at the University of South Carolina. An expert on African comparative and international politics, he has taught at the University of Yaoundé, Cameroon, as well as the University of Nigeria, Nsukka; Somali National University, Mogadishu; and the University of the Western Cape, South Africa. In addition to his numerous publications on Cameroon subjects, Dr. DeLancey has served as editor of the *African Studies Review*, associate editor of the *African Book Publishing Record* (*ABPR*), and as a board member and treasurer of the African Studies Association (U.S.A.). From 1993 until 1998, he was chair of his department. His major publications include *Cameroon, Dependence or Independence* (1989), *African International Relations* (1997), and *Historical Dictionary of International Organizations in Sub-Saharan Africa* (1994). He has also published numerous articles in professional journals.

Mark Dike DeLancey (B.A. Oberlin College; M.A. Harvard University; A.B.D. Harvard University) is presently engaged in a long-term study of the influence of Islamic culture on palace architecture in northern Cameroon. He has lived in Cameroon, Somalia, Nigeria, and Egypt for much of his life. He served as an apprentice to a wood-carver in Cairo for several months and studied Islamic architecture at American University in Cairo. He has published several reviews and essays.